MEDIEVAL SWORDSMANSHIP

To all those who have ever dared to lift a blade in contemplation and wonder.

MEDIEVAL SWORDSMANSHIP

Illustrated Methods and Techniques

John Clements

Paladin Press • Boulder, Colorado

Also by John Clements:

Renaissance Swordsmanship: The Illustrated Use of Rapiers and
Cut-and-Thrust Swords

Medieval Swordsmanship
Illustrated Methods and Techniques
by John Clements

Copyright © 1998 by John Clements

ISBN 1-58160-004-6
Printed in the United States of America

Publisher's Cataloguing-in-Publication
(Provided by Quality Books, Inc.)

Clements, John.
    Medieval swordsmanship : illustrated methods and
techniques / John Clements. -- 1st ed.
    p. cm.
    Includes bibliographical references.
    ISBN: 1-58160-004-6

    1. Swordplay.   I. Title.

U865.C59 1998   796.86
             QBI98-1657

Published by Paladin Press, a division of
Paladin Enterprises, Inc.
Gunbarrel Tech Center
7077 Winchester Circle
Boulder, Colorado 80301 USA
+ 1.303.443.7250

Direct inquiries and/or orders to the above address.

PALADIN, PALADIN PRESS, and the "horse head" design
are trademarks belonging to Paladin Enterprises and
registered in United States Patent and Trademark Office.

Illustrations (except the historical ones) were created by the author.

Visit our Web site at www.paladin-press.com

Contents

Introduction 1

Chapter 1: The Medieval Combat Environment 7

Chapter 2: Medieval Fighting Manuals 11

Chapter 3: Medieval Swords 29

Chapter 4: The Making of Medieval Swords 47

Chapter 5: Swords against Plate Armor 51

Chapter 6: The Fate of the Medieval Sword 57

Chapter 7: Forms of the Medieval Sword 61

Chapter 8: Medieval Shields 87

Chapter 9: Sword & Shield 109

Chapter 10: The Long-Sword 179

Chapter 11: Practice and Sparring 251

Advice to the Reader 259

Afterword 263

Appendix A: On Obtaining a Real Sword 267

Appendix B: The Problem of Stage-Combat 271

Appendix C: Methods of Weapon-Sparring 279

Appendix D: Blunt Steel and Plate Armor Sparring 285

Appendix E: Medieval Fantasy
        and "Boffer" Sparring Methods 289

Appendix F: The Importance of the Full-Leg Target
        in Weapon-Sparring 293

Appendix G: Kneeling Down in Weapon-Sparring Rules 299

Appendix H: Weapon-Sparring in Martial Arts 303

Appendix I: Understanding Swords and Martial Arts in America . . . 309

Bibliography 313

Warning

Neither the publisher nor author of this work will be held responsible in any way whatsoever for any physical injury or damage of any sort that may occur as a result of reading and following the advice or instructions herein. Before attempting any physical activities described in this book, the reader should consult with a qualified physician. In any form of weapon sparring always use safety equipment and remember, never strike at a person with a sharpened blade.

Acknowledgments

ratitude for their help with this work must go to the members of the Historical Armed Combat Association (HACA), all my students from classes and seminars, and all my old Medieval Battling Club members over the years. Particularly I must thank Andy, Chris, Christian, Fred, Joe, Justin, Mark, Matt, Mike, Rick, Russell, Pat, Paul, T.J., Tom, and especially my good friend and sparring partner, Todd Palmer. Gratitude must be offered to my student Mark Bertrand for his great help in formatting this manuscript and to the great people at Paladin Press. I wish to acknowledge my debt to the many fellow scholars and students of the sword around the world with whom I have corresponded, including Christoph Amberger, author of *The Secret History of the Sword*; sword researcher Matt Galas; Steve Hick; Stephen Hand; and Professor Sydney Anglo, to name just a very few. I also offer my thanks to the many historical reenactment organizations in Britain, Australia, Germany, and Italy.

I must give special thanks and appreciation to the venerable Hank Reinhardt of Museum Replicas Limited for his years of divulged wisdom and mentoring. Additionally I must thank all those loved ones who tolerated my madness, particularly my dearest Pamela. Finally, I must acknowledge all my fellow Medievalists and hoplologists (students of arms and armor), whoever they may be, who have committed themselves and worked so hard to explore our Western martial heritage, particularly the renowned authority Ewart Oakeshott, without whom we would all be quite bewildered.

After many years of studying, training, and teaching, my motivation for producing this work is threefold: genuine love of the craft, a sincere desire to educate, and frustration at the disturbing lack of basic understanding frequently encountered. Study of Medieval swords and weaponry is an intellectual and physical challenge. In a work of this magnitude there are bound to be errors. Often our information is only as good as our sources and cross-references. To those who find factual errors in this work, I apologize. Further, whenever we are dealing with archaic terminology from languages we are not proficient in, there are bound to be times when words get butchered.

My interest in this work is not in regurgitating the available historical texts verbatim, and this book is not a point-by-point analysis of all the major swordsmanship manuals from the Middle Ages. Not every technique or principle illustrated here has a reference in a specific manual or a specific historical Master. Instead, to realistically present the overall nature of the weapons and the nature of their use, this book distills and presents discernable, pragmatic, and very real techniques and concepts from the historical manuals. The basis of my perspective is years of training with and handling of historical arms and many years of earnest sparring and study. Naturally, therefore, this book does not follow an academic, scholarly approach alone, but more or less a martial one, which the subject demands. The study of a true martial art is not a literary pursuit; it is a practical one. You cannot "armchair" it. Anyone who has studied a martial art in depth knows that at least 80 percent of it can never be put into any book. This much is obvious with regard to Medieval or Renaissance fighting methods; besides, the works of the historical Masters are hardly complete or comprehensive, which is also obvious.

I have no doubt this work will evoke considerable controversy among members of certain Medieval societies, re-creationists, and martial artists. To those who disagree with my presentation and findings, I welcome comments. Historically, exponents of different schools and styles disagreed vehemently and rarely endorsed one another. But although practitioners are free to make any claim they wish about handling and using historical arms, in the end they must be prepared to prove their case in the "courtroom of combat"—in other words, through demonstration and serious contact-sparring.

For the most part, this work presents what are the established and accepted theories about Western sword history. My additional speculation and conjecture are tentative opinions and beliefs, but opinions and beliefs based on almost two decades of personal hands-on study, training, and experimentation in the use of all manners of swords and weaponry. We must always be prepared to accept most things historical as temporary, pending further investigation. They are rarely certain beyond all doubt. All we can hope for is future confirmation or clarification and that we haven't repeated information that has been found to be incorrect. Martial knowledge itself must, in part, always remain theory, and sometimes we must follow our instincts. This is precisely why neither historical research nor martial arts is an exact science.

Author's Note

Occasionally, one hears people ask, "Why bother studying swords at all anymore, why not just use a gun?" There is an obvious fallacy in this question that assumes we are using swords for killing or even for pure self-defense. Comparing swords to guns is like comparing horses to cars. Cars are an infinitely superior mode of transportation; however, there is still much to be said for the enjoyment of rearing and riding fine horses (indeed, there are still things horses can do better and more efficiently than automobiles). But edged weapons are the great equalizers. They have an inherent power. Sharp steel is sharp steel, and whether you cut with strong force or massive force the human body will often hardly notice the difference. It doesn't matter whether you have an average build or look like "Conan"; a sword can still cut through your flesh and bones. If the same armor were to be worn, the results would not be much different from one person to another. No matter how skilled you might be with your blade or weapon, you could be hurt or killed almost as easily as anyone else. The ability to balance the chances in combat between those who may not have been equal in strength, speed, stamina, or agility made swords so valuable. Their ability to unleash death is what made them so respected.

As a result of both their variety and their heroic status, Medieval (or *Mediaeval*, the British variant) swords are among the most popular of historical weapons. For admirers of swords, a good point at which to begin is with the weapons of Medieval Europe because their use includes all the necessary fundamentals and is quite free from stylistic formality. Indeed, some people are drawn to Medieval swords because of this very fact. Of course, this lack of any truly definable and established tradition also allows for a great deal of "interpretation." This also leaves room for the assertion of virtually any notion, no matter how nonsensical, about technique or method, because there is often no real way to disprove it. However, the burden of proof is on those making the assertion. It is one thing to speculate and demonstrate viable, working theories with historical support and physical examples and quite another simply to make vague or untestable claims about fighting.

The term *Medieval sword* is used throughout this work to refer to the long slashing & cutting swords and the long cutting & stabbing swords common throughout Europe from roughly 800 to 1500 A.D. This definition is merely for convenience in discussing the methods and techniques of Medieval swordsmanship, sword & shield use, and related weaponry. Therefore, I have made an effort here to refer consistently to a generic "Medieval sword" form such as the "Norman" style (Oakeshott's Type X or XI). This form consists of all the qualities typically associated with the swords of that age. The emphasis here is on the use of sword & shield during the "mail period" (approximately 800 to 1300 A.D.) more so than during the later "age of plate" (roughly 1300 to 1500 A.D.).

For the original illustrations included in this work, I have tried to avoid as much stylistic influence as possible, and I merely display the mechanical application of techniques or concepts in their proper tactical context. Most illustrations use the perspective of a right-handed fighter. Whether for single-combat or mass battle, the emphasis is on those techniques that would apply in battle with actual, sharpened steel weapons. The whole body was considered a legitimate target, and distinctions between (or effects of) various grades and types of armor are noted only when relevant and practical. I have made no attempt to approach the subject with regard to the unique conditions of knightly tournaments and have made no reference to describing techniques for use in any manner of staged performance.

Throughout this book I advocate *contact-weapon sparring* because of the value of weapon-sparring in general and because it is directly related to understanding the use of the Medieval sword. It should be obvious that it is chiefly through safe sparring that any practical fighting experience is gained with historical arms and armor. This is thoroughly explored throughout the book. I have been active in numerous forms of contact-weapon sparring for many years and can strongly affirm its value to any of those not already convinced.

The numerous footnotes accompanying the text contain a considerable range of information and editorial content that should not be overlooked. At the end of the book are appendixes that contain a range of relevant material and commentary that does not directly fit into prior sections. Their purpose is to better connect concepts between diverse portions. Because historical Western fighting skills have yet to be fully reconstructed and reestablished as legitimate martial arts, this material is necessary to address many issues raised by the wide variety of approaches now being pursued.

Throughout the text, I have intentionally used the term *swordsmanship* rather than *fence* or *fencing* (from the root word *defence*, referring to the *art* of the sword). Though *swordsmanship* and *fence* can be synonymous, the word *fence* is too closely tied to *fencing*, which is now almost exclusively associated with the modern sporting form. The modern version of fencing with foils, épées, and sabers is far removed from its martial origins in the Renaissance "Art of Defence." Swordsmanship, therefore, more aptly describes the craft of historical fencing as the martial skill of using the weapon.

Interestingly, the term *swordplay* (from as early as 1000 A.D.) was in use long before the term *swordsmanship* (as recent as 1851) or even *swordsman* (only as far back as c. 1680). The obscure term *swordman* (as opposed to *swordsman*) was used as early as 1387. A student of the craft was often called a *scholar*. A swordsman was a *fencer* (*fechter, skirmator, escrimador*). The unique English term *sword-player* appeared around 1538 but never became very widely used. In an age when your life could depend on skill at arms "swordplay" once had a connotation very different from what the word "play" now has. To "play" at swords meant to practice seriously. But today it often denotes the lighthearted or even the theatrical form rather than the historical martial art. We also know that experts of Medieval and Renaissance fighting arts considered themselves to be far more than any simple "fencer." Thus, since word meanings and connotations change over time, the generally understood term *swordsmanship* is used here.

Frequent use is also made of the male gender in referring to handling weaponry and fighting opponents. No effort has been made to be gender-neutral when discussing historical combat or modern practice. Additionally, since historically Medieval warriors were virtually all male, I use these terms for convenience. Certainly the term *swordsmanship* can be read as being genderless and meaning *swordpersonship*, or simply *sword-skill art*.

Regardless of people's gender or any other physical attributes, when they take up a weapon they become fighters and targets. It is as such that they should be evaluated. Nothing more, nothing less. One might say an opponent is "good for a 12-year-old," but saying that someone is "good for a female" is as inappropriate as saying that someone is good for a male or for being tall or for being short or for being blind or for being in a wheelchair. Some people, because of size, build, fitness, or attitude, are simply at a disadvantage when fighting and weapon-sparring: this is true whether such a state is their natural condition or because of something else. Whatever the case, the cause is irrelevant on the battlefield, and neither excuses nor special considerations should be made because of handicaps. Skill is skill. The practice of historical-fencing or real swordsmanship is not about accommodating participants, building self-esteem, or feeling good; it is about functioning effectively (even if only in simulation). This kind of combat simply cannot be made "accessible" for everyone without eliminating the very struggle for commitment and discipline that it embodies. Training in a martial art is a personal undertaking that demands each individual's full efforts.

In a violent age when warriors could expect to walk out the door at any moment and enter combat, it is reasonable to believe that they were not concerned in their learning with the "style" or "form" of any one school or instructor. Rather, they were concerned with practical methods of pragmatic fighting—in other words, with acquiring the personal skills to simply protect themselves and defeat enemies. This view is apparent from the fighting manuals as well as the literature of the period and was not to change until the advent of civilian schools of dueling in the Renaissance.

Preface

"Who can separate a man from his sword?
One is worth nothing without the other."
—Kalebipoeg, Estonian epic

This work is meant to serve as a reference for Medieval sword enthusiasts and to aid serious study in the reconstruction and replication of historical European fighting skills. It is also intended as a guide to dispel the many myths and misconceptions permeating the subject of Medieval swords propagated by fantasy and popular media. The focus of this presentation is on the function and use of the sword & shield and the long-sword. This book emphasizes the historical lethality of sword fighting rather than the modern re-creational aspects. Its intention is to describe Medieval European sword skills as a true martial art. This book should serve as a source for all those people who have asked, "What's a good book on Medieval swordsmanship?" To which for years I could only reply that there wasn't one. The emphasis in this work is primarily on foot combat with sword & shield by dismounted warriors and *milites* (knights and professional men-at-arms) from roughly 900 to 1450 A.D. This 550-year period was filled with savage, almost constant warfare in Western Europe. Somewhat less emphasis has been placed on knightly foot combat of the late 1300s and 1400s, when fighting in full plate armor became more common, fewer if any shields were used, and axe and pole weapons were more prevalent.

Because it is impossible to "teach" swordsmanship or fighting skills from a book, all that can be done here is help the reader to think clearly about how to proceed in a useful direction. Also, some small but profound lessons can be passed on regarding certain fundamental concepts and ideas of practice fighting with archaic weaponry. This can lead one further and not only show there was a great deal of skill involved in the historical craft, but to suggest that there is indeed a "higher" way to follow for those practicing today. My approach to this guidebook is therefore not so much scholarly as martial. The material should provoke both thought and research (practice) and perhaps even some needed debate.

This book is also a companion to my earlier work, *Renaissance Swordsmanship: The Illustrated Use of Rapiers and Cut-and-Thrust Swords* (Paladin Press, 1997), which, incidentally, was begun after this work was already nearing completion. Readers familiar with my previous title may notice that small portions of that text have been included here and many ideas are presented again. Although I was reluctant to reproduce earlier material, in certain cases it was unavoidable because it was originally written for this book. Also, many universal concepts of swordsmanship mentioned in that prior effort apply equally (if not more so) to Medieval swordsmanship, and excluding those ideas would have been a disservice.

As with that earlier publication, this book is primarily aimed at four different audiences:

1. Fellow students and scholars of the Medieval sword, who will welcome material aimed directly toward their special interest
2. Novice practitioners, both individually and in various organized groups, who have for so long been without realistic guidance or a comprehensive reference in pursuing historical-fencing
3. Students of traditional Asian martial arts, who so often are sadly ignorant of their own martial heritage and, as a result, have either dismissed it as inconsequential or accepted blindly the nonsense so often seen in film and television
4. Complete neophytes, who by reading this may develop an interest and gain respect for what so many already pursue and enjoy

In addressing these different audiences some portions will speak more to each reader than others.

Another motive for producing this work was the realization of just how much effort and time is required to gain a comprehensive knowledge of the nature and working of Medieval swords. Quite often I am dismayed at the lack of even basic information possessed by many enthusiasts, including members of re-creational combat groups and living-history societies. I am continually surprised at how many people say they "train" or "practice" with European weapons, only to learn upon examination that they (a) don't do any contact-sparring, (b) have never actually cut with a real sword, and (c) only play with stage combat props or sticks rather than historically accurate reproduction blades. There are many obvious aspects to the modern replication of Medieval swordsmanship so fundamental that, when presented with them, some enthusiasts will feel resentful at having so easily ignored or dismissed them in the past. Becoming a skilled practitioner of Medieval swordsmanship requires far more than mere

costumed theorizing and armchair research. It demands extensive physical training in handling a weapon and considerable fighting practice. The magnitude of the subject and the spread of the various resources necessitates a committed, long-term effort to acquire any expertise. There are sources involved that many practitioners simply do not have. This material, therefore, is meant to concentrate and shorten the learning process. Unlike the modern study of popular Asian fighting arts, there is not a great deal of accurate information or quality instruction readily accessible for this subject.

Considering just how deeply Medieval swords are embedded in our popular culture and our fantasy, we would expect that a more serious and accurate martial understanding of these weapons would exist. This is obviously not the case. Unlike its Eastern counterpart in Japanese samurai swordsmanship (kenjutsu), there really is no cultural interest group (or virtual lobby) that has preserved and now actively promotes the traditional craft of Medieval European war arts or knightly fighting skills. Instead, we mostly have performers and actors with assumptions derived chiefly from modern sport fencing and the stylistic notions of historical-fantasy organizations. Therefore, part of the purpose of this book is to provide a more coherent martial appreciation of the function and use of Medieval swords through examination of period sources and current re-creational practices.

However, this book is not meant to be an all-encompassing instruction manual or a how-to on Medieval swordsmanship (far from it). Unlike other works on Western swords, it was written from the perspective of, and with regard to, the historical function and use of the Medieval sword. It approaches the material not from just a military history point of view, nor as theatrical stunt or fantasy playing, but as a legitimate martial art.

It is somewhat ironic that the English phrase *martial art* (from the "arts of Mars," the Roman god of war) has now become virtually synonymous with Asian fighting art. However, given that Medieval fighting systems, by definition, do indeed constitute true martial arts, the phrase is in every way appropriate and must not be allowed to be exclusive.[1]

---

[1] Tell traditional martial artists (i.e., students of Asian systems) that your style is "Medieval" and you can usually watch perplexity followed by smirks come across their faces. Even stating that one is a "swordsman" rather than a "fencer"—a word that denotes the modern sport form—is today an unusual statement for any martial artist to make.

Indeed, the very term *martial art* was used in the West for a considerable time. Its first recorded instance is likely from the 1639 *Pallas Armata* (a much undervalued book on rapier and sword). In it, a poem by a student to his Master of Defence contains the following lines:

> *In a plain way that famous martial art*
> *Of fencing, which by charge and*
>   *toylesome payne*
> *Thou hast attain'd, and thriv'st to make us gaine.*

As with *Renaissance Swordsmanship*, this book is also not intended directly for fight choreographers, though they may certainly benefit from it. It offers information distilled from historical sources and modern study. I should add that there are sure to be many who will find this book somewhat controversial. There are those enthusiasts who must come to realize that the rule structure they find reasonable and under which they may have had almost exclusive fighting experience represents only one interpretation of what the practice of Medieval swordsmanship and combat was, and can be, all about. Additionally, those who regularly enjoy games of fantasy swordplay or live-action Dungeons and Dragons-style role-playing adventures will likely find little in this work that will translate directly to their method of fantasized, "magical" play-fighting. These issues are themselves addressed more directly and separately in the appendixes, which appear after the illustrated section. The concern in this work is about the use of real weapons—lethal techniques, their reconstruction, and their safe simulation.

In the great number of scholarly works on Medieval military history and the art of war in the Middle Ages, little attention is paid to the martial skills of fighting at the time. Often, the Medieval warrior's craft is reduced to the idea that combatants merely bludgeoned one another or hacked and slashed savagely. This is a myth that is unsupported by historical information, archeological and iconographic evidence, or modern reconstruction. Many of the opinions of historians and academicians stem from a lack of enthusiasm for the expert application of Medieval weapons and a "sport-fencing" viewpoint. There is far more involved than just the collector's curiosity, the living-history reenactor's research, or the theatrical actor-combatant's quest for thrilling performance. The martial artist practitioner or student of the sword has a very different vantage point.

Fundamentally, this book is not specifically about Medieval warfare or Medieval arms and armor in general, but about Medieval swords and swordsmanship, because you really cannot study one without the other. Although the two have been presented separately again and again, doing so is like writing about cars without ever mentioning driving. For too long-swords and swordsmanship have been separated (luckily by authors who were honest enough not to try writing about a subject in which they had no experience). Unfortunately, virtually every book dealing with the Medieval sword or Medieval weaponry ignores the subject of use—swordsmanship. Virtually every book available on European arms and armor describes swords from a museum curator's point of view. That is, they describe merely the "evolution" of the weapons, paying particular attention to the craftsmanship, artistry, and design of hilts. This is the typical art historian's approach, and it is understandable, because the authors are, for the most part, not serious martial artists. (How many of them have tested or even handled the weapons they study, let alone ever practiced with one?) Many books describing swords and Medieval combat were also written in the decades before active students of the sword had begun to seriously practice and train with replica weapons. The opinions of many authors reflect a fundamental misunderstanding of the nature of fighting or of a martial art.

These books tend to focus their attention on form rather than function. Few of the works available describe in any detail or accuracy the "why" of weapon design. What good does it do for a student of the sword to know great details about pommel decorations or blade inscriptions, but not know the reason why a certain sword was fashioned a certain way and how that affected its use? Going back the last 150 years or so, scholars and researchers of this subject have approached these warrior tools essentially as art historians, antiquity collectors, and archaeologists (with occasional input sought from sport fencers and theatrical performers). Up until the past few decades many researchers simply did not have access to a wide range of materials and sources.

Those now studying the actual craft as a martial art have principally had to rely on limited and sometimes biased references. Only a few books give information about function or use and usually only in a passing remark on the armor the weapons encountered. Although the influence of armor on weapons is very important, such an exclusive focus is misleading. The majority of such books also ignore or at least only make brief reference to the few surviving historical manuals on Medieval fighting, and such books are neither intended for nor written by practicing swordsmen. Although some works have also been produced on stage-fighting theory and theatrical techniques for European swords, there are next to none on the undistorted historical skills and their actual martial application. Much study has additionally been done on blade metallurgy, but little on purpose or utility. A good deal of that which has been presented about function has been aimed more toward the limited applications found in theatrical stage-combat.

Much work has also been done to classify and categorize the Medieval sword according to blade shape, length, and hilt design (guard, handle, and pommel). As interesting as all this is, it does not directly concern a study of sword use. After all, it is the blade and how it is used that determines hilt configuration. Following this pattern, the authors of most books on Medieval swords are obsessed with hilt descriptions and every minute change in their ornamentation. They detail the artistic styles and patterns, often giving only passing thought to the swords' functional purpose. Although the ornamentation is important, the authors write as if it alone is the history of the sword rather than concerning themselves with the actual blade of the weapon—which is the whole reason for the thing. When the swords themselves finally are mentioned, there is barely even reference made to such important factors as blade length, weight, or cross-sectional shape. Even more rarely is there any mention of the weapon's feel when handled.

Much misunderstanding of this subject can also be traced to works from earlier in this century that have been continually re-referenced and republished despite their compounding of inaccuracies and near obsolescence. These works still continue to misinform the uninformed, and in many of them the authors want to see clear demarcation between styles of swords, countries that used them, and the periods during which they were popular. They envision a simple linear evolution from one type to another. This is just not the case with European swords (or most arms and armor, for that matter). Sword types popular in one region for a certain length of time may not have appeared in another for quite a while. The duration that a type might be in use in one place could be very different from its duration in another.

For example, a type in use in southern Germany for a century might have fallen out of favor in northern Italy 50 years earlier and would not even appear in Scotland for another 75 years. As some styles fell into disfavor, others arose. These were gradual changes. Good blades often survived and were passed down. There is evidence that a piece could be in use for some 50 years or more. However, fine blades, being prized, were generally well used. Being used, many were lost or ruined in the process. Some weapons in museums or private collections have actually survived because they were hardly used. This may be because they were of poorer quality as much as because they were exceptional and prized. Many pieces have been originally misidentified or poorly cared for, thereby making careful study more difficult. In the study of swords, new research becomes available, revisions are made, and more questions arise all the time. Thus, what matters is an understanding of the art of using them in the first place. Although it is important to know the details of a subject, we should not allow them to become the subject itself. Thus, it is impossible to ignore fighting techniques when discussing this subject. Yet, this is precisely what the vast majority of authors of works on Medieval swords and arms and armor have been forced to do either out of disinterest or ignorance or both.

Therefore, there is really no need here to continually describe in great detail the ornamentation and decorations on historical sword hilts or blade inscriptions. This is all well worth studying and can be quite interesting, but has been done to death already. It also happens to have no direct concern to sword function and use. Students of arms and armor should become familiar with it on their own through available sources. Similar things can be said about the subject of metal forging and sword manufacture, including metallurgy (which, although important, is probably of more interest to those actually making blades). Despite what may be seen as deficiencies, we do, however, owe the authors and scholars of all these earlier works a tremendous debt. It is chiefly through their research and scholarship that we now have swords, weapons, and armor classified and dated for us. They have presented us with an invaluable foundation for study and reference. But when it comes to function and use or methods and techniques, that is a different matter. For the most part, all that has been offered in this area is the typically inappropriate theories of theatrical stage-combat (a problem addressed at length in its own appendix).

Because there is no one source that is trusted, because there is no one authoritative reference to turn to, people are free to suppose almost any assertion about European swords and their techniques, including making up countless ideas ignorant of history, archaeology, or even practical utility. It seems that Medieval sword fighting is often viewed as a wholly subjective matter consisting merely of brute force and ferocity and failing to lend itself to reasoned analysis and discernible principles. Both are equally inaccurate. It can be quite pitiful when leading sport-fencing experts (experienced only with flimsy foils, épées, and sabers) reveal their prejudices with laughable statements about how Medieval swords "weighed 10 pounds" or could only be used for "clumsy bashing and chopping."

People in this activity are notoriously afraid or unable to ever say, "I don't know," about some aspect of Medieval swords and weapon use. This problem is further confounded by the diversity of Medieval-fantasy organizations that conduct fictional, often juvenile ways of weapon-sparring with little regard for the historical reality that inspires them. Still other groups, attempting to simulate styles of actual historical combat, may succeed in different degrees, but nonetheless are forced by habit and safety concerns into a particular style of practice that may or may not be wholly legitimate. The efforts of many historical role-playing groups, and even some living-history organizations, through their emphasis on the romance and fantasy of historical reenactment, have at times retarded the interpretation and replication of actual Medieval fighting arts. Similar criticism can be applied to the stage-combat community and its distortions and traditional misrepresentations that have little or no place in historical fighting or the practice of a martial art. But all this is something that students of the subject must deal with themselves. Whether done by an individual or a group, the sincere, earnest practice of any martial art must be at its core a very personal undertaking.

One of the objectives of this work is to dispel as many of the errors and myths as possible (and, it is hoped, to not add any to them in the process!). As already mentioned, the popular media and Hollywood productions are notorious for misrepresenting Medieval combat (and history in general). Additionally, it seems the Asian martial arts community holds many erroneous and naive assumptions about European arms and armor that are continually accepted without question. In promoting the art of Medieval swordsmanship today we often encounter three distinct communities: students of traditional Asian martial arts, who are predominately unaware of the history of Western martial culture; theatrical-combat students, who apparently need to understand how much more there is to the art than pretending; and, finally, modern Olympic/collegiate fencers, who must often be educated that their refined sport is not innately "superior" to earlier, more brutal methods. Addressing the ignorance of each of these communities while respecting the desire of serious students for detailed information is no small task.

Just as with the subject of my previous book, which attempted to describe the use of Renaissance swords and rapiers, this material originally began from a series of discussions and practices among friends and fellow practitioners. It was clearly obvious that no one person or group had all the answers, and many had serious misconceptions. Often, experience obtained from different individuals or organizations resulted in contradictory understandings. After years of comparing anecdotes, sources, and experiences, I began to realize that far more research was necessary. Eventually, the accumulated information and experiences formed the basis of a series of classroom lectures and demonstrations. This led to still further research, which in turn helped produce a more defined, yet by no means complete, body of knowledge.

As with my study of Renaissance

swordsmanship, it was not easy in this subject to avoid the haphazard trial and error approach, the hearsay, and the sheer fantasy currently out there. As with many of my colleagues and fellow students of the sword, we must split our time between research and practice (some much more so than others). Dividing attention between the literary investigation and the physical interpretation is challenging. Of course, when one is unburdened of concern for the physical training and martial study of the craft, all efforts may be directed toward academic discoveries. The reverse, however, is not true.

Investigation into the practice of how Medieval warriors and knights used their swords and handled themselves in combat requires study in a wide range of fields. It is an area that includes elements of history, art, military history, historical literature, archaeology, languages, anthropology, sociology, psychology, physiology, kinetics, martial arts, fencing, metallurgy, and physics. Still, scholarship and research alone are insufficient for a proper understanding of the craft. Reading and reasoning are vital elements, but they are hardly enough to produce understanding, let alone skill. There is an old saying that those who study books will know how things should be, while those who study people will know how they really are. One cannot learn how to play tennis, for instance, merely by reading about it. Swinging a racket and hitting a few balls help, but to understand it you must actually play at length. So it is with swords and swordsmanship to an even greater degree.

This work is therefore the product of extensive (sometimes obsessive) research and hands-on practice in contact-weapon sparring and training and cutting with historically accurate replica weapons. For too long I have wished for such a book. Finally, after years of disjointed research, personal study, and discovery, I realized that I was able to effectively write the thing myself. As with my earlier book, it was written mostly because it did not already exist, yet was certainly needed. In addition to the material on Medieval swords, it is also my intention to describe the fundamental use of the Medieval shield, one of the most common instruments of war through the ages and one that reached its highest form in Western Europe. The shield has been undeservedly overlooked as a weapon and tool of martial study. It

seems right that its use be described here in terms of Medieval European combat.

Further, it is my hope that this work will inspire increased contact-sparring and practice-cutting among all manner of sword students and medievalists. Active, serious sparring is crucial in developing the sense of distance, timing, and perception necessary for effectively understanding swordsmanship. It is really only through fighting practice, preferably full-contact and with full-body targets, that one gains the physical skills and mental attitude to properly understand and apply weapon techniques. It has been said that the very value of contact-sparring is precisely in the spontaneous, unrehearsed application of realistic techniques with countertiming (that is, against the actions of the adversary rather than with his active cooperation). Although ignored by some, the importance of practice-cutting in weapon training also cannot be understated: virtually everything revolves around it, and all else is secondary. Practice-cutting is a vital element for fully understanding any edged swords, but it is a notoriously neglected area within the study of Medieval swordsmanship today.

As a fighting tradition in Europe, Medieval swordsmanship and fighting skills were eventually to be transformed into those of the Renaissance methods. Today, no direct lineage back to true historical schools or instructors really survives. But through the efforts of specialist scholars and devotees the legacy of these warrior arts can and is being recovered. A growing interest in the actual Medieval fighting arts from the 700s to 1400s has succeeded in creating a new standard for scholarship and study. Today, practitioners of historical Western swordsmanship are reviving and reconstructing the knowledge and skills of these once sophisticated and highly effective martial arts. They are not trying to just reinvent or merely interpret, but to replicate and rebuild the art. It is my sincerest hope that this book will encourage further exploration and serious sword training among its readers and help divert efforts away from mere costumed role-play and pretend performance.

John Clements
November 1998

Introduction

"With two thousand years of experience behind us we have no excuse, when fighting, for not fighting well."

—T.E. Lawrence

There really is no such thing now as a "traditional Medieval European sword art." What there is consists of a collection of reconstructed techniques and movements based on conjecture and analysis of historical arms, armor, art, and literature from several centuries. One may ask how—without any surviving traditions, established schools, or accredited instructors—anything legitimate can be redeveloped or reclaimed. The answer is through serious, long-term practice and study. The chief tools for this are examination of historical arms and armor; extensive training and test-cutting with historically accurate replica weapons; research of the surviving historical manuals and texts; and earnest, realistic contact-sparring with realistic but safe simulated weapons.

Since no historical schools of European martial arts exist today to pass on their learning or tradition (excluding the modern forms of sport-fencing and cane fighting), enthusiasts have had to rediscover skills virtually on their own. A few manuscripts and instructional materials have survived, but most of the information they offer, though important, is only rudimentary. Some of the greatest insights have come (naturally) from studying the actual historical weapons themselves and then doing hands-on training and

cutting practice with accurate replicas. Accurate reproductions of all types of arms and armor have been available for decades (as have quite inaccurate ones, unfortunately). Among the primary tools of investigation have been archaeological analysis, study of Renaissance fencing manuals, battle reenactments, experiments with safe sparring weapons, and contrasting techniques with Asian martial arts and modern sport-fencing. Through physical exercises, academic research, and pure supposition many dedicated individuals and groups are continually working to rebuild these lost skills and reclaim our Western martial heritage.

Today, the modern replication of weapon arts from the Middle Ages has its own distinct character. Its unique martial spirit is neither that of modern sport-fencing, with its gamelike sporting conventions and refined etiquette, nor that of Asian fighting arts, with their cultural and metaphysical components. As a Western martial art form, Medieval swordsmanship differs from its Asian counterparts in many substantial ways and cannot be approached from the same perspective. It is much less structured, involves less etiquette, has no ritual or ceremony, and is without established hierarchy. Western fighting arts are far less defined, and in many ways their replication is still in its infancy. With each passing year there are more discoveries and insights into their practice. But Medieval swordsmanship is far from whole or complete. Historically, it focused purely on utility. There are no ranks, no belts, and no certificates . . . only you and your skill. It is a martial art form, which can and should be viewed within its own historical and cultural contexts. Certainly it can be venerated for its Nordic and Celtic elements of striving against adversity or honored for the knightly chivalric ideal of prowess, charity, piety, humility, and loyalty. Still, we must have no delusions concerning the differences between idealistic practicing of a martial art now, as opposed to training in a fighting method for real combat back then.

The techniques of Medieval European sword fighting have often been described as hardly subtle. The winner it seems *usually* was the biggest and strongest warrior who could keep pressing a slashing and smashing attack. However, although power and endurance were certainly prized, they were clearly not exclusive factors. Medieval combat was by no means untutored or devoid of mastery—far from it. Any experienced medievalist training today can attest to that. Medieval swordsmanship does indeed consist primarily of a "hack-and-slash" style, and its techniques are not flashy or showy. However, it should not be interpreted as being artless or without technique as is so often depicted in movies. Although strength, stamina, and ferociousness were—and are— valuable factors, there can be no doubt that the same can be said of quickness, coordination, and nerve. Those who think the Medieval sword & shield employed just a "wham-bam, whack-whack" fight are greatly misinformed. Those who think the use of the Medieval long-sword merely involves brutish hacking are also laboring under a tremendous delusion. How such beliefs can be held independently of those who assiduously study and train in the subject as a true martial art is due to misinformation from watching too many movies.

Without going into the history of warfare, it's important to state that it is a myth that fighting in Medieval Europe was entirely crude and cumbersome and was never an art. It is perhaps true that only in a cultural context it cannot compare to the systematized traditions of feudal Japanese fighting arts or elements of Chinese martial traditions. However, there is sufficient surviving evidence that (when paired with contemporary research) has given us a much better understanding of the function and use of Medieval European arms and armors to confirm that they were highly effective and dynamic skills at least as rich and distinct as any in Asia. This experience spans many varied lands from roughly 500 to 1500 A.D.— 1,000 years of warrior cultures. There can be absolutely no doubt that fighters from these years seriously practiced and mastered the warrior craft. They learned to skillfully fight in terrain and climes ranging from the desolate, icy north to deep forests and mountainous valleys, the warm Mediterranean coasts and seas, and even into the deserts of the Middle East.

Throughout the Medieval period, training in arms was a requirement among most all Northern peoples for the sons of knights and other nobility, and also for foot soldiers and even the common folk. It is not difficult to imagine that—as is the method in most cultures—these skills were taught within the same household and among relatives. The professional man-at-arms must have also been an invaluable and common source of passed-on knowledge. Professional masters and teachers of weaponry and swordsmanship were not uncommon. For example, there was the long-lived guild of St. Mark in Germany, a collection of fencing schools run by common citizens and soldiers. The English, too, had their own *Schooles of Defence* that survived well into the Renaissance. They continued for some time to teach the older Medieval swords and weaponry. There were also teachers of clandestine schools of arms and even traveling professional fighters who for money would act as "stand-ins" during trial by combat.

Many of the instructors of various fencing guilds, especially in Italy and Germany, would also tutor the upper classes and aristocracy. Training for war and tournament was an everyday fact of life for knights, especially. These were not skills just for use in the local village or backwood paths, but intended for the battlefield complexities encountered with whole armies at war. The details we have of such practices and methods are unfortunately sketchy, at best. A good deal of it is only conjecture. As is not the case with many of the ancient weapon arts of Asia, we have little surviving knowledge of what actual methods of training and fighting were for the

Medieval warriors of Europe other than some of those used for tournaments.[1] Even the terminology used in training and fighting itself has not survived intact. However, again, in contrast to our knowledge of Asian martial arts, we do not have to rely entirely upon unwritten traditions inherited person by person for all our knowledge of Medieval methods, since there actually were numerous technical manuals on fighting published during this time.

In noticeable contrast to some of the well-preserved Asian fighting systems, there are no national styles and traditional ethnic or cultural forms for European methods to continue as an art. There is no real Celtic or Norman or Frankish style, no purely Germanic or Flemish method, no Lombard or Burgundian system, and no authentic Saxon or Angle form to follow. Although many peoples and ethnic groupings did apparently have something of their own favored national arms, the differences appear likely to have not been major.[2] It is possible the differences were more cosmetic than technical. It is very difficult to separate the weapons a people used from the societal and historical conditions that prompted their development.

Because of this, differences in opinion, technique, or method can now often be a subjective matter of personal preference among students of Medieval arms and armor. Debate, therefore, tends to revolve around just what is historically accurate for what people, under what conditions, during which portion of the Medieval period. In other words, it's not just about who used what types of sword or shield or helmet, but why and how they originated and used them. However, the fact that there are no issues of ethnic and cultural pride to interfere with the study of Medieval swordsmanship and combat skills is actually a benefit to objectively reconstructing them. There can be little doubt that the warring peoples of the Middle Ages likely had their own regional and perhaps even ethnic differences in their methods of fighting. Though they surely varied, they must have

done so only within the parameters of what was both reasonable and functionally possible for the weapons they employed and the adversarial conditions under which they were used.[3]

As a martial art form, the modern replication and practice of historical Western sword skills as of yet cannot really be clearly separated into different "styles" (e.g., the German or English schools or the French and Italian methods). There are certainly very clear differences in the surviving teachings of various masters, but insufficient knowledge and detail so far prevents a true reconstruction of the techniques and methods of any one entire system that would then enable any "distinct style" of swordsmanship or fighting to completely reemerge. Considerably more research and study will be needed. Until such a time, there is instead a more or less general body of knowledge that includes techniques and principles that, in themselves, may be a composite of any number of Medieval nations and regional schools or individual masters. Anything else is only superficial.

The incomplete nature of this subject does offer an exciting sense of discovery and inquiry on the part of its followers. In fact, there is a vitality in the many modern interpretations and approaches to Medieval combat as practiced and reenacted today. For decades now, there have been dedicated Medievalists and hoplologists across North America and Europe in many different organizations. They have researched, studied, and practiced in order to reconstruct our Western martial heritage. It is a challenging task with no clear consensus in many areas and subject matters. As with any area of historical study that involves archaeological and scholarly investigation, there is a great deal that must always be viewed as tentative, pending future discoveries and understanding. Within the subject of using historical arms and armor there is also a very unique and very active dimension to the research. This dimension involves considerable athletic participation and physical re-creation.

Unfortunately, when this dimension is combined

---

[1] It must be recognized that the historical Medieval tournament is certainly not equivalent to the Medieval battlefield or even to single trial by combat. Also, any single particular historical tournament reference is not representative of all tournaments. Tournament conditions and rules varied among regions and countries at different times and evolved over generations, becoming more ritualized and less martial as time progressed. For example, though there are references to forms of tournament combat where rules were invoked to avoid strikes below the waist and to the legs, this was not always so.

[2] Except more perhaps for some concepts among Italian, German, or English schools during the late 1400s and more into the 1500s.

[3] When we consider the great diversity among Asian fighting arts, with their dozens and dozens of styles and substyles, this is not at all surprising.

with the high level of fantasy and role-playing that is such a strong element with many enthusiasts, it tends to romanticize and cloud the details of accurate reconstruction and realistic practice. The various methods of Medieval combat simulation or weapon-sparring that are currently being pursued by groups and individuals do not always lead to very similar (or realistic) experiences and conclusions. Any one method or manner of reconstruction may emphasize certain aspects of Medieval swordsmanship or battle that others may not. What they all have in common are their nonlethality and their emphasis on safety (to one degree or another) when conducting mock fighting or sparring. Regrettably, such factors as ignorance, familiarity, pride, self-interest, and even indifference can all prevent practitioners from exploring other options in their weapon practice and free-sparring.

In a sense, modern researchers doing training or reenactments really cannot hope to even approach, let alone surpass, those historical fighters who trained virtually every day for real combat, with real weapons, to actually kill. Historical men were real warriors who over hundreds and hundreds of years passed on lifetimes of accumulated experience, both good and bad, learned in life-threatening warfare and duels.

How can individuals playing around on weekends ever imagine we could duplicate their fighting capacity or even dare assume to innovate fighting techniques? Through exercises and practice drills with replica weapons and our modern advantage of safe sparring, the most that can be reasonably achieved is a facsimile of what these warriors did. Safe contact-sparring, in which one can be "killed" yet remain alive and safe to learn and improve, is the sole means at our disposal for realistically emulating the warrior skills of the past. It is through contact-sparring that we can only speculate about what appears to be practical and realistic techniques for offense and defense with Medieval weaponry. The rest is fairly self-evident after we become more skillful and experienced.

By studying the weapons, the armor, the historical accounts of battles, the manuscripts and manuals, and the artwork on tapestries, effigies, and sculpture, we can come to a reasoned composite of how men fought and killed with these vicious

implements. We can also gain insight by analyzing the literary accounts from battles, duels, and tournaments. Additionally, we have the opportunity to practice cutting with replicas of actual swords and weapons. Test-cutting and sparring use the same movements and teach perhaps the same physical mechanics encountered in battle. Only the emotional content of facing death and taking life is missing. That is not to belittle the importance of such psychological factors at all. Quite the contrary, they are paramount.

Being really threatened with death, the prospect of being maimed, pain, and fright must surely totally change one's outlook in combat. The level of adrenaline increases, and the emotional responses of rage and panic come to the forefront. This is quite different from the friendly and occasionally chivalrous encounters of modern enthusiasts (despite the intensity and effort that may be encountered in such competitions). This reality is seldom reflected in the practice of any modern martial art, Asian or Western. Regardless of skill and physical conditioning, the individual must be psychologically equipped and ready to handle the stress and danger of combat. It is precisely the absence of such emotional elements of real fear and anger that enables us as modern practitioners to enjoy our hobby, sport, research, martial art, and our "blood lust."

Consequently, no discussion of Medieval swordsmanship would be complete without placing it in context to modern *swordplay*. The notion is sometimes still fostered that the modern form of collegiate/Olympic sport-fencing is somehow a more highly developed "science" of sword fighting than anything that previously arose in Europe. This is just not so. Nor is it true that Medieval or Renaissance swordsmanship can be reconstructed by simply *deconstructing* classical fencing movements and slightly altering them (the approach used by countless fight directors and choreographers). One cannot ignore the tremendous changes that European fighting arts underwent during the Renaissance. The methods of earlier Medieval combat were profoundly altered by new conditions. Further developments continued under the unique social and military conditions that followed in the 1700s. Yet, an attitude has grown among some that modern sport-fencing is more sophisticated and therefore somehow "superior" to anything that preceded it. This indirectly stems from a bias held by the upper classes that had originally developed *small-sword play* (a descendant of *rapier fencing*) into a refined and elegant gentleman's art. In the scientific approach to its game, classical sport-fencing has never entirely escaped this pretentious view.

The sport of modern fencing is a highly specialized skill constructed for a specific set of contrived circumstances, featherweight tools, and sporting rules. Although the basic movement form uses highly sophisticated mechanics, it is by no means a "higher evolved" form of fighting. Swordsmanship is not a linear progression toward some ideal form. The old idea of heavy, cumbersome chopping blades evolving slowly into the refined, featherweight, slender small-sword is a historically and militarily ignorant notion. Indeed, much of sport-fencing's rules, constraints, limitations, and other artificial constructs would be highly detrimental (if not useless) with Medieval weapons. Not only that, they would be severely impaired when faced with the simple addition of a shield, the inclusion of virtually any armor, or even the free use of the second-hand or companion weapon. All the game of modern fencing really does is to very usefully break down certain movements, actions, and concepts into identifiable principles (based primarily on concepts devised in the 1700s, formalized in the 1800s, and then codified early in this century!). This technical view can of course help analyze and examine almost any form of sword fighting. But modern sport-fencing (which just barely qualifies as a true martial art) developed from urban weapons of self-defense that were employed under conditions very different from those used in the typical Medieval battle or tournament.

When all the fencing books written by fencing masters going back the past 200 years are examined, they are dismissive and ignorant of and condescending toward Medieval and Renaissance fighting. Yet some people now expect us to believe that the end product of centuries spent moving further and further away from battlefield effectiveness and street-level lethality (resulting in today's sport) is going to help us understand Medieval or Renaissance methods. The assertion that modern fencing coaches

have some de facto authority over skills in which they have little practical experience ends up obscuring any real value the coaches might actually have to offer. Being a competent sport fencer could certainly help make it easier for someone to learn Medieval swordsmanship, but it is not at all a prerequisite. Looking at it as such could even be a handicap to proper understanding.

There are those who even believe that, other than sport-fencers and stunt actors, there can't really be skilled Western swordsmen today. They think that because there are no longer any real historical schools or accomplished "masters," as there are for Asian martial arts, that no one can possibly know anything significant. They believe all of us are just playing and cannot learn something real about such long-dead skills without the formalities and methodologies such as found in traditional Asian fighting arts. They cannot understand that there is *something* for others to understand. They don't realize that there are people who really can and do train with Medieval (and Renaissance) swords, and that they practice test-cutting and indulge in forms of intense free-sparring.[4] They also do not know that such people study in depth the historical manuals of the old "forgotten" Masters. They do grasp that these students of the sword practice and train in manners far different from those of modern fencers or actors in movie and television fight scenes. Across North America alone, there are thousands of such enthusiasts, and among these there are perhaps only a few dozen who possess skill and martial knowledge of an exceptionally high degree.

Yet to one degree or another we are all amateurs in the pursuit of this martial subject. No one can be "expert" unless he has actually fought and killed with a real sword. To call someone "master" of a fighting skill when you are even less qualified to know the difference than he is a hollow label. For someone to claim "mastery" himself without a true authoritative mentor or guide to qualify him is equally a sham. Thus, in a very true sense there *can be no true masters* of Medieval or Renaissance swordsmanship today in the same manner as there are for Asian martial arts. All there can be now are students and scholars of Western martial culture who study and train in *historical fencing* until they

---

[4] Whereas sparring in general is any manner of intentionally noninjurious fighting practice, *free-sparring* is that in which each party openly tries to "defeat" or best the other as an outcome.

seriously accept for themselves the title of *swordsman*. Even then they must continually demonstrate and amend their knowledge.

Considering all this brings some likely questions to mind. Exactly how do we know what we think we know? Who today has had to repeatedly defend his life against a long cutting blade? Certainly, no one has fought for real with Medieval swords or a sword and shield for more than 300 years. Is there anyone living who knows for sure exactly how Medieval warriors fought? No. Are there any authentic, surviving skills that continue to be passed on today? Not exactly. Does this mean that we can't be sure of how they genuinely used their weapons or how they actually fought? Not entirely. Does this mean we can never know authentic or real techniques? Well, only in a sense. So then, *can* we rediscover or even reinvent techniques; *can* we develop true ability? Yes, of course we can. It is indeed possible for individuals without the benefit of an established "school of fighting" or the tutelage of a "trained master" to develop effective and formidable historical Medieval fighting skills to a high degree. There are many Medievalists and martialists across the nation doing so. Some have been active for decades. It is not easy and it takes considerable practice and exceptional dedication.

Exactly who is there today who can be recognized as expert in the function and use of Medieval swords and weaponry? Who would there be to even qualify or certify such knowledgeable individuals as such? Certainly not those with doctorates in Medieval studies nor the curators of museum arms collections nor those proclaiming certificates in theatrical fight direction. Sport-fencing instructors are also way out of their league in this, and masters of Asian martial arts are in another ballpark entirely. There are no official governing bodies or authorities with say over who is or isn't accomplished in the craft. There is no means by which others can really declare anyone a "master." Those with proficiency in the antagonistic application of historical European arms and martial skills must, for the most part, be recognized by self-appointment and popular acclaim. Expert practitioners of Medieval fighting skills today must develop and practice their ability in the same essential manner as their ancestors— through practical hands-on application (non-lethally of course). Our knowledge is incomplete, but it is by no means superficial. Expanding and refining it is a continual process of research, training, and experimentation.

The simple, powerful techniques of the Medieval sword developed in history because of the necessity to defend oneself and defeat the enemy. The moves are those that the natural biomechanics of the human body allow and for which the tools were shrewdly designed. Their techniques and tactics are a matter of physiology and psychology. The method of discovering, practicing, and applying the most effective and efficient of these against someone else doing the same is what we wish to study in the form of our Western martial heritage—the *Medieval Art of the Sword*.

CHAPTER ONE

The Medieval Combat Environment

The idea of the "Middle Ages" is exclusively a Western historical concept. It does not apply to other regions of the world. The word *Medieval* itself has even been called merely a convenient adjective for referring to the time span of the Middle Ages. The era of the Middle Ages is made up of those centuries between the "fall" of the Roman Empire in the West (no one had really noticed it fell) and the resurgence of civilization and culture that came to be called the Renaissance.[1] This "middle" time span also includes the Dark Ages (about 476–1000 A.D.), so called because the light of knowledge and skills was dimmed in the chaos that followed the gradual collapse of the Western Roman Empire. The Medieval period itself is often called the Middle Ages, indicating that it came between the glory of Rome and the rise of Renaissance Europe. It has been described as one long conflict between kings and popes and bishops and lords. Essentially, kings and bishops wanted weak popes, while popes and knights wanted weak kings. This situation, combined with religious and ethnic strife, territorial disputes, cultural clashes, invasions, plagues, disputed successions, and assorted rivalries, created an environment of constant violence. Much of Medieval society was based on warfare as a way of life.

The Medieval knight was by no means the sole practitioner of swordsmanship or user of swords and shields. The feudal system by nature pressed free men into military service. Bearing arms was itself synonymous with freedom, but not just knights and freemen were armed. The common folk were not all helpless peasants. They too were frequently armed against bandits and even to defend the realm when called upon. Often they were required to be ready and equipped (but not nearly as well as the warrior class).

It is important to realize that the nature of Medieval warfare through the centuries was not static and fixed, but had diverse and evolving patterns. Wars tended to be short affairs, and sieges of castles and fortresses were far more common than field battles. Sieges were what Medieval warfare actually revolved around. Surprisingly, full-scale battles were not all that common. Opposing sides could not always meet on equal terms, and the consequences of doing otherwise could be disastrous. Medieval combat was a violent, jumbled, and bloody affair. Far more than any mix of single engagements, battle was

[1] Historians first used the terms *Medieval* and *Middle Ages* as early as 1453. The exact dates are arbitrary, and the era begins more or less with the collapse of Roman political control and cultural dominance.

a chaotic and crowded clash of rushing and blundering armed men. Shields and shafted pole weapons clashed as spears, arrows, and axes flew back and forth. Weapon met weapon, and men grappled. The screams and yells of the living and the dying mixed with the sounds of horses and clanging steel. Some men stood firm, some fell, and some ran. Usually, one side finally broke and was either routed or withdrew. It is worth stating, though, that feudal warfare itself was not a primitive or disorganized affair by any means. It involved a good deal of documented strategy, tactics, maneuvers, and spying. Even horse archers and mercenaries were in use. As warriors, Medieval knights in particular were far from being undisciplined and rash. They prized cunning, stratagem, and prudence, but these were elusive qualities.

The mounted knight was not nearly as dominant over footmen and archers as is commonly believed.[2] Foot soldiers, including spearmen and archers, had virtually equal roles. Each type of fighter filled a need and mutually supported the others. Although in any particular battle one type might prove more effective or even decisive, this would not render the others obsolete or irrelevant. Medieval warfare was also not really any more "chivalrous" in its character than warfare of any other period of history. The notion of the chivalric knight in shining armor valiantly sparing the weak in favor of challenging his fellows is hardly much more than myth. Although there are numerous accounts of quite chivalrous behavior by knights during wars, there was always a disparity between ideals and practice. Medieval swordsmanship, or the art of sword and shield, need not be concerned closely with knightly chivalry.[3] It can be separated from it as easily as Japanese kenjutsu or kendo from feudal bushido or modern sport-fencing from the Renaissance *code duello*. Indeed, awareness of this separation is a sure way of approaching study of the skill as a distinct and self-contained fighting art.

Especially during the period from 700 to 1000 A.D., battles were fought mostly on foot. This age was primarily the time of mail-clad Frankish, Viking, Saxon, and Norman warriors armed with axe, spear, long knife, and sword. Even the Franks and Normans, who were among the first to rely extensively on heavy cavalry, used foot soldiers. Horses were still used more for transportation to the battlefield. But from the time of the Normans, and up to about 1350, mounted warriors did dominate. This has been described as originally a reaction to the mobile forces of Viking, Muslim, and Magyar invaders, who could not be easily combated on foot alone. If the average warrior couldn't afford a horse, though, he fought on foot.

Of course, after 1200 A.D., it was common for knights to fight mounted rather than on foot (although, it's documented that a large number of battles even before 1200 were won through the use of dismounted knights). Knights often trained for war in small tactical horse units sometimes called *corrois*. Swordsmanship and mounted combat are certainly not exclusive practices, but rather complementary. Although the issue of mounted combat is well outside the scope of this examination of Medieval swordsmanship, its significance should at least be addressed. There are major and obvious differences between mounted fighting and combat on foot. There are differences of height, reach, momentum, movement, and permissible technique. The horse itself serves as an obstacle to the rider for many actions that would be appropriate for foot combat (horizontal cuts and certain parries or thrusts, for instance). But by standing in the stirrups when fighting rather than sitting in saddle, a warrior could strike downward with great momentum. A horse also allows for other actions effective only from the back of such an animal. However, the sword was very much the principal cavalry weapon, more so than even the lance or spear. Only the sword—not the spear, axe, or mace—could be used easily against foot soldiers as against other mounted fighters in both melee and charge.

Today, mounted performance riders and Medieval

---

[2] The belief that cavalry dominated Medieval warfare is incorrect, as is the belief that the charge was designed specifically for use against infantry. The main activity of cavalry combat came by using sword and mace *after* the initial clash by spear and long lance. The shock of a clash itself was rarely sufficient to break a wall of foot soldiers on its own, either on the first or succeeding charges.

[3] A typical knight's notion of chivalry in battle was for the most part limited to his social equals—other knights—and not for those beneath him. If they were captured, other knights (and sometimes clergy) could be ransomed. Common foot soldiers, men-at-arms, peasants, infidels, and all others were typically slaughtered and were themselves rarely able to capture and ransom knights.

cavalry reenactors can do only rudimentary, even simplistic combat routines and stunts on horseback. There are just too many inherent dangers to the horses as well as the riders (from being thrown as well as being struck). Anyone who has never ridden a horse cannot imagine the physical demands that it places upon the rider. Those who have never stood close by a horse as it charges past can also not understand the speed and momentum that such a large, heavy beast can generate. Ignorance of both of these, combined with general inexperience in Medieval warfare disciplines, leads to a profound naivete among many enthusiasts.

The shock value of knightly heavy cavalry with spear and sword and couched lance was often decisive and devastating (although, it could also be a disaster). However, due to the combination of effective archery and massed spearmen, knights and the far more numerous men-at-arms eventually began again to fight dismounted more and more. Massed archery became more and more common as did heavier armors for most all warriors. After this, other factors began to intervene more until formations of pikemen and firearms forced even greater changes. This is a simplistic view, but because this book is not a treatise on warfare it will suffice for our purposes. The subject of Medieval warfare is one that rightly must be studied separately.

Throughout the study of swords and archaic fighting, we must also keep in mind that there has always been a noticeable difference between fighting in mass battle and fighting one to one. Unlike single combat or small skirmishes, stances, footwork, and cuts usable are all typically much more restricted in mass combat. More precisely, there is in single combat the opportunity for the application of more specific and focused action.[4] Mass battle's chaotic rush, though certainly favoring the more highly proficient warrior, can still be a matter of luck and circumstance. It has been often repeated that it doesn't matter if you're Conan or Lancelot, if that next arrow or spear has your name on it, you're done for. Anyone who has ever participated in group-

sparring will understand this completely. What matters most often is the attitude and reaction of clashing groups on the whole more than whom you have at your side or are directly facing.

Individual combat, on the other hand, is well known for allowing greater use of expertise and developed skills. Although further arguments could be made either way here, doing so would digress too far from the subject at hand. The point, then, is that one often has to make a distinction between single and group fighting when talking about the use of a particular weapon, technique, or tactic. One can apply much the same method of fighting whether fighting a single duel or rushing a dozen opponents. However, there are indeed differences in the nature of a melee as opposed to individual combat and duel. It is naive to believe otherwise.

There can be no doubt that techniques have a time and place for their use and that the crowded clash of mass combat is a severe limitation on many. Group-sparring (or the re-creation of a mass battle) has its own dynamic that cannot be fully comprehended unless one has experienced it firsthand. It could be compared to two cars racing one another on a track as opposed to rushing around in congested city traffic. You have a lot more things to watch out for on urban streets and yet far fewer things you are free to do. Although it has been said that on a strategic level one-on-one is basically the same as a thousand against a thousand, this is not exactly equivalent to the physical actions of applying individual techniques. A famous swordsman once said, "One fighting 10 is the same as 10 versus 100 or 1,000 versus 10,000." It is merely a matter of discerning and applying the common principles.

Although great ability can transcend situations, and overall fighting is much the same whether one fights 10 or 10 fight 100, there is still a noticeable contrast between single and group fighting. If a warrior armed with a dagger fights one armed with a spear, the fight will invariably go to the superior fighter despite the spear's arguable advantage. But if 100 spearmen engage a group of 100 with daggers,

---

[4] This is something often witnessed in kenjutsu, Japanese swordsmanship. Apparently, this was realized once swordsmen in that country began to focus on perfecting their craft as a higher end in itself rather than only a war-fighting skill. During the era of the Tokugawa peace (in the 1600s), without constant warfare to occupy them, samurai began to seek other justification for their skills and training efforts. They began to place more focus on elements of personal spiritual and character development in the practice of their craft. In this we see the beginning of martial "arts" in contrast to martial "skills." A similar occurrence took place in Europe during the Renaissance with regard to the personal dueling weapon *par excellence*, the rapier.

the encounter will likely unfold very differently (assuming consideration for, among others, formation, terrain, leadership, training, and morale). Since most historical combat was of the massed variety, most information derives from such. But in the case of modern enthusiasts and martialists, it is single combat or small-group skirmishes in which the majority of our experience and opportunity lies. Therefore, when necessary, this work will defer to that distinction while attempting to keep it in historical focus.

Medieval combat is a complex and varied subject. It is one that cannot be approached in isolation from its many parts. Fighting among chain mail-clad warriors of 1066 was not exactly the same as that of foot knights in 1425.[5] The complex factors that involved mounted warriors and archery, for instance, cannot be ignored. Yet in a study of foot warriors and their weaponry as presented here, that is precisely what must often be done. All that can be said is that we are recognizing this limitation and, it is hoped, placing the use of the Medieval sword in proper relation to a larger whole.

[5] The term *chain mail* is itself something of a misnomer and redundant since *mail* means the chain form of linked-ring armor. The term actually was first used for mail in the mid-1700s. Mail, as the armor is known (from the Old French word *maille*, meaning mesh), has been around for well over 2,000 years. Likely invented by the Celts, it was used extensively by the Romans. Its thousands of small, interlocking rings (usually individually riveted) created a highly flexible armor offering excellent protection against cuts and slashes. However, it gave little protection against concussion blows or stabs. Its links could even break off and be driven into a wound, causing terrible infection. Mail was expensive, time consuming to make, and cumbersome when worn in large amounts. But it was one of the most popular and effective defenses throughout the Middle Ages. Strangely, the word *mail* itself was apparently not first used until the early 1200s. The term *plate mail*, although not historical, is sometimes used to refer to a composite of plate armor worn with mail underneath or occasionally to mail with additional plate pieces attached.

CHAPTER TWO

Medieval Fighting Manuals

The reputation of the Middle Ages often suffers from coming after the achievements of the Roman Empire on the one hand and before those of the Renaissance on the other. Medieval society acquires additional prejudice from association with the term *Dark Ages* as well as from events as diverse as the plagues, the Inquisition, and the Crusades. Although *Medieval* is frequently used today to mean antiquated, backward, or even barbaric, it in fact refers to a time of fairly sophisticated technical and mechanical achievement. The fighting implements and talents of Medieval European peoples were not those of some oppressed peasant farmers, Iron Age nomads, or semi-isolated tropic islanders. They were the well-reasoned implements and disciplined products of vigorous, technically skillful, heterogeneous cultures. Such wide arrays of formidable mechanisms were not produced through mere fortune and accident. All romance and myth aside, Medieval society was highly martial, and its impressive legacy flows from both the savage dynamism of Germanic and Celtic warrior tribes and the ordered might of the Roman war machine.

One of the most obvious questions to ask about this subject is, "Why aren't there any historical works on fighting from the Middle Ages?" This is a good question. The answer is very simple on the one hand and rather complicated on the other. There are certainly few historical sources for descriptions of how Medieval warriors handled their swords and weapons or developed their fighting skills. Firsthand descriptions of battles are very rare, and the few that do exist offer few details on the fighting (at least not from the point of view we would have liked). Even less detail is recorded on the effects and wounds caused by weapons or of the resistance of armors. However, anyone who might believe that there are no actual Medieval fighting manuals or that there are no real historical sources for Medieval martial arts is entirely ignorant on the subject.[1]

One possible explanation for the general lack of historical works on Medieval sword use or fighting skills is simply that they did not write much on the subject. Although general society in the Middle Ages was certainly illiterate and hand-produced books were limited, there are perhaps other reasons for the apparent scarcity of texts on fighting. For the most part, books were rare. An activity as common and familiar as weapon use was limited to the fighting classes of

---

[1] This is but an example of what J. Christoph Amberger, publisher of the historical sword journal *Hammerterz Forum*, has called the "secret history of the sword."

society. Those who did most of the scribe work during the time were typically monks, whose interests did not typically include the details of how to fight. They were concerned far more with laws, official documents, and theological matters. Furthermore, those who would be the most interested in such a subject (knights and men-at-arms) were themselves generally illiterate and not that concerned with "bookish" learning. Why spend time reading about a subject that you had real-life experience in almost daily and had been exposed to since childhood? It might perhaps be the equivalent today of someone spending the effort to create a detailed Internet Web site dedicated to how to dial your telephone or how to park your car. For such pragmatic skills, there was so much everyday opportunity for experience both in battle and tournaments, as well as many veteran teachers around, that spending time in scholarly learning for such a self-evident subject would have surely been an aberration.

Much of what warriors learned was passed down from person to person between households or clans or from father to son. Being mostly illiterate, Medieval people were much more interested in illustrations than in text. This is reflected in the range of scenes that can be found showing battles, tournaments, and single combat in all forms of Medieval art. A good deal of scholarship has already been done in this area. Additionally, Medieval artwork is thematic and not very representative, with elements often presented according to social or theological importance. When it came to depicting combat, those who paid the artisans to produce such works were hardly interested in accurately illustrating fighting "technique" for posterity.

Among the best sources we have for information on the early use of sword & shield and for early Medieval armor and weapons is the famous Bayeux Tapestry. The tapestry is a large embroidery created to celebrate William the Conqueror's invasion of England in 1066 and his subsequent victory at the Battle of Hastings. In its many panels can be seen Saxon warriors with axes, spears, swords, and round shields. Few have armor. The Normans are shown in mail armor, mounted and on foot, with kite-shaped shields, swords, lances, spears, clubs, axes, and bows. The combat is mostly that of a mounted charge against an infantry shield wall, but some insightful

exchanges on the ground are also shown. For information on fighting in later centuries we have such sources as Froissart's *Chronicles*. Between 1370 and 1400, the poet historian Froissart wrote detailed but secondhand accounts of battles from the Hundred Years' War (1337–1453). Beautifully illustrated editions of his writings were later produced, but they reflected the methods of fighting of their own era rather than that of which he was writing.

On the subject of fighting or sword use, the literature of the Medieval period offers dismally few useful references. In contrast to works on methods of the later Renaissance, there are very few historical references on Medieval fighting in existence. However, there are indeed some rare works that have survived. For every one that has survived, we can assume there were several more that did not. We also have no way of knowing how many works have been lost or destroyed in the intervening centuries. The lack of any references to such works within Medieval literature itself may suggest that manuals on how to fight were indeed uncommon. Although these manuals show a range of rudimentary techniques, they reveal enough in their text and illustrations about the basic form and stances of sword use that a great deal of knowledge can be inferred from them by those of sufficient understanding and proficiency. These Medieval works, along with literary descriptions of battles at the time and depictions of fighting in books and artwork, provide for us a firm foundation on which to add our hands-on experience.

The oldest surviving historical manuscript we know of is very likely the *Anonymous Tower Manuscript I-33*, a German work in Latin from the late 1200s on the use of the sword and buckler. Rather than theory, this unusual work is on actual weapon use, and its method closely resembles that of later Renaissance styles. It also reveals several subtle differences between the Medieval and later Renaissance sword-and-buckler styles. The Medieval method, using wider, heavier blades without the fingering grip, had to deal with a greater range of armors and weapons. The manual's movements clearly reflect this. It teaches many involved actions, including a large amount of thrusts (particularly to the face), cuts to the shin and feet, and an array of sword parries and buckler strikes.

Another of the oldest manuscripts may be the

obscure Milanese Del Serpente's alleged work from 1295, *On the Art of Fencing*. Later works on fighting arts include the many German *Fechtbuchs* (actually *Fechterbücher*), or fight books. One of the earliest of these is Johannes Liechtenauer's *Fechtbuch* of 1389, actually compiled by Hanko Doebringer. Liechtenauer (or Hans Lichtenawer) is considered the father of the German school of swordsmanship. A whole series of fencing manuals are based on his work. Doebringer was a priest who at one time appears to have studied fighting under this grand *Fechtmeister* (fight master) and whose teachings he later compiled. It is one of the earliest European works on techniques and methods of fighting instead of just theory, but only portions survive and the rest is reportedly now lost and nonexistent. Liechtenauer himself appears to have studied under such earlier masters as Lamprecht from Bohemia, Virgily from Krakow, and Liegnitzer in Silesia.

Another manual of great significance for the single sword is the *Flos duellatorium* (*Flower of Battle*) from 1410 by the Italian master Fiore dei Liberi. This work, primarily on the use of the long-sword or Italian great-sword, is highly significant because it offers a contrast to exclusively German systems. Dei Liberi studied swordsmanship for some 50 years but was originally taught by German masters and states their influence in his verses. His techniques reveal many aspects, including point attacks and disarms. The techniques and stances shown by dei Liberi for the unarmored great-sword offer an understanding of later Renaissance fighting postures for the single sword. He also covers other weapons and unarmed techniques.

Many of the later Renaissance fencing manuals included some portion of single long-sword fighting, such as the Italians Marozzo in 1536 and Lovino in 1580. Particularly important are the efforts of Germans, including Paulus Mair's huge work of 1550, Joachim Meyer's *Fechtbuch* of 1570, and also Jacob Sutor's *Fechtbuch* of 1612. There are numerous other Renaissance *Fechtbuchs* that include the long-sword, such as the one by Joerg Wilhalm in 1523, Hans Lebkommer's in 1530, *Der Alten Fecter an fengliche Kunst* and *Fechtmeister Kal*. Lebkommer's is actually the work of Christian Egenolph and, as

with many of the others, includes materials from earlier works on the sword, such as those by Andre Pauerfeindts in 1516 and Sigmund Ringeck, circa 1440. The material includes the use of the sword, *Falchion*, and other weapons and now consists mostly of various editions from the 16th to 17th centuries.

Another useful source is the *Codex Wallerstein* from the mid-1400s, which features drawings on long-sword use and other fighting skills. There is also the rare, anonymous Burgundian manuscript from the 1400s, *Le Jeu de la hache* (*Axe Play*) on the use of the pole-axe. Many works on swordfighting also typically included the use of other weapons. Of course, various Viking sagas and Old English poems also offer some important clues and insights into the use of sword and shield. We can also examine the rare anonymous *Harleian Manuscript 3542* (*The Man That Wol*) on the use of the two-handed sword, which was written in Middle English. Many of its archaic technical terms are indecipherable or at least open to considerable interpretation, but some major themes can be identified in this oldest English work on sword use.

Another major work, which retains elements that reflect more the nature of late Medieval fighting, is the more widely known *Fechtbuch* of Hans Talhoffer from 1443. His work was reprinted many times during the 1400s but now consists of various editions from the 16th and 17th centuries. Master Talhoffer, likely a student of Liechtenauer, reveals an array of great-sword techniques, sword-and-buckler moves, dagger fighting, seizures and disarms, grappling techniques, and the Austrian wrestling of Otto the Jew. The work also describes methods of fighting against pole-arms. Like many others, Talhoffer's manual includes fighting with swords while unarmored as well as in full plate. His methods reflect somewhat those of the coming Renaissance with its changing forms of warfare. Talhoffer also covered material relating to dueling and was greatly concerned with secrecy in both the teaching and learning of his skills.

The Germans and Italians were particularly industrious in the 1400s and early 1500s in producing books on their sword arts.[2] The manuals by Italians include Filippo Vadi's treatise on long-sword/great-sword, *Ars gladiatoria* (1480 or 1495), and Diego de Valeria's treatise on arms, also from the late 1400s.

[2] The question arises as to whether they were propelled to write so much as a result of a different social environment or whether theirs just happen to be the texts that have survived more intact.

Both show something of the emerging focus on civilian swordsmanship and the transition toward the cut & thrust forms of the early Renaissance. Pietro Monte, a master and scholar who wrote extensively on martial arts and weaponry, produced his own book on swordsmanship and other weapons in 1509.

There are more than a dozen other significant German works remaining on long-swords/great-swords and two-handers that have yet to be fully analyzed. Many of the works show apparent influence from one another. In the early 1500s the Augsburg master Gregor Erhart wrote a work on the great-sword, *Falchion*, spear, and dagger, which is now reportedly lost. Erhart advocated a method called *ernst fechten* (fighting in earnest). Also, Peter von Danzig produced a book on the long-sword in 1452, and Johannes Leckuechner published a *Fechtbuch* around 1482. Leckuechner added the machete-like *Messer* into his teaching. Another German master, Peter Falkner, produced his *Fechtbuch* in 1490, and H. von Speyer offered one a year later in 1491. Another major source that has survived is that by the great artist Albrecht Dürer from 1512, featuring drawings of techniques for the long-/great-sword. A whole book could be written on the great German sword masters alone (and deservedly so). But this task must be left to others more intimately familiar with their works.

There is also another important element to consider in researching Medieval fighting arts. As one begins to study in depth the many diverse manuals on combat from the later Renaissance, something begins to emerge. Medieval warfare obviously underwent changes in the 1300s and 1400s and even more in the 1500s. As we know, individual combat itself changed with the development of articulated plate armor and the weapons associated with fighting both in it and against it. We also know that the Renaissance Masters of Defence began to systematically study and analyze swordsmanship and fighting. We know they likely raised it to a higher degree of sophistication and effectiveness than ever before in Europe. This came about as a result of the convergence of numerous factors. These include the discarding of heavy armor brought about primarily by the spread of firearms and the reduced role of an individual warrior's skill in arms on the battlefield, as well as the rise of an armed urban middle class.

Specialized schools of defense and other fighting guilds began to thrive under these conditions. In this environment their students and masters discerned numerous techniques and principles, which they rigorously studied and practiced.

But just how many of these principles were their own innovations and discoveries, and how many were merely refined from Medieval concepts? Like much of the progress in Renaissance learning and scientific advance, it could very well be that they based much on what had already been commonly established for centuries. Despite the introduction of plate armor for some combatants, would the nature of fighting with a shield and sword really have changed fundamentally from, say 1100 to 1550 A.D.? In that 400-year span, did the techniques for striking and parrying and cutting and evading alter significantly? Did a Renaissance soldier wearing a few pieces of plate armor or just light leather in 1520 move and fight noticeably differently than a mail-clad knight of 200 to 300 years earlier?

We cannot also discount the information that may be gleaned from a close study of those Renaissance manuscripts (such as Marozzo's *Opera nova* of 1536) covering the use of the sword and buckler or small shields (or targes). Though Renaissance sword blades were lighter and the thrust was used to a far greater extent, it takes no stretch of the imagination to see how their techniques and concepts were carried over from earlier times. The intervening years of plate armor and great-swords could not have completely eliminated the prior centuries of sword & shield skills from each generation. By dissecting those few Renaissance shield techniques hinted at in various works we are able to better validate information from other sources.

Thus, the question arises as to how many of the concepts and techniques revealed in early Renaissance fighting manuals were actually of Medieval origin. We can never know for sure, but it would seem reasonable to imagine a great deal of them would be. There are only so many ways you can strike with a bladed weapon. The basic cuts would not have changed. Cuts must surely have been made with nearly identical footwork as well; the human body can only move in a certain manner. Nor should the stances and defenses of carrying a shield be all that different.

It doesn't seem realistic to believe that the

fundamentals the early Renaissance masters built upon were entirely of their own invention and not following the patterns of their great-grandfathers. Instead, they must surely have called upon a long-established foundation from the Medieval fighting methods, which date back to the Dark Ages and beyond. Such basic concepts must have included ideas such as attacking on the pass, the use of traversing side steps, the coordinated use of a shield when striking a blow, and the idea of countercutting or counterstriking the opponent. This line of thought is in keeping with descriptions of combat dating back to early Viking sagas.

This is also consistent with the descriptions of techniques in the late-Medieval Italian and German treatises on the subject. When we understand the use of early Renaissance cut & thrust sword forms, the use of the Renaissance sword & buckler, and the employment of pole-weapons, this makes even more sense. After all, the history of arms and armor is one of established continuity marked by sudden developments of necessitated innovation. Even then, changes were slow to catch on. This is entirely consistent with the practices of the old English fighting masters. The London Company of Masters guild resisted for some time the encroaching system of the Hispano-Italian rapier in favor of their traditional methods. Similar circumstances existed in German fighting guilds.

There is no doubt that the Renaissance Masters systematized and innovated the study of fighting skills, particularly swordsmanship, into sophisticated, versatile, and highly effective martial arts (culminating in the development of the civilian dueling weapon, the vicious thrusting rapier). A good number of the developments in Renaissance fighting methods resulted from the demands of urban encounters and dueling rather than those strictly from battlefield conditions. But it makes no sense to assume that they were able to achieve their advances in a vacuum. No tradition of fighting or methodology of combat exists by itself. It comes into being as a result of environmental pressure as only a processing or refinement of what existed previously. The English master George Silver even stated this familiar refrain in his *Brief Instructions on My Paradoxes of Defence* of 1599: "There is no manner of teaching comparable to the old ancient teaching."

What can be discerned in late Medieval and early Renaissance manuals cannot have been really all that different in form and in function from what was developed for the use of earlier Medieval swords and shields. The differences in regard to the earlier period must surely lie in the overall attitude toward the study of the craft and the specific techniques developed (e.g., fighting in a shield-wall or defending against massed cavalry charges).

After one has handled accurate reproductions of the weapons, shields, and armors of the Medieval era and then contrasted them to those of the early Renaissance era, this becomes much clearer. Those who have typically focused exclusively on an archeological and inconographical interpretation of arms and armor have been able only to discern general and obvious changes in them over time. The ideas and principles behind their employment are much subtler and cannot be uncovered without extensive hands-on training and martial practice. They do not come through scholarship alone or theatrical playing. That there is a direct and discernible link between the more sophisticated Renaissance fighting systems and the fierce methods of the Middle Ages should be obvious. But just what links the two is important when trying to accurately reconstruct in detail the general techniques of Medieval combat on foot with swords.

The authors of the few surviving late Medieval and early Renaissance martial works were likely not setting out to provide a coherent body of knowledge on the common method of how to fight in full armor. It may very well be that instead the authors had begun to see the need to describe techniques for fighting other than those of the traditional means of combat. Older methods must no longer have been as applicable or valid. This may very well be the case, given that these surviving works on the fighting of the time do not attempt to be all inclusive, but only offer certain fundamentals and insights.

It seems that most Americans—in fact, most Westerners in general—possess a profound ignorance of their own military history and martial culture. There are a great many myths and common misconceptions about historical European fighting skills and arms and armor held even by experienced fencers and many experts of Asian martial arts (this is particularly so for the Renaissance systems). It is no surprise, then, that one can go down to any local bookstore and see shelf after shelf of books on supposedly "secret" Asian fighting arts, yet find a complete absence of titles by the many celebrated European Masters. Indeed, how many other famous works are still shrouded and untranslated from old German or Italian? The teaching of popular Asian martial arts today relies, for the most part, on traditional transmission from one practitioner to another. This process is said to pass on the system of fighting unchanged and whole over generations (although sociologists tell us that this "oral tradition is by its very nature fluid and mutable with each generation"). In our equivalent Western arts, we do not have this personal connection to the past, but we do have something else: detailed technical manuals complete with illustrations. In the classic Western approach to learning we have at our convenience almost two dozen manuals to guide our replication of historical European martial arts. We can examine in their own words and pictures the methods and techniques of historical experts. However, as vital to the study as these manuals are, they are incomplete, superficial in areas, and filled with archaic terminology. Still, they are a prized resource for which the historical weapon arts of other cultures have nothing comparable.

Outside of historical-fencing enthusiasts and re-creational or living-history societies and literary academics, few people are aware of the multitude of instruction manuals by European Masters from the later Middle Ages and Renaissance. These experts developed and taught a craft that they had learned through life-and-death encounters. Their works reveal a variety of weapons and unarmed techniques as well as the trend from the powerful Medieval long-sword to the early Renaissance cut-and-thrust style and then the methodical thrusting of the rapier. These various manuscripts are invaluable resources to direct and guide the study of Medieval fighting skills and swordsmanship. They present us with sophisticated aspects of our Western martial heritage and so are richly deserving of careful study. Historians and scholars have so far been negligent in doing so. Most if not all of these books are generally unfamiliar and not commonly available. Some texts exist only through microfiche or photocopies of older publications. A few have also become available on the Internet. Sword students and scholars around the globe are at work reading and interpreting them.

There is no doubt there were considerable innovations in the study of fighting and swordsmanship in the Renaissance. But there should also be no doubt that they built upon what had already been there for some time. Building upon past methods, whether they are practical or idealized, is a tradition in most all fighting arts. The process of change within the methods is nearly always a gradual and selective one. We know, for example, that the English followed some of their old fighting traditions well into the 1700s and 1800s, as did the Germans. They did not discard or ignore, but rather used, borrowed, adjusted, adopted, and in some cases certainly improved (or at least refined) what was known and had already been done for centuries. They did not make up their methods from scratch but utilized their own formidable martial past. It is this very Medieval martial culture that we will explore in this work.

Medieval artwork, which is a primary source of knowledge of swords and swordsmanship, varies from the cartoonish to the highly representational.

The Victorian-era ideal of the chivalric knight in shining armor is more widely known and of greater influence today than is the less romantic but historical reality of the professional warrior class.

Not all Medieval artwork consists of simple illustrations; much is specifically descriptive of fighting techniques, especially with regard to the use of Medieval bucklers, or small hand-held shields. The fundamentals of their use are not all that different from those used for their larger versions worn on the full arm.

A rare German manuscript on sword and buckler use from the late 1200s reveals the sophistication of fighting skills that were well known and practiced at the time. This short, illustrated manual is indicative of the approach of and attitude toward warrior skills.

Shown clearly is the use of the flat of the blade, and not the edge, in parrying, as well as the reliance on low strikes and rising cuts.

The familiar fighting postures or stances of high, low, middle, and back are repeated. The noticeable fighting distance and the use of passing footwork reveal a great deal about the nature of personal combat at the time.

The considerable use of straight and angled thrusts, as well as visible attempts at parries, completely destroys the assertion that such concepts were not fully conceived until the later Renaissance.

Attacks, counterattacks, and parries both high and low to the arm and leg (as well as the head and torso) are described and depicted as very basic actions. Although fairly commonplace at the time, this level of coordinated, technical application of weapons by Medieval warriors is something not generally realized or appreciated.

The sophistication of Medieval fighting arts was probably nowhere greater than that for the long-sword. This weapon was the subject of intense study and use for hundreds of years, particularly in Germany and Italy. Seen here in illustrations from one Italian manual on fighting are only a few of the standard fighting positions or guards with the weapon. As examples of the depth of martial understanding then known, the drawings alone say far more than words. Although they were presented at a time when such weapons had lost relevance on the battlefield and were impractical for urban self-defense, the early Renaissance master Marozzo included material on great-swords in his work. His terms for postures and cuts correspond closely to those described by Medieval masters of the long-sword.

As both aesthetically impressive and technically accurate, the drawings in many of the German *Fechtbuchs* are unequaled anywhere in the world of illustrating historical martial arts. These are from the well-known artist Dürer. As with many of the Medieval German *Fechtbuchs*, definitive translations and respectable interpretations, though sorely needed, are still being awaited.

Shown here are examples of the effort put into such works during the age. These are but a fraction of Talhoffer's invaluable manual from the mid-1400s.

Once again, the emphasis is placed on thrusting as well as cutting with counterattacks and deflecting actions. Most distinctive are the distance of the combatants and the passing of one leg forward or backward with each attack or technique.

Also noticeable is the emphasis on close-in movements and techniques, including the use of the hilt to trap or deflect the opponent's weapon and especially the use of kicking, grappling, and wrestling moves.

As in many of the Medieval fighting manuals, close-in actions involving grabbing the adversary by hand or binding and trapping with the hilt make up a large part of all techniques described by dei Liberi.

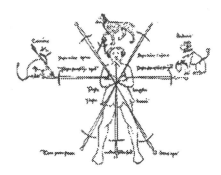

A diagram of dei Liberi's cuts, which were very similar to those devised by later Renaissance masters.

Many manuals contain a range of no-nonsense grappling and wrestling techniques, including kicking and disarming moves. These were clearly not taught as incidentals but rather were worked into their fighting repertoire. Dagger fighting was also considered another important aspect.

The various guards and fighting postures are depicted in virtually every conceivable way. Even without their accompanying text, such depictions reveal a deep understanding of sophisticated fighting concepts that, unfortunately, are seldom associated with Medieval warriors or European arms and armor.

The Medieval long-sword and great-sword have a distinct beauty and artistry in their use that come across in the artwork accompanying many versions of Talhoffer's work.

The flow of movements is far more than mere technical execution of violent actions. This flow is an example of the very definition of a martial art.

Late Medieval sword and buckler.

Talhoffer offers instruction in many weapons and fighting skills other than the long-sword. He includes sword and buckler, dagger, pole-axe, wrestling, and combat on horseback, as well as describing methods of preparing students for judicial duels.

Combat against multiple opponents.

Training with the single sword. Note the placement and angle of the high-attack position and the low-attack posture.

25

From later German *swordmakers* we have still more illustrations of techniques from the traditional system of swordsmanship.

The use of countercuts, feints, preparatory actions, and false attacks are covered as is the less tangible elements of knowing and learning your opponent.

With each illustration the actions of two fighters are typically described with comments and explanations from the master. Note here the attack to the foot (no foot equals no standing and no fighting).

Again, the illustrations themselves speak volumes to today's student of Medieval swordsmanship. Note the distance and footwork in each, as well as the apparent technique being executed.

The examples we have of using long-swords, great-swords, and even true two-handers are not restricted to Medieval sources alone.

Great-sword or true two-handers?

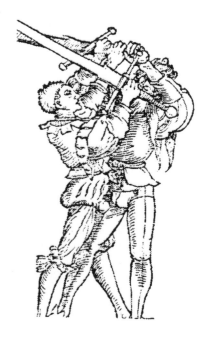

Joseph Swetman's 1617 *Schoole of the Noble and Worthy Science of Defence*.

Much can be learned from later Renaissance sources and English manuals. Many of the Renaissance Masters of Defence kept alive the "old traditions" of long cutting blades and respected their battle potential at the very time they taught the new rapier method.

Fencing practice with Renaissance Italian two-handed swords from Lovino's manual of 1580.

From Jacob Sutor's book of 1612, which includes the older methods.

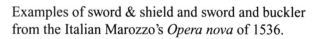

Examples of sword & shield and sword and buckler from the Italian Marozzo's *Opera nova* of 1536.

CHAPTER THREE

Medieval Swords

The Medieval sword has a long and noble heritage behind it. A great deal has been written about its history. Throughout the Middle Ages, the sword was more than a mere weapon. It was the particular weapon of leading warriors and of knighthood. Starting around 1000 A.D. early knights began to revere the sword over all other weapons. It was the very symbol of the knightly warriors and their badge of rank. The sword was their emblem of authority and power. Of all the weapons used by Medieval warriors, only the sword (and the dagger) was carried in its own case and worn. No other weapon was as important, as valuable, and as personal. No other weapon was as anthropomorphised. It could be a sign of a man's wealth and status and his taste. It could be an object of precision workmanship and a family heirloom. At birth a child was sometimes even given his sword along with his name, or his sword was offered later at his coming of age.

The sword was never the primary battle weapon, however. That role belonged to the spear and, to a lesser extent, the axe. On the early Medieval battlefield the axe and spear were actually more common than the sword; later, however, specialty pole-arms and other hand weapons were plentiful. The sword may not have been the most common weapon of the Middle Ages,

but it was certainly the most celebrated. An entire book alone could be written on the romance and lore of the heroic Medieval sword. Yet, although the Medieval sword is common in many books, games, films, television shows, and works of art, it is a greatly misunderstood object. It is routinely represented and handled incorrectly.

What can be said about Medieval swords does not really take all that long, and yet it is not that easy to compile. Essentially, all we are talking about is simply a long, doubled-edged bar of tempered steel with a handle. Yet above all else it is a practical instrument of violence. Swords excelled at one thing: *killing*. As one learned authority often likes to say, "They were instruments of death designed to kill young men, and they did this quite well."

It is important to first define what it is we are discussing. The typical sword of the Middle Ages can be called, simply, the Medieval sword. In fact, to be more precise when we talk of the Medieval sword we are really talking about Medieval swords, plural, for there are several varieties. Medieval swords existed in great varieties over more than nine centuries. A wide range of sword types were used throughout the period. But the "generic" Medieval sword can be generally described as a long, thin, straight, fairly wide blade with two parallel edges and a simple cross-guard (or "cruciform" hilt). Despite the consistency in European swords over the Medieval centuries, experimentation was almost constant. Warriors and knights might even have owned several kinds of swords, being expert in the subtleties of applying each. Most were one-handed weapons capable of both cutting and thrusting. Their blades ranged from wider cleaving ones to thinner, stiffer, and acutely pointed ones. Those with gently tapering blades are often considered the classic "knightly" sword. Many were longer and suited to use with either one or two hands, while still others could only be handled with both. Such specialized designs represented a very sophisticated and inventive response to the hazards of battle against the arms and armors of a range of peoples.

Terminology for Medieval swords (and many other weapons) is not an exact matter. Swords can be classified (typically by blade or hilt design) into a great many categories by curators, collectors, and military historians. Our Medieval warrior forebears did not distinctly clarify differences between classes of swords for us. Often they were not consistent or didn't agree themselves. Plus, word meanings can change over time. Scholars and arms experts over the last century and a half have tried to categorize and classify items according to various criteria of design, age, function, nationality, and style. Curators, collectors, and historians included their knowledge, and then theatrical choreographers and fencers added their own opinions. All this now makes applying historically accurate terms challenging for students and scholars of the sword. However, re-creationists and sword enthusiasts today typically prefer the actual historical terms as much as possible.

Identifying Medieval swords into general forms is not always easy, because two different swords might be identical in their blade length and style but not in their handle, or vice versa. Some swords that survive in collections and museums are the sole existing representatives of their style. These models often will have been given their own unique name based on where they were found. Others survive as samples of a particular common pattern. Acknowledged expert Ewart Oakeshott, unquestionably the leading authority on Medieval swords, divided the many types into two major categories based on blade styles, those from circa 1050–1350 and those from circa 1350–1550. But

these divisions, like so many, are a synthetic construct to help us appreciate their attributes. Oakeshott also developed a useful classification system for Medieval swords based on variations of blade width and length and formation of fullers, handles, guard styles, and pommel designs over the centuries. For example, similar swords might be called Type XII, Type XVI, XVIa, or Type XX. There are more than 20 of these classifications within Oakeshott's typology. A Medieval sword can therefore refer to any variety of single-hand blades or those with hand-and-a-half or double-hand grips. It should be pointed out, however, that the familiar term *hand-and-a-half* is itself not historical and is actually another creation of modern collectors. Although certain German versions of the term were used in the late 1500s well after such swords were past their military value.

The origin of the word *sword* is obscure. It may come from the Scandinavian word *svaerd*, or the Anglo-Saxon *sweord* or *suerd*, or possibly the old Germanic *svert* or *swerdom*. It may also originate from the Old English and Scotch *swerd*. Originally, the "w" was pronounced in most of these versions. In various languages a sword might also be referred to as *schwert*, *svard*, *suerd*, *swerde*, *swerd*, *espada*, or *éspée*. Historically, they seem to have been most often referred to as just *swords*. When carried by mounted knights, it could be called an *arming sword* to distinguish a shorter, thrusting, "antiarmor" blade from longer types. In contrast to a sword, a long-sword (*langenschwert*, *spada longa*, or *esapadon*) has both a long blade and a long grip. The line between what constitutes a Medieval long-sword/war-sword and a great-sword, or between a great-sword and a two-handed sword, is not always clear. Long-swords can include the classes great-sword, bastard-sword, and estoc. Two-hander can refer to a great-sword alone or later on a specialized true two-handed sword. During the 1300s, a long bladed weapon usable in two hands was commonly referred to as a *sword of war*, or a *war-sword* (*épée du guerre*). The largest might also be known as a great-sword (*grete swerd*). In later Elizabethan times, older one-handed Medieval blades became known as *short-swords*, while great-swords were often called two-handers, and the bastard and war-sword variety were referred to as *longe swordes*.

Today, it is generally acceptable to distinguish between shorter single-hand swords and long-swords (also called *war-swords*) and between great-swords and two-handed swords. The term bastard-sword was not used until around 1450 and appears to have referred primarily to longer, typically tapering swords with special half-grips more so than to wide blades. An Italian long-sword or great-sword might also be known as a *spadone*. A few types of particular swords not fitting the generic form of the Middle Ages were the short, cleaver-like *Falchion*, the Bavarian *Dusack*, and German *Messer* and later the narrow, edgeless *estoc* for use against full plate-armor.[1]

The familiar term *broadsword* is commonly misapplied as a generic synonym for Medieval swords or for any long, wide blade in general. Although the first actual appearance of the term may be from one of William Hope"s various "Scots Swordsman" works (circa 1710), it did not take on its popular meaning of referring to Medieval swords until the 1800s. The term likely originated in the 1600s as a way of distinguishing between newer civilian small-swords and the older rapiers. During Hope's time a gentleman's blade had become the slender small-sword, whereas the military still used a cutting blade. Those cage-hilt and basket-hilt swords used by cavalry starting in the 1640s were also broadswords in form, as they were gripped and used much as earlier Medieval swords. Modern use of the now popular misnomer, *broadsword*, actually originated with Victorian-era collectors in the mid-1800s. Fascinated by all things Medieval, they described swords of earlier ages as being "broader" than their own thinner contemporary ones. Many military blades of the 1700s and 1800s, such as spadroons, cutlasses, hangers, and straight sabers, are also classed as broadswords. But the weapon known as the true broadsword is in fact a form of short, basket-hilted, naval cutlass developed around 1630.

Thus, to refer to Medieval swords, whether of the one-handed or hand-and-a-half variety, as broadswords is inaccurate. This is commonly done everywhere from Dungeons & Dragons to video games and by everyone from fantasy sword merchants to stage performers, collectors, and even

historical combat societies. It is generally accepted, but it is not correct. Most Medieval blades may be broad and they may be swords, and everyone may understand what the word refers to, but broadsword is not an appropriate historical term. Besides, a great many Medieval swords are quite tapering with fairly narrow blades. In an effort to bring more accuracy and scholarship to this subject, the term *broadsword* will not be used in this book, and others are encouraged to avoid it as well.

The quality of Medieval swords is often unfairly disparaged by those with little factual knowledge about them. They are sometimes unjustly classed as little more than sharp iron tools. This is absolutely false. The level of metallurgy in Medieval swords has been underrated. It may not have always been exceptional, but it was the highest known in Europe at the time and was more than adequate for the needs of the time. Indeed, Arab sources at one time even acknowledged that Norman swords were the best in the world that they knew of. Recent chemical analysis of Arabic Medieval armor revealed it to be substantially weaker than its equivalent European iron and steel.[2] This contradicts assumptions that because of the superiority of forms of Damascus steel in certain blades, all other Middle Eastern arms and armor must have been of similar quality.

Part of the reason for such ignorance regarding the general caliber of Medieval swords may lie in the scarcity of finer examples. Unlike feudal Japanese swords, which are often in immaculate condition because they have been well cared for over generations, Medieval swords did not enjoy such treatment. As armors and methods of warfare improved through later centuries, swords of many types and styles were discarded, abandoned, or reworked. Unless well-known or richly decorated, for the most part Medieval swords were not looked upon as objects of any particular artistry, history, or interest until the 1800s. Another reason for bias connected with the characteristics of Medieval swords may have much to do with inferior modern reproductions, which are so prevalent, and possibly

---

[1] It is worth noting that some surviving forms of Medieval swords were more ceremonial and decorative, serving only secondarily as self-defense tools if at all. There are even children's swords made for royalty that have survived.

[2] The Saracens too complained that the mail of Crusaders was so tough that their arrows would not penetrate. Others tell of warriors fighting on with 10 or more arrows stuck in their armor.

even poorer Victorian-era replicas and forgeries.

There is, of course, diversity among forms of Medieval sword and certain corresponding changes in use among them. It is important to comprehend that the development of different forms of Medieval sword was not one of linear evolution, but rather a process of adaptation, a series of responses and developments to changing forces. Their designs were changed to meet the necessities of fighting other weapons and defeating armors. When one form of Medieval sword was deemed effective and useful it was imitated and followed until some other adaptation or transition was necessary. It must be understood that in between these distinct classes there were typically many transitional designs with features of each as well as noticeable leaps and gaps between forms. This often makes definitive labeling impossible. For our purposes here, a simple definition of those within the major "families" will suffice. After all, knights and warriors at the time were not trying to make swords fit into one "official classification" or another, but rather were having them made in the pattern of known and effective forms that would suit their own preference.

We recall that European swords of the Middle Ages have their origin in the longer Roman blades that were themselves likely influenced by the longer Celtic and Germanic ones. The late Roman *spatha* eventually became somewhat more popular among the legions than the short, stabbing *gladius*. The Byzantine cavalry adopted a similar long-sword, the *spathion*. These long, slashing, "barbarian" blades often bent in the midst of battle and needed to be immediately straightened (this says something about their quality, but also of the value even a poor sword has as a weapon).

The ancient Celts most likely initiated the advent of the longer slashing sword over the short thrusting one. Dark Age swords also differed from the Saxon/Germanic *scramaseaxe* or *seax* (from which the Saxon people derived their name). This was a popular single-edged long knife or short-sword that eventually fell out of use. They are known to have had versions with both single and two-hand grips (such as the smaller *handseax* or Norse *skalm*, and the larger *longseax*). Such swords were also in use among the Huns and Norsemen. During the Dark Ages the Byzantines and the Franks also adopted

longer blades. They were suitable not only for strong slashes against armored foes, but also for fighting from horseback (the new manner of warfare, which provided a foundation for feudalism). The Scandinavian and Anglo-Saxon long blades make up the forerunners of the "typical" Medieval sword.

As fighting in the early feudal period began to involve greater and greater mounted combat, such longer swords as the *spata* of the Frankish cavalry must have become more commonplace. Swords with dulled or rounded points, usable only for cutting, seem to have been dominant at first. Swords with sharp points able to stab into mail and heavy leather were obviously recognized as more versatile and soon became common. There is proof that swords made only for cutting coexisted side by side with those also capable of thrusting. Interestingly, this actually appears to hold true through the majority of the time period. Starting with Frankish swords, the blade began to be made with more of a tapered shape, which made them more maneuverable without loss of cutting power. There is also evidence that they began to be made less thick toward the point for the same reasons (what are known as *distal* tips).

Surprisingly, the Roman way of war actually had little influence upon the arms and armor or the fighting methods of early-Medieval warriors. For this, they followed the patterns of their more "barbaric" ancestors. It is not hard to imagine that early European warriors, who tended to prefer individual combat and mounted fighting as opposed to fighting in an organized body, would favor a longer, hacking blade. In the tighter formations of a Roman legion or phalanx, a shorter thrusting-style blade makes more sense. On the other hand, when one is as likely to engage in personal single combat as much as a group skirmish, a sword with greater reach, which allows natural strength to be applied in cutting, is eminently practical. This is particularly so when a good portion of the opponents faced might be armored and not equipped with their own swords, but with axes, spears, or even clubs. For those who could afford them, the sword was by far the weapon of choice.

In the early Middle Ages weapons and armor were almost prohibitively expensive (swords alone might be worth from 7 to 20 cows). Full sets were the prized possessions of kings and nobles, who gave them to their followers. Really only the landed nobles could afford to properly equip themselves, and it was usually a duty to do so. During the Dark Ages, metal armor was a rarity for the average warrior. In fact, some early artwork shows warriors fighting essentially unarmored and even barefoot. This continued even into the 1000s. Still, it was the wearing of mail armor that was the main factor influencing the standard design of Medieval swords.

The advantage of a sword weapon on the Medieval battlefield was simple and obvious: the long blade offered a substantial length to defend with while its edge had a large killing area. It could kill and wound by a striking blow or cutting hit, by a pulling or pushing slice, and by a thrusting stab. It could successfully face shields and many armor types. Held at the end of its grip, it traveled through a centripetal arc that created a blow of great force. In this way it made maximum use of its considerable reach. Despite its length, it could still be used close in, and its large guard could bludgeon as well as protect. Overall, there was no other hand-held (non-firearm) weapon so versatile that offered such a balanced offense and defense. It has been said that while the sword was not the perfect Medieval weapon in all circumstances against all possible opponents, it was surely the one that had the greatest potential in the greatest range of encounters. Considering the historical diversity of sword forms worldwide, there can be little doubt of the truth of this statement. For those who could afford them, the sword was the weapon of choice.[3]

Swords are very personal weapons, and, being such, there is rarely any exact standardization among them (each might even have its own sheath that would fit no other). Though they differ, they do so only within certain defined parameters. Blades, guards, handles, and pommels might all be nearly exact from one to another. Most were made entirely as one-of-a-kind pieces, but within a given style or design. Variety among Medieval swords is as much a matter of artistic and cultural choice as of technical necessity on the part of the user (i.e., opponents and armor faced). Differences in sword

choice among warriors was a matter of personal strength, agility, and fighting style. Sometimes a warrior used only what he could afford to obtain or what had been given to him.

Tracing the history of the Medieval sword is not a matter of linear progression. Primarily this has been done through tracking changes in blade and hilt design, but this is never exact. A type of sword or a hilt popular in one region for a certain length of time may not have appeared in another for quite awhile. The duration that one type might be in use in one place could be very different from its duration in another. For example, as stated in the Preface, a type of sword in use in southern Germany for a century might have fallen out of favor in northern Italy 50 years prior and not even appear in Scotland for many more years. As some styles fell into disfavor, others arose. These were gradual changes. Adding further difficulty is the fact that to suit fashion or taste, original blades might have their mountings (guard, handle, pommel) periodically replaced. In later centuries this was not uncommon.

Good blades were passed down within households or to retainers. During the Dark Ages weapons would sometimes be removed from graves after decades and still be in perfect condition. However, good blades, being prized, were usually well used. Being used, many were lost or ruined in the process. Archeological finds have shown a great variety in types found at the same locations. Other finds have discovered bundles of swords that were nearly identical, indicating they were from the same manufacturer who was turning out multiple copies of one particular design. Some archaeological finds have revealed swords clearly from the same maker but where each piece is distinct and individual.

The number of antique Medieval swords in existence today probably numbers only in the tens of thousands.[4] The moist climate of Europe is not the best for preserving steel, and in recent centuries the

---

[3] However, the axe had always been popular as well as relatively inexpensive regardless of armors faced. Light, fast ones with fairly thin, wide blades were common for centuries. Others had smaller, heavier heads with back-spikes, whereas still other forms (both long and short) made excellent throwing weapons. Some axes were specific for war while others were tools adapted to the purpose.

[4] The only Medieval swords that have survived are either those found in archeological sites (bogs, riverbeds, and burial grounds) or those that were kept preserved in castles, private armories, churches, and other institutions. The condition of these swords ranges from pristine to well worn and rusted to "excavated condition" (badly deteriorated).

weapons had not yet acquired their archeological and antiquarian value. Because of the low number of pieces of quality condition, each individual sword find is of great significance: it may be the only example of its kind surviving. In fact, some of what we know about the Medieval sword is limited to study of a single sample weapon. We cannot know for sure whether such a piece is a typical example or a truly unique specimen. Those swords identifiable in artwork only occasionally offer details to expand our knowledge much further. There is also some degree of uncertainty as to whether many weapons surviving in museums and collections are representative of those swords that were intended primarily for fighting on foot or for both mounted and foot combat. Historical artwork depicts many types of blades used for both. Also, over the centuries some blades in collections have rusted or deteriorated so that their tips have rounded or broken off. It may even be the case that there are also those unusual swords that were for fighting under some specific rules of tournaments (i.e., they might be blunted or of different weight).

A great deal of our knowledge of Medieval arms and armor comes from pre-Christian ("pagan") graves and from manuscript drawings, sculpture, and other art. Only a smattering has been gleaned from literary accounts. Little on combat was written down, and archeological evaluations on battlefields yield very little. Also, information on the sometimes unique conditions of knightly tournament contests cannot always be translated into battlefield terms. Museum collections of arms and armor today are often difficult to trace, and they contain many obscure items (hence the reason many of their pieces have survived: they were relatively unused). In the past few centuries interest in Medieval arms and armor waned, and a good deal of knowledge was either forgotten or just never preserved. It is only recently in this century that a more thorough, scientific study of the subject has been undertaken and many new resources have come to light.

Interestingly, unlike European sword forms, which adapted to meet developing challenges, Asian sword styles remained fairly constant, changing little. Japanese swords in particular followed essentially the same established, dependable, all-purpose designs for centuries (a testament to their capable design).

Whereas Asian swords tended to follow something of a "one-model-fits-all" approach to the problem of effectiveness, European swords, facing wider arrays of armor challenges, responded with a specialization of designs. Thus the concept of the "Medieval sword" does not really represent one singular type. By contrast, in referring to "the Japanese sword," we are dealing with a weapon that was fairly uniform and unchanging for centuries and whose subtle differences are really noticeable only to trained experts. Similarly, with few exceptions, Chinese swords have from ancient times consisted of either a chopping saber or a slender, one-handed, cut & thrust sword with straight, parallel edges.

Why it was almost exclusively Western Europe that produced such diverse and original sword forms was the result of several factors. Without a feudal structure elsewhere, a warrior elite who could afford the investment in equipment and training simply did not arise. Those civilizations in hotter climates also did not produce heavy armors, which demanded still further responses. Instead, slashing and slicing methods developed using one-handed, single-edged blades curved for maximum effectiveness. Few kinds of true chopping or cleaving sword blades arose outside of Medieval Europe. Nor were there many two-handed forms or specialized thrusting swords. Naturally, not having the necessity for a shield-countering, armor-defeating weapon, few cultures developed versatile, armor-piercing blades (or the prerequisite metallurgical technology).

The sword, more so than any other weapon, was a personal and noble one. The idea of a sword did not just happen; it wasn't just "invented." The weapon's origin was a gradual process unlike the concept of a club, spear, or knife. The notion of using a long piece of sharp, firm metal to hack and cut came about out of the use of longer knives to stab and block. Cutting came later as metallurgy improved to allow a reliable and lengthened blade. Some swords are merely a sharpened piece of tempered iron with a handle attached. Others made for war and battle tested in skilled hands are something far greater and deadlier. Though produced by relatively simple technology, Medieval swords were indeed sophisticated weapons. The skill by which they were used was equally so.

Finally, one thing that is not usually pointed out is that a great number of Medieval swords on display in museums and armories are often the "prettier" ones rather than the more common warrior blades. Institutions customarily select their pieces based on appearance and historical relevance (although finer swords are rare, and an institute sometimes must take whatever it can get). Frequently, a weapon that might feel great to a swordsman or be of major interest to a practitioner now may not be placed on display at all and instead will remain in a cabinet in the back. It might be considered too plain or too ordinary simply because its art or design doesn't seem very significant and doesn't interest a curator or historian. The pieces that do get displayed then end up in reference books as the prime examples and standards for modern students and swordsmiths to go by. Perhaps in the future, this will begin to change, and collections will also showcase certain swords for their inherent martial value.

DEVELOPMENT OUTLINE OF MEDIEVAL SWORD FORMS CA. 500–1500 A.D.

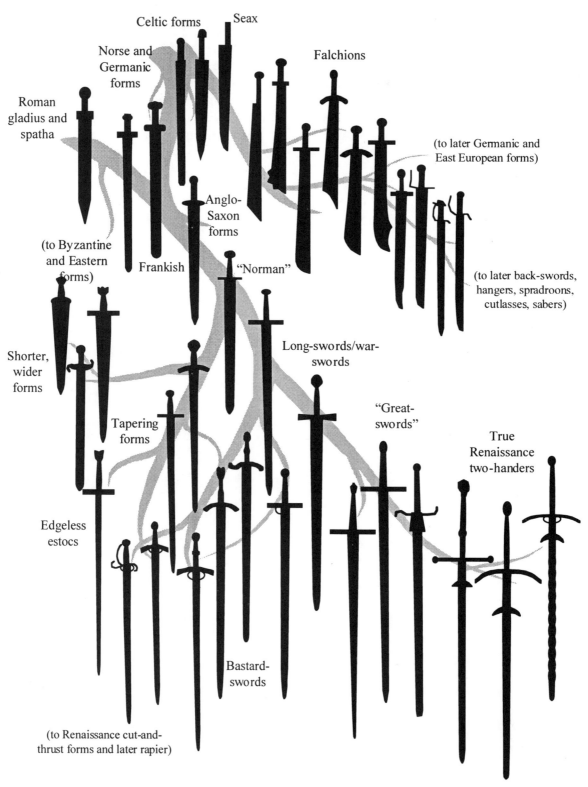

Celtic forms

Seax

Norse and
Germanic
forms

Falchions

Roman
gladius and
spatha

(to later Germanic and
East European forms)

(to Byzantine
and Eastern
forms)

Anglo-
Saxon
forms

Frankish

"Norman"

(to later back-swords,
hangers, spradroons,
cutlasses, sabers)

Shorter,
wider
forms

Long-swords/war-
swords

Tapering
forms

"Great-
swords"

True
Renaissance
two-handers

Edgeless
estocs

Bastard-
swords

(to Renaissance cut-and-
thrust forms and later rapier)

An outline cannot completely show all the relationships among all sword types. Some elements cross over among different classes, such as length and hilts between tapering hexagonal or diamond blade shapes. This chart emphasizes blade function and not simply hilt design.

The typical Medieval sword was designed for one-handed use and fighting with a shield. Lengths ranged from 35 to 43 inches long, with roughly 5 to 8 inches of this being hilt. The average weight was between 2 and 3 1/2 pounds. This style evolved from Celtic, Germanic, late Roman (the *spatha*), and Anglo-Saxon forms. The Viking and early Frankish forms (the *spata*) are also considered to be more direct ancestors. This common form was a one-handed weapon used for hacking, shearing cuts, and also for limited thrusting. The familiar type of Medieval sword consists of either a wide or a narrow blade with a short handle for a one-handed grip. Many styles and forms of these swords simply do not and did not have their own definitive name. The variety of their hilts could be considerable while differences between their blades might be subtle (such as in width, taper, or fullers). Virtually all are straight with two parallel edges. Some blades were just as long as those for long-swords but with single-hand grips. Viking and Anglo-Saxon swords are more distinctive in their design. Their blades tend to be wider and shorter with single, large fullers while their hilts tend to have smaller guards and distinct pommels.

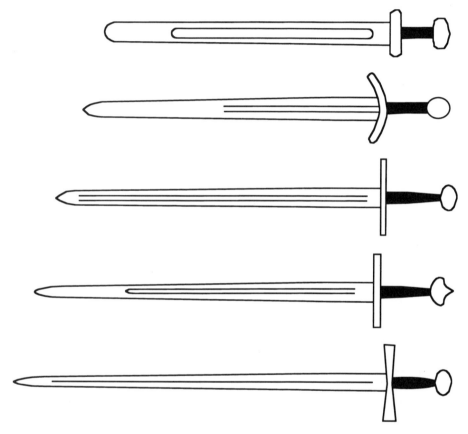

The term *arming-sword* is not very descriptive of any singular sword, but did at one time apparently distinguish a shorter, thinner, pointier one-handed sword for fighting plate armor from those war-swords or long-swords. The term is recorded in 1431 but was surely in use much earlier. They can also be classed as *riding-swords* (also a *parva ensis* or *épée courte*). It is this form which is so closely associated with the idea of the "knightly sword" (circa 1300). Arming-swords might also be carried bare without a sheath in a metal ring at the waist. There is also evidence such swords may occasionally have been worn by knights at court. Stiffer blades of a more flat-diamond shape with central ridges, or *risers,* have been dated to as early as 1250. A variety of one-handed swords with wider, tapering blades and sharply narrowed tips came back into use from about 1350 to 1520 to combat the mixed armors of mail and newer plate. These cut-and-thrust style blades were wide and heavy enough to fight through mail, but were pointed for facing plate. They were ideal for the close, crowded battlefields of mixed armor found in the 1400s. They were popular in mostly Western and Southern Europe. During the 1400s some of these swords included protective guards with finger-rings or side-rings, which led to the *close-* or *compound-hilt.*

LONG-SWORDS

The various kinds of long-bladed swords with handles long enough to be used in two hands are deemed *long-swords*. Long-swords, war-swords, or great-swords are characterized by having *both* a long grip *and* a long blade. First recorded in English about 1450, the term *long-sword* was undoubtedly used earlier, at least in Germany. We know that at the time they did distinguish war-swords or great-swords (*grant éspées* or *grete swerdes*) from "standard" swords in general, but long-swords were really just those larger versions of typical one-handed swords, except with stouter blades. They were "longer swords," as opposed to "single-hand swords" (or just "swords"). The term *war-sword,* from the 1300s, referred to larger swords that were carried in battle. They were usually kept on the saddle as opposed to worn on the belt. They were effective when the bearer fought on foot or when mounted.

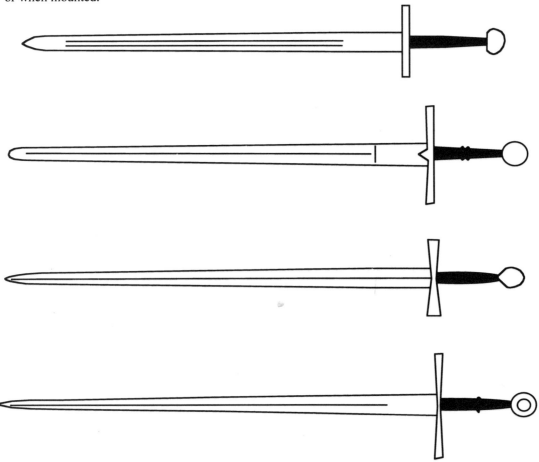

Their blades might be wide and flat or, later on, more narrow and hexagonal. Those of the earlier parallel-edged shape are known more as *war-swords*, while later the thicker, tapering, sharply pointed form were more often called *bastard-swords*. Long-sword blade lengths ranged from approximately 40 to 48 inches long, with roughly 7 to 9 inches of this being hilt. Average weight could be from 2 1/2 to 3 1/2 pounds. Using two hands on these longer weapons allowed for a stronger blow against armored opponents (often not employing shields). Long-swords (or war-swords) eventually helped lead to improved armor, which, in turn, led to the development of larger swords. Longer swords were also necessary on horseback, since larger war horses were then being used to accommodate more heavily armored riders as well as the animal's own armor protection. Sitting higher up called for a longer weapon to reach opponents on foot and on the ground. New evidence suggests such swords were in use as early as circa 1150.

GREAT-SWORDS

Originally the term *great-sword* (or *grete war sword*), also first used in the 1300s, only meant a war-sword (long-sword), but it has now more or less come to mean a subclass of those *larger* long-swords/war-swords that are still not true two-handers. These blades are long and weighty enough to *demand* a double grip. They are swords that cannot be used in a single hand. Although they are "two-hand" swords, great-swords are not the specialized weapons of later two-handed swords. They are antecedents to the even larger Renaissance versions. There is evidence that such weapons may have been in use as early as 1180. At the time, a Medieval great-sword might also be called a *twahandswerds* or *too honde swerd.* The term *two-handed sword* or *two-hander* (German *Bidenhänder*) is really a classification of sword now frequently applied to both Medieval great-swords and Renaissance swords (the *true* two-handed swords). Great-swords are the weapons often depicted in various German sword manuals.

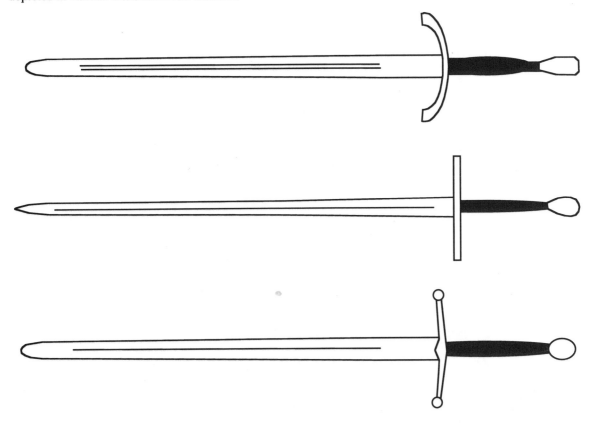

Blade lengths of these great-swords ranged from approximately 44 to 53 inches, with roughly 7 to 9 inches of this being hilt. Average weight ranged between 3 and 4 pounds. Whereas other long-swords could be used on horseback and some even with shields, great-swords were infantry weapons only. Their blades tend to have rounder tips with fullers typically along half their length. These larger swords capable of facing heavier weapons, such as pole-arms and larger axes, were devastating against lighter armors. Long, two-handed swords with narrower, flat hexagonal blades and thinner tips (such as the Italian *spadone*) were a response to plate armor. Against plate armor such rigid, narrow, and sharply pointed swords are not used in the same chop-and-cleave manner as with flatter, wider long-swords and great-swords. Instead, they are handled with tighter movements that emphasize their thrusting points and allow for better use of the hilt. Such weapons saw more use in the later Middle Ages and early Renaissance. The most famous great-sword is the early Scottish *claymore,* circa 1300. The later two-handed claymores of the 1500s and 1600s are not quite the same as their earlier predecessors.

BASTARD-SWORDS

Later in the mid-1400s a form of long-sword with specially shaped grips for one or two hands (a "hand-and-a-half" sword) became known as a *bastard-sword*. This may be because it was neither a true one-handed or great-sword/two-handed one and thus not a member of either "family." Since newer types of shorter swords were coming into use, the term *bastard-sword* came to distinguish this form of long-sword. Bastard-swords typically had longer handles with special "half-grips" that could be used with either one or both hands. These handles have recognizable "waist" and "bottle" shapes (such grips were later used on some Renaissance two-handed swords). The unique bastard-sword half-grip was a versatile and practical innovation. Although, once again classification is not clear since the term *bastard-sword* appears to have not been entirely exclusive to those swords with hand-and-a-half handles as older styles of long-sword were still in limited use. Bastard-swords varied, and they might have either a flat blade or a narrow hexagonal one for fighting plate armor. Some were intended more for cutting, while others were better for thrusting. Blade lengths were typically that of long-swords, at 40 to 48 inches. At 3 to 3 1/2 pounds, they might be slightly heavier than long-swords with simple cross-guards. Their method of use also differed by the significant addition of a compound-hilt of *side-rings* (anneus) and *finger-rings* (annelets). The compound-hilt developed out of the need to protect the now exposed fingers and allowed for the useful technique of *fingering the ricasso* to control the point in stabbing. Warriors were also going more and more without heavy gauntlets, and these newer hilts offered greater hand protection, particularly against intensifying attacks by thrust. Bastard-swords continued to be used by knights and men-at-arms into the 1500s and were particularly popular in Germany and Italy. Their hilt style led to the shorter *cut & thrust* sword forms of the Renaissance. Strangely, in the early Renaissance the term *bastard-sword* was also sometimes used to refer to single-hand arming swords with compound-hilts. A form of German arming sword with a bastard-style compound-hilt was called a *Reitschwert* (cavalry sword) or a *Degen* (knight's sword).

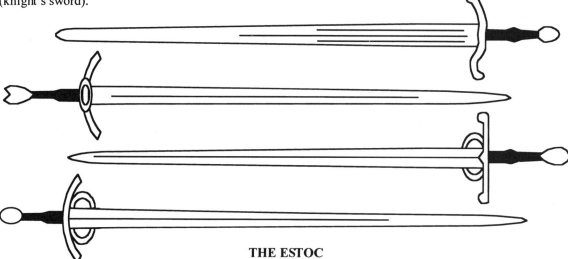

THE ESTOC

This was a form of specialized long-sword with a very rigid, pointed, edgeless triangular or square blade designed exclusively for fighting plate armor by beating on it and thrusting into its openings and gaps. The estoc was essentially a thick armor-piercing rod with a hilt. The guard might be cross-shaped or even a round wooden disc. It could not cut but could be used almost like a club. Called a *stocco* in Italian and a *tuck* in English (the root word is derived from the Old French *estoque* (to thrust; English rapiers are sometimes mistakenly referred to as *tucks*). A German version was known as a *Dreiecker*. Though long, some could be used in either one or two hands, with the second armored hand often gripping the blade itself. Occasionally, estocs are confused with hunting weapons known as *boar-swords*, which have a similar shape but a flat, spearlike tip. Those estocs (or tucks) that endured into the early Renaissance were shorter and one-handed, often with bastard-hilts.

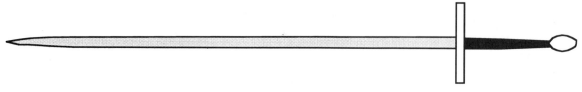

TWO-HANDED SWORDS

These swords first developed from great-swords designed for fighting heavier armor and existed in several sizes and forms. Although their method of use *was* different, it is important that the Renaissance two-handed sword be included here for reference and contrast to the Medieval great-sword two-handers of the same name. Technically, *true* two-handed swords (*épées a deux main*) were actually Renaissance, *not* Medieval weapons. They are really those specialized forms of the later 1500s and 1600s, such as the Swiss/German *Dopplehänder* (both-hander) or *Bidenhänder* (double-hander) or *Zweihander/Zweyhander* (three-hander), which are relatively modern not historical terms. Starting around 1480, English two-handed swords were sometimes referred to as *slaughterswords* after the German *Schlachterschwerter* (battle swords). These weapons were used primarily for fighting against pike-squares, where they would hack paths through lopping the tips off the poles. In Germany, England, and elsewhere, schools also taught their use for single-combat. Typical blades could be up to 6 feet long, often with ring-hilts and particularly long handles (14 to 18 inches long). Weight generally ranged from just over 3 1/2 pounds to 5 pounds or more. Some blades were quite slender for their size, while others had rounded, blunt points. True two-handed swords have compound-hilts with side-rings and enlarged cross-guards of up to 12 inches. Most have small, pointed lugs or flanges protruding from their blades 4 to 8 inches below their guard. These *Parrierhaken,* or parrying hooks, act almost as a secondary guard for the ricasso to prevent other weapons from sliding down into the hands. They make up for the weapon's slowness on defense and can allow another blade to be momentarily trapped or bound up. They can also be used to strike with. The most well-known of *twa handit swordis* is the Scottish *claymore* (Gaelic for *claidheamh-more* or great-sword) that developed out of earlier Scottish great-swords, with which they are often compared. They were used by the Scottish Highlanders against the English in the 1500s. Another sword of the same name is the later Scots basket-hilt broadsword (a relative of the Renaissance Slavic-Italian *schiavona*), whose hilt completely enclosed the hand in a cagelike guard. Since the late 1700s both swords have been known by the same name.

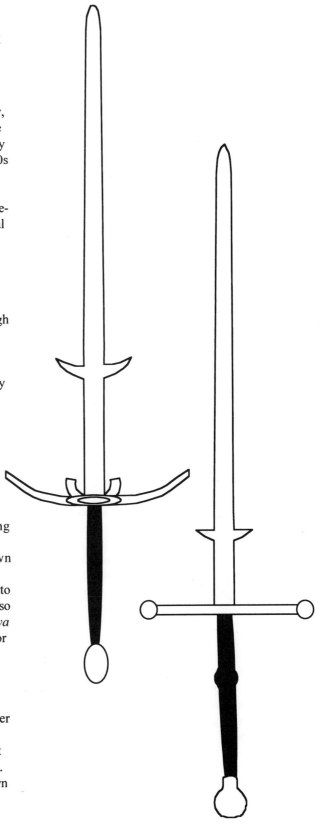

The later true two-handed sword did not abruptly appear because some warrior suddenly realized a bigger sword was better or because someone finally realized that he could swing a heavier blade. There have probably always been those fighters, usually of great size and strength, who prefer the devastating effect of a larger, heavier blade. Perhaps being less quick or agile, their natural inclination might rightly be to take advantage of their strength, or maybe they were both strong and fast and chose to focus on offense. Physically, the warriors of the Middle Ages were not all that different from those in other times, when such large swords were not known. Where there is no need for powerful, heavier (slower), double-hand-gripped swords, there simply aren't any. What started to change during the mid-to-late Middle Ages was the nature of some of the fighting. At the end of the Middle Ages and into the early Renaissance there was also the increased necessity for a bladed weapon capable of reaching and severing the shafts of long pole-weapons (e.g., pikes, halberds, glaives). These weapons were increasingly common on the battlefield, and two-handed swords could chop off their ends and allow fighters to get in past them. This trend in warfare was to increase dramatically during the Renaissance. The fact that more and more warriors were also fighting dismounted in plate armor and without shields meant that two-handed swords were used even more. Bigger, longer swords were increasingly needed to smash, dent, and crack plate armor. By their sheer size and weight, such swords demand that both hands to be used. Their ricassos were often covered in leather wraps. These helped the grip when held there and also acted to protect the blade when being carried over the shoulder (they were too big to wear in a sheath, but the Scots carried theirs slung over their back).

A two-hander or even a slightly smaller great-sword is intimidating. To be wielded it requires a strong and powerful fighter. The devastating chops and hacks such a weapon can make as it sweeps out in a wide arc takes considerable effort. Such a blade could easily take off both of a man's legs at the thigh and surely bring down the biggest warhorse. Medieval two-handers, evolving from great-swords, tended to have smaller hilts, and their blades were more reminiscent of those developed to fight plate. True two-handed swords, as distinct from Medieval long-swords or even great-swords, found use for defending passageways during sieges and for special banner guards on the battlefield. But in the early Renaissance they became common for fighting pike formations and for single-combat duels. Several varieties were used by the Swiss-Germans, Italians, French, and even Spanish (the Swiss apparently were not recorded as having used the weapons in battle until 1495). Some may have even been made purposely large simply to impress people. Those of the Renaissance ranged from swords indistinguishable from their Medieval counterparts to ones with enlarged complex-hilts and waved (or "flame") blades. Certain flame-bladed two-handed swords have come to be known by collectors as *flamberges*, although this is inaccurate. Such swords developed in the early to mid-1500s and were more appropriately known as *flammards* or *flambards* (or the German *Flammenschwert*). The term *flamberge* was also later applied to certain types of rapiers. The wave-blade form is visually striking but really no more effective at cutting than a straight one.

Today, a good number of reproduction two-handers can be found that either are far too heavy (6 to 8 pounds) or far too flimsy. Care should be taken in examining whether one is an accurate replica or a cheaper fantasy version. There were also huge two-handed blades known as *bearing-swords* or parade-swords (*Paratschwert*), weighing up to 15 pounds, which were intended only for carrying in ceremonial processions and parades just to impress onlookers. These are sometimes confused with real swords and have given rise to the myth of two-handers being impossibly sluggish, ponderous things (which, if they had been, their users would not have stood a chance in battle).

THE FALCHION

From at least 1200 A.D. on, this less common form of wide, heavy, single-edged, slightly curved sword was favored for the horrendous power of its chopping blow. The falchion (pronounced fal-shun) was neither greatly prized nor known for high quality (few examples survive today). Being forward weighted/balanced at 3 to 4 pounds, as well as being wider and heavier than typical straight, double-edged blades, falchions were much less maneuverable and were not used in the same manner as more familiar Medieval swords. In fact, the falchion was little more than a meat cleaver, possibly just a simple kitchen and barnyard tool adapted for war and hunting. The term *falchion* has come to be applied to any form of wide, machete-like Medieval chopping sword. Their name may come from a French word for sickle (*fauchon*) or the British *faussart*, which is itself related to the Latin *falx*. Its name might also be related to a hooked pole-arm, the *falcione* or *falco*. Its name may even be connected to the ancient single-edged Spanish convex-sword, the *falcata*. It has been suggested that it originally was the Czech *tesak*. This term was later transformed to the German *Dusack* (or *Dusagge*), a similar cleaver-like sword. There are also references to the falchion later being called a *malchus* or *storta*. It has been claimed as possibly being related to one-edge versions of the old Dark Age long-knife, the *seax* (*sax* or *scramaseax*). The falchion also bears strong resemblance to the later Germanic *Messer* (knife), another type of wide single-edged, machete-like weapon.

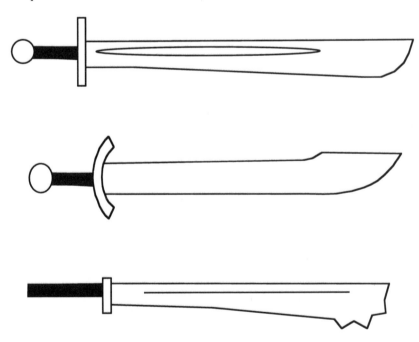

Some early falchions had no guards, but most later ones had straight cross or "s" guards. Falchions seem to have been among the first European blades to have knuckle-guards added to their hilts, which started around 1450 and may have something to do with their lack of agility. The falchion is sometimes considered a form of back-sword, since it has a single forward edge with a thicker, unedged back side (a reason for its powerful chopping cut). Most falchions are much wider at the lower end, adding greater weight to their strong hacking chops. Almost all are suited to single-hand grips, though a few have room for two. Artwork often depicts falchions in use by non-Europeans and employed against armored opponents as much as commoners.

Because of its similarity to the scimitar, the falchion is sometimes said to have been introduced to Europe from the Middle East after the first crusade of 1096. However, the weapon is definitely European and dates from at least 1063. The earliest falchions were straight with curved points, and most were without any fuller. Their backs were also typically straight but could be slightly curved. Still others had convex blades with slender or even wide, triangular points. A few types also had angular, back-clipped points, making them suitable for shallow thrusts. This short back portion was also sometimes sharpened. The falchion was a far better footman's weapon than a mounted warrior's. This makes sense: it cannot be used to thrust or draw-cut well on horseback. It is also possible that, unlike other swords, they were useful as general tools outside combat.

The popularity of the falchion diminished in the 1400s with the increasing use of full plate armor. But, as were two-handed swords, falchions were more prevalent during the Renaissance. Indeed, we see mention of the falchion in the 1500s as a weapon other than the "sword" with which to be proficient (once again underscoring its handling differences from thin, straight, two-edged blades). Some varieties for the nobility were even highly decorated (possibly emulating similar Middle Eastern swords). Today there are very few surviving examples of falchions. Falchions may very well be the original ancestor of the cutlass and sabre/saber (or *sabel*). The term *falchion* itself has come to be applied to any form of these heavy, machete-like chopping weapons. Other forms of slender, curved blades were known from as early as 1400. Depicted in historical artwork are also a few other rare and unusual varieties of singled-edged Medieval chopping swords.

Swords of the early Medieval period (roughly from 500 to 1000 A.D.) tended to be shorter, wider blades with single, wide fullers. Some Dark Age swords were surprisingly light and short, at around 28 inches and only 1 1/2 pounds. Sword types during the 1100s began to be more uniform across Western Europe. Those of the 1200s began to diverge into a number of discernible types. From around 1000 to 1250 A.D. the "standard" form of sword was from 32 to 36 inches long with a single or double fuller running the length. It was essentially a cutting blade for slashing and hacking against mail and leather armors, but those with thrusting points were also known. Handles were between 4 and 6 inches long. From the mid-1200s, blades capable of thrusting and cutting became more common (i.e., they then had sharply pointed tips). It has been suggested that improvements in metallurgy at about this time allowed for the creation of the thinner, harder metal necessary for a sharp, narrow, thrusting point. That this then coincided with the advent of tougher armors that were harder to cut through likely cannot be just coincidence.

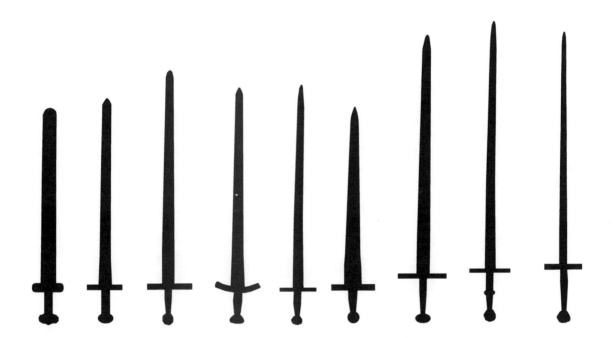

By the 1300s, the strictly cutting, double-edged sword was out of general use. A sword also capable of stabbing through spots in armor was needed. A sharply pointed, gently tapering style of blade became more common than those with parallel edges. Swords of the early 1300s had also begun to extend in length to about 38 to 48 inches, and many had acquired grips for both hands. Pommels were made larger and heavier to counterbalance the increased weight. At this time, the cruciform-hilt was still standard, as it had been for the previous 200 years or so. The standard single-hand sword certainly did not go out of use, and a variety of different designs were in simultaneous use. Indeed, there are references in the 1300s to cavalry across Europe being armed with two types of swords: a one-hand cutting/slashing blade and a narrow, lighter one intended more for thrusting.

Whatever its design or form, a sword was always considered a weapon of great value and importance. The Vikings so prized theirs that they often named swords with such expressive names as *foe of mail, leg biter, wolf of the wound, serpent of the wound, battle snake, snake of the shield, fire of the shields, the byrnies fear, gnawer (skrofnung), viper (nadr), hole maker (naegling)*, etc. In the 900s some Anglo-Saxon swords were recorded as having the value of 120 oxen or 15 male slaves. A Medieval knight's sword could cost the equivalent in modern value of tens of thousands of dollars.

Swords of the 1400s were made more specifically for warriors on foot and less for fighting from horseback. This is evident in their size, handle length, and weight. Because of the improvements in plate armor, blades made primarily for cutting or hacking were unable to penetrate effectively. From the late 1300s through the 1400s, their use changed from primarily cutting to thrusting and cutting. A more rigid blade, diamond-shaped in cross-section, with a raised center for reinforcement, was more effective. It was also heavier and harder to wield. Its tapering blade with a hard, narrow point allowed for stronger thrusts (into the joints and weak points). While swords of this form developed, the older forms did not disappear entirely. They still found many adherents and uses both by, and against, lighter armored fighters. During the 1400s, a variety of short, stabbing swords (and very long daggers) for use against heavier armor also came into use. These forms of one-handed blades, wide at the shoulder and ending in fine points, were popular with foot soldiers and pike-men. In the crowded crush of pole-arms, these were quick, maneuverable, and able to stab into heavy armor as well as hack at lighter forms. However, they lacked reach, momentum, and striking area, and did not cut power. The names of some of these swords included the Italian *couteau, corta, cousteu, coltello, spada,* and even *spade* (from which the playing card suit gets its name). Many of these "short" swords are exclusively one-handed weapons and are not suitable for any two-handed use (and indeed make little sense employed in that way). This trend continued somewhat into the Renaissance, but longer cut & thrust swords (as well as large slashing blades) were still the norm.

The change from wider blades with parallel edges to narrower, tapering ones was significant because it affected both handling and cutting. A narrower blade shape has slightly less weight and a better balance that allows for a quicker switch from a cutting angle of attack to a more horizontal stabbing motion and back again. Narrow, tapering blades have a balance and center of gravity somewhat closer to the hilt, and this encourages greater speed and agility in certain techniques. When thrusting or parrying, shorter, quicker movements of the arm are possible—and are therefore more deceptive. On long-swords and great-swords, such blades allow for powerful, deceptive thrusting against heavier armors.

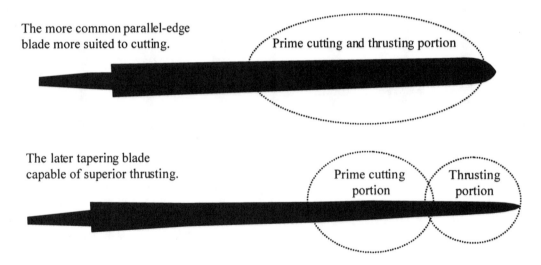

The more common parallel-edge blade more suited to cutting.

Prime cutting and thrusting portion

The later tapering blade capable of superior thrusting.

Prime cutting portion

Thrusting portion

No names have been given to these forms of blade (other than the Oakeshott Type XII and XV), and none will be presumed here. It is important only to understand that there were the older hack/slash and stab variety and the later antiarmor cut & thrust category.

Most swords after 1350 had grips that could accommodate both hands, and short-handled, single-hand grips became much less common. Many bastard-swords also reverted to a flatter, wider, fullered blade capable of better cutting. Interestingly, starting about 1450, shorter swords capable of easily cutting and thrusting once again became common. They were needed against lightly armored foot soldiers. At the very time that plate armor was reaching its highest forms, many foot soldiers were discarding more and more of their armor because of the changing nature of warfare.

CHAPTER FOUR

The Making of Medieval Swords

The best swords were excellent weapons capable of causing tremendous wounds. They were not easy to construct, and the finest ones could last for generations. It is no surprise that a certain amount of mystery surrounded both their making and their use. But only a portion of this sword lore survives for us today. Our knowledge of just how Medieval swords were made does not come from historical literature directly describing their manufacture in detail. Instead, it comes from a wide range of sources—literary, artistic, archeological, metallurgical, and technical. What is clear is that, unlike other weapons, a sword could not just be "put together"; it had to be forged and carefully tempered. It was not just a long knife on a shaft, as with a spear, or a heavy stick with a metal end attached, as with an axe or mace. It required a laborious and skillful process. Sword construction and metallurgy are complex and involved. There were undoubtedly a multitude of methods and techniques to the craft over the centuries. The final purpose of each was to create a strong, light blade capable of holding a good edge.

The quality of steel in Medieval swords could vary from weapon to weapon. It depended a great deal on its heat treatment. Steel first needed careful forging and tempering (quenching and reheating). Steel is iron with a higher carbon content and is much stronger. Steel was made from selected iron ore by repeated heating in a hot charcoal fire. The addition of the carbon molecules improves the alignment of iron molecules (carbon content of swords then ranged from a respectable .75 to 1.2 percent). The raw metal was worked by hammer into a bar. A sword might be constructed from several separate pieces of iron and steel, each carefully hammered on. These were then "welded" together by hammering them when yellow hot (one X-ray of a Viking sword revealed it to have been forged from 58 separate pieces). Separate bars were also sometimes then added for the edges. Finally, while still hot, the blade was worked into final shape and tempered by quenching (rapid cooling by plunging into a liquid bath). The steel was hardened by heating the shaped blade to a bright red color and then plunging it into a liquid bath (which could be oil, water, wine, honey, urine, or blood). This made the steel hard but also brittle. To temper it, the blade was then reheated to carefully soften it. A fine balance was needed between hardness on the edge for cutting and softness in the body for flex and durability. The tempered blade was then polished (sharpened) by stone wheel.

Sometime about 500 A.D., the Vikings began to obtain harder blades that were able to hold better edges by repeatedly folding and beating higher carbon iron. Dark Age swords were usually forged by bending together rods or strips of soft and hard steel. These were twisted and hammer-welded into bars in a process known as pattern welding. Blades from about 300 to 900 A.D. were of this construction. Pattern welding was not really a manner of "welding," but rather a method of repeatedly heating and hammering twisted rods of metal. It is sometimes known as "false Damascene," but this is a misnomer because it is its own distinct method and not necessarily an inferior one. (The term came from the fact that the twisting of pattern welding creates a unique, highly distinctive design in the metal that can be made to stand out through the use of acids. During polishing, this results in a variety of beautiful patterns in the exposed metal of the fuller. A decorative mosaic, which in some literature is described as scalelike or snakelike—called *mal* or *moel* by the Vikings—can be made to appear.) Eventually, easier methods of forging strong, flexible blades other than by pattern welding were discovered. In the 900s, a laminated or "piled" sword blade was made by repeatedly folding layers of soft, pure steel and mild, harder steel (carburized iron). Some were made by twisting bars of hard and soft steel and then beating them. Due to improved smelting technology of ferrous metals, later blades from about 1000 to 1500 A.D. were made of a single bar of higher quality steel.

In the 1300s, the introduction of water-powered bellows for blast furnaces and water-powered triphammers for forging both allowed for the creation of better iron and steel. Improved methods of production may have well allowed for more blades of a reliable and reasonable quality to be manufactured in less time than with the older methods. Apparently, older methods took longer and could result in a blade whose quality might just as likely be poor as exceptional.

When forged, the metal of a good blade had to be free of flaws and impurities that would cause it to break. Even finer, hand-forged blades can suffer from hidden imperfections, which can cause cracking or fracturing. Because the exact factors that made up a good sword were not fully understood or comprehended, it was a matter of intuition and instinct on the part of the maker. At the time, these swordmakers had no true "science" of metallurgy and did not know about carbon content, exact temperatures of heat, or specifics of tempering. Workability, hardness, and strength all had to be judged from experience. The swordmakers' craft was almost entirely skill and superstition. Not knowing the precise factors that made a fine blade added a definite air of mystery and magic to a good weapon, which is why the greatest swords were often thought to have mystical properties. The quality of steel, amount of impurities in it, manner in which it is worked, and length of time for cooling and heating are only some of the many critical factors involved.

The strength of steel is a matter of its metallurgical composition, as well as its tempering. Inferior steel can still be good if well tempered, but poor tempering can ruin even the best quality steel. Tempering of a sword was a careful, demanding process, an art in itself. In simplistic terms, the heat treatment must be just right. Poor heat-treating prevents proper flexibility. Too little and the sword will be soft and weak-edged, too much and it can be brittle and fragile. Good steel contains a variety of minute trace elements and other metals that add to its strength and flexibility such as carbon, silicon, manganese, and even some chromium. The percentages, though, can vary greatly and seriously affect the quality of the resulting blade.

The making of a fine sword would typically involve the skill of several men, which might include a forger, a shaper, a finisher, a temperer, a polisher, and finally a cutler for the hilt. However, sometimes these functions would be done by the same man. Naturally, the quality of Medieval swords varied. Even a good swordmaker's product could vary from one blade to another, sometimes greatly. Usually a smith was inconsistent. A maker might produce a good piece one month and a poor one the next. Respected smiths were those whose weapons were consistent and trustworthy. On some blades, the name of the maker was proudly inlaid in the fuller. Understandably, names of better smiths were even forged. For the most part, major centers of sword production in the Middle Ages arose in Germany, Italy, Spain, and France, as well as elsewhere. Some leading sword-making towns existed from Roman times through the Renaissance.

There is a wide variety of steels and tempering methods now used in modern reproduction blades, and quality varies considerably. Many blades today are made by the stock-removal process, in which a steel bar is ground down into shape and then tempered. Some are made simply by grinding and filing a bar of good, preforged, commercial spring steel (so named because it is suitable for use in many types of industrial bar springs). This ensures some quality in the metal and saves the maker from the art of actually forging and tempering, but it also means that the sword is not made in the traditional manner of real ones. Many replica swords now are also not fully tempered but are simply case-hardened. A case-hardened blade is one made with a core of soft, malleable iron inside a very thin "skin" of harder iron with a higher carbon content. Some modern reproduction swords are now conveniently made from modern stainless steel. Stainless steel contains such trace elements as chromium to give it that "shine" and prevent tarnish, but they also weaken it by affecting the steel's grain. It comes in a variety of hardnesses for swords (for example, 420B, 440A, and 440C). Whereas carbon-steel blades must be quenched for tempering, stainless steel is typically air-hardened (left in the open to cool). Swords made from stainless steel can hold a decent edge but not as well as carbon steel, nor are they as flexible. They are also certainly not historical.

Today, swordmakers often create simply whatever they can sell or whatever they like or can manage, and the typical purchaser will accept whatever he can get. Few swordmakers are still able to follow more traditional methods and processes. Some can make blades that have exceptionally sharp edges but that can't flex well or take a beating. Others will make a blade with good flexibility but no ability to keep a decent edge. Combining the best qualities in a blade is not easy to master. But because few who purchase such swords will actually ever bother to cut with them or even test their resilience, blade makers seldom must account for deficiencies. Knowing the exact numbers of modern metallurgical ratings and

technical scales is not vital to the average student. All the student really needs to know is whether the steel in a sword is equivalent to the historical kind or whether the manufacturer significantly modified it in order to save a step (see Appendix A).

Of course, in the ages when warriors relied on their swords daily and were near the top of the social pyramid things were different. Continual communication between warrior and swordmaker would ensure the best design for the job (if not the best quality individual sword). There was obviously a constant feedback from those who created the weapons and those who used them and whose lives thereby depended on them. This produced a sort of natural selection that could ensure a minimum of expected quality. It has been said that once real swordsmen in the West stopped doing real sword combat or earnest practice, it can be no surprise that swordmakers stopped making real blades. The cycle of feedback from skilled users to skilled makers had ended. Unfortunately, this is as true today as it was hundreds of years ago when it first began to change.[1]

Sword design follows from need and technology, and sword techniques reflect design. A weapon is devised to suit needs and is then used according to how it handles. For the Medieval sword the workings of this dynamic produced designs and qualities that were both practical and lethal. All the while armorers kept up the effort to improve defense through better means of protection (which in turn necessitated changes in sword designs). In all its various forms and versions the Medieval sword is a fairly simple, even somewhat crude object of clear and lethal practicality. Although there are many notable exceptions, overall the swords of Medieval Europe perhaps tend to be less elegant than those of other contemporary cultures. Instead, they are austere, functional tools from the clashing societies of a brutal age. This is reflected by the esthetic simplicity and symmetry of a straight blade intersected by a simple cross-guard.

---

[1] This is a phenomenon repeated more than once in history and most notably during the U.S. Civil War. Blacksmiths called upon to quickly produce swords without prior experience had their products end up in the hands of untutored, less-than-expert users. The results were hardly impressive, with few recorded wounds from sword encounters being made during the entire conflict.

CHAPTER FIVE

Swords against Plate Armor

The manner in which swords were used was certainly not standard throughout the entire Middle Ages. On the one hand it can be argued that all Medieval fighting is pretty much the same because it came down to a lethal clash of arms and men. However, upon closer examination we can see the major differences and subtleties of its form as it changed over the centuries. It can be said that the majority of Medieval combat more or less involved the familiar form of mail-clad warriors armed with shield, spear, axe, and sword. Everything else was minor.

Although the emphasis in this book is not on plate-armor combat, its significance and great importance to swordsmanship must be addressed. As has been well documented and examined elsewhere, armor for both infantry and mounted warriors varied considerably during the Medieval centuries. It ranged from quilted garments to soft and hard leather to shirts and coats of mail to additions of metal plates, and eventually led to fully articulated suits. Armor was never standardized or uniform throughout regions and eras, but was rather a matter of personal choice and affordability. It is therefore difficult and risky to make broad generalities or draw too many firm conclusions.

Plate armor today is synonymous with the image of the chivalrous knight. Indeed, much of Medieval plate armor is ingenious and unequaled anywhere in the world. But when talking specifically about the use of metal plated armor (or "plate armor") in Medieval fighting, it is important not to lump it all together under the cliché of the "knight in shining armor." Plate armor existed in countless varieties, and the later style of fully encasing, fully articulated plate armor must be distinguished from the earlier forms. The early forms consisted simply of the addition of metal plates over a mail *byrnie* or *hauberk*. The plates were placed on the most common target areas (initially the knees, elbows, and shoulders). Other forms attached metal plates to coats of leather or cloth. The variety of styles and patterns for all this was immense, and it is not critical to discuss them.

Plate armor was not by any means adopted simply because knights were obsessed with personal safety, and Medieval warriors did not adopt plate armor purely in response to self-defense needs or some primitive survival fear. If that had been their motivation, they would not have been out giving battle in the first place. Against the terrible weapons they had to face, knights wanted to be as effective as possible on the battlefield, and the solution they perfected was plate armor.

After perhaps a generation of experimentation, the adoption of plate armor occurred fairly rapidly, perhaps in less than 50 years. The adding of small sheets and pieces of shaped iron to reinforce mail in the early 1300s was a reaction to the use of such deadlier weapons as halberds and other heavy pole-arms. Even in the hands of common foot soldiers and peasants such fearsome weapons could cut through mail with great ease. Starting about 1350, full plate armor developed primarily as a defense against the increased use of mass archery in battle. The effectiveness of longbows and crossbows forced the adoption of sections of connected, hinged plates made from high-quality iron. For better coverage and greater mobility, these plate sections were strapped and jointed on their own. The inclusion of shin, thigh, and arm pieces with hip, torso, and collar protection eventually produced "full" plate armor and the problems associated with fighting both against it and in it.

It is essential to realize that throughout the Middle Ages, plate armor (used specifically by knights and wealthy men-at-arms) represented only a fraction of the armor types worn. Plate was the exception, not the norm. In fact, even during its heyday plate armor was apparently worn by perhaps only some 5 percent or so of warriors, and even then it was worn mostly while fighting *mounted*. Therefore, it is not representative of "Medieval combat" as a whole. There is a difference between the earlier man-to-man Medieval fighting (with lighter leather and mail armors), which went on for well over 500 years, and that in the later "age of plate." The difference between the two is significant and often blurred by misconceptions in popular media and also in some current efforts to re-create safe methods of historical sparring. It is fairly obvious that the virtual invulnerability created by heavier plate certainly did alter both the swords used and the manner of fighting of almost all warriors. Essentially, the improvement in armor started to alter the effectiveness of swords, and a process of reaction and response ensued. In many ways, the introduction of full plate armor was not just an evolution in defense itself, but a reaction to the deadliness of more powerful weapons.

It has been firmly established (although it is often overlooked) that most swords have little value against plate armor. They simply *cannot* and *do not* "cut" into it. As a result of the improved defense offered by heavier armors in the mid-to-late Middle Ages and even into the Renaissance, warriors began to rely on a variety of other weapons for bringing down a heavily armored foe. A range of weapons came into wider use against plate armor. Often preferable to swords for fighting heavy plate were axes, clubs, hammers, heavy spears, flanged maces, and stiff daggers. It seems that severe concussion blows ordinarily could do far more damage than an edged weapon. Quite common were heavy axes, halberds, and pole-axes with blade heads especially able to dent, gash, or pierce heavier armor. With their powerful thrusts, glaives, bills, or heavy spears could also be extremely effective. Flails and other flexible chain weapons were capable of generating blows of incredible force. They could also rend armor, thus creating further openings. In any case, a warrior in full plate could always be dismounted or pulled to the ground by a variety of hooked or pronged pole-arms or other weapons. Once down, they might then be pummeled and struck until beaten to a pulp inside (his armor might even still be left largely intact). In fact, beating on a heavily armored fighter in this way was often imperative, since he could still get on his feet fairly easily and continue fighting.

What is pure fiction, however, is the myth that such an armored warrior would lumber around awkwardly. What good would it do to be able to withstand blows, but be unable to get at the opponent? After all, these warriors trained for years to be able to fight wearing this armor. A knight in full plate might even charge and grapple with another to take him down and drive a rigid dagger into his faceplate or visor. Both might wrestle with each other for a moment before one managed a fatal stab to the armpit or throat.[1] Although the fiction of the slow, staggering, dismounted knight weighed down by heavy plate armor has been discredited and mostly dismissed, there is a certain small truth in it, which is now safe to admit. There is a definite difference between the agility and speed of a man in full plate and those of one in lighter armor or none at all.

Additionally, with jointed plate armor there are

---

[1] This form of armored plate-versus-plate combat is difficult to safely simulate realistically, but a number of ways have been developed for doing so. Several groups of "live-steel" and plate-armor fighting exist around the United States and Europe. Unfortunately, for safety concerns many major techniques specific to this kind of fighting must be omitted (e.g., stabbing to exposed gaps).

limitations to the mobility of the arms in striking certain blows and to the usable footwork. Of course, an armored fighter who is fully aware of these deficiencies can make up for it by focusing on those techniques that are more applicable. The disadvantages in tactical flexibility are made up for with the armor's *overwhelming* defensive value. This is self-evident by the increasing number of foot soldiers who adopted forms of plate toward the end of the Middle Ages and into the early Renaissance.

Although it has been demonstrated that plate armor is not as debilitating or restrictive as popular myth once purported, it is nonetheless clearly not as mobile as much lighter armors. One need only conduct practice cutting with live blades while in full armor to understand some of the differences in angulation, flow, follow-through, and recovery. Handling a sword when in armor is not precisely the same as doing so when unarmored. Experiencing the opportunity to spar in plate armor against opponents wearing little or no armor will also reveal just how significant a difference in speed and agility there truly is. Just as quickly, it will also reveal how well-protected a combatant in heavy armor can be. Of course, one-on-one bouts and massed group battles are different affairs, and not all conditions are equal. There is a time and place for each weapon and each armor—which is precisely why such a variety of each existed.[2] In the massed crush of poles and missiles, plate armor's protection had great worth. This was probably even truer when riding against a prepared force of foot soldiers or another lance-bearing knight.

Of course, there were always individuals who, because of personal taste, physique, or finances, preferred lighter armor and the fewer penalties that go with it. A faster, more agile fighter can avoid and evade a better armored attacker and deliver his own faster, more careful strikes. Nature and history would seem to favor the protection of armor, but there is no foolproof law or rule at work. Victory is mostly a matter of skill, but also of luck. There was no surefire means of offense or a perfect method of defense. It all came down to the individual warrior and the circumstances he found himself in. There has been the suggestion that for the armored nobility of Medieval Europe, staying alive was more a concern

than killing the opponent. Thus, the immediate concern of defense may have very well transcended offense. To a certain degree, with the near invulnerability of full armor comes the capacity to survive combat with one's social inferiors, as well as the more romantic idea of testing one's might against social equals. Whether this attitude existed generally among the warrior class and was influential in the development of full plate armor is highly debatable. It may be a result of the wearing of full plate armor rather than its cause.

It is well known that as armor improved in the mid-to-late Middle Ages and the development of fully articulated metal plates became more common, newer forms of swords did eventually appear. The advances in armor defense necessitated a change in swords as it had other weapons. This offensive reaction to the defensive "challenge of plate" was a gradual process. Traditional blades designed mostly for cutting continued to be widely used. But a good many swords of the later Middle Ages were clearly made for fighting heavily armored opponents. The standard flatter blade could not chop through plate, and its thin tip (rather than puncture) would only glance off. For fighting full plate, sword designs became more rigid and capable of striking harder, jarring *blows* rather than just making *cuts*. The blades needed to be even more resilient to withstand this. This was achieved through a more hexagonal or diamond cross-sectional blade shape with a raised center ridge, or "riser." This increased the blade's strength and its rigidity for bashing and denting tougher targets. Swords of all lengths, both short and long, changed to adopt this newer antiarmor model of blade.

Correspondingly, some forms were made longer and somewhat heavier with thinner, sharper points for more effective thrusting. Additionally, some shorter, single-hand forms also became narrower. All these swords have thicker but sharply tapering tips for getting into the weaker gaps and joints between plates (such as to the underarm, face or visor, palms, back of the knee, inner thigh, and groin). The idea was now to beat aside the adversary's weapon and open them to a thrust driven into the armor's gaps and joints. On a solid, forceful stab some of these

---

[2] In the late Middle Ages and early Renaissance there were, of course, forms of special plate armor specifically created for the tournament joust. This kind of "tilting" armor was heavier and far more restricting than that meant for battlefield or for use on foot.

blades can indeed pierce through armor. There are several literary accounts, as well as scenes in artwork, showing points of these swords puncturing chest or back plates.

Later Medieval swords also tended to have hand-and-a-half or two-handed grips. These were necessary not only because of their increased striking power, but also because with the wearing of full plate one had *less* need for a shield and so the second hand was often left free for use. Longer grips capable of being used with two hands had first come about because of the need for giving more forceful blows against increasingly tougher armors. Larger swords were also needed that were sturdy enough to stand up against increasingly more frequent heavy weapons (e.g., pole-axes, halberds, war hammers). A double-hand method of gripping allowed still heavier blades to be handled, which in turn further required better armor.[3] Still, shorter, more agile thrusting blades were also popular. In a tight situation or close-up fight they could be very useful for stabbing into the vulnerable spots of armor.

These changes in sword forms affected application. We know that in many schools of fighting differences were clearly noted between methods of both armored and unarmored combat. With better protective armor, somewhat less attention needs to be given to defense, and this can result in the committal of more audacious attacks. Knowing you have a certain degree of invulnerability when fighting in plate armor can allow greater freedom in action and aggression. To have to face such a well-protected, confident adversary could be quite intimidating, and this was no doubt a factor. With two equally armored adversaries, this could result in much closer contact between weapons and combatants. A variety of techniques were devised for fighting close in with the newer long-swords. Although one could not cut a plated opponent, just forcing him to move and block

(or just knocking him around) could open up a vulnerable target area to a thrust. Of course any powerful strike, even if it couldn't cut, would still deliver tremendous force to a very small area. Sometimes this could be enough to slow, stifle, or stun the plate-armored opponent if not outright injure him. Beating the opponent senseless was a reasonable tactic whatever the weapon used. It is also important to remember that, despite facing more heavily armored foes, a warrior often still needed a stout cutting sword effective against common, less well-defended adversaries (whether they were the preferred opponent or not).[4]

There is even considerable reason to believe that swordsmanship on the whole actually deteriorated in Europe with the ascendancy of full plate armor around 1350. Why concentrate on sword skill when the weapon is all but useless against heavy armor? Why worry about encountering a skillful swordsman if your armor is almost invulnerable to cuts?[5] Heavier armor demanded heavier blades, more powerful blows, and brutal stabs, not precise cutting strokes. Because blows must have been intended less to cut the adversary than simply to beat on him, better results would have been achieved with a mace or axe than with a heavy sword—and without the need for the motion of cutting. The careful and deliberate techniques of sword & shield or single-sword fighting in more vulnerable armors are just not as relevant (which may explain why the limited visibility of most great-helms was so acceptable for a time).

All this is not surprising, considering that plate armor hinders certain movements and that heavier blades allow for less agility and dexterity in numerous techniques. Fighting in plate armor may have contributed to any drop in swordsmanship among the knightly classes in favor of other weapons. But combat under such conditions calls for different blade designs and a different method of handling

---

[3] It is worth mentioning that there was a variety of larger two-handed forms and that these were primarily used during the Renaissance. True two-handers did not originally appear exclusively to face plate armor, and their use continued long after plate had declined.

[4] To generalize for a moment, it is known that the Medieval knight had a preferred adversary in that of his social equal. Fighting commoners for soldiers offered little prestige unlike that possible against other knights. Additionally, a knight beaten for capture by another knight might expect (or hope) to be ransomed. Commoners could not ransom their social betters, nor did they have much hope of selling off captured armor. There was also a certain degree of animosity or at least resentment at work between the classes. Commoners could usually expect to receive little mercy if they were defeated or captured.

[5] It can even be reasonably argued that common soldiers and fighters had to develop better fighting skills because of their own lack of armor. This was certainly the case with civilian fighting in the early Renaissance.

them. Thus it may not be proper to describe these changes as a deterioration of swordsmanship so much as an alteration of their skills. Certainly focusing on close-in stabs and knocking strikes when wearing full plate is a different "style" than when using sword & shield in mail.

The increasing vulnerability of heavy cavalry (mounted knights in armor) to longbows, crossbows, pikes, and newly emerging firearms precipitated the development of plate armor and the trend by many knights to fight more and more on foot. The wide use of fully articulated plate armor by foot soldiers in the 1400s gave rise to a changing style of fighting and of wielding long-swords in two hands. A method emerged that used actions specific to facing stronger armors with specialized antiarmor blades. Rather than making attacks and cuts in a standard hack-and-cleave manner, there was a much greater use of tighter, closer motions and thrusting. This style clearly involved moving in shorter striking arcs, making greater blade and body contact, knocking and hitting with the guard or pommel, and even grasping the blade in one armored hand. This change in style is evident from many of the fighting manuals and paintings of combat from the time. It also makes sense, given the nature of a long, cutting blade faced with stronger armor. Under such fighting conditions, most swords began to be used that were not all that different from such specialized weapons as the estoc and pole-axe.

Strangely, the overall weight of some of these later long-swords and great-swords seems to have decreased. Although they originally were heavier sword forms, some of the more pointed, more diamond-shaped ones were lighter than earlier flat blades of similar length. This may likely have been specifically because they became used less and less for cutting and needed greater tip agility. This, in turn, must have further

improved their effectiveness in thrusting attacks (holding a long, heavy blade horizontally for stabbing is not easy). Their manner of use undoubtedly involved little or no slicing (draw-cuts) and far less actual hacking, and instead relied on clubbing strikes to wear enemies down and open them for stabs to the vulnerable spots. Grabbing the blade in the middle to shorten its reach and aid stabs was also a common technique. Eventually, this led to a rigid, triangular form of sword weapon called a *tuck* in England and Germany and *estoc* in France. In Italy it was known as a *stocco*. Such a "sword" was far more of a hilted metal club/spear than an actual blade weapon.

Ironically, improvements in missile weapons and heavy pole-weapons (which themselves had come into still greater use because of the challenge of plate armor) eventually caused improvements in plate armor itself.[6] This is not hard to understand. After all, full plate armor did not just pop into existence because someone suddenly realized such superb protection could be built. For the most part, the technology had always been there, but the need for such an encumbering (and expensive) defense had not.[7] *It was the increasing need by knightly warriors to protect themselves against these deadlier weapons that first spurred the increasing development of plate.* This simple dynamic is often forgotten in the study of the use of Medieval arms and armor. Further improvements in mail reinforced with plates was a reaction to the increased use of such weapons, which, in turn, subsequently encouraged their continued development and use. There was (as always) a symbiosis at work between offensive and defensive implements: the need for plate armor forced developments in Medieval metalworking skills necessary to produce it. The development of sword forms better able to fight it and their corresponding skills were never far behind.

---

[6] Plate armor was not eliminated because of the use of the longbow either. Both the longbow and the crossbow were highly effective at penetrating it, but they did not render it entirely obsolete any more than they rendered unarmored infantry obsolete. It was the inevitable deployment of effective, widely used firearms that was to eventually make full plate armor irrelevant.

[7] The Romans, of course, had forms of overlapping plate armor (such as the *lorica segmentata*) as well as molded single pieces and mail.

CHAPTER SIX

The Fate of the Medieval Sword

What eventually happened to Medieval swords? Why did such varied forms give way to others such that we must now refer to them as *Medieval*? The answer has to do with the changing social circumstances and new forms of warfare that developed during the early Renaissance. The use of heavier armors declined as firearms became more prevalent and effective. The need to fight against massed shield walls, heavy cavalry charges, and plate-armored opponents was to give way to fighting formations of halberds, long pikes, and ordered lines of muskets. The swords of the Renaissance then developed methodical styles in an age when swordsmanship on the battlefield had begun to lose its relevance.

It is important here to make a contrast to the developments in swords during the Renaissance so as to better understand why Medieval swords were designed and used as they were. Fundamentally, there arose during the Renaissance a distinction between those swords intended for war and those for personal self-defense. Social forces had begun to allow common citizens to not only be able to afford and in many cases legally own their own swords, but to wear them in the crowded cities. The breakdown of the old feudal order also limited the avenues for both redress of personal

grievance and exhibition of martial skill. Consequently, there was an immense rise in the number and frequency of both street-fighting and private dueling. This, in turn, caused a renewed interest in the "Art of the Sword." Combined with the new "sciences" then coming into vogue, a much more systematic approach to studying swordsmanship swept Western Europe. New Schools of Defence offering instruction in numerous fighting arts sprang up all across the Continent. Swordsmanship was then raised to a higher degree of study than had previously existed in Western civilization (for a detailed picture of this see *Renaissance Swordsmanship*).

It was in this environment of the early 1500s that swordsmanship in Europe became the "noble science of fence." During the Renaissance, swords transcended their use as weapons of war to become civilian tools of personal self-defense and, with that, keepers of personal honor. This was not the case in previous centuries. An edict from as early as 1286 in England forbade private schools of fence within the city of London—ostensibly to control "civil strife" customarily seen to be "associated" with such activities. The Renaissance, however, gave rise to more legitimate and, in many cases, more respected schools of the *noble science*.

Under these circumstances sword blades changed once again. The focus shifted to include urban self-defense instead of battlefield utility or tournament. The cut & thrust swordsmanship of the early Renaissance consisted of a sophisticated, highly developed, and effective system of armed combat that evolved from Medieval swords. They are considered "transition" weapons from Medieval cutting forms to the later thrusting rapiers (for which they are typically misidentified). They are characterized by a narrower, tapering blade, often with a stronger cross-section and fitted with a swept- or compound-hilt. Cut & thrust swords were used mainly by lightly armed footmen as well as civilians in the 1500s and 1600s. Such swords were employed against a range of armored and unarmored opponents. They were battlefield weapons that found increasing use in personal single combat. The cut & thrust form allowed for a highly underrated method of swordsmanship consisting of a versatile and well-balanced combination of penetrating stabs with more classical cuts and slashes. They were popular for sword & buckler and sword & dagger fighting, which provided the foundation for the thrusting rapier.

These swords also fully utilized the unique one-handed gripping method of wrapping the index finger around the quillon and ricasso. It provided superior point control and agility and was to be developed even further with later Renaissance swords and rapiers. During the Renaissance, the use of the thrust began to dominate the cut for civilian fighting. The primary reasons for this have to do with the environment in which the weapons were relied upon and certain mechanics of use. The more refined techniques of Renaissance cut & thrust swords provided a foundation for those of later centuries, such as cutlasses, hangers, and spadroons. These, in turn, became European stick-fighting martial sports during the 1700s and 1800s (such as "cudgeling," "singlestick," "backswording," and "la canne").

Other forms of cut & thrust swords, more closely related to Medieval blades but with basket and cage hilts, emerged for mounted combat during the late Renaissance. These were held in a single-fist grip and employed in a manner similar to that of earlier Medieval swords. However, the Renaissance cut & thrust sword as a military arm was eventually to be replaced by the *hand-gonne* and the curved cavalry saber, both more suitable for later mounted armies. As a personal weapon of urban self-defense it was also to be eclipsed by the dueling tool par excellence, the vicious and elegant rapier.

The thrusting rapier was a distinct sword form and fighting method. Rapier fence was an innovative, sophisticated, and highly effective form of personal combat that was both efficient and deceptive in its lethality. Its introduction as a civilian weapon was a gradual process that was highly controversial at the time and often violently disputed. The rapier first developed out of, *and in response to*, civilian use of cut & thrust swords, and only *later* did it find use against other rapiers. Its early proponents were undoubtedly already experts in the use of cut & thrust style swords. The rapier produced a lethal method of personal swordsmanship that emphasized agility, cunning, and finesse over strength and ferocity. It required careful practice and quick reaction. In a skilled hand it is a highly formidable weapon, particularly against those unfamiliar with its virtues. The rapier's thrusting, piercing style also represents one of the most innovative and original aspects of European martial culture. As a weapon for personal single combat and dueling the rapier was unequaled for almost 200 years until the ascension of the dueling pistol.

It is also important to realize that the art of rapier fence cannot be studied or understood exclusively from the perspective of modern foil or épée fencing. Although similar, the two have a considerable gulf between them. Being longer, heavier, stiffer, and sturdier than today's sporting versions (épées and foils), true rapiers cannot be used in the same flimsy manner (and vice versa). The modern sport reflects only a small portion of rapier ideas and owes far more to the later form of lighter small-sword than to the earlier rapier. Many of modern sport fencing's ideas developed fairly recently in the 1700s and 1800s, whereas many of its rules originated early this century.

Throughout the age of the Renaissance various experts, or Masters of Defence, began to teach fencing and fighting both publicly and privately. Such masters as Agrippa, Morrozo, Saviolo, di Grassi, George Silver, Joseph Swetnam, Capo

Ferro, Fabris, Koppen, Meyer, Alfieri, and many, many others became highly regarded experts. They looked upon their craft seriously, earnestly, and with careful consideration. These martial arts masters consisted of both gentry and commoners. Many traveled and tutored widely. Italian and Spanish instructors of the new rapier were among the most admired; in Germany, there were long-lived fighting guilds such as the *Marxbrüder* and the *Federfechter*, which specialized in many weapons, including two-handed swords and, later, rapiers. In England there was the Company of the London Masters of Defence, a fighting guild with origins dating back to the Middle Ages. Teaching a variety of swords, weapons, and unarmed techniques it prospered for more than 100 years.

These various Masters of Defence also produced more than 100 detailed, often well-illustrated technical manuals on their fighting methods. These manuscripts, published in the 1500s and 1600s, are invaluable resources on Renaissance swordsmanship. These many works were produced by professional swordsmen and cavaliers who fought and killed in countless duels and battles. Their manuals present us with a portrait of their highly developed and innovative martial arts and reveal swordsmanship at the time to be systematic and highly dynamic. They are useful sources for tracing earlier methods of fighting. The Renaissance masters were not always clear or complete in their ideas and sometimes even contradicted one another. But their works describe to us well-reasoned and effective fighting arts that were founded upon the experience of their Medieval forebears. Following the older traditions, they built upon the legacy of arms and armor and skills of their ancestors and adapted to the changing times. Sadly, due to historical and social forces, the teachings and skills of the Renaissance masters fell out of common use, and no traditional schools of instruction survive today. What is left now of their knowledge in the overly refined sport of modern fencing is so far removed from its martial origins that it only remotely qualifies as any form of Renaissance "swordsmanship."

Thus to reiterate, the Medieval sword did not really become "extinct" so much as it was transformed (it did not "evolve") to meet changing requirements. After all, swords did not get sharper, stronger, or especially more effective after the Middle Ages. They did not evolve as guns did to become more accurate, of longer range, and with faster rates of fire with each successive generation. It is wrong to view swords in this way. What happened to swords after the Medieval period was their being changed because of differing social and military conditions, as well as fashion to a smaller degree. This transformation must be viewed in the context of the new methodologies of warfare, technological advancements, and societal changes that first began to emerge in the late 1400s and early 1500s. The Medieval sword cannot in any way be viewed as a failure for having faded into historical obscurity or given way to Renaissance methods. Nothing that had successfully been in use for more than 900 years can be labeled a failure. Medieval swords and the arts of using them were appropriate and very effective for the environment of their age. They were not "stepping-stones" to deadlier forms or superior styles. For their time and conditions they were not only sufficient but quite formidable. Their legacy was influential and long lasting.

Forms of the Medieval Sword

THE MEDIEVAL SWORD

The Medieval sword is fundamentally a metal blade intended for cutting or cutting and thrusting. No two swords are exactly alike. Although there are a vast number of styles of Medieval swords, they vary only within a set of limited characteristics.

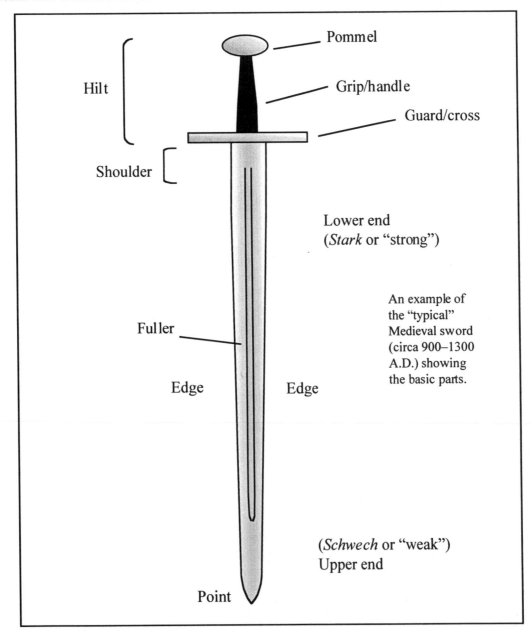

Hilt

Pommel

Grip/handle

Guard/cross

Shoulder

Lower end
(*Stark* or "strong")

Fuller

Edge   Edge

An example of the "typical" Medieval sword (circa 900–1300 A.D.) showing the basic parts.

(*Schwech* or "weak")
Upper end

Point

Fundamentally, a sword as a weapon has three main functions: cutting, thrusting, and guarding. A sword is used to hack (or slice), stab, and block. Some designs perform one function better than the others. Few do all equally well. The nature of a sword's design depends on the use to which it will be put (i.e., the type of weapons and armor to be faced). A Medieval sword's primary purpose is cutting. Parrying and receiving blows on a blade are secondary functions (although one would never know this from the ubiquitous, stereotypical examples typically offered by theatrical swordfights and stage performers).

There are a number of important generalities that can be made about the Medieval sword. Most Medieval swords are broad, two-edged blades either nipped at the point or gradually tapering, with straight, cruciform-hilts. Their lengths vary, but for the most part by only a few inches (excluding exclusively two-handed versions). They are commonly double-edged. Only a straight blade allows for a double edge, permitting the other to be used when one is dulled, worn, or chipped. It ensures that when handled quickly either edge is instantly at the ready. It also allows for the possibility of a reverse or back cut (using the "false edge"), although this is mechanically weaker than simply turning the angle of the wrist to cut with the forward edge.

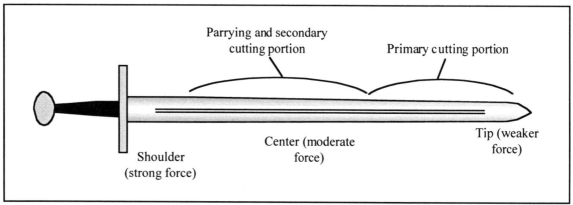

The typical Medieval sword blade is generally of a wide design, channeled or fullered. Its wide blade can deliver a shearing cut that makes a large, devastating wound. It is sturdy enough to beat or chop on thick pole-arms and metal-rimmed shields. A wide blade also allows for repeated sharpening and grinding to remove gouges and nicks. A blade-heavy weapon has merit in its stronger hacking blows, although it is much less maneuverable—and this can be more crucial when attempting to hit. The level of metallurgy during the Middle Ages virtually required a minimum width to produce a blade capable of making strong blows while still retaining something of an edge. Standard length was that which could comfortably fit the user and varied with purpose (and metallurgical skill). Swords varied in length often because the fighting men themselves varied in size. The swords generally had to be wielded with one hand, and when used by mounted combatants, needed to reach far enough to strike standing targets. When used by men on foot, they needed to be long enough to reach up to mounted adversaries. When used against an adversary with a shield, the sword typically had to be able to reach the opponent's legs, head, and weapon arm. Often their length was that which could fit from the hip to the ankle when worn vertically on the belt (approximately 36 to 40 inches). This length was ideal for use with a shield by a warrior either mounted or on foot.

Swords had to be light enough to be carried and used relatively all day in combat. They had to be well balanced and agile enough to fight with effectively. This is in stark contrast to what is depicted in countless Hollywood films and TV swordfights. Upon first hefting an accurate replica of a Medieval sword, many people are surprised by its relatively light weight and comfortable balance. Too often people are conditioned by the myths and fantasy perpetuated by choreographed swordplay in which the weapons supposedly weigh 10 or 20 pounds. People are also more used to the feel and weight of inaccurate weapons, such as those commonly found at cutlery shops and Renaissance fairs. Medieval swords were not the laboriously heavy things displayed in most movie scenes or sold at so many flea markets, malls, and knife shows. The majority of the cheap replicas available today are thick, inflexible, poorly balanced, and much too heavy. But even a light, maneuverable weapon can certainly feel quite heavy to an inexperienced arm or after hours of use. For those with no real experience in handling authentic swords, it is difficult to grasp just how different the steel is in a cheap, soft, heavy blade and a light, hard, well-balanced one. The considerable differences are most readily apparent when practicing cutting on various test materials as opposed to merely banging around blunt blades. It is only by handling and extensively practicing with real swords that a student can come to understand what they can and cannot do. Everything else, though useful and instructive, is still just supposition and conjecture.

Swords were handmade objects and as such—though precise and exact—were never quite 100 percent symmetrical. They were not modern machine-made instruments and so reflect the skill and hand-craftsmanship of each artist involved.

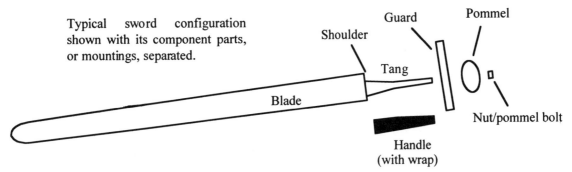

Typical sword configuration shown with its component parts, or mountings, separated.

Terms such as *foible* and *forte* for blade areas are inaccurate for Medieval swords and actually apply to Renaissance sword forms. *Foible* is a Renaissance term for the upper portion near the tip on a blade, which is weaker (or "feeble") but has more agility and speed. The lower portion does most of the attacking. The forte (also called *prime* or *fort*) is another Renaissance term for the upper portion on a sword blade. The lower portion closer to the hilt has more control and strength and does most of the parrying.

The tang (or "tongue") is the hidden unedged portion of a blade running through the handle, to which the pommel is attached. The origin of the term *tang* is obscure. The corner portion of blade where the tang connects is called the *shoulder*. Blades are sometimes slightly thicker and wider at the shoulder to increase their strength at this stress point. The sword's tang also must be wide enough at the hilt to withstand the stress and torque of being quickly swung and then stopped. It must be wide enough and long enough not to break under stress, but not so much that it alters the balance and weight of the weapon. Tangs usually would taper toward the pommel but could also be parallel and even widen in the middle. The qualities of the metal for the tang are somewhat different from those required for the blade, and the metal is sometimes of a softer temper in order to absorb the vibration and shock of a blow without breaking. The tang may be wrought from the same single piece of metal as the blade or a separate piece of metal welded on after the blade was forged. Sometimes a fuller would even extend into the tang. Typically, the end of the tang was made to pass through the pommel, where it was then hammered down to rivet the entire hilt against the blade's shoulder. The cross-guard also would have a slit chiseled in it to be able to slide down the tang and fit against the shoulder.

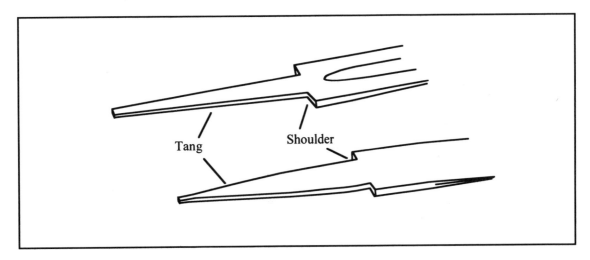

Cross-sectional samples of a variety of "typical" Medieval sword blades. Although there are a wide range of blade shapes with no single one being the "norm," the majority fall into the patterns below. The cross-section of a blade typically would change slightly along its length and was not uniform from from hilt to tip. Note the variety of fullers ranging from wide and shallow to narrow and deep. Those blades of earlier centuries are flatter with wider fullers, whereas later ones began to take on raised ridges and more diamond-like shapes.

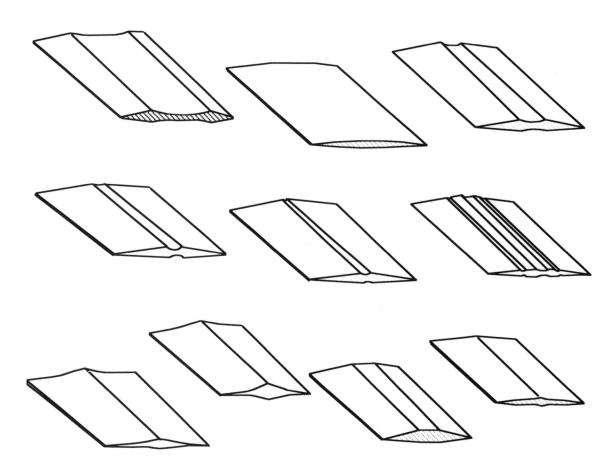

The cutting power and resilience of a sword are particular to the shape of the sword's edge. To cleave and sever armor, flesh, and bone, a sword needs to be flat with thin, very acutely angled edges. A thick blade with a more obtuse edge angle cannot cut very well. A steeper edge angle does not allow for as sharp a cut, but does create a stronger shape that may improve strength for the flat to parry. But the lesser the edge angle, the finer the edge that can be applied. The finer the edge, the sharper the cut, but also the easier the edge can dull, chip, or fold. A sword had to be capable of being resharpened or repolished repeatedly, and each time it is reworked, a little more metal is ground away. Though it can certainly be very sharp, a Medieval sword does not require a razor edge. The sheer inertia of such a thin piece of tempered metal striking a body can deliver a terrible blow. All that force is directed onto a very small portion of the contacting edge. By being thin and wide at the point of striking, a blade does not have to push as much material aside and so can cut much deeper.

A Medieval sword's edge is more like that of a "chisel" than that of a modern butcher knife. On a blade of softer temper, an edge will not usually "bite" (cut into) mail armor or even thick leather. An edge can be very sharp but still not be hard enough. The blade had to be well tempered and the edge kept properly polished. Some of the cheaper modern replica blades have crudely ground edges. Rather than a smooth, clean polish they are rough with noticeable tool marks. Such edges will never cut properly. The flaws and deformities in their surface will minutely catch and drag on material, thereby distorting the effect and power of cuts. It has been suggested that failure to hold a particularly sharp edge on many Medieval swords was one possible reason for a straight blade design, but the evidence for this is flimsy. It has also been suggested that a straight, dual-edged sword lends itself more to a style of fighting that emphasized chopping blows over slicing cuts. Against tougher targets, it's reasonable that perhaps a user would make up for some of the weapon's inherent lack of cutting strength by using his own raw strength. It has also been suggested that northern Europeans in general tended towards larger physical builds that may have further encouraged this.

Although they are obviously designed not to, all swords *can* break. Many broken blades are shown littering the ground of battles in Medieval artwork. If hit exceptionally hard on the flat, a sword can bend too far and simply snap. If struck on the edge at a damaged spot or an internal forging flaw, a blade will crack and break. Since many, if not most, blades after 900 A.D. were made by welding a sandwich of plain (softer) iron between two steel skins, there would be a minute seam down the center edge. This seam could cause a blade to break when the edge became too damaged.

Flexibility of a Medieval sword should be substantial. A test bend should flex approximately 3 to 6 inches and return true.

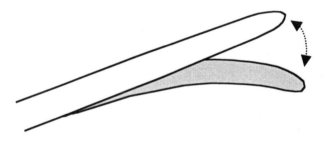

Flexibility is a crucial characteristic in the steel of a good sword blade. A sword had to be made shock resistant (flexible), and it needed resilience to resist fractures. Flexibility is required for the metal to withstand the repeated impact of blows. It is also crucial that a blade be flexible so that when striking the resistant edge of a shield it can twist and bend without distorting or staying bent from the shock. To achieve this, it cannot be too thick. Unlike the naturally supple wooden hafts of other hand weapons, a flat metal bar will bend or snap under the stress of impact unless it is tempered. Swords can be made with various tempers and hardnesses, but the harder the steel, the less inherently flexible the blade is. For flexibility a "spring" temper is typical. When struck hard the blade must give way (flex) and then return true (spring back) to its original shape without deforming or permanently bending. A good spring temper allows it to do this without breaking or warping. Today, because of poor tempering (or none at all), flexibility is routinely absent in many of the cheaper reproduction and fantasy swords. A good blade should be able to repeatedly flex out of line at least 3 inches and return perfectly. Viking blades were known to flex 6 inches or more.

A blade must be light and agile so that it can easily change direction, reverse momentum, and quickly recover from a strike or parry. A light, strong blade can simply outfight a heavier, slower one. The quicker sword will cut circles around it. A wider blade cuts smoother and more effectively. A narrow blade can sometimes twist and turn, causing the force to be distorted and turned away.

In contrast to a straight, double-edged blade, a curved sword has a single edge that can give it a much longer bevel for a better cut. With only one edge, its shape can also allow a thicker back or spine for greater strength. Unlike a straight edge that must meet its target at a direct angle, a curved edge essentially slices as it cuts and because of this can deliver a larger wound for its weight and size. But its curvature does make it less effective for thrusting, and the wider a blade the less maneuverable it is for guarding and parrying.

67

The *fuller* is a hollow central groove or shallow channel running down the length of a blade. During the Medieval period, a blade's fuller may have been known as the *hollow*. Its purpose is to lighten a sword without reducing its width or cutting edge. It also adds strength and rigidity without increasing weight or inhibiting flexibility. Fullers varied considerably, and not all blades need or have one, as it is possible to make them only on better steels. Fullers may run the whole length of a blade or only a portion of it. Blades might have a single, deep, narrow fuller or a shallower, wider one. They might be on both sides of a blade or only one. Some might have two or three fullers which might even taper together into one another. Some fullers may start at the hilt, while others start nearer the middle. They may reach to the point or stop well before it to allow it thickness for extra strength. Usually a deep fuller lightens a blade on the lower half, but to keep rigidity it will stop short toward the upper half. Occasionally, very slight fullers will serve only a decorative function. The fuller is sometimes mistakenly called a "blood run" or "blood-groove," although these are misnomers because blood does not run down the fuller, which actually serves no such purpose having to do with wounds or sticking and has absolutely no relationship to whether a blade will cut well or not. Deeper, thin fullers are also sometimes referred to as *flukes*. The opposite of a fuller is a *riser*, which improves rigidity on narrower swords and those used for fighting plate armor. Risers are sometimes referred to as *ribs*.

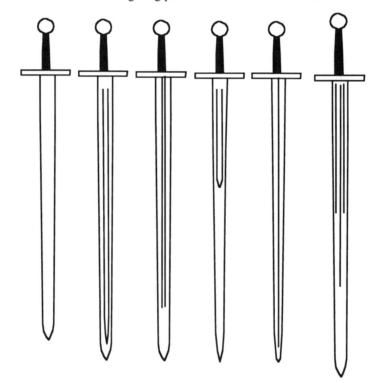

Samples of some of the various types of fullers that can be found on Medieval swords.

To digress for a moment and address something slightly off the subject, consider the often-heard phrase *double-edged* or *two-edged sword*. This expression is commonly used nowadays to refer to something that has both good and bad effects, that hinders as much as it helps, or that works equally against the person using it. This is a ridiculous misidentification *and a highly misleading notion* that says a great deal about ignorance of swords. A double-edged sword *in no way whatsoever* harms the user any more than a double-barreled shotgun endangers the shooter. No sword with two edges will cut or injure someone swinging at something else. The very act of using a sword to attack removes this possibility. There is just no physical possibility that, in the course of employing a sword for any attack or parry, the back edge facing the swordsman can be pushed in against him or slice him. Yet, unfortunately, this familiar and illogical phrase has become embedded in our popular lexicon. It's time its use was abandoned for the nonsense it is. Double-edged swords (as opposed to single-edged ones) do not cut "both ways." They *only* cut one way at a time, the direction in which they are used.

The shape of a sword's point is particular to its penetration. Many Medieval swords lack tips for effective thrusting, relying instead on cutting edges for strong hacking blows. Others have points readily able to pierce armor, including mail. Later Medieval swords had thicker points specifically intended to pierce mail links or the joints in plate armor.

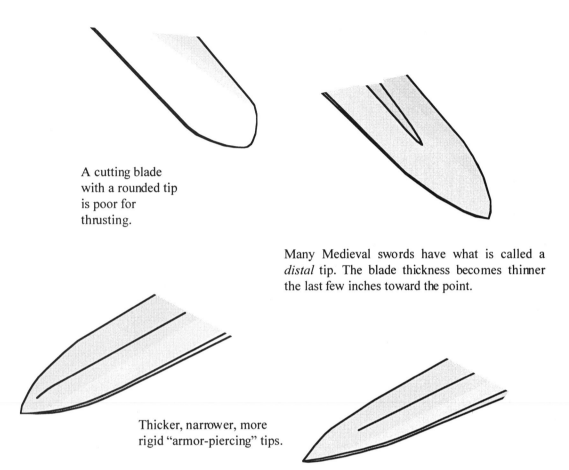

A cutting blade with a rounded tip is poor for thrusting.

Many Medieval swords have what is called a *distal* tip. The blade thickness becomes thinner the last few inches toward the point.

Thicker, narrower, more rigid "armor-piercing" tips.

Those swords intended for hacking and chopping have broad blades usually unpointed (rounded or with dull tips). Those that are for cutting and thrusting tend to have slightly narrower blades with angled or tapered tips. A narrower blade will often be lighter and have a deeper fuller. Those that are for use against tougher armors, rather than a fuller, will instead have a *riser* or center ridge. Such tips were also ideal for splitting and bursting the links of mail. Some early Medieval swords are more suited to cutting only than to cutting and thrusting; a few even had points unsuited to effective thrusting. All this appears to have been a matter of personal preference, style of fighting, and local custom to some degree. Although it would seem that armor would be a factor in this, it appears not to have had much effect; varieties of swords coexist regardless of the forms of armor available.

Interestingly, many historical depictions of early Medieval combat show swords with seemingly rounded or blunt tips being used for thrusts. In many cases such blades are shown stabbing clean through mail-covered bodies and heads. Although some early blades were incapable of stabbing, the apparent lack of a sharp point on some depictions may very well be the fault of the artist doing the rendering; illustrations sometimes do not provide a detailed representation of the swords.

The *hilt* is the lower portion of a sword consisting of the cross-guard, handle/grip, and pommel. Most Medieval swords have a straight or *cruciform-hilt*. The cruciform-hilt style was almost universal throughout all of Western Europe. The term *hilt* is an old Saxon word coming from a Viking name for the cross-guard, *hjalt*. Although it is a sword's blade that is the determining factor of its use and classification, the hilt is the more recognizable and familiar element. Often considered heirlooms, swords could be in use for considerable time and have their hilts and handles replaced on several occasions during their lifespan. It was with the earlier swords of the Dark Ages (particularly the *Carolingian* ones) that the hilt features classically associated with Medieval swords became fully defined. The straight, sturdy guard and enlarged pommel were a result of a heavier blade intended for solid, shearing cuts. The straight crossbar guard developed from the stubbier, smaller guards of earlier swords. Such guards ensured a strong hilt and good grip (it also kept moisture out of the sheath when the sword was inside). The cross-guard began to take shape with the adoption of the long, slashing sword during the Dark Ages. Larger, sturdier guards helped improve the balance of the heavier blade while protecting the hand from glancing blows and from being knocked into shields. Indeed, in all iconographical sources, *there is no real indication of a cross-guard used for directly parrying a sword blow.* They are shown being used only to trap and bind opposing weapons.

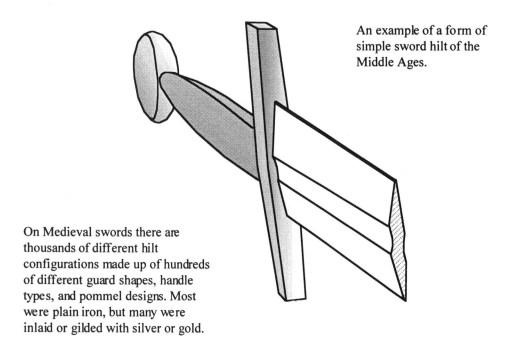

An example of a form of simple sword hilt of the Middle Ages.

On Medieval swords there are thousands of different hilt configurations made up of hundreds of different guard shapes, handle types, and pommel designs. Most were plain iron, but many were inlaid or gilded with silver or gold.

The bar guard (or cross-guard) on the hilt of Medieval swords is more properly known as simply the *cross*. The simple crossbar or cruciform shape is the most common and practical. A Renaissance term for the straight or curved cross-guard was the *quillon* (possibly from an old French or Latin term for a type of reed). The term *quillon* was not first used until perhaps as late as circa 1570 and, though useful and popular, is inaccurate in reference to Medieval swords. Guards varied in width and length, and over later centuries various styles came and went. Both pommel and guard were typically made of steel; rarely were softer metals used. The steel might be gilded or otherwise decorated. Like a pommel, a guard also acts as a counterweight to balance the hilt with the blade. A blade-heavy weapon can be clumsy and slow; a hilt-heavy one can be weak and slow.

Guard length is a factor of the balance required by the blade as well as personal taste. The earliest Medieval swords (like those of the Vikings and Anglo-Saxons) with their small, simple, stubby guards reveal that a guard is essentially a hand-stop. The primary purpose of a guard is to prevent the hand from slipping down the blade when stabbing and thrusting. Its secondary purpose is to protect the grip from smacking into a shield. Its final purpose is to prevent other weapons from striking the user's hand.

Examples of "typical" hilts showing only a range of common guards types.

Not all guards had squared-off and rectangular cross-sections; many were varieties of octagonal, hexagonal, and pentagonal shapes. Some styles were more exclusive to certain types of long-swords. Early Saxon and Viking sword guards might be made of separate pieces riveted together. Viewed from the top, their design might be triangular, tapered, or bow-shaped. Several guard and pommel types are unique, while other types are fairly common. The Church later encouraged the cross style as a way to remind knights of their piety.

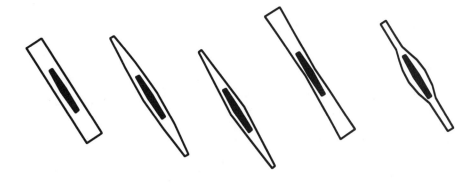

On the center of some cross-guards were small cusps (called *ecussons* in the Renaissance period) intended to help lock the sword into its sheath and keep out moisture.

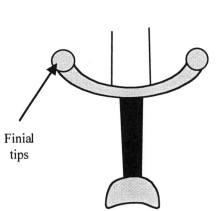

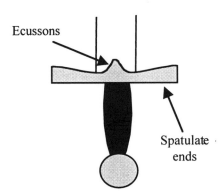

Finial tips

Ecussons

Spatulate ends

A few guard styles also had small recessed crosses cut into their ends.

Scrolled or curved guards and downturned tips were known on Viking swords as far back as 900 A.D. They first emerged on Medieval swords around 1150 but were quite rare until the late 1300s. They are purely decorative, with no functional value. They really do not offer *any* greater ability over straight guards in trapping or binding another weapon. The same can be said about straight guards with bent tips.

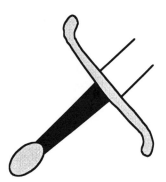

Curved "s" guards appeared around the 1420s, and they, too, are purely decorative and do not offer any improved defense. Many styles of these became common in the Renaissance.

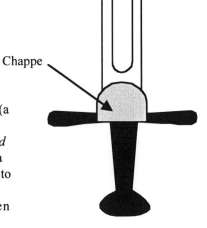

Chappe

Starting in the mid-1200s, a small leather piece called a *chappe* (a cape) was sometimes added to a guard. The chappe helped to protect a blade from moisture when it was sheathed. A *garnished* hilt could refer to one with a chappe or a *binded* grip (one with a special wrap). On some modern replica blades today, hilts seem to be one of the more difficult parts for manufacturers to produce accurately. The hilts are notorious for being substandard and even falling apart during even light use.

Beginning in the 1400s, the Medieval cross-guard underwent major changes as result of new ways of employing different blade forms against various armors. Earlier, about 1320, small, extra guard rings called *finger-rings* (or *annelets)* began to be added to hilts. These small loops, or branches (also called the *arms-of-the-hilt*), extend toward the blade from the cross. They were intended to protect the index finger when it is wrapped over the guard (later, more elaborate hilts were devised specifically with this in mind). Using the lead finger in this way allowed for the gripping technique of *fingering.* This technique was a result of the increasing need to control the tip in both stabbing attacks and in parries against them. The finger extends around the guard to allow for greater point control and a better grip.

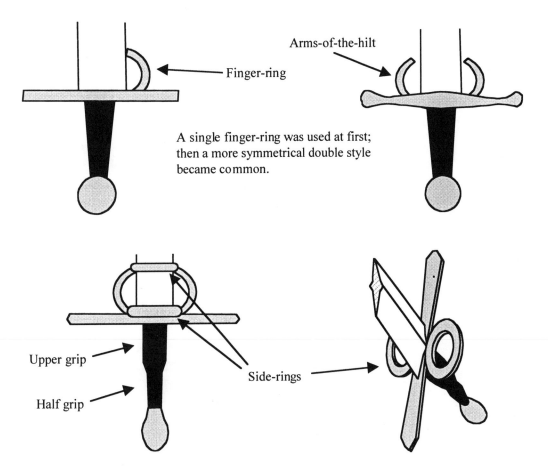

Arms-of-the-hilt

Finger-ring

A single finger-ring was used at first; then a more symmetrical double style became common.

Upper grip

Half grip

Side-rings

Side-rings or *ring-guards* (later called *anneus* or *ports*) developed around the 1420s. They were also designed to further protect the hand and fingers (particularly when not wearing gauntlets or heavy gloves). They, too, are typically found on bastard-swords as well as Renaissance two-handed swords. Some swords will have either finger-rings or side-rings while others will have both. The combination of both finger-rings and side-rings appeared on bastard-swords by the 1460s. The knuckle-bar or knuckle-guard did not appear until about the 1470s. When combined, they are often referred to as either a *close-hilt, compound-hilt,* or *compound-guard.* Often, these compound-hilts can add considerably to a sword's weight and detract from its thrusting agility (the reason for adding the guards in the first place). Although limited to a few swords of the late Middle Ages, these were common fixtures on Renaissance cut & thrust swords and later rapiers.

The simple cruciform-hilt should not be viewed as partial or "incomplete." It was fully developed on its own. Like swords, Medieval hilts did not "evolve" to some superior ideal form so much as later adopt additional attributes better suited to more diverse needs.

The dull portion of a blade just above the hilt became known as the *ricasso* by the end of the 1400s. The origin of the term is obscure. Short ricassos of 1 to 3 inches first appeared on blades around 1200 A.D. and later were a common feature of most Renaissance swords. The ricasso is intended for fingering and is left unsharpened to prevent injury to or irritation of the finger. Ricassos can be found on many bastard-swords and two-handers, where they can extend from 6 to 10 inches. Those on great-swords and two-handed swords are sometimes called a *false grip* and allow the entire second hand to grip and hold on. Not all swords with hilts capable of using the fingering grip had a ricasso. For maximum effectiveness, a blade was generally sharp its whole length; this could also prevent it from being grabbed near the hilt. Even some blades with compound-hilts are also sharpened where their ricasso would be. (This may be because the hilt was added at a later date, for reasons more of fashion than function). There are a very few great-swords with flared ricassos.

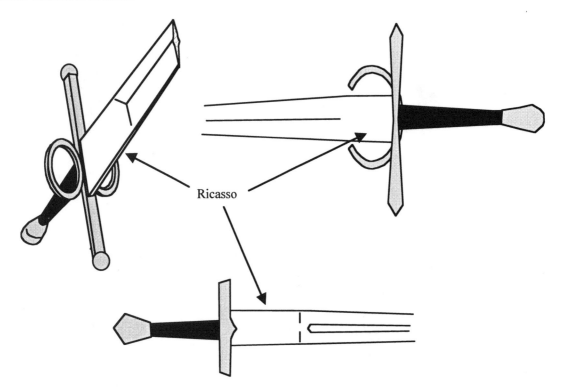

Ricasso

Unlike those for civilian and courtly wear of the later Renaissance, Medieval swords tend to be plainer and less ornamented, although there are many notable exceptions, including those for royalty and early Viking blades. With few exceptions, Medieval swords were not carried by civilians or warriors not in military dress. Medieval Christian swords were typically blessed or inscribed with religious or biblical quotations. This, of course, was done to "protect" the user from curses and devils. The fashion of adding inscriptions on blades fell out of common use around 1300, because the newer flat-hexagonal or diamond blade shapes could not easily be inlaid with writing.

The use of *basket-hilts* or *cage-hilts*, consisting of various swept bars and rings, was a much later development. Beginning in the very early 1500s, some forms of complex guards were given additional enclosed bars and knuckle-guards. These were especially popular on back-swords. Saberlike "bell" guards did not develop until later in the 1500s. They are in no way related to any Medieval swords; they are variations of Renaissance compound-hilts. Occasionally, practitioners today will use them for safety purposes since they offer better hand protection. However, this comes at a price: basket-hilts are by nature much more restrictive of the grip and do not accurately reflect the subtleties involved. Because they are also heavier, they significantly alter the balance (and therefore the handling) of a blade. Basket-hilts and cage-hilts are not Medieval.

The pommel (Latin for "little apple") was a solid metal shape that acted as both counterweight and hand-stop. It prevented the hand from slipping off the grip when striking. The pommel also keeps the hilt firmly attached to the blade. The pommel fits tightly over the end of the tang holding the handle to the hilt and the hilt to the blade. Without an appropriately sized pommel, a sword would be poorly balanced and very clumsy. As has been well documented, a great variety of pommel styles developed, almost all of which were matters of fashion and personal taste. There are more than 40 types of pommels that have been classified. Their names are more or less modern designations given by collectors and curators. Some pommels are specific to single-hand swords and more comfortable than others against the palm. There are those that are suited to single-hand swords and those that are more appropriate for larger blades. Flat ones were simply not intended to be gripped by the hand or possibly were even designed with armored gauntlets in mind. Over the centuries many forms and styles became popular in different regions. Like guards, pommels have been used by historians as an aid in classifying sword types and approximating their age. It is notoriously difficult to date Medieval sword guards and pommels or even blades with any certainty of when they first or last appeared in any century. Dates are frequently subject to revision.

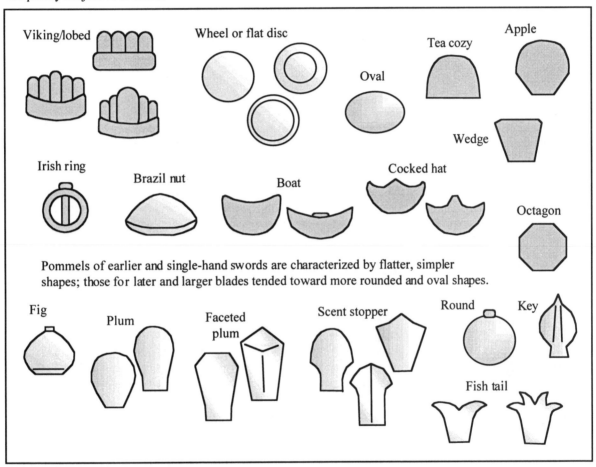

Viking/lobed Wheel or flat disc Tea cozy Apple Oval Wedge

Irish ring Brazil nut Boat Cocked hat Octagon

Pommels of earlier and single-hand swords are characterized by flatter, simpler shapes; those for later and larger blades tended toward more rounded and oval shapes.

Fig Plum Faceted plum Scent stopper Round Key Fish tail

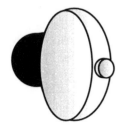

Pommels were attached in a variety of ways, such as by weld, rivet, or screw, or were simply hammered on. Some were fixed by having a hole bored directly through them and then having the end of the tang heated or just hammered over cold. Sometimes the pommel included a small rivet (capstan rivet) called a pommel nut, pommel bolt, or tang nut. Some blades have pommels made out of the end of the tang itself hammered flat. Saxon and Viking pommels often had separate "caps" riveted over them.

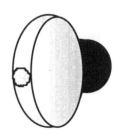

There have been a variety of handle designs in use over the centuries. Many designs were determined by fashion as much by the requirements of the blade. Whatever their shape or length, almost all conform to eight standard patterns. Their names are, for the most part, modern labels. Grips are designed for how a sword is held. Although a *handle* can be called the grip, the *grip* itself is actually the *wrapping* on a handle. Wooden handles, as well as those of horn or bone, can be slippery in a bare, sweaty palm. Metal rings or leather or wire wrapping was therefore used for a better hold. Many grips were bound in this way to offer a better grip when wearing a leather glove or iron gauntlet. Grips might also be covered in such material as linen, velvet, cord, or leather. Some might have an under layer with a thong or wrap of leather. The word *grip* is also used as a term for any method of holding the weapon. Handles themselves were usually of wood, bone, horn, or ivory and could be made in two halves shaped to fit around the tang. They were then tightly glued together, sandwiched around the hilt. After 1250, handles were usually hot-bored (or burned through) onto those blades with tapering tangs. This provided a far better fit.

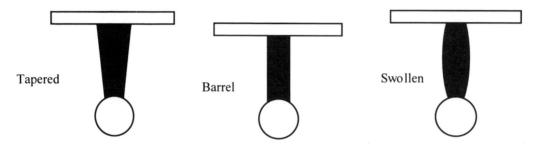

Tapered   Barrel   Swollen

On a cutting or slashing sword, handles are not usually round at all, but oval or somewhat flat. Rounded handles have a tendency to slip in the grip when cutting strongly and when parried hard or struck at a weak angle. A flatter, squared-off shape allows for a stronger grip and fits the hand more naturally. Swords used more or exclusively for thrusting (e.g., rapiers) tend to have rounder handles because of the manner in which they must be gripped and the position in which they are held in the palm. Today, many inaccurate reproduction swords and fantasy pieces, regardless of their design, are made with round handles. On bastard-swords and two-handers of the 1400s handles might also have been octagonal or rounded-off squares.

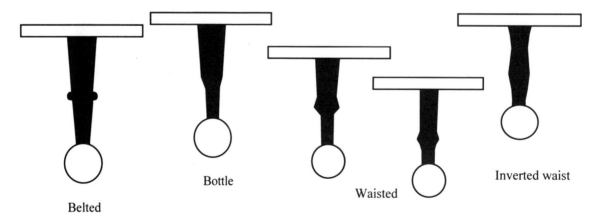

Belted   Bottle   Waisted   Inverted waist

A long handle (sometimes referred to as a hand-and-a-half grip) enables the extra weight of a somewhat larger blade to be easily handled. It also allows for the advantage of using both hands when the other one is not carrying a shield or secondary weapon or if it becomes injured. Against heavier armors a two-hand grip can be necessary for greater blows. Longer handles sometimes had *belted* grips with small notches or knobs in the middle and allowed for somewhat better control when held with one hand or two. This was the early development of the half-grip. Double-hand grips are sometimes thinner near the pommel or can have a *waisted* shape. The taper of a waisted handle allows an excellent grip whether held by one or two hands. Not all long handles are always the so-called "hand-and-a-half" grips; many are designed intentionally for two hands. True hand-and-a-half handles are more those that taper toward a shorter, thinner "half-grip."

76

The method of holding a Medieval sword is that of a "fist" grip. It is held with the edges lined up parallel with the knuckles. This ensures that the weapon doesn't hit flat and is aimed for the correct cutting angle. A proper grip is crucial in using a sword. If a grip is not strong and secure, a blow will be weak and cut poorly. When the sword is gripped, it should not be held too tightly or too loosely. Too loose and you can be disarmed; too tight and the arm will soon tire. A sword can also be knocked out of a tense hand.

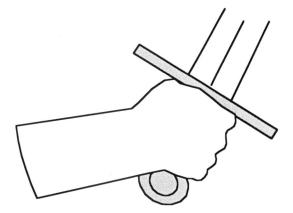

The cross-hilt of a Medieval sword allows for a closer grip as the side of the thumb and index finger tighten up against the hilt. The top of the hand rests flush with the cross-guard. For a firm grasp, it snugs and even rides up past the guard a few centimeters. This occurs only with a cross-bar hilt. The guard should be felt comfortably against the hand, but not completely pressing it. In the standard method of gripping a Medieval sword, the palm and little finger rest against the pommel to improve the hold. Alternatively, even on some short handles, the grip or pommel could be held by the second hand for leverage.

Most Medieval swords, intended for use with a shield, are suited to only one-handed use. That is, their short handles are sized to fit only one hand securely and comfortably. The sword itself is balanced and weighted for wielding in one hand. Some swords do have handles that, although short, can allow the second hand to grab on (even though they are not true two-hand or even half-grips). This often depends on the pommel shape because some are easier for a second hand to hold than others.

The balance of a good sword is subjective to some degree. The sword should not feel either blade or hilt heavy. When held, it should just feel "there." The finest real swords have a "capable feel," befitting their obvious function. Good balance should allow the weapon's natural center to focus on a cut. Usually, a Medieval sword's balance will be on the blade about 3 to 6 inches from the guard.

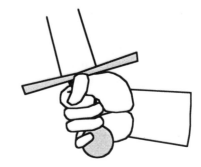

Illustrations from as early as 900 A.D. even show the pinkie finger stretched out loose and extending past the pommel (this is sometimes mistaken as being "on" or over the pommel).

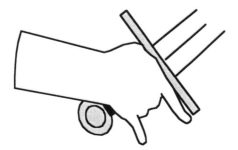

Historical artwork also shows swords gripped with "loose" fingers. In a strong hand, this loosening of a finger or two on the grip acts to naturally release tension in the hand. It is a simple action that can help prevent wrist fatigue as well as aid the weapon's mobility and balance . . . *in a strong hand.* Often only the lead or pinky finger is left "off the grip."

Historical artwork shows both early and late Medieval swords being gripped by the pommel just as the wielder strikes. When striking in this way, it's possible to extend the reach of a swing a few valuable inches by sliding the hand down the grip at the last second and grabbing the pommel. This is sometimes known as "slipping," as the Vikings were alleged to have done. It allows for an additional snap of power at the instant of contact. However, loosening the hold in this way can cause it to be knocked from the hand should it be blocked or strike a resistant target. Holding the blade at the pommel end to increase reach may sometimes be referred to as *pommeling* or *palming.* This is possible on those blades with longer handles and rounded or oval pommels suited for grasping.

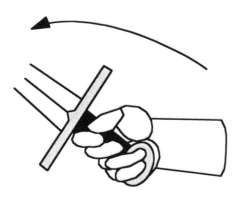

Slipping the pommel in a blow.

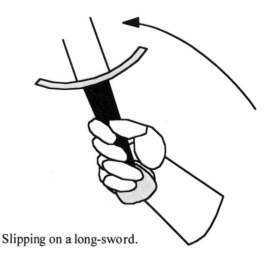

Slipping on a long-sword.

Medieval artwork also depicts a few swords being gripped in the middle of the handle with the hand flush with neither the guard or pommel. Although somewhat weaker, this grip is perfectly suited to cutting and parrying, allows "slipping" the handle, and will not cause the lead knuckle to chafe against the guard.

When the opponent is on the ground, the weapon can be switched around and held inverted for a downward stab. This is also useful when close in, and the second hand, if it is armored, is free to grab hold of the blade itself.

A long handle or one with a half-grip can be held by a single hand. For balance, a grip closer to the guard is preferable, but to use its length on certain cuts a grip near the pommel is also possible by either hand.

The grip for a Medieval sword is not at all like that used today in sport-fencing. In contrast, modern saber fencing places the thumb on the back of the handle, as was common with many 19th-century swords. Modern sport-fencing sabers are extremely light, thin, flexible pseudo-swords. The saber's bell-guard (or *caprice*) evolved from the knuckle-bars and basket-hilts of Renaissance military swords. Saber fencing itself developed only in the last century from a combination of sources. It is not a direct descendant of Medieval (or even Renaissance) methods. It is its own stylized athletic game derived, in part, from methods devised for cavalry sabers, cutlasses, and back-swords of the past two centuries.

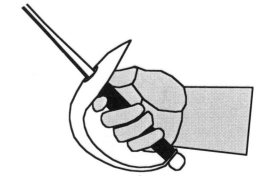

79

There are also some depictions of short handles held by two hands, with the second hand grasping more of the pommel than the handle. Even on the short handles of many single-hand swords both hands could be used (but for effectiveness and agility, such a weapon was designed with one hand in mind). Doing so can become necessary when the swordsman is tired or injured, when his other hand is empty, or when he is striking against tougher armors.

Unlike with the double-hand grip used with Japanese *katanas*, in which the second hand holds the bottom of the handle (or *kashira*), the pommel on the Medieval sword is not normally held. This is as much due to differences in hilt design between the two types of weapons as with their styles of cutting. A *katana* uses a sort of torquing motion with the wrists and a pulling action as a cut is delivered. Many practitioners attempting to use Medieval long-swords and great-swords in a "kenjutsu style" will adopt long handles and use this method. Practice at actual cutting with accurate reproductions of sharpened Medieval swords, however, will quickly reveal the necessity for a different grip. The handling and the balance of a longer, straight edge require a somewhat different cutting motion. You cannot hold the pommel on all swords when gripping the weapon. Only those pommels designed for it can be held. When the pommel is gripped, it can improve maneuverability or thrusting power.

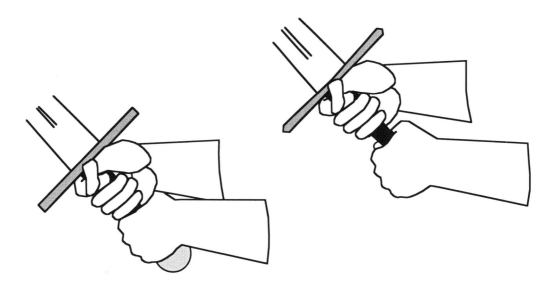

Not all long-sword handles are held with the hands close together. Some are long enough to allow for a space of an inch or two between the hands. On great-swords this is necessary for the balance and action of a larger blade. Different hand positions are also used when changing to certain stances or delivering particular cuts.

Often overlooked and undervalued is the Medieval sword's unique capacity to use the gripping technique of fingering the crossbar. Fingering was not uncommon during the Medieval period (it was in use by the Franks), and it can be seen in both early and late Medieval art. However, it was far more common in the 1400s, particularly among the Italians and Spanish. At one time it was known as the "Italian grip." It has been suggested that it came to Europe by way of Persia or even India, or that it came to Spain from the Middle East. This would seem very unlikely, because none of the swords from these areas use finger-rings nor are they used with much of a thrusting style of fighting. Wrapping the finger around the guard greatly aids in thrusting and can improve gripping, but it does expose the finger. Extra guards were therefore required to protect it. Fingering is not possible on all swords nor when wearing mail mittens or heavy gauntlets.

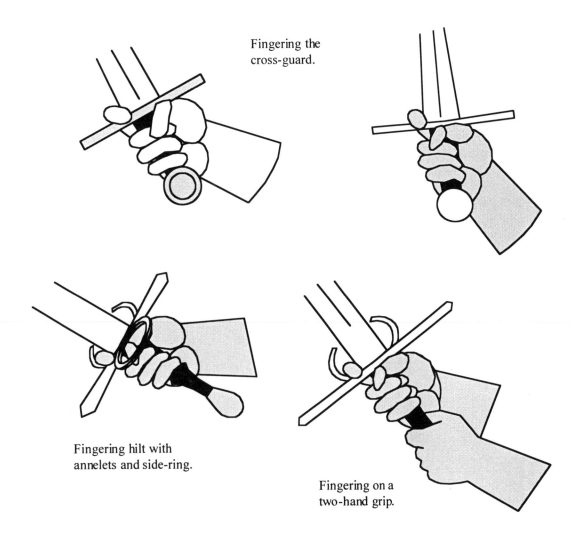

Fingering the cross-guard.

Fingering hilt with annelets and side-ring.

Fingering on a two-hand grip.

Although fingering has its disadvantages with most Medieval swords (there is the danger of losing a finger, and it also slightly diminishes cutting power), it does improve blade agility and is also useful if the hand becomes tired. These are important factors when using a sword more for stabbing attacks. This unique and innovative form of grip, known since ancient times, also became quite common in the Renaissance with cut & thrust swords and was later essential to the use of the rapier. Many bastard-swords have single or double finger-rings. For some time they have been incorrectly called the *pas d'ane* (likely from the Old French for *donkey step* or *mule foot*, which they seem to resemble). The finger-ring was the first sign of the changes which led to the characteristic *compound-hilts* or *complex-guards* of cut & thrust swords and rapiers in the 1500s and 1600s.

A Medieval sword's cross-guard was not really for protecting the hand. This is a common misunderstanding. Certainly, it does offer some defense against the shafts and hafts of other weapons, but clearly it is not very extensive. If it had been used for defense against blades we would expect surviving historical swords in collections and museums to have considerable and noticeable scarring on them. They do not. This lack of expected trauma (nicks and gouges) can only be explained by understanding how the weapons are actually used. The same can be said for the blade's shoulder above the hilt. Modern practice with replica swords also reveals that protecting the hand from cuts is a minor and secondary function. Instead, *the function of wide Medieval cross-guards seems to have been for preventing the user's hand from slamming into or hitting against the flat of an opponent's shield.*

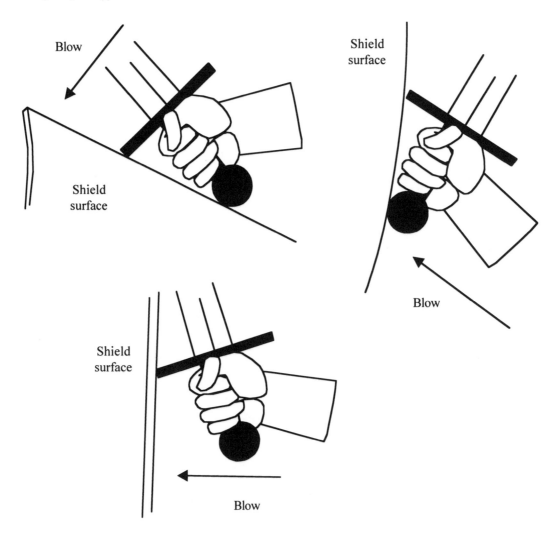

When you strike as an opponent uses his shield to parry, there is a chance that your knuckles and fist will knock forcibly into the opponent's shield as your blade comes down or is parried. This can also happen as an opponent uses his shield to smash forward. Although warriors might wear mail mittens, heavy gloves, or even armored gauntlets, having the hand smash into the face of a shield can cause injury, upset any recovery or renewal of attack, or even force a disarm. A long cross-guard (whether straight or slightly curved) helps prevent this. Pushing against an opponent's shield with the hilt offers stronger leverage than is possible by using the center or end of the blade. However, on long-swords and great-swords (to be examined later) a longer, slender guard has application in binding and trapping. The proper use of a sword's cross-guard will be addressed in detail in the section on fighting with the sword & shield.

We call the metal crossbars on Medieval swords "guards" for a reason. They do guard the hand. Although a Medieval-style cross-guard may at first impression seem not to offer significant protection to the hand, this is not entirely so. The simple crossbar of the Medieval sword is sufficient defense for preventing opposing weapons *only* from slipping down, bumping into, or sliding against the hand *when the sword is used in the proper manner*. If this were not so, then the simple cruciform-hilt would surely not have survived as a standard for hundreds of years (practitioners who insist upon using historically inappropriate basket-hilts —which did not even appear until around 1510 at the earliest—entirely miss this). It must be remembered that hand armor was not universal throughout the entire Middle Ages. Although they added excellent protection, mail mittens and metal gauntlets were certainly not available to or used by everyone.

The fact is that Medieval artwork is virtually devoid of any rendering of hands or fingers being injured during combat as a result of the insufficiency of cross-guards. A cruciform-guard on a sword provides quite suitable and adequate protection—given an experienced user who knows how to handle it. With centuries of ingenuity and effort behind their arms and armor, there can be little doubt that the absence of enclosed hilts during the majority of the Middle Ages was not due to any ignorance on the part of Medieval warriors and weapon smiths. Nobody woke up one morning and suddenly realized he could build a better sword-guard. Prior to their development as protection for the fingering-grip (a reaction to the need for increased thrusting against plate armor), large cross-guards were simply not a necessity.

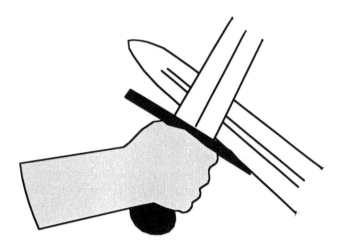

83

There are thus numerous reasons that can be offered as to why the Medieval sword's cross-guard design is both substantial and beneficial: (1) It allows both edges to be easily accessible by a simple turn of the handle (a necessity when one edge is dulled or damaged). (2) It allows for limited use of the "fingering" grip (for thrusting precision or when the arm is tired). (3) It allows another blade to be "unhooked" from a bind. (4) It facilitates lining up the knuckles with the edge for easier aiming and cutting (thereby avoiding hitting flat or off the mark). (5) Its flat shape is comfortable against the side or hip when worn. (6) When two blades are locked close together, it can be used to hit the opponent in the face. It is no difficult matter to imagine all these reasons being the forces behind the continued popularity and practicality of the cruciform-hilt during the Middle Ages (not to mention on swords throughout much of the Middle East and elsewhere). Ancient Greek and Roman swords, being shorter and meant for thrusts (with a few notable exceptions) just did not need very developed guards. For the majority of swords from the mid-1500s and after 1600, the cruciform-hilt was to become largely ceremonial, deferring to the newer compound-/complex-hilts that were more appropriate. Many European swords of the 19th century also reverted to simple bar guards.

An enclosed guard would seem to make sense on a cutting blade, but it is uncommon among swords of the world. If the enclosed guard was truly a significant advantage over the cross-guard we would expect to have seen it develop not just in Europe, but also in Asia, Persia, or India, on whose swords it was noticeably absent. There must be a practical reason for this, and a good part of it has to do with weight. For the most part, such hilts are just too darn heavy. The relatively small and virtually inconsequential guard, or *tsuba*, on Japanese katanas also serves as an example. In the case of the katana guard, the hand is held slightly different because of the grip required in its formidable method of swordsmanship. The shape of the katana handle is also different from that on Medieval swords. Similar to Medieval swordsmanship, kenjutsu generally involves multiple, two-handed strikes and sweeping, aggressive pulling cuts or forward pushes with the hips. A variety of thrusts are also used, especially against armor. Yet, a kenjutsu swordsman's hands are not in any great danger of being accidentally hit. Considering what little hand armor samurai had, this should seem remarkable. One wonders how they managed to keep their fingers protected from such strong attacks with only a small hand guard for defense. Can it be simply because their schools of swordsmanship taught proper cutting and defensive movement? Again, the answer lies in the proper manner in which parrying should be done with any long-sword (i.e., focusing on either avoiding or redirecting and countering an adversary's weapon, rather than stopping or meeting it). The idea is not to *rely* on the guard for defense anyway (since an opponent can take advantage of that), but instead to learn how to evade and counter or properly parry blows. This is the case with the cruciform-hilt of Medieval swords.

CARRYING THE SWORD

Swords were carried in a *sheath* or a *scabbard*. A scabbard was generally a hard, rigid case of wood or stiff leather. Most consisted of two thin wooden slats glued together and wrapped in leather. A sheath was either a stiff leather case or a soft, flexible leather cover. The inside of each would often be lined with sheepskin, lightly oiled fur, greased cloth, or felt. A sword case would typically have a metal cap or binding at the end called a *chappe* and another at the mouth called a *locket*. The chappe helped prevent the scabbard's end from being worn down and kept the sword's tip from poking through. The chappe originally meant a flap extension of the grip itself. The locket was a metal lip intended to create a firm fit for the sword and keep moisture out. The fit and shape of the cross-guard itself also prevented water or sweat from running in. Occasionally, small rings or "lockets" were attached to a sheath or scabbard to enable belts and cords to fit through. Typically a sword was worn vertically from a belt resting on the left hip at the waist (provided the weapon was not too long to draw). The belt was sometimes double wrapped and had a leather or metal holder or frog. Prior to 1100, swords were often worn from a baldric over the shoulder and resting on the hip. A dagger was often worn on the opposite side and thereby provided a convenient counterbalance. When wearing plate armor, a sword might be kept bare in a metal ring on the belt of a knight. This was for quick drawing during tournaments or battles (it also kept the scabbard out of the way).

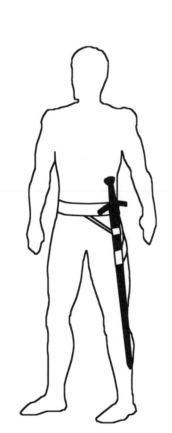

Swords were worn over the shoulder from a hanging baldric and vertically against the hip from a specially wrapped waist belt. The hilt would fit against the body just above the belt. Longer blades might be worn more forward and diagonally from a belt with straps and rings connecting to the scabbard. Swordsmen who were on foot or horse would typically draw their swords from their case with a straight upward motion.

CARE OF A FINE BLADE

The microscopic pores of a blade will trap moisture and cause tarnish, rust, and corrosion that will eventually weaken a blade. Constant cleaning, oiling, and repolishing are necessary. If left on, even the acids and salts in common sweat will soon cause rust spots. Even blood has to be wiped off. The higher the carbon content of the steel, the more susceptible it is to corrosion. Modern replicas can be kept clean by simple household utility oil and a soft cloth. Special preservers are also available. Sharpened blades also need the occasional scratches sanded out.

CHAPTER EIGHT

Medieval Shields

MEDIEVAL SHIELDS

Like the Medieval sword, the Medieval shield existed in great variety over many centuries. It too is a familiar object that has been frequently undervalued and historically unappreciated. Just as do swords, shields still appear in our modern world on many familiar icons from badges to emblems, insignia, and medals. Yet, little detail has been written about them. To understand the basis of Medieval swordsmanship we must understand the shield. Again, as with Medieval swords, we should refer to shields in the plural, for there were many types that saw use during the period. Medieval European shields were by no means uniform or universal. Several varieties were in use in different regions at any one time during the Middle Ages. They ranged from large oval and round forms to teardrop and triangular shapes to small hand-bucklers. There were also free-standing walls, an array of concave jousting versions sometimes used on foot, and many other unusual styles. Like swords, shields were personal, functional items but also ones influenced by changing fashion and custom. They can all be classed into just a few general types.

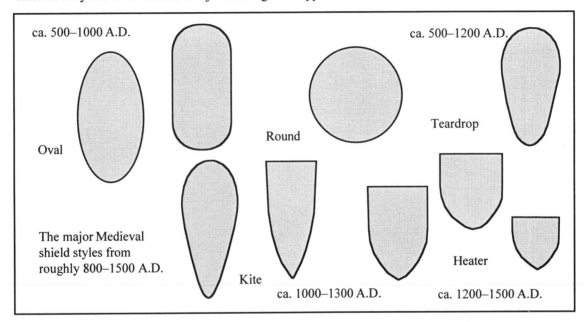

ca. 500–1000 A.D.   ca. 500–1200 A.D.

Oval   Round   Teardrop

The major Medieval shield styles from roughly 800–1500 A.D.

Kite   Heater

ca. 1000–1300 A.D.   ca. 1200–1500 A.D.

Medieval shields were used for one very practical reason: they were needed! Weapon blows were devastating in their effect, and armor alone was simply not sufficient on its own (at least not until the later advent of full plate). What is more, shields work. They are very, very good for defense. When combined with a sword, axe, or spear they are excellent defensive weapons in either mass battle or single combat. The most obvious value of a shield is that it protects from missile attacks—arrows, spears, axes, and rocks. In all its varied forms, the Medieval shield can be used passively and actively, defensively and offensively, whether the swordsman is mounted or on foot. For hundreds of years, the sword and shield went hand in hand and were very likely considered integral.

Due mainly to the rise of heavy cavalry and the coming of plate armor, shields underwent several changes during the Middle Ages. The earliest types owed much to Celtic, Germanic, and Roman influences. Later styles were developed by the Franks and Normans and over time were modified into new styles that then became widespread. Although there is no direct evidence, it is reasonable to think that there were shields intended specifically for foot soldiers and those intended for use both by warriors on foot and horseback. The size of shields, even more so than even swords, must have been a matter of personal taste and custom as well as what was required for battle. Although historical artwork tends to depict shields in any one illustration as being of a standard one-size-fits-all, several sources from the 1400s show that the variety of shield shapes and sizes during the late Middle Ages was considerable and unique (though many were specialty "tilting" or jousting shields and targes). By the late 1400s, shields for heavily armored knights on horseback were no longer a necessity.

Although they were all used in a general way, each type of shield that developed did so for a particular manner of combat. There are trade-offs with any size and shape of shield and these factors had to be weighed in relation to the user's personal preference. More importantly, consideration had to be given to the nature of the fighting to be encountered (e.g., mass warfare, small skirmishes, single combat, mounted charges, massed pole-arms, hails of arrows or crossbow bolts). Many of the more unusual shield designs were not for foot-combat; rather, they were specifically designed for use with lances on horseback.

Anatomy of a Round Shield

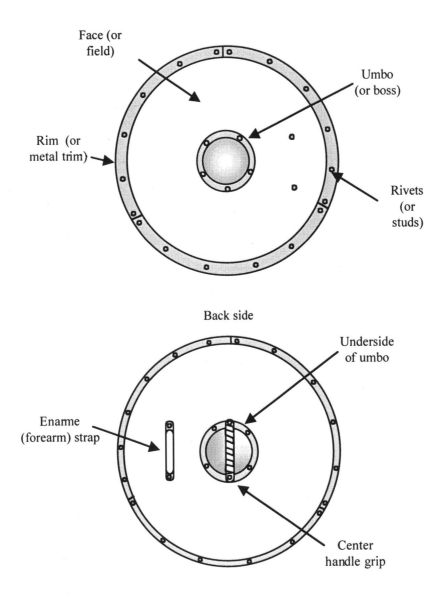

Shields were not intended for long-term use, just to endure as long as they lasted. Some were even made to be disposable. Once the wood was too severely damaged or worn, it was discarded and only the metal pieces (and possibly the straps) were saved for reuse.

Shield grips came in two styles: those with a single, rigid central handle held in one hand, and those with two or more leather arm straps worn on the forearm. A single-center grip allows the shield to be more maneuverable and kept farther out from the body. These were typically the shields of foot soldiers. Their fixed handles were usually made of wood or metal and attached with rivets over a hole in the middle of the shield. Protruding over the handle on the front of the shield was a protective, bowl-like, metal cup called an *umbo* or *boss*. Umbos were found typically on infantry shields, whereas smaller bosses were often only decorative. Umbos were between 4 and 6 inches across and made of approximately 16- to 18-gauge steel. Most were round, and many were slightly pointed. Blows could be taken on the umbo and strikes made with it. Most early shield styles, primarily round and oval forms, had umbos. Later shapes relied on forearm straps, with their bosses simply attached to the face of the shield and not offering any hand protection. By the mid-1200s, umbos on shields became ornamental only and eventually disappeared. This may have been a result of more and more shields being held on the arm by straps (which was more appropriate on horseback) rather than from central handle grips. The increasing curvature of shields (to fit closer to the body) also somewhat limits the use of a central grip. Umbos were also the basis for small hand-shields, or *bucklers*.

The Backs of Typical Arm-Worn Round Shields

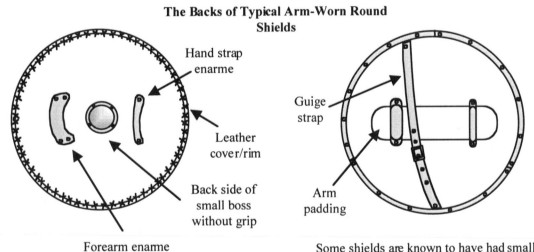

Hand strap enarme

Leather cover/rim

Back side of small boss without grip

Forearm enarme

Guige strap

Arm padding

Some shields are known to have had small padded armrests made of cloth or animal skin.

When worn on the arm, special straps called *enarmes* (or *braces*) are required. Carrying a shield on the arm allows it to be held close in against the body and suits it to both mounted and foot combat. It also allows the user to fight much closer to an opponent. The arm straps and grip would be riveted on and placed slightly off center in the middle of the shield (at its center of balance). By the 1300s these straps sometimes had adjustable buckles to improve their fit. Some shields had both arm straps and a rigid hand grip. The handle might be made of wood, stiffened leather, or leather-covered metal.

Some examples of typical umbos. They might range from fist-sized to 6 or 7 inches in diameter. Most were round, but some were more pointed. Earlier umbos were typically made of separate pieces of iron riveted together.

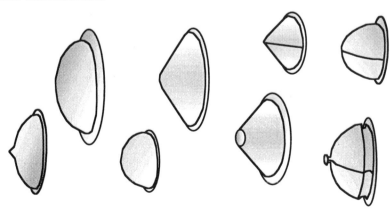

Shields were usually made by gluing planks of wood (from 4 to 7) side by side, though a few seem to have been made of single pieces. They might typically weigh from as little as 5 pounds to as much as 14. Early Medieval shields may have been made with a layered construction technique, like that used for modern plywood. One layer of alder wood was glued to one of oak. Others were made like plywood by laminating two or three layers of wood together, each with the grain in opposite direction for strength. Lime (linden) and poplar wood appear to have been the most common. Later shields were apparently made of thick willow or poplar. We cannot know precisely, because being made of perishable wood and leather, very few such shields have survived the ages. Shields could range in thickness from lighter ones of just under 1/2 inch to heavier ones of more than 1 inch. On average, they were from approximately 5/8- to 3/4-inch thick. Later shields, such as *heaters,* were between 1/2- and 3/4-inch thick. The front and back were usually covered in linen, parchment, or rawhide, which were glued or tacked on.

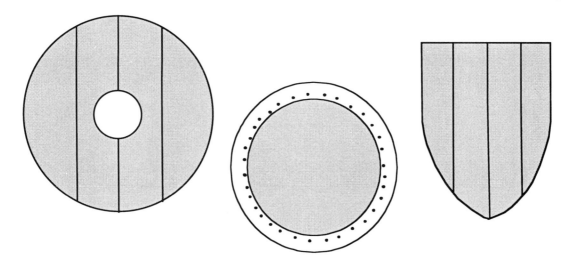

It is sometimes believed that Medieval shields were made of metal. This is a myth fostered by movies and television. Although small, hand-held bucklers are themselves of steel, such larger metal shields would be far too heavy and impractical for Medieval combat. Wood was a much more appropriate and practical material to use. Some jousting shields were all metal or reinforced with metal plates. Only in the later Renaissance did some large metal shields find limited use against pike formations.

Example of a metal trimmed edge.

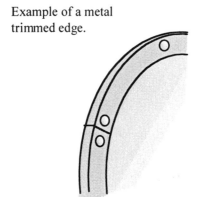

Many forms were only of leather-covered wood, while others had a protective trimming or rim usually made of iron. A leather cover helps protect the shield and absorb the impact of blows, whereas a metal trimming strengthens the shield. These rims were approximately 3/4 to 1 1/4 inches wide. There is actually no direct proof whether shield trims were always made of metal or whether some were of hardened leather. On some forms, extra bands of metal or leather were placed across the shield's front, or face. Some had additional metal fixtures and plates for decoration and to increase strength.

One of the most common shield shapes of the Middle Ages, and of history in general, was the round shield. It could range in size from as small as 14 inches to as large as 3.5 feet. A flat, round shield measuring approximately 28 to 32 inches in diameter and weighing from 8 to 12 pounds was among the earliest Medieval forms. They were highly popular with the Celts, Vikings, Saxons, Franks, and numerous Roman-era tribes. Round shields were used by many ancient civilizations, particularly the Greeks. Both center-gripped and arm-worn styles were used, with the center-gripped being more common. A round shape is an agile form suited to many sizes and ideal for both group battle and individual combat. It can easily be raised and lowered or used to strike out with. Considering that creating a round one is more difficult than building a square or rectangular one, there must be a reason. One obvious answer is that a round shield is maneuverable and allows the user to easily charge and run while carrying it. Unlike with many larger forms and other shapes, a round shield makes it easy for the bearer to run without knocking his legs into it. For foot soldiers, a round shield allows blows to slide off and be easily deflected. As with their swords, the Vikings regarded their shields highly and even gave them colorful names on occasion. Small round shields were also used by the Franks both on foot and while mounted. These were similar to ones favored by the Byzantines and the late Roman cavalry (determining whether a small round shield in Medieval artwork is a buckler or an actual arm-worn shield is not always easy). Oval-shaped shields had been popular since ancient times and were used by Germanic tribes as well as the Celts, Vikings, Saxons, Franks, and even the Normans. Oval shields can be used effectively while fighting both mounted and on foot. Use of round shields generally declined as Medieval warriors adopted newer designs better suited to both foot and mounted fighting. But the popularity of round shields reemerged in the 1400s as mounted combat lost value and foot soldiers rediscovered their versatility.

Classic round shields, such as those used by the Anglo-Saxons and Vikings, shown here in metal rim and untrimmed leather-covered versions.

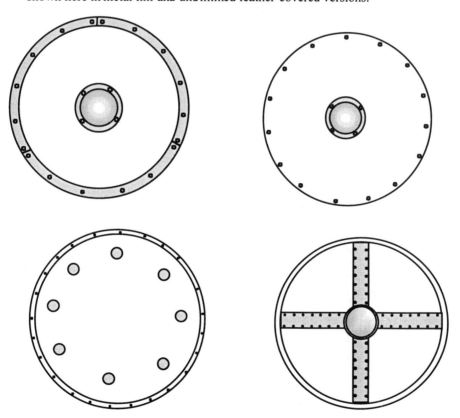

Round shields might also have large metal studs or reinforced metal plates riveted on, although these appear to have been somewhat rare.

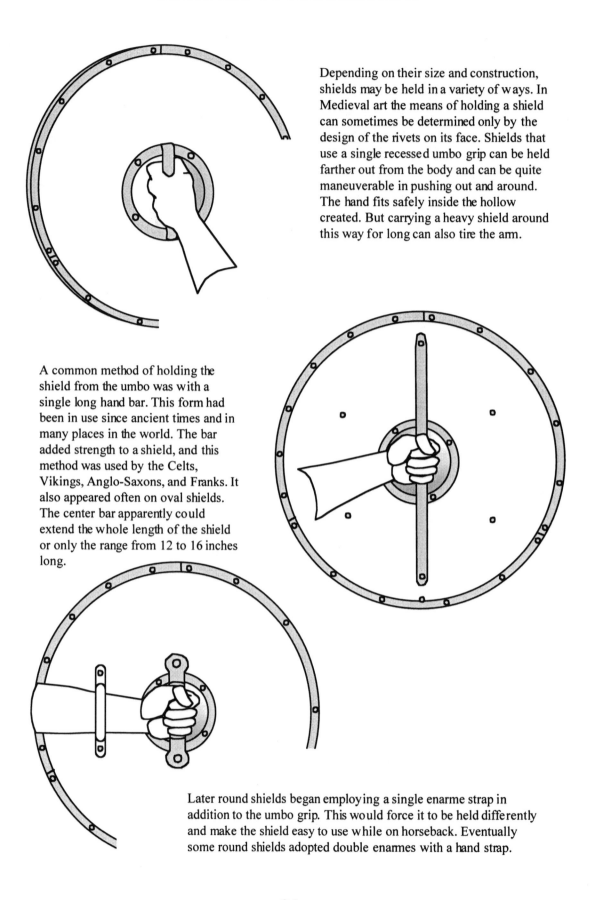

Depending on their size and construction, shields may be held in a variety of ways. In Medieval art the means of holding a shield can sometimes be determined only by the design of the rivets on its face. Shields that use a single recessed umbo grip can be held farther out from the body and can be quite maneuverable in pushing out and around. The hand fits safely inside the hollow created. But carrying a heavy shield around this way for long can also tire the arm.

A common method of holding the shield from the umbo was with a single long hand bar. This form had been in use since ancient times and in many places in the world. The bar added strength to a shield, and this method was used by the Celts, Vikings, Anglo-Saxons, and Franks. It also appeared often on oval shields. The center bar apparently could extend the whole length of the shield or only the range from 12 to 16 inches long.

Later round shields began employing a single enarme strap in addition to the umbo grip. This would force it to be held differently and make the shield easy to use while on horseback. Eventually some round shields adopted double enarmes with a hand strap.

Among the most popular Medieval shield forms was the teardrop or *kite*-shaped shield. The kite shield is an extremely effective design. The earliest depictions of these shields come from a manuscript of 983 A.D. At first they were only round shields with elongated bottoms or tapering oval ones. The longer and more pointed variety is often called the Norman shield, although it was even used at times by Saxons and Vikings. They were approximately 20 by 45 inches in size, were flat to slightly curved in cross-section, and weighed from 8 to 10 pounds. This typical form was ideal for use on horseback because it fitted the shape of the horse's neck and offered coverage for the rider's leg. The arm does not have to move to provide protection for the legs, which would be hard to do when holding a horse's reins in the same hand. When the swordsman was on foot it also provided great protection from the chin down to the knee and was good in a massed "shield wall" formation. With only a slight up or down movement it could easily protect either the head or the shin without exposing the other; such superb protection makes up for its lesser mobility—it does not have to be moved as much. Unlike with a round shield, when the swordsman is charging or running long distances the kite-shaped shield must either be held more horizontally or lifted up out of the way to prevent the legs from hitting into it. Longer shield styles are often dominate in cultures where warfare is based more on use the of spear and javelin.

Early kite shield shown with boss and leather face covering.

A later version showing rivets of the back-side enarmes and straps.

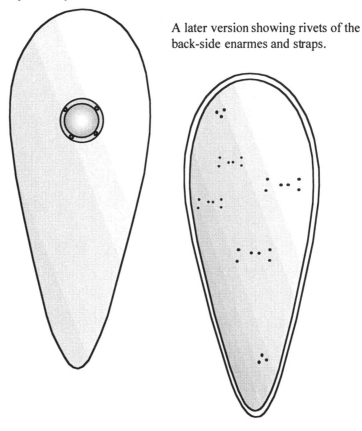

As with round shields, no one precise size was standard. One surviving kite shield from the mid-1200s reaches from shoulder to knee on a man 5'8" (which was about average for a male of the time). Medieval shields were made in both flat and convex forms (bending slightly to form a bowl shape). They could be shaped by steam-heating them in a vise. Although flat forms were easier to make and appear to have been more common, convex styles offer better defense and later became very popular in many shapes.

At first, both center-gripped and arm-worn kite styles were used, but the latter was better suited for mounted combat and became far more common. Most kite shields, as with nearly all shields worn by straps on the arm, do not have a boss. Early kite shields had vestigial bosses that were now too small for a hand to grip inside. The bosses might have had some limited use in striking and blocking, but they were unnecessary for shields carried by enarmes. The continuation of small umbos on kite shields is evidence of the use of a shield's flat side, as well as the edge, to block with. Otherwise, retaining a boss was not really necessary. Bosses were later discarded on the smaller and more maneuverable triangle shields that tended to be used by warriors in heavier armors. This makes sense since both the warriors and their armored opponents would not find a center grip necessary or consider blows by the umbo very threatening.

Kite shields at first had round tops, but by 1150 they had gradually flattened out. It has been speculated that this change may have been to improve visibility. A flattop shield design has little effect on defense even though making it somewhat easier to look over the top of one. However, a rounded top in some ways is better at deflecting blows off its curved rim. The idea that after hundreds of years, knights suddenly decided they could not see well over the rounded tops of kite shields makes little sense. The change in the kite shape to a flattop may very likely have had much more to do a simple preference by better armored knights for a smaller shield. Armor was improving, and there was greater use of fully enclosed helms and additional limb protection. Since fighting against plate armor involved greater use of stabbing attacks with the sword, the larger shields must also have been somewhat cumbersome for this. The kite shape was used into the 1200s until smaller, shorter, more triangular forms began to appear.

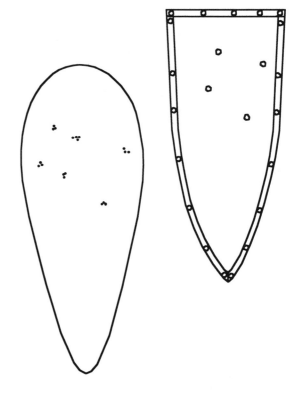

One useful development was that of a curved shield with a convex bowl shape to better protect the body. Although the Vikings, Anglo-Saxons, and Franks used only flat shields, the Normans were among the first to begin to use ones warped to form a closer form-fitting shape. This was an idea dating back to ancient times and one used extensively by the Romans. The ancestor of the kite shield may be the Frankish teardrop or "casket" form, which is itself likely related to the oval Roman *cliepus*. The cliepus developed as fighting in the late Roman Empire's armies became more individualized and based less and less on formations. The cliepus was used by both Roman cavalry and infantry.

Kite shields were held in a variety of ways, and their grips were much more individual. Typically, the straps or enarmes are positioned so the arm is held with the fist angled up and the elbow down. This is less stressful than trying to hold it horizontally. This is also the basic position it would assume on horseback.

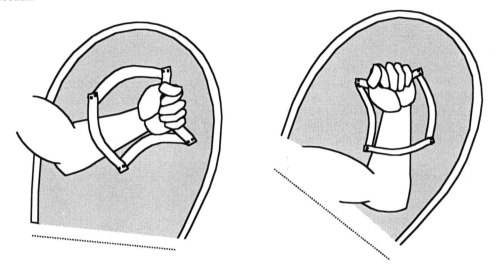

Several depictions of kite shields show them carried from "square" strap arrangements and by at least two different methods. This square strap system may have offered a universal means of gripping. Many portions of the Bayeux Tapestry even show mounted Normans holding kite shields sideways from S-shaped diagonal straps. On average, enarmes appear to have been from less than 1 inch to almost 2 inches wide and from 8 to 12 inches long.

Another unique method of carrying a shield is by twisting the arm through the main strap to create tension that ensures a tight, solid hold.

It must be realized that just as some swords are depicted out of proportion in Medieval artwork, shields are also shown as unrealistically small or large. This seems particularly true of kite shields. Some of the most accurate kite renderings from the Bayeux Tapestry are shown as only being large enough to cover from just above the shoulder down to mid-thigh. In other works of art kites extend from the chin to the knee. However, they are certainly not the gigantic "wall" shields extending from mouth to ankle that are sometimes used unrealistically by some modern Medieval combat enthusiasts.

The handle straps might also be in a unique double-crescent form. As the hand grasps each loop the tension between the two gives a very secure grip. This type of grip appears quite frequently on many Medieval shields and is well suited to sweeping blocks and deflecting parries.

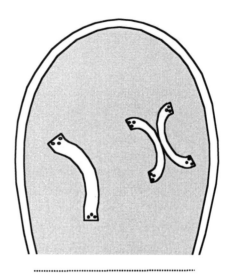

There were a range of different ways that shields might be held, depending on whether they were primarily infantry or cavalry shields. One arrangement better suited to mounted use had two arm straps and a double-crescent grip in a vertical position. There were also shields with only a single arm strap with two hand grips.

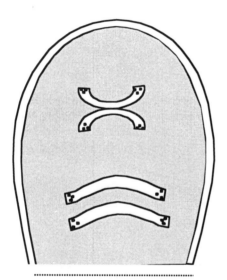

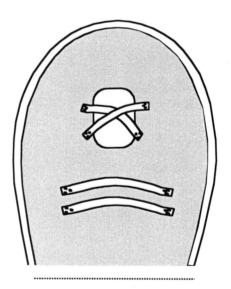

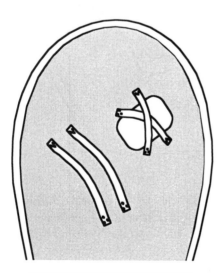

Other arrangements had two hand grips in an "X" arrangement and a pad for the knuckles. They are seen in both vertical and diagonal positions.

Soft leather handles on most shields make more sense than any type of solid, metal, or wooden ones. The soft handles are not likely to cause injury should the back of the shield be knocked into the face or the body, and they are also safer when the shield is used on horseback or carried slung over the back.

Some forms had two arm straps while others had three. On those with three enarmes, a mounted rider could let go of the third strap (to control his horse's reins) but still be able to hold onto his shield by the other two.

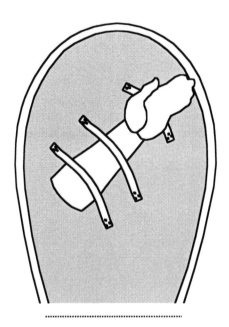

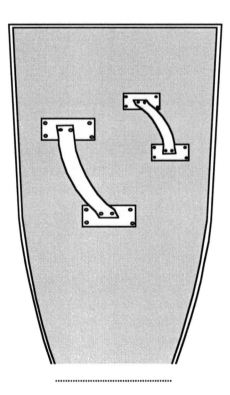

It is difficult to fully realize how a Medieval shield is handled and employed without the benefit of examining and practicing with a historically accurate reproduction. Many people are surprised at how heavy and solid they truly are but also how effective at safely covering the body from attack. Getting the chance to bang away with a real sword on a real moving shield is an edifying experience for any Medieval sword & shield practitioner.

The two-enarme version is a fairly standard form of shield grip and existed on many types.

For many shields it was common to have a long, extra shoulder strap, called a *guige*, that was used primarily for hanging the shield when not in use. The guige could also be used for carrying a shield around the shoulder and neck, as was depicted frequently in Medieval art. A shoulder strap allowed a shield to be carried much closer when the swordsman was in tight mass battle or even worn on the back when he was on horseback. It also gave the shield arm more freedom to assist in holding a spear, carrying a second weapon, or holding the reigns or a lance when the swordsman was on horseback. At certain times a shield could also be worn on the back when fighting with two-handed weapons. To keep the shields out of the way when not in use, guiges could be wrapped around the straps or even the handle. Some also had buckles that allowed them to be drawn up and shortened so that they were out of the way during battle. It may also very well be that guiges were detachable options on some shields, used according to whatever the requirements at the time were. Since not all shields had guige straps, it may be that they were a matter of personal choice.

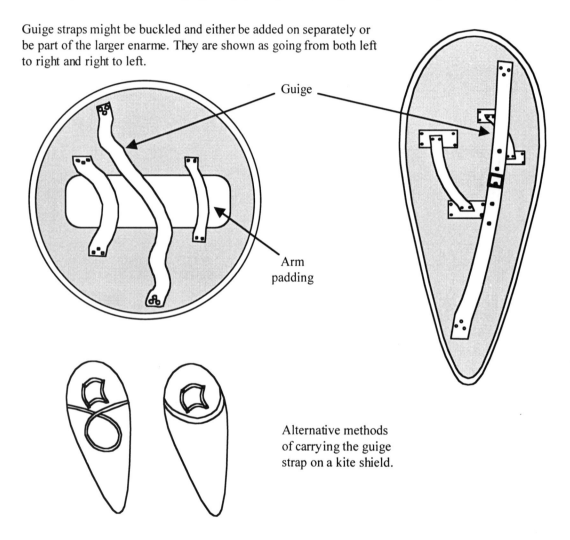

Guige straps might be buckled and either be added on separately or be part of the larger enarme. They are shown as going from both left to right and right to left.

Guige

Arm padding

Alternative methods of carrying the guige strap on a kite shield.

Although some pictorial evidence does show shields around the neck of figures lined up preparing for battle on foot, engaging in tournaments, and assaulting unarmed victims, it would seem very unlikely that a shield was worn on the back when in the midst of close foot combat. Guige straps are shown more often being used during sieges where the combatants use both hands to handle various implements rather than fight in group melees. Shields are also seen held by guiges when they are not immediately in use (such as when the swordsman is at rest, awaiting an enemy formation at a distance, or indoors). Art works do show soldiers using spears and other pole-arms who have their shields on a guige hanging off their shoulder. In this way the soldiers could fight without completely discarding their shields, which might be needed later.

Under certain conditions, hanging the shield from the shoulder might be a practical means for a warrior to protect himself against missile weapons without having to actually hold it in his hand or wear it by his arm in front. But modern experimental re-creation has shown that doing so restricts the free movement of any weapon and also hampers the ability to properly handle the shield defensively. Guige straps shown are rarely, if ever, seen on round shields or those types smaller than heater shields. Guige straps appear most often being used by spearmen fighting with kite shields. This makes sense because they would need both hands for fighting and could leave the shield hanging in front of them.

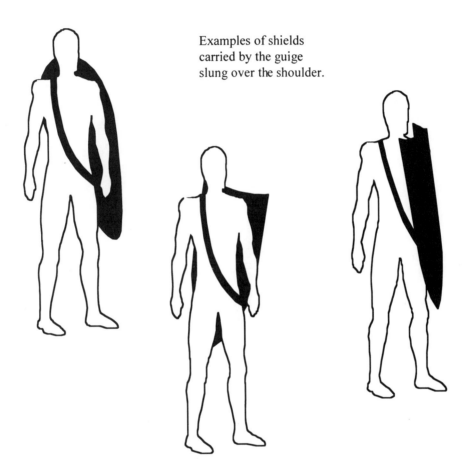

Examples of shields carried by the guige slung over the shoulder.

There are also indications from several sources, including the Bayeux Tapestry, that shields were sometimes worn on the back from guiges by mounted warriors. This is presumably to keep the shields out of the way, but may also be to protect the warriors' backs when they were turning and riding away. There are other illustrations showing swordsmen fighting on foot with long-swords and concave kite or heater shields slung over their backs. There are even illustrations of kite shields worn on the back while a one-handed sword is wielded with both hands. To Anglo-Saxon and Viking warriors, the slinging of a shield on the back during combat may have even been considered an act of great bravery. To Norman knights and later men-at-arms, it may have been just an occasional convenience (particularly when they were using longer blades or retreating from missile weapons).

By about 1250, somewhat shorter shields of a more triangular shape and with flatter tops emerged from the larger kite styles. The *heater* style (so named by modern curators for its resemblance to an old flatiron) is the shield so classically associated with the Medieval knight and heraldry. They could weigh from 3 to 6 pounds and range in size from approximately 20 by 30 inches for larger ones to 14 by 18 inches for smaller shields. At first, they too were flat, but after 1300 or so heater shields commonly were convex. Ones with concave curving tops came into use between 1250 and 1300 and offered still better handling and protection. It has been suggested that the change to smaller shields was the result of the use of great-helms, which offered superb protection to the head, face, and neck, thereby rendering a large shield less vital. Also, the increased use of couched lances in tight cavalry charges made a smaller shield less crowding for mounted knights. The heater shape also was shorter, making it easier for the warrior to run and charge with when he was on foot. Small heater shields continued in use until the 1400s.

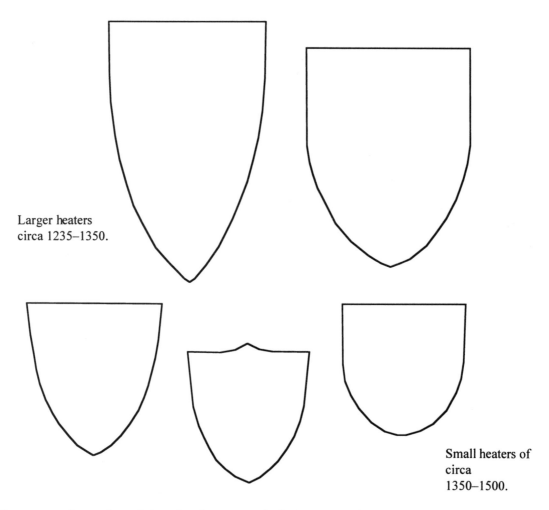

Larger heaters
circa 1235–1350.

Small heaters of
circa
1350–1500.

Heaters came in a variety of sizes, but they progressively became smaller and less pointed. Some suits of plate armor were even made slightly thinner and lighter on the shield side, because there was less need for protection there. But this changed as shield sizes got progressively smaller in the later Medieval period. As a result of improved plate armor, many fighters simply had less need for a shield. Consequently, shields were made smaller for the better-armored fighters. Smaller shields protect less area, but they are more maneuverable; hence, they allow for better weapon employment. Shields were also made thicker. The smallest, lightest heaters allowed the warrior to release the second hand for use on a weapon. These smaller buckler-sized heaters were in use as early as 1280. Some Italian cavalry of the 1300s also used a small shield called an *ecu*.

Front and side views
showing typical convex
curvature on a heater.

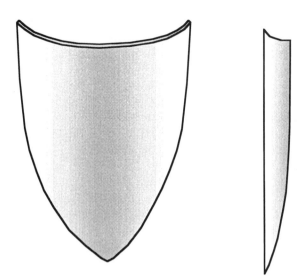

Various straps on heater shields. The first shows a
three-strap arrangement with short guige. The second
shows crescent grips on a small heater, and the
third depicts a standard two-strap arrangement.

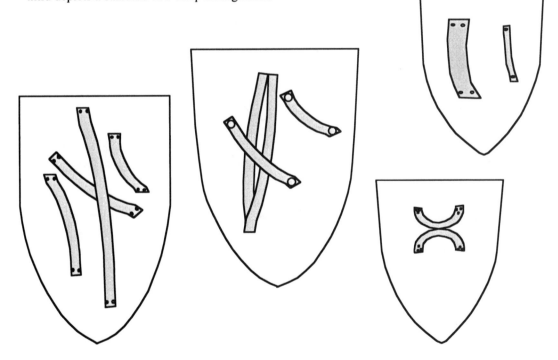

Medieval shields in general are well known to have been brightly decorated with crests and other
symbolic devices. Shields of most Medieval cultures were often painted in bright colors to signify
different ethnic or family groups. Later they distinguished individuals and had coats of arms and
heraldic insignia (which became popular since knights wearing closed face helms had difficulty
identifying one another).

It can be assumed that as the earlier kite shield transformed into the heater shape, there must have been versions in between the two styles. Indeed, in artwork of the Medieval period, shields are rarely present after 1450 and even then are quite small. The development of flattop heaters from larger kite shields is likely the result of increased fighting on horseback and the use of improved armor. Smaller shields are known to have been used by a wide range of mounted warriors, including Roman cavalry, Asiatic horsemen, and Arabic warriors. The kite shield was well suited to fighting on horseback, yet not all of the horsemen's opponents fought the same way; they often preferred shield walls, which the horses had difficulty charging into. But when an enemy was using his own cavalry and mixed forces, a more maneuverable and faster shield made more sense for fighting both mounted and on foot against similarly equipped opponents. This is also evident by the popularity of round shields. Thus the development of the heater shape was most likely a response to the need for a more versatile shield. As fighting into the 1300s and 1400s involved more and more foot combat by better armored warriors, the heater style was made in smaller and smaller sizes. One reason for the decrease in shield size and its later abandonment had to do with the need to use both hands on the weapon to make stronger attacks on tougher armors. It has also been explained that with better armor there is less need for a shield. Contrarily, another explanation proposed may be due to the increased use of such weapons as long-bows, crossbows, and heavy pole-arms that were capable of damaging or defeating shields. When the warriors were in heavy armor, carrying the weight of even a small shield around would have been an encumbrance.

  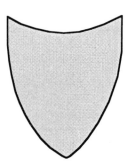

Since so few shields survived, it is not always easy to tell whether certain shields in Medieval artwork are being shown as really flat or convex shaped in two-dimensional front view.

Perhaps because their users were so highly individual, Medieval shields tended to avoid clipped or cutout shapes, such as those used by ancient cultures and which are more suited to close group formations. However, some more unusual cutout shapes and small, stylized heaters did find use as jousting shields. They are not directly related to the use of swords and, therefore, are outside the scope of this study.

A great number of those partaking in less historical approaches to Medieval combat re-creation or who are doing fantasy play-fighting will create all manner of shapes for their shields, regardless of a complete lack of historical support. This is unfortunate because historical designs were deemed effective for a reason, whereas fantasy shields may often work only under pretend play-fighting conditions. There are authentic replicas of many types of Medieval shields available from several manufacturers. Practice versions suitable for sparring with wooden, metal, or padded weapons can be made out of materials ranging from plywood to wooden boards, steel plates, and foam-padded plastic.

Small hand-shields, or *bucklers*, were also used extensively during the Medieval period, beginning as early as 700 A.D. The Medieval buckler was essentially an enlarged umbo with a single handle. The English word *buckler* is derived from an Old French word for the metal boss (or umbo) on a shield. Italian bucklers were known as *bochiero* or *rotella*. Technically, a shield is large and is worn on the arm or carried by the hand, whereas a buckler is small and is only held in a single-hand fist grip. Bucklers were usually made of all metal (roughly 16 gauge), but also of wood with iron reinforcements. They were typically round, approximately 8 to 18 inches in diameter, and weighed under 4 pounds. Others might be star shaped, square, or even triangular.

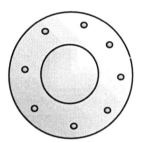 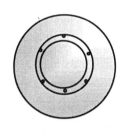

The buckler provided a convenient and effective defense against cuts and thrusts and was easy to carry. They were known to be popular among foot soldiers and archers. There are a number of illustrations showing bucklers being used with typical Medieval swords by both knights and men-at-arms. Sword and buckler fighting was said to be a common pastime in Northern Italy from the 1000s to the 1300s. It was also a traditional weapon of English commoners into the early 1600s.

The buckler had its own distinct method of use, which was different from that for shields. A buckler was held in a fist grip and used to smack, deflect, or punch at blows and thrusts. The edge could also be used to strike and block with. Bucklers are weapons in their own right, being useful for punching and hitting an opponent (in the Renaissance many were equipped with long spikes). Typically, a buckler is held at arm's length or close in by the face or chest, and parries were made with the fist. When both hands were needed on a weapon, the swordsman could conveniently wear the buckler on his belt or hang it on the sword scabbard. Bucklers were also used for practice and teaching purposes, particularly by the Germans, Italians, and English. This is likely because they require more finesse and thus make good training tools. Their use continued into the Renaissance, during which they became more common and existed in greater variety. For a time, they were even carried by civilians around town.

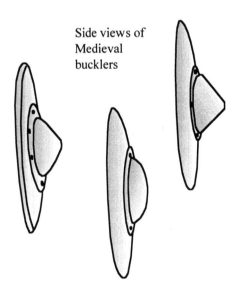

Side views of Medieval bucklers

Another type of small Medieval shield was the *targe*, or *targatt*, associated most commonly with the Scots. Unlike bucklers, targes were worn on the arm, as were typical shields, and ranged in size from 20 to 23 inches. The word *targe* comes from the Norse *targa* and is the origin of the word *target* (archers once practiced with stuffed dummies that had targes hanging from them). Targes could be made of iron, plain wood, iron-plated wood, or leather-covered wood. Some were also covered with metal studs or spikes. Worn on the arm, they could be round or square and usually had two buckled adjustable straps. They were also flat rather than convex. A form of Scottish targe, sometimes with a center spike, was a popular shield for hundreds of years. A form of German jousting shield was also called a targe. A few forms, such as the later Italian *rondache* (rondash), had built-in gauntlets or mail mittens. The rondache was often concave and made of wood, iron, or iron-plated wood. Many of these types of shields also included padded armrests. There were also types of decorative targes used by swordsmen and cavalry for parade only. Some forms of steel battlefield shields from the later Renaissance are often classed as targes or targets.

There was a specialized form of immobile ground shield called a *pavise*, said to have been first used in Pavia in Northern Italy but in use since ancient times. These were stationary protections for archers and crossbowmen during sieges and were known as *mantlets*. In the 1400s special Italian foot soldiers called *pavesari* used them. A German form of pavise was the *Setzschild*, a type of tall infantry shield that sat on the ground. Like other pavises, it was not for carrying in a melee or single combat, but for hiding behind during sieges or when firing missile weapons. A pavise might also be variously known as a *bellifortis*, *barlache,* or *bretasche,* and several shapes and sizes were known to be in use into the 1600s.

 Interestingly, as stated before, evidence shows that shield size actually *decreased* during the later Middle Ages. It makes sense that there was simply less need for a shield as defense when armor could do the job. There was also even greater reason to decrease the weight then being carried. Later Medieval warriors in heavy armor seem to have had a preference for the maneuverability advantage of *not* carrying a shield over the defensive benefit of having one. When warriors were fighting in heavy armor, having a second hand free to use on a weapon must surely have been more important than defending with a shield. Even when Medieval warfare changed to reflect more the old phalanx-like tactics of Greek and Roman armies with their massed pole-arms, shields in general became less common. This is also true of Medieval Japanese and a few other Asian armies where hand-held shields were almost unheard of. There are some references in the 1100s to a rare type of large "table top" dueling shield, called a *talevas* (*tavolaccio* in Italian). It may also be the same as the *taboloclium amplum*, a large, rectangular Italian shield with angled corners of the 1200s and 1300s. The use of such huge shields seems to have been an aberration resulting from conditions of trials by combat. It was used, however, in sieges and tower defense. There was also the *targiam*, a rarer form of large cavalry shield, which saw limited application.

It would appear that a good number of today's Medieval combat enthusiasts fighting under certain organized rule systems use large, *historically inaccurate* shields. In fact, there is a noticeable tendency for some practitioners to favor unrealistically large shields. There is a serious misconception about the prevalence and utility of such shields, despite the fact that such large sizes are all but fictional for the Medieval period. Examples of such extralarge shields for foot combat cannot be found in art or literature of the period. A shield that is too big is simply a hindrance: it is heavy, immobile, and can end up keeping your own weapon from your adversary as much as his from you. A good opponent can not only "hide" in front of your large shield himself, but also force you to risk exposure when looking out from behind it. The reason some enthusiasts favor such extralarge shields is due more to the rules they spar under than any historical precedent. Those sparring systems that do not include the lower leg (from the knee down) as a target area force fighters to stand very close to one another. Since neither has to move his shield much (if at all) to protect his lower legs (or even to maneuver), a large shield just kind of hangs there covering everything. From this position (of "hiding" behind a large shield) and under these types of sparring rules, combatants must step up point blank, shield to shield, and "snap" their weapon around or over the top of the opponent's shield. This is all they really *can* do in this situation.

However, once practitioners widen their sparring rules to include the full leg and any exposed hand/grip, a more realistic fighting distance emerges and the vulnerabilities and deficiencies of this limited method become clear. A fighter with a longer blade and faster (smaller) shield will be able to take out his opponent's legs (despite his larger shield coverage) while still protecting his own. Thus, the whole fight essentially becomes one of judging distance and timing, while getting the adversary to open up his own shield through the use of footwork and feints. To be convinced of this only requires practitioners to experience free-sparring under particular, historically based conditions: use only shields of realistic and accurate weight; include the *full* body as target (especially the shin, knee, foot, and hand); and don't allow a "wounded" combatant to fight from a sitting or kneeling position—especially while his attacker is forbidden to rush in or encircle him. Large shields are favored by many ill-informed enthusiasts today because of the advantage they are given under specific sparring rules where fighting is conducted on the knees or sitting down. This is hardly historical, let alone realistic (see Appendix F). If one constructs artificial sparring rules in an effort to re-create notions of "chivalrous" tournaments, for instance, then large shields can seem very effective indeed. However, it must be realized that under rules that restrict certain hits or techniques for safety, large shields will certainly appear very effective—*under those specified, limited conditions*—but this should not be viewed as validating something that has *little* historical validity.

Only the ancient Romans really used large shields (in their "shield-wall" formations), and this was because of both the type of warfare they practiced and the manner of opponents and weapons they faced. Even the largest rectangular Roman shield (*scutum*) extended only from the shoulder to just below the knee. These shields were not intended to withstand the powerful, cleaving blows of Medieval swords, massed long-bow fire, or charges of heavy lance-bearing cavalry; rather, they were designed to counter only the short swords, slings, and spears of their day. The same can be said for earlier Greek shields. This is precisely why the Romans were able to use such large shields. For the most part they did not do much individualized combat, but fought in organized groups of mini-phalanxes. With a large shield, although the body is well protected under some conditions, the quick maneuvering necessary in single combat or group skirmishes is impractical, and offensive options are thereby diminished. Also because of the nature of their fighting, the Romans rarely employed effective slashing cuts, which would have also affected the size of shields they chose. It is interesting to point out that today modern riot police in many nations use large shields and short clubs, along the lines of the Roman model while others use smaller round shields and long sticks. As with the Romans, this is because their opponents are disorganized mobs fighting as individuals and hurling missiles. The police are also more defense oriented and, like the Romans, seldom need to do more than break up and rout their enemy. The use of larger shields will be addressed again under the section on fighting techniques.

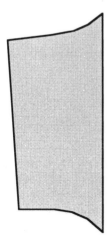

Two examples of the many styles of large "winged" Medieval shields with raised left corners or sides. Somewhat rare, they were occasionally used in the 1400s by front-rank troops in Italy and Eastern Europe. Other large, unusual Medieval shields include special types of German dueling shields, which had points at each end and were held by a long central bar. They could be used as weapons on their own. As with some other shields, they had a center "spine" or fold in which the handle-bar fit.

The shield is among the earliest and most obvious forms of personal defense. Almost every culture has developed some form of it. The shield was used in the earliest civilizations of Sumeria and Babylon. They were widely used in ancient China and India, as well as in Persia, Malaysia, Indonesia, Africa, the Asian steppes, and even parts of South America. There are a few forms of Asian small shields that are seldom seen, but their use seems to have been preserved for little more than dancelike operatic routines. Usually, shields were lacquered wicker, wood, stretched hide, or treated leather. In the crowded clash of battle with spears and arrows, holding a deflecting cover makes great sense for a warrior. In the push and shove of mass warfare there might be fewer opportunities to employ one's weapon, but a shield will get almost constant use. In closer combat, the utility of the shield is evident in the way it allows a warrior to block slashes and thrusts while still permitting counterattacks. It is with the many classes of Medieval shields and the highly developed method of employing them that these ancient tools were undoubtedly represented in their most effective form.

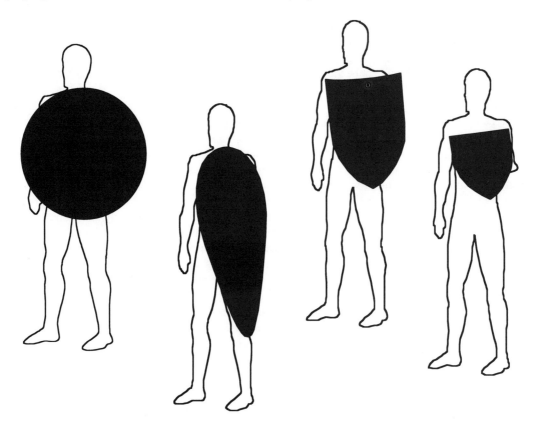

Examples of the area covered by different shield designs.

The shield itself has become an emblem that is somewhat synonymous with the idea of the Middle Ages and the chivalric knight. Since ancient times the shield has been an important symbol of defense, guardianship, and resistance. When a Viking died in battle he was carried off on his shield, much the same as the ancient Greek hoplite was carried. In Germanic culture, a warrior was admitted to the ranks by being ceremoniously handed his shield. The word *shield* has even gone from noun to verb. Eventually, with the changing nature of warfare, the Medieval wooden shield fell out of favor. It saw only limited use in the Renaissance and finally continued only for parade use. The coming of firearms eventually rendered it obsolete as a implement of war, but prior to this it was an ancient and highly prized tool. For centuries it was extremely effective and achieved its greatest form and application when combined with the Medieval sword. Study of this most simple, yet formidable instrument can be a fascinating martial exercise today.

CHAPTER NINE

Sword & Shield

SWORD & SHIELD

NOTE: It is nearly impossible to describe in words and pictures alone enough detail to instruct in technique or proper movement form. These examples are meant to be informative, not representative of all possibilities. They are general, not universal or definitive, fighting instructions. The attempt will be made here only to reference certain basic concepts and principles of Medieval sword & shield fighting. For purposes of general instruction and education of historical sword and shield use, two types of Medieval shields are illustrated throughout. These types are the medium-sized round form, sometimes called a Saxon or Viking shield, and also the larger teardrop- or kite-shaped form, usually called a Norman shield. Additionally, these two types are shown in both the single-handle center-grip variety and the more familiar full-arm strap form. To best demonstrate major principles and techniques, the round shield held in a left hand is used as the primary example. The sword will be considered to be that of a generic "Type X."

There is no real record in the *early* Middle Ages of swordsmanship itself (or any other fighting art) being considered as a separate, independent skill. Rather, it was thought of as one of many from the Art of War. But the sword, unlike other weapons such as axes, spears, bows, and daggers, which were tools or had hunting application, was always exclusively *a weapon of war.* Battle was its very reason for being (with the possible exception of trial by combat and tournaments). It was a personal weapon of war. It was not to transcend this role until the Renaissance.

Virtually every hand weapon of Europe during the entire Middle Ages—whether axe, spear, pole-arm, mace, or flail—was utilized in respect to the effective combination of shield & sword. Yet the sword & shield has never before been addressed in detail as a martial art's weapon combination. Considering the familiar image of the sword & shield in Western culture and its close association with the very idea of the Medieval warrior and knight, it is time its practice be presented in all of its lethal aspects. Shield use is not complicated: there are really only a few simple principles that apply. However, because of stylistic notions or ill-conceived sparring rules, practitioners often misapply these principles. Understanding of the fundamentals for fighting with the Medieval sword & shield must begin with the position of the body and the weapons.

FUNDAMENTAL STANCES

We will refer to those ready positions for striking a blow and defending as *postures, stances,* or *guards*. No terms for sword & shield stances really survive from the period. There are a few German and Italian terms for a single sword that, although not entirely comparable, are useful to extrapolate from. The Renaissance term *ward* for a fighting posture did not come into use until the 1500s, and the word *guard* itself was not used until after 1600.

The basic sword & shield stances are ones that naturally use and allow for the intrinsic movements of the body. They follow from the natural mechanics of raising a weapon to strike or parry while moving. Their purpose is to threaten *all* targets of an adversary's entire body, while defending *all* of one's own. There are three primary positions for the sword & shield: *high, middle,* and *back*. There are no stances that do not fall into one of these three. Each can easily be raised or lowered to assume the others, and each has its own advantages of offense and defense. Whatever stances are personally favored, they are really only slight variations of one of the three.

Just what a shield is and does must be understood to properly use it to its fullest capacity. A shield is an armament, but a defensive one. It is a form of weapon. More accurately, it *is a shield,* a subclass of weapon. It defends, it protects, it literally "shields." A shield offers considerable enhancement of a warrior's defense, especially for unarmored or lightly armored fighters. At the same time, it scarcely diminishes a warrior's offense.

A shield can eliminate almost half the body's targets and allow a weapon to remain hidden and ready to strike from an indirect position (particularly against an adversary's legs). A fighter using a shield can step right up with virtual impunity and deliver a wicked and swift blow from seemingly out of nowhere. A shield allows a fighter to close in against pole-weapons and to charge or hold under assault by arrow and spear. It can also be a weapon in itself, and likely no warrior thought of it only as an implement of passive protection.

Taking a ready position with the shield & sword requires a stable yet flexible stance. Although a stance must have energy and intensity and allow for free, instantaneous action, it must not be uncomfortable or stressed. It should not feel unnatural or inhibit freedom of movement, but rather encourage it. The position should be one that is simply based upon the mechanical requirements of defending with the shield while attacking with the sword. Fighting postures or guards must allow for the greatest possible freedom of action. They must provide for mobility and balance both in attack and defense. Mobility is crucial since it permits coordination, accuracy, and speed. A stance must also allow economy of motion (efficiency in action). Stance is the foundation from which we fight and utilize technique. Techniques should be applied easily and with the least amount of movement necessary to deliver a strike, make a parry, or distract the opponent.

Ideally, a person's stance will reflect his center-of-gravity, agility, and level of balance. Too often fighters who are slow-footed or weak-kneed make excuses for habitually faulty footwork instead of making the effort to exercise a strong, proper stance. The back should be straight yet slightly forward and not hunched over or rounded. The shoulders should not be slouched, nor should they be too tense. A tense, improper stance will lead to quicker muscle fatigue, as well as rob one of speed and power.

The knees should be bent slightly to allow for sudden motion. Too little of a bend creates stiff, slow movements. Too much bend can also create slower movements and limit range rather than offering springiness. For beginners, time is required to become accustomed to moving and fighting with the knees slightly bent. For balance and mobility both feet should be firmly on the ground with the majority of the weight on the balls of the feet. Often the heel of the rear foot can be raised slightly to aid momentum. The lead foot should point toward the opponent, and the rear foot should be at roughly a 45-degree angle. This allows for maximum mobility both linearly and laterally. One needs to be able to quickly move in or out and side to side. The feet should be roughly shoulder distance apart for maximum balance and agility. At times they may necessarily become closer or farther apart, depending on the action being committed. Essentially, the idea is to not exaggerate or minimize their position.

Above all, your stance should avoid being static and rigid. It must not be stiff or slow. Although there are slight variations in stance and footwork from person to person, the idea is not to violate the basic principle of generating mobility, stability, and power from a well-balanced and fluid position. Judge the value of a stance based on this principle.

The first stance is the *high* guard, probably the most common position. This is undoubtedly the most natural and sensible stance. The high guard is foremost an offensive fighting stance. It is the stance that occurs immediately when we raise a weapon to deliver a strong blow. It offers a threatening weapon ready to strike behind the circumspect protection of the shield. It presents an aggressive attitude of provocation. The sword can make a powerful strike vertically, diagonally, or horizontally with almost equal ease. It is the most practical and useful in the majority of situations. In many ways it can be argued that the high guard is fundamental to shield & sword use. All other variations are only forms of this basic fighting position.

The weapon is held in the basic "45-degree" posture or "on-guard" position. The hand should be positioned above the forehead so the pommel is just within peripheral vision. The edge faces vertically upward, and the hilt is "aimed" at the adversary. The arm is poised to strike but not in either a stressed or an overly relaxed manner. The sword arm is not "cocked" to "snap" out, but rather readied and supple to make a shearing cut with a quick, sharp blade. The shoulder is not tensed, nor is the hand gripping too tightly. The same can be said for the shield arm.

When using a shield, to achieve maximum reach and better agility the lead leg is that on the shield's side. This "forward stance" is to keep the body behind the shield as well as allow the hips to turn. From this position, maneuvering can be done with either leg stepping forward or falling back with the cut in order to add power. As a blow is thrown, the rear foot can step or *pass* forward to add force and reach. This is usually done just as the shield is raised, lowered, or pushed forward. As with a boxer, the legs are planted firmly, but not heavily, in order to provide maximum agility.

From here the sword can simply be lifted at the elbow or shoulder to make any strike, thrust, or draw cut. All parries and attacks are applied in conjunction with your properly stepping in to or out of the opponent's own action. The fighter is ready for instant action to strike, parry, rush forward, or break in to a run.

Held in the standard "forward" manner, the shield can block to any area high or low, left or right. It is in a position to allow the sword to strike from behind as it uses its full defensive capacity. The shield can receive blows on its face, stop them with its edge, or be moved forward to deflect and knock them up, down, left, or right.

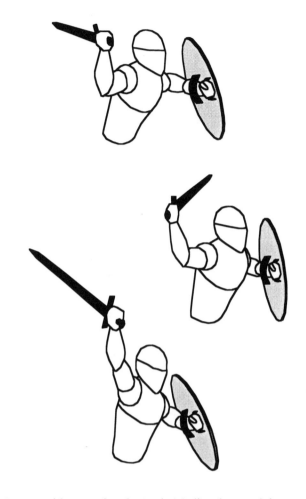

The foremost purpose of a sword & shield stance is to attack. Defense is secondary, and the shield's leading position assumes most of that role on its own. Slight variations of the high guard are understandable as the blade is brought up to strike or returns after other actions. However, the sword should not be kept behind the head or leveled horizontally. In generating power for cuts or when returning along the line of another blow, the sword may very well be pulled far behind the back with the point down. At other times, when cutting around to the left, the blade must come from behind the head. The arm might also be raised higher and straighter to fully extend the reach on a particular cut. These positions are often captured in historical artwork. But they are not the ready position of the high guard itself or proper fighting postures on their own. Only the centered 45-degree position of the high guard is suited to freely and quickly cut equally to the left or right without "telegraphing" it to the opponent.

It goes without saying that early Medieval artwork is known for its stylized perspective and renderings. Proportions of people, horses, weapons, and buildings are often notoriously out of scale. Because of this, accurate dimensions of swords are often indeterminable. They are sometimes shown as clearly being too short, too long, too large, or too wide in proportion to figures and surroundings. The details of early Medieval artwork cannot always be taken at face value. However, late Medieval and early Renaissance artwork is actually quite detailed and realistic. Overall, artwork and sculpture of the period and actual surviving specimens of weapons are among the most valuable sources of information. Among the various illuminations, paintings, and embroideries can be seen the basic sword attacks, parries, and primary stances or guards (middle, high, back). It also can be persuasively argued that there is a good deal of significance in Medieval art and literature that can remain obscure and elusive to those ignorant of the techniques and martial concepts of historical swordsmanship and weapon use.

115

The second stance is the *middle* guard. This is a viable position with the sword held forward (at a 45-degree angle). This position, though seemingly awkward or impractical, is equivalent to the standard middle guard position for holding a single long-sword in both hands. In this case, the second hand instead holds the shield, vastly increasing defense. This is a posture rarely understood or used by modern Medieval combat enthusiasts, yet it appears frequently in Medieval artwork. It is a natural position for warding and guarding, as well as threatening. It is a somewhat "neutral" position and presents a defensive and "expectant" attitude. This position can be assumed from holding the weapon high, low, or point down. The middle stance also allows the sword itself to be used in defense to parry.

In the crowded rush of mass combat, the middle guard is quite useful in closing in and thrusting or just tangling up an opponent.

In the middle stance the hand and hilt are protected behind the shield while the point of the sword threatens an adversary's face and throat. From here the sword can quickly be lifted to the high guard and cuts can be delivered or the sword can be pulled back to the low back guard. The blade can also be raised or lowered to parry. As with the high guard, the blade is held with the edge vertical, aimed forward. Though fewer cuts are possible than with the high position, this guard also has uses in stabbing under an opponent's shield or weapon, thrusting at his face, or suddenly trapping or binding him. The weapon may also be pushed forward to make a draw-cut or pulling slash on the adversary's hand or face. It is a deceptive and practical position that does not tire the arm and works well when you are close in. Fighting from this position does require practice, because it is not as instinctive as the others. Even from this position the weapon can still quickly be lifted up to generate the necessary force for effective blows. It is no problem for the sword & shield in the middle guard to be used in a manner consistent with that of the high guard.

The third stance is the *back* guard. This is a "low" stance with the sword held behind and low (again at roughly a 45-degree angle) with the tip facing backward. This is a naturally strong stance for cutting under and around. The back guard is a deceptive and somewhat countering stance with an inviting and intercepting feeling. The weapon is kept seemingly out of the way and hidden but is actually poised to immediately deliver a powerful cut. In readiness, the posture is slightly forward with the rear leg slightly back. This is a position that occurs when a weapon is pulled back to deliver an upward cut from underneath. It also allows a deceptively wide "cut-over" to the opposite side. From a back guard the blade may strike diagonally, horizontally, or vertically, or even suddenly turn inward for a thrust. It is a versatile and useful guard. Almost every attack from this position is made with either a passing step of the rear leg or a forward step with the shield side.

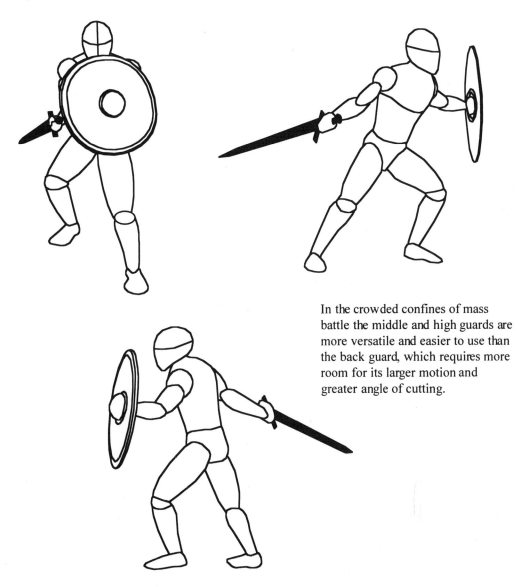

In the crowded confines of mass battle the middle and high guards are more versatile and easier to use than the back guard, which requires more room for its larger motion and greater angle of cutting.

The arm is relaxed but not limp, and the palm is turned up with the edge aimed off to the right. The back guard is another posture rarely understood or used by modern Medieval combat enthusiasts, but it (like the middle guard) makes great sense and appears frequently in Medieval artwork. This is a fundamental position but also one that is less familiar to those who do not practice using full-body target areas (lower legs and feet). Again, this guard is equivalent to the standard back guard position for holding a single long-sword in both hands.

Each of the guards can transition in a quick, fluid motion to any of the others as needed to threaten, strike, parry, or recover. The idea is not to focus on any of the guards as a physical position, but rather on the dynamic of all their attitudes and potential offense and defense. Indeed, the idea of "fixed" guards or set, systematized postures for the shield was not devised until the Renaissance. Information about guards prior to this indicates that they were seen simply as readily apparent natural "positions" for fighting.

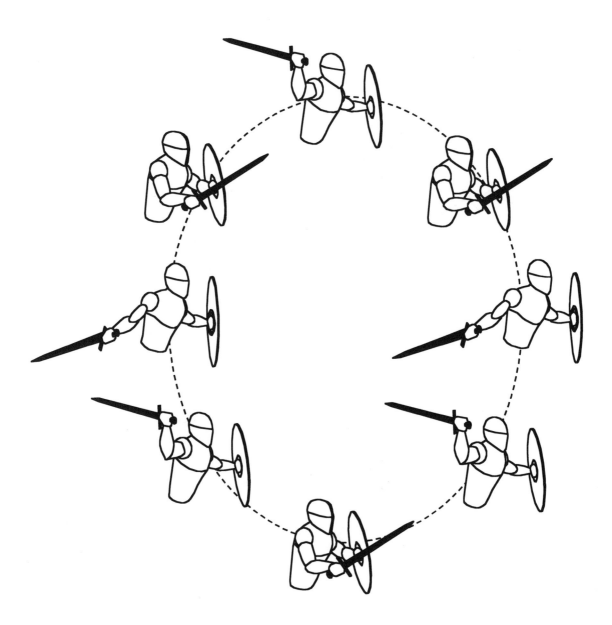

High guard can drop to middle. Middle can pull back to back. Back can raise to high, which can move to middle again. Middle can lift to high, and high can fall down to back. Back can assume the middle. Each transition can be smooth and quick in preparing for an attack or a parry.

Examples of fundamental weapon positions using an arm-gripped or strapped shield. Many of these can be transitional motions between cuts and actions as well as ready stances for attacking or defending.

Historical illustrations contain many depictions of warriors with sword & shield in positions that are clearly transitional. Often it is not possible to tell precisely whether the warriors are in the middle of striking a blow, altering guards, or hesitating or pausing. Understanding the fundamental movement of sword cuts will reveal just when such pictures are showing actions already in motion and when they are showing preparatory positions.

The middle guard with "point-on" in preparation for a thrust or recovery.

A back guard is ideally suited to deliver cuts from more indeterminate angles. As the tip is raised to strike or just assume a high guard, there may be a span when it is momentarily in neither position.

When coming around or "following through" from another cut or action, the arm is sometimes pulled farther back for greater power. This should not be mistaken for placing the arm statically into this position from inaction or holding it there as a "ready position." The weapon does not need to be held this far behind, but it may be suddenly pulled back to roughly 45 degrees just before a strike. This announces the attack and unnecessarily forewarns the adversary. Ideally, the energy of a blow should *already* explode without additional lift or windup before it is committed. Even a subtle *precede* (a telegraphed motion or "tell") before an action can alert the opponent.

Here a strike is being started from the high guard, and momentum has just been committed.

FUNDAMENTAL MOVEMENT AND FOOTWORK

Quick, efficient footwork is vital to any form of swordsmanship or fighting with hand weapons because movement itself is fundamental to all combat. Movement is done to close the range or maintain range with an adversary. We advance to strike or feint and create openings for a strike. We move backward to avoid being struck but also to invite an attack we can then counter. We also move diagonally and sideways to do all these things.

The proper positioning of the feet is that which is most natural to the human body. This consists of the "45-degree foot" stance. The lead foot points toward the opponent while the back foot or rear leg is placed at 45-degrees to it. This positioning has counterparts in boxing and many martial arts. It is far more versatile than the perpendicular "L" position of the feet in modern fencing. The "L" stance, used to offer a "thin" target toward the opponent, was developed in the early 1700s and has application only for the particulars of thrusting fence. In contrast, the 45-degree foot position allows the easiest movement and application of the body's weight in stepping in to and out of strikes, as well as avoiding blows. The hips and shoulders can be brought into alignment with any cut, while the feet can easily shift to face any direction. In this position either leg can easily assume the lead and *pass* forward or back. As a human walks forward in a natural gait, the feet do not move parallel but will turn out to this 45-degree position. The motion of moving with a shield & sword in combat is done in a similar manner. This position also lets the legs lift up or sidestep to avoid low blows and allows for the shield to be better employed in protecting them. Unlike the "L" stance, it also permits easier movement to turn and cut or parry within 360 degrees of action (a necessity against multiple opponents).

The feet positions of the "standard" forward stance with a shield (shown as from a right-handed fighter). The heels are not parallel one behind the other, but rather shoulder width apart.

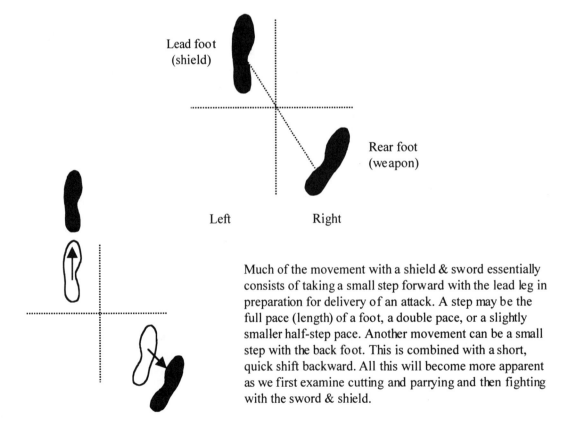

Lead foot (shield)

Rear foot (weapon)

Left   Right

Much of the movement with a shield & sword essentially consists of taking a small step forward with the lead leg in preparation for delivery of an attack. A step may be the full pace (length) of a foot, a double pace, or a slightly smaller half-step pace. Another movement can be a small step with the back foot. This is combined with a short, quick shift backward. All this will become more apparent as we first examine cutting and parrying and then fighting with the sword & shield.

120

Advancing to strike is accomplished by *passing*. A pass may be made from either side. The leading leg may pass backward, or the rear leg may pass forward. In a forward pass a strong advancing step is made with the rear leg so it "passes" to the front. The shield leg pivots slightly on the ball of the foot as the rear leg steps to become the new lead. Advancing this way allows for the simultaneous committal of a strike as you move. From the new stance the action can be repeated with the shield side to continually push forward, or it may suddenly reverse and fall back. The value of quickly passing forward is to add force and reach to an attack. The action is similar to that used in Renaissance cut & thrust swordsmanship, in which most cuts are made "on the pass." This became the basis for the more involved footwork of those methods.

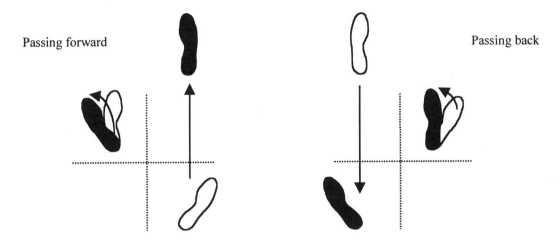

Passing forward   Passing back

Just as with passing forward, the leading shield leg can also drop back ("pass back") to reverse the stance. At this same time the rear foot simultaneously turns slightly to become the new lead. This action can be repeated immediately from the new stance to allow for a smooth, well-guarded back motion or retreat. This manner of backing up also allows one to instantly move forward again on the attack. Blows may be delivered continually in the process. Pulling the shield away like this as you drop back is also a form of shifting to bring the weapon forward. The value of this reversing or quickly falling back is in its withdrawal of the body from the opponent at the same time the weapon is brought around to counter his attack.

To maneuver, the rear foot may quick-shift to a slightly wider stance by taking either a short step back or a cross-step to the side. This can be done in conjunction with a parry or a blow, in preparation for a larger step, or in anticipation of a forward or reverse pass. The lead foot need not remain static for this and can also make a quick, shifting step or small hop.

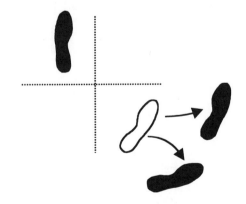

It is important to note that although many of the drawings here show fighters only from the waist up (to save space), this should not be misconstrued as emphasizing only arm movements. Almost all actions require some footwork. Virtually every time you move your weapon to attack, parry, feint, or perform any other action *your feet should move in some way as well.* Footwork is integral to arm motion and weapon movement. It cannot be neglected. As with all other actions, footwork should be natural and not rigid or predictable. Avoid both the deliberate, rhythmic style of theatrical fighting and the planted, unmoving manner used to ensure a safety distance between performers.

121

Movement is crucial to fighting. With shield & swordfighting, footwork takes on the primary purpose of closing the distance to strike or moving to evade attacks. One steps in to hit or steps out of an attack and counterstrikes. While the natural movement of running (or bursts of trotting) can be applied, specific stepping motions are more applicable once engaged in fighting. Passing forward to strike or recover and passing back to parry or counter are fundamental to using the shield & sword. Ideally, they are done best from the high and back guards. The footwork appropriate to the hacking, slashing, and thrusting style of sword & shield fighting is not nearly as involved as that which would later be devised for the cut & thrust forms of the Renaissance. During the Medieval period, there was no need for it. The steps employed when using Medieval weapons are simple, natural, and effective.

With the use of a shield a standard forward step can be made with the shield leg leading.

In either forward or backward movement, the rear leg can lift in a small "hopping" motion.

To recover from the "reverse stance" after a forward pass, the lead (sword-side) leg can drop back to its earlier position or the rear (shield-side) leg can advance on its own pass. Passing with the shield from the rear can be done to recover, parry, or even knock into the opponent's body or strike against his weapon.

A primary means of moving to strike by passing forward. The rear (sword-side) leg steps forward in coordination with a *simultaneous* motion of the arm and weapon. As the hips twist, the swordsman maintains the shield's forward-facing position by a small turn of the shoulder.

The opposite action of stepping in with a passing attack is to drop the lead (shield) leg back. The shield-side leg falls back simultaneously with a strike timed in reaction to the adversary's attack or forward motion. This has the result of pulling the body away from the strike and out of the line of attack. At the same time, the counterblow is delivered to the oncoming opponent. The shield may also be defensively lifted, pushed out, or held firm.

The action of stepping out of the attack with a pass back deceptively shifts the fighting distance while twisting the hips to add force to the counterblow. It takes the lower leg out of the way while also allowing a counterblow to easily target the adversary's lower legs or his extended weapon arm. It is also more difficult to be counterattacked with this action than with a forward passing attack.

The pass back results in a reverse stance with the sword leg leading and the weapon immediately assuming either a high, back, or middle guard. The shield is still maintained in front. From here a pass forward can be made from the shield side to reestablish a forward stance, or the sword side can pass back for the same result. Which to use depends on whether an attack is being pressed or the adversary is attacking forward. Fighting is not exclusively a matter of either pressing forward the attack or falling back from attacks. Rather, both are to be applied as necessary, depending on the nature of the adversary's fight. Generally, the weapon is moved *simultaneously* with any footwork. Other times, the weapon may move first, followed almost immediately by stepping.

An example of the sequence for a simple forward pass.

In the act of maneuvering (e.g., passing forward, passing back, sidestepping and evading) there should be no extraneous movement or dancing about. These concepts of footwork and movement are common to many forms of swordsmanship and weapon fighting.

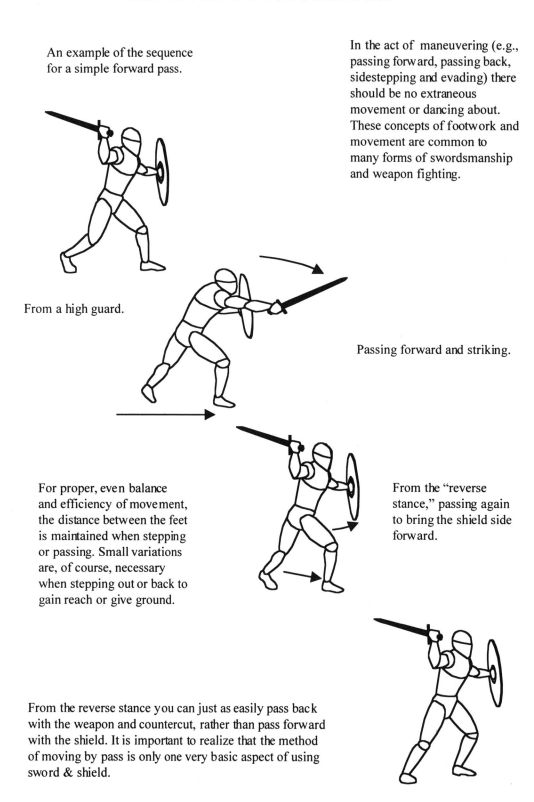

From a high guard.

Passing forward and striking.

For proper, even balance and efficiency of movement, the distance between the feet is maintained when stepping or passing. Small variations are, of course, necessary when stepping out or back to gain reach or give ground.

From the "reverse stance," passing again to bring the shield side forward.

From the reverse stance you can just as easily pass back with the weapon and countercut, rather than pass forward with the shield. It is important to realize that the method of moving by pass is only one very basic aspect of using sword & shield.

Recovering to a shield-leading forward stance at high guard.

In addition to stepping while evading or delivering cuts and thrusts, there are other movements that are used as needed. These may involve small hopping, leaping moves and even lunging forward with either leg. Although the formal "lunge" as a distinct action was not developed until the more refined methods of the Renaissance, similar action using one leg to stretch out in a large, quick step are evident in several Medieval fighting manuals. Such action is not as long as that required with a thrusting sword, but a form of lunge step does have application for sword & shield fighting.

Similarly, there are numerous occasions where to suddenly cut or parry in a new direction a step must be taken to pivot on the balls of the feet in a turning or spinning motion. Turns are often required to the left, right, or to the rear when facing multiple opponents. The idea is to move in a quick, efficient, and balanced manner that uses the motion of the turn itself to aid the direction of the cut or parry. Again, the simple rule is to follow the 45-degree stance and shift back and forth diagonally or laterally with passing steps. This cannot be explained in detail but requires individual examination.

Keep in mind that Medieval fighting is not an orderly affair. Attacks may come from *any* direction, and combat is not "linear." The simple footwork and stances used with sword & shield allow for easy 360-degree shifting to meet adversaries in any direction and execute cuts and parries against them. A firm stance and practiced footwork are necessities in order to strike strongly. You do not want to throw or pull yourself off balance as you swing.

TARGETING

In describing the use of the sword & shield, one must address a number of interrelated elements, including cutting with a sword, blocking with a shield, and the nature of sword wounds and their effects. Each of these must be looked at before the methods and techniques of the fight can be studied.

Against sword & shield, the preferred target areas are not easily exposed. The shield's coverage can be substantial. The primary areas to strike are the head and collar, lower legs, arm and hand, shoulders, thighs, and hips.

The central vulnerabilities are on the arm at the wrist, inner elbow, and underarm. The legs are particularly vulnerable at the shins and calves and the sides or backs of the knees. The ability of a wider cutting blade to dismember human limbs is typically underestimated. Yet, unarmored limbs need not be dismembered or hacked to the bone to be rendered useless in a fight. They could also be effectively immobilized with simple slicing flesh wounds. If ligaments or tendons are cut, such wounds could permanently disable a warrior.

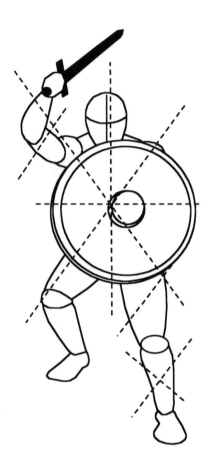

Medieval shields were generally tough and well made. Shields could not be split or chopped away as easily as is commonly believed or often shown in movies. Because not all shields were constructed of uniform materials or with equal care, claims of "shield splitting" cannot be fully evaluated except in light of what we do know from historical accounts and experience with modern replicas. Certainly it is possible that a particularly fearsome blow with a heavy axe or great-sword on a weaker or older shield could be enough to render it useless. This is still far from destroying a new shield by raining a few blows on it. Shields were designed to withstand this very thing, and constructing one to such a standard was not especially difficult. Medieval artwork shows only a very few shields being damaged by weapons. The Norse sagas do give a few examples of Viking duels in which shields are splintered and broken. But this form of combat duel consisted mostly of each side taking turns whacking at the other. The quality and construction of those particular shields is also not fully known as with other cases. It can be reasonably assumed that, like many early Viking shields, they were not metal trimmed or metal reinforced. In any event, the act of purposely "attacking" the opponent's shield to "destroy" it is itself something of a myth.

Depending on the stances used by an adversary, as well as the shield he carries, the targets accessible can vary considerably. Targets are subject to change from moment to moment as each fighter moves and acts. As a result of either the opponent's attacks or your own, other targets may suddenly open up or can be made vulnerable for a brief instant. This is part of the nature of fighting in general.

The major sword & shield guards revealing some of the more open or vulnerable targets are indicated by the dark areas.

Historically, a warrior would *avoid* hitting his enemy's shield if at all possible. Swords can cut into the edges of untrimmed shields. The bare wood would let a blade bite into it a few inches, and for an instant the sword would stick ever so slightly. Even if this occurred for only a second, it could be critical. Until the sword was pulled free this would leave the warrior quite vulnerable. There is even reason to believe that for this very reason shields *without* metal rims were sometimes favored. But shields were often metal rimmed, and it did no good to hack your sword's edge against it. Striking the metal trim could damage a blade's edge, and, more importantly, a hard blow might once again cause the sword to get stuck and slow down the weapon's recovery. It served no purpose to intentionally hack away at the edges of an opponent's shield like this, and in the process you might easily open yourself up to a counterblow. Instead, the idea is to force the adversary to react and create an opening as he must move his shield in defense. Unlike in the movies, fighters would avoid a shield in favor of feigning attacks and then cutting at the opponent's head, neck, hand, forearm, and especially his shin and ankle. Reenactment fighting today that uses blunt blades to beat on shields often overlooks these elements.

Major sword & shield guards revealing
more open or vulnerable targets are
indicated by the dark areas.

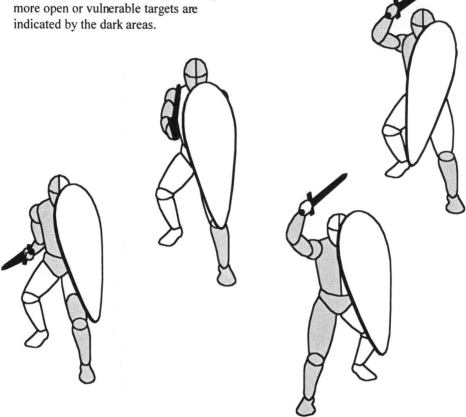

If possible a fighter would also avoid hitting body armor. But encountering mail and leather armor was almost universal. Mail was stripped from the dead after battles and salvaged for reuse. It was also handed down so that with each successive generation more and more was accumulated until it was quite commonplace on the battlefield. Mail, hard leather, and even soft leather armors could easily protect against draw-cuts and pressed slices. Their defense against concussion blows or blunt trauma was much less (although layers of soft padding helped). Their resistance to cutting blows or hacks and chops was another matter.

Mail armor could be cut, but only if strongly hit on the proper angle. To cut strongly with a flat, wide blade against mail armor you cannot bend the wrist. The arm must be straighter and somewhat rigid. If a blow against mail is not struck squarely on, the sword's edge will skip and not cut. When mail is struck properly, the blade will receive little or no damage even if hit forcefully. The links of mail would be cut or snapped, and often the rings even driven into the wound (which if not immediately lethal, could cause serious infection). Interestingly, softer metal links of untempered mail could wrap around a blade's edge as it cut and actually be harder to penetrate than tempered wire (or hardened mail). The softer rings will bend and deform first and in the process thereby better resist a cut. Tempered mail, though tough, would often crack and snap more easily from a blow, allowing the cut to push through. The wearing of mail itself would not really affect the bend of the elbow or the movement of the arm in striking. A mail byrnie (coat or shirt) is very flexible, the sleeves are loose and wide, and its overall weight is not burdensome. Forms of *lamelar* armor, made of small plates or scales laced together, were also commonly used. Lamelar armor has greater resistance to impact than the linked rings of mail, but is much less flexible, is subject to greater wear and tear, and can be more easily punctured.

128

WOUNDS

Swords can kill by laceration (cutting flesh and bone), by thrust/stab (puncturing organs), and by impact (blunt trauma). However, it is notoriously difficult to try to make broad generalities or draw too many firm conclusions about the wounding effects of swords. Still, a considerable amount of information is revealed from historical sources.

There are many depictions in Medieval art of armor (both mail and leather) and helmets being split, pierced, and rent. Heads are shown decapitated, skulls cleaved from crown to lower jaw, and arms and legs completely severed. Medieval literature often describes combat as being decided by a single crucial blow that cleaves the adversary's mail, helm, or shield. Viking sagas describe legs cut off either above or below the knee from a single-hand stroke. Skeletal remains from various battle sites show warriors losing both legs at the shins from the same blow, as well as hipbones being sheared clean through. We also know that the Vikings especially targeted the knee and ankle. Icelandic sagas offer accounts of bodies cut in two across the waist with one stroke and heads cleaved down the middle so each half fell on opposite sides.

Still other accounts tell of an English knight who had his "*hipbone cut away*" by a Norwegian axe. In the Icelandic saga *Droplavgarsona*, there is described a duel in which "*Grin carried two swords and could fight equally well with both hands. He brandished a sword in his left, but with the right he struck at Gouss and cut off his leg above the knee.*" Another account describes a duel in which one Helgi cut at one Hiarrandi "*and struck his thigh; the sword went through to the bone but would go no further and glanced off behind the knee, and the wound put him out of the fight.*" The historian John of Antioch, writing in the 600s, tells of a blow he witnessed as follows: "*He leaped upon him and dealt him a blow with his sword upon the collar bone. . . . It was a killing blow, and the weapon pierced Adovocar's body down to the hip. It is said that Theodoric exclaimed, 'In truth, the wretch has no bones!'*" A much later account of the battle of Barnet in 1471, when there were fewer shields in use and plate armor was at its peak, tells of warriors wounded "*mainly in the face and the lower half of the body.*" Another records a knight removing the foot of his opponent with a blow. Corpses from battle sites also show terrible wounds to the teeth, and such injuries are described in literature. Artwork clearly shows sword thrusts of all types as going though bodies, heads, and thighs. In summary, there is no doubt whatsoever that in the hands of skilled warriors Medieval swords were fearsome in their killing power.

A powerful and mortal blow may be dealt by which the adversary will surely perish, yet for several seconds he may still fight on and deliver a lethal blow of his own in return. A stroke should instantly dispatch the adversary or at the least incapacitate him from continuing (such as by dismembering a limb). There are many instances recorded of armored knights not being killed by any one single blow, but by a series of blows as well as through loss of blood. Many are said to have collapsed from fatigue rather than injury. Blows to limbs would either fail to incapacitate, or they dismembered and caused death outright. One account from 1380 of a duel in plate armor describes a knight who received a spear thrust clean through his thigh. Although he later lost the encounter, he was said to have "*reeled with the blow but did not fall.*"

However, the sheer force and cleaving potential of swords is often just not fully appreciated by most enthusiasts. Many practitioners today doing forms of contact-sparring or just playing with sticks are naive as to the true power of cuts. It is unfortunate that they cannot witness the sight of a fresh cow femur sliced in half by a single stroke of a sharp replica sword. Or, better yet, have the opportunity to cut with an accurate reproduction blade on a fresh side of beef. The magnitude of the wounds the weapon makes in the meat is frightening, and it is a sight that few, if any, stage or film choreography has yet to properly display. Theatrical swordfights also rarely show the real effects of cuts on a body or limb. They prefer instead to feign kills by stabbing, abdominal slicing, and occasionally decapitating.

Historical chroniclers do not give very detailed descriptions of the close combat or melee of Medieval battles, but enough is provided to understand the brutality and lethality of the arms employed. Strangely enough, there is not a great deal of detailed evidence about the wounds caused in Medieval battles. Modern experiments offer us some insights, as do archeological finds.

As have been well documented, the famous excavations at the site of the Battle of Visby (Wisby) on Gotland, off the coast of Sweden, have revealed a tremendous wealth of archaeological evidence about the nature of Medieval battle wounds (as well as armor). In July 1361, a small peasant force was defeated in three battles by Danish soldiers. Over 1200 corpses were left in grave pits outside the city of Visby. Likely because of high temperatures on the day of the summer battle, the corpses were not stripped of their armor as was usual but quickly dumped in mass graves. The mass graves show a wide range and diversity of armor types. Everything from soft and hard leather to differing sizes of mail and "coat-of-plate" was discovered. No two pieces are identical, with each having been made for the individual. Both noble and commoner appear to have been armored at least in some way.

Most interesting is what the skeletal remains of the Visby site reveal about their wounds. Excavations and forensic examinations of the skeletal remains were made and the injuries to bones recorded in detail. More than 450 skeletons showed tremendous injuries. Of the more than 1,000 corpses, the majority had major limb wounds. About half or more of the corpses also appear to have died as a result of head wounds, but 70 percent or so of those suffered *serious leg wounds as well*. It would seem the combatants were first receiving attacks to their lower legs that, causing them to either drop or lose their guard, then opened them up to a lethal head blow. In other words, a low strike below the shield followed by a high one above it—*probably one of the most natural and innate sword & shield techniques*. Analysis reveals that many wounds were to the high left, indicating that numerous attacks were made from right-handed swings cutting high to low. This is understandable when we consider low feints made against shields were followed instantly by high attacks on the resultant opening.

The shinbones and leg armor of many skeletons were nicked and cut into. More than 70 percent of the corpses had wounds to their *lower* legs; about 12 percent had wounds to the thighs only. One man had both legs cut off by an apparent single blow. Helmeted skulls were found that had been cleaved clean through, and others had parts of their craniums sliced off. Most of the Visby remains, however, show no bone trauma; suggesting that they died of soft-tissue damage or flesh wounds (arrows, spears, slices, and stabs). Considering that they were still wearing armor, this fact could also be the result of either blunt trauma or thrusts. There are also many indications that individuals died from wounds delivered to their backs, likely while retreating or fleeing.

Recent study speculates that the Visby excavations say a great deal about the overall importance of attacking the lower legs in Medieval combat. More than 75 percent of blows to the left shin of the skeletons were made to the outer side. More than 70 percent of those to the right shin were made against the inner side. Thus, it is easy to see that the casualties received their wounds when standing in a familiar, left-leg-forward sword & shield stance, as well as making passing steps onto their right legs. More than 90 percent of those skeletons showing wounds to the right thigh had them on the inner side as well. When fighting sword & shield, this is unlikely to occur except as a result of either making passing moves to bring the right leg forward on an attack or to falling back onto it when countering.

CUTTING

There are eight cutting angles for any attacks. These are simply the natural directions for optimally hitting the body with a weapon and effectively cutting with a sword. These eight cuts were not as systematically codified during the Medieval period as they would later become in the early Renaissance. The idea of *inside* and *outside* areas had not yet been devised, nor had the various cuts been given individual names. Also, the urge to describe Medieval swordsmanship in terms of classical (18th- and 19th-century) fencing concepts should be avoided. Instead, attacks can be separated into those that strike high or low (over or under) and left or right.

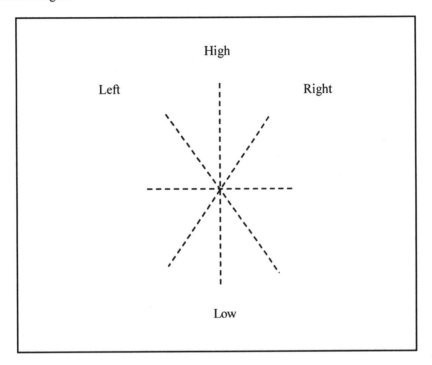

Using a Medieval sword is about delivering cutting blows, not just whacking with it. Obviously the *edge* must hit with force to cut or slice. Sword blows are about cutting, trying to cleave and shear into flesh and bone. It is not simply hammering with the weapon or "throwing the blade out there." Cuts are not just hits that are "snapped out" like a simple stick fight. They are strikes that are meant to deeply sever by their thin cutting edge. Provided no bones or major arteries are severed, the human body is capable of taking considerable laceration to flesh and skin yet still survive and function. But a single, powerful, cutting blow can easily have an instantaneous killing effect.

It is helpful to stop and make a few points of semantics: the terms *hack, slash,* and *cut* are often used synonymously, but mechanically it is good to distinguish between the blows and strikes of a sword. To *hack* or *chop* means essentially to hit or whack strongly with any edged weapon. To *cut* with a sword refers to an ideal cleaving or shearing blow. To *slash* means more or less to slice with the tip or edge, i.e., a dragging or sliding cut. A slash can also be a slower pulling or pushing draw-cut.

For the blades of straight Medieval swords, cuts with the tip alone are less effective than using the wider second quarter (down from the point) where more force can be applied. The optimal striking center where the most weight and force can be delivered with the least reverberation of the blade is known as the *point of percussion*. This section is a natural feature of any sword or weapon and can vary from sword to sword, depending primarily upon its balance. With a straight, doubled-edged sword, the point of percussion is commonly about the first 6 to 10 inches below the point.

131

What is important in learning swordsmanship is what is apparently most often ignored: cutting. It is no surprise how many Medieval combat enthusiasts and practitioners of martial arts who, while having sparred for years and owning real blades, have never attempted to do any serious cutting practice. Not test-cutting with a sword is like practicing driving without ever starting the car. Of course, not every enthusiast can get his hands on a decent sword, get it sharpened, and then locate substantial items to test-cut. This is unfortunate, because cutting, like free-sparring, reveals a multitude of weaknesses, bad habits, and incorrect techniques. It has the capacity to reveal many obscure and subtle, but still vital, elements of swordsmanship. In a sense, it shows one what most swordsmanship is all about.

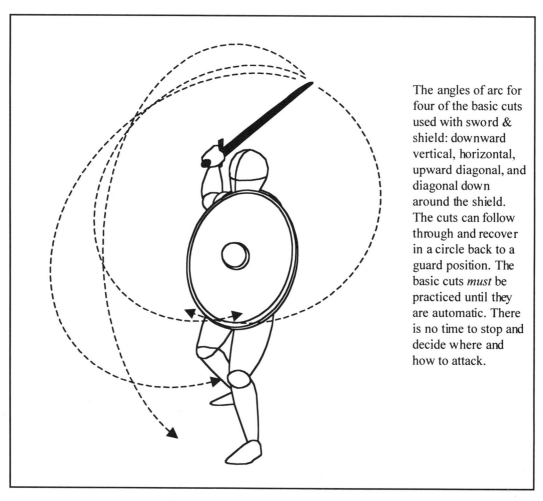

The angles of arc for four of the basic cuts used with sword & shield: downward vertical, horizontal, upward diagonal, and diagonal down around the shield. The cuts can follow through and recover in a circle back to a guard position. The basic cuts *must* be practiced until they are automatic. There is no time to stop and decide where and how to attack.

True swordsmanship is not about "touching" or making "hits"; it is about killing and wounding by slashing cuts and shearing hacks. It is possible, though, to develop the correct striking motions and defensive moves without actually having a fight with sharp steel blades. In fact, this is how our ancestors must have at least partially trained and taught. This is understandable; real weapons are too dangerous to use in mock fighting and too valuable to ruin in hours of practicing. But realize that they surely supplemented their practice (however it was conducted) with live-weapon training. At the very least we know this much alone from tournaments. Cutting and striking with real weapons had to be done to learn to do it for real. Waiting to learn through actual battle was too late. It is not unreasonable to conclude that light practice fighting was done with dulled weapons and wooden versions. Since at least the time of the ancient Greeks, wooden weapons of all manner have been used for practice in Europe. Sometimes they were even wrapped in cloth padding. Renaissance Schooles of Defence are known to have used wooden weapons (variously referred to as *wasters, bavins,* and *cudgels*) as well as blunt (or "foiled") blades.

Medieval swords are designed primarily for striking with the full arm in a wider arc from higher positions. Generally, cuts can be delivered in one of three ways: (1) Cuts from the shoulder or "full-arm," which, though slower, have the most power and are the hardest for an opponent to anticipate. They are the most instinctive and capable. (2) Those made from the elbow or "half-arm" are quicker but have less power and are perhaps better suited for draw-cuts and close-in moves against unarmored target areas. (3) Cutting from the "wrist" is the quickest, but also by far the weakest. Such actions would typically be ineffective against armor. Paradoxically, even though it's easy to cause a wound by the sheer cutting power inherent in a sword's blow, to do so intentionally and consistently (especially in the heat of battle) takes considerable training and practice. One must do more than just hit the target. One must also injure it. What matters in combat is not style or form or even specific technique, but rather survival—and this means defeating the opponent through violence. With a sword this meant cutting.

For contrast, in modern sport saber fencing, the main force of "cuts" is generated only by the wrist with emphasis on the use of the fingers. Strikes are not delivered from the elbow and certainly never from the full shoulder. The intent is to not in any way injure the opponent or use "force," but only finesse. The result of this transformation from the idea of cutting with a bladed weapon to essentially that of a sporting slap with a flat, bendable metal rod is a significant mutation of ancient sword techniques. Do not confuse the "touch cutting" manner of modern sporting sabers with the strong, earnest cuts of real weapons or even the forceful hits of today's full-contact weapon-sparring.

Practicing at the *pell*, a
standing wooden target.

Although one can indeed train seriously through the use of sticks or padded weapons, there is a significant advantage gained in understanding swordsmanship through the use of actual swords. Naturally, real swords provide insights into their handling and function that simply cannot be discerned otherwise. This applies not only to the area of practice-cutting, but also to the general mechanics of moving, parrying, and recovering. When test-cutting with a live blade (assuming it's a replica of proper weight and balance), suddenly everything becomes clearer and can seem obvious, practical, and effective.

It is surprising how many people say they "train" or "practice" with European weapons, only to learn upon examination that they (a) don't do any contact-sparring, (b) have never actually cut with a real sword, and (c) only play with stage-combat props or sticks rather than use historically accurate reproduction blades. Apparently, most practitioners today rarely have the opportunity to learn to cut properly or even to train with quality live blades. Others spend a good deal of time only whacking at static targets. The best training is obviously one that combines safe, realistic contact-sparring and frequent cutting practice.

Cutting effectively with a sword (or any bladed weapon) is not as easy as one would imagine. You don't just pick up a sword and swing it around. Learning to strike to cut effectively requires practice. That is why actual cutting exercises with a sharpened blade on test material is so important (something notoriously overlooked in Western swordsmanship). A blow may be well placed and well timed yet, because of inexperience, hit at an angle that deflects it or does little damage. A blow may hit but because of insufficient power, not penetrate deeply enough to prevent the adversary from responding. A blow may hit and cut well, but because of the swordsman's lack of skill no follow-through or proper recovery is made, and one is left vulnerable. Without practice at test cutting, the fundamentals of using a sword cannot be fully understood. Some would go even further and argue that cutting is the most important thing. Otherwise, one may know how to parry and strike, how to move and evade, but still be ignorant of how to deliver a clean, precise, killing cut.

The difficulty of properly making a strong cut, as well as the ease with which it does incredible damage, has been greatly distorted and misrepresented by video games and fantasy role-playing games. To box, you have to throw punches. You have to learn to hit by hitting a bag and other targets. So it is with swords. You must practice cutting. Otherwise it is like trying to learn to box without ever really punching anything. You cannot become a skilled marksman by just shooting a squirt gun, and you can't fully understand swordsmanship without practice cutting with real swords.

For modern students there are a wide variety of materials that can be suggested for test-cutting (training with a sharp sword to strike practice targets). Suitable materials are those that are substantial and will not cut too easily, but will also not damage a blade if a cut is made incorrectly. Ideally, 1- to 4-inch fresh bamboo is excellent, but it is rarely available in most parts of the country. There are other tropical plant stalks that make good substitutes. Cardboard mailing tubes of 3 to 5 inches in diameter and 1/4-inch thickness make good targets, and they are commonly available. Newspaper rolled up to 1 to 2 inches in diameter and then wetted are also appropriate. Watermelons are worthwhile test targets, as are pumpkins and other large squashes. Large plastic milk jugs or juice cartons filled with water are also recommended. Tightly wrapped dense foam rubber and even rolled-up straw mats are useful. Each of these different test target materials offers slightly different feel to the swordsman. The purpose of good test-cutting materials is to reveal whether the blow was effective and properly delivered. This is indicated by whether the cut itself was complete and straight with no twisting or tearing.

A warning on cheap reproduction swords: Cheap replica swords suffer from a multitude of problems that make them unsuitable (even dangerous) for cutting practice. First, they cannot hold a good edge (a problem only if you intend to practice test-cutting). Even when well-sharpened, they will not hold an edge for very long—assuming you practice cutting with it. Because so many cheap blades have weak, inferior tangs, they can also break at the handle when swung with force. The torque of stopping and then reversing for a parry or recovering from a strike can snap them. Some blades will even warp from test-cutting or the mere act of swinging. If these cheap blades are used to actually parry another blade during practice, the result is usually traumatic, causing major gouges and nicks. Sometimes the blade can even be permanently bent or even broken in the process. Quality reproductions do not function like this. Practitioners are strongly advised to acquire only the best historically accurate swords for training.

For maximum effect and edge alignment, the cuts are delivered on roughly a 45-degree angle. This inclination is best suited for the body to turn the hips and shoulders into the blow for power, as well as allow the arm to follow through and recover around or reverse back.

The Major Cuts as Made from a High Guard

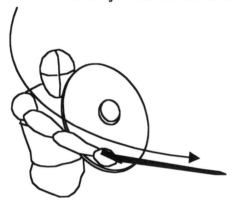

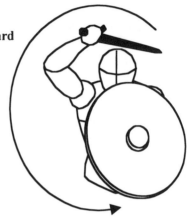

Horizontal right-to-left cut aimed primarily at the waist, hips, or thigh. This is also more effective made from the high guard.

A diagonal right-to-left cut aimed primarily at the head or neck/collar. This is the strongest and most common cut. Variations may also be thrown at the exposed arm or shoulder and even aimed as far down as the leg. This is most effective from the high guard. A vertical downward cut is made in the same manner.

A diagonal right-to-right upward cut is aimed primarily at the lower leg and thigh but may strike under the shield into the groin and abdomen. This is most effective from the back guard or back stance.

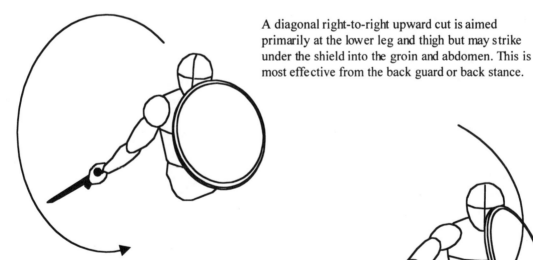

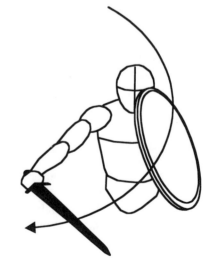

A diagonal left-to-right cut over the shield is more difficult because of the shield's location. However, it can be aimed primarily at the head, neck/collar, and exposed arm or shoulder. If delivered with a forward pass and outward shift of the shield, it can also hit to the lower legs.

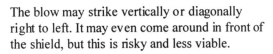

The blow may strike vertically or diagonally right to left. It may even come around in front of the shield, but this is risky and less viable.

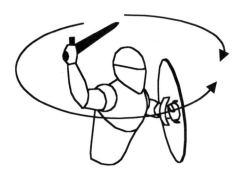

Cutting from the central high guard position, the blow can cross over to come around diagonally either from right to left or left to right over the shield. This can be used in deceptive feints or false attacks.

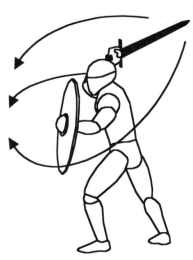

Cuts delivered from the back stance can be made with a step of the shield leg (forward or back) but are more effective counterattacks when made with a pass.

Perhaps two-thirds of the blows in early Medieval literature from 700 to 1000 A.D. describe cutting strokes thrown vertically toward the head, causing decapitating and amputating slices. The Danish historian Saxo Grammaticus, writing on sword combat in the 1100s, stated: "... *in the ordering of combat, men did not try to exchange their blows thick and fast; but there was a pause, and at the same time a definite succession in striking; the contest being carried on with few strokes, but those terrible, so that honor was paid more to their mightiness than to the number of the blows."* Froissart later wrote that a knight in 1381 fighting peasants *"began cutting and thrusting all round ... he cut off a foot or hand or an arm or leg with every stroke."*

Cuts from the middle stance must first pull back to gain momentum, but with passing steps are effective and efficient. Considerable practice is required to make them quickly and deceptively.

Again, it is important to understand that virtually *no* cut is delivered statically from a still position. Attacks are with the lead foot stepping in or one leg making a passing step. Both feet may also simultaneously "hop-step" forward or backward. Attacks are also made with a movement or shift of the shield to protect the body and prevent exposing a target.

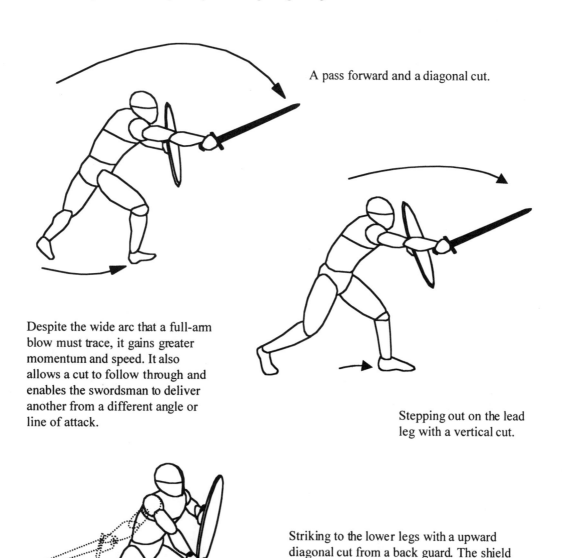

A pass forward and a diagonal cut.

Despite the wide arc that a full-arm blow must trace, it gains greater momentum and speed. It also allows a cut to follow through and enables the swordsman to deliver another from a different angle or line of attack.

Stepping out on the lead leg with a vertical cut.

Striking to the lower legs with a upward diagonal cut from a back guard. The shield may be lowered or raised to intercept an incoming blow at the same time. The rear leg may pass forward, or the shield side leading leg may step ahead.

Full-arm cuts may be best applied in conjunction with evading and countering. Cuts from the half-arm can best be applied immediately after parrying, deflecting, or evading. The combination of the three striking methods with their different ranges and speeds is what can overwhelm and outmaneuver an adversary. It goes without saying that these cuts all can involve faking actions and timed stepping.

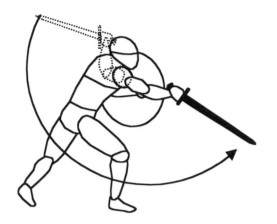

The basic cutting motion of a sword is not from the wrist. It involves the arm and shoulder. The arm does not "punch"; it makes a cut with the weapon. The arm is not completely straightened either. Some bend and flex must remain for the suppleness needed both for correct focus and recovery. Do not make your arm limp; try to feel the force of the cut flow through your arm and weapon and then to the target. In all striking, your body's momentum must blend with that of your weapon. The feet, hips, shoulder, arm, and wrist must all move in smooth sequence. Striking more effectively also involves good *aim,* and this can only be obtained with long-term practice. Aiming the sword is really a matter of aligning the edge to cut.

Passing forward with a low cut from the high guard and the shield sliding out and to the left block.

A low cut from the high guard with an advancing step by the lead leg and shield, and kept at the ready.

Low cuts can strike diagonally upward or come in at horizontal angles. They can easily cut to the shin, knee, thigh, or hip.

When employing a shield in the left hand, the majority of cuts are delivered from the right, but a few can even be made from the left. From the high guard, a cut can be made around to strike left to right as the shield drops to parry a low attack.

Focus is an important element in striking correctly. Ideally, simultaneously with the motion of striking, one focuses the point of impact of a cut or blow slightly "into" or just beyond the target. If the strike is a cutting slice, it is just as quickly followed through with a forceful pulling motion and brought around fully with the momentum. If it is a hacking blow, the strike should be just as quickly withdrawn and recovered to a guarding position in preparation for either a renewed attack or a parry. Proper focus of a strike not only enables real cuts to have power or precision, but also assists in developing control for nonlethal contact-sparring.

If a cut connects, there is the need to *follow through*; if it misses there is a need to *recover* the guard (or prepare for a parry). Recovery, returning to a guarded ready position, is important after making any single attack or parry. To continue an action or to change to another often requires an intermediate move. Proper recovery can be made by returning a strike or swing on the same line of its attack (a "return in line") or by a follow-through bringing it fully around. Following through uses the strike's own natural momentum to transcribe a path that can turn into yet another strike or stance.

Another element that can affect the power and delivery of a strike involves expressive vocalization or, rather, yelling with the attack. Just at the point of striking, tension is created in the arm, and the breath is forcefully exhaled with a loud vocal sound from the gut. Quick exhalation like this is natural under physical exertion and can be practiced to help tense the muscles of the chest and abdomen into yielding more power to a strike (this is common in Asian martial arts but hardly exclusive to them). It is perhaps the equivalent of a lion's roar that momentarily both startles and alerts its prey to an attack. The primal, guttural yell that assists blows is not only physical but also psychological, causing the adversary mental distraction while aiding one's own effort. The Vikings are known to have terrified their enemies with strange howling cries and yells as they fought.

Although the vast majority of Medieval swords have two edges, only one is employed at a time. The edge facing away from the body and toward the opponent is the leading edge (later called the "true" or "right" in the Renaissance schools of fence). The closer edge facing inward is called the back edge (or later on, the "false edge"). Almost all cuts were made with the leading edge. The back edge is seldom used to strike with. Back-edge cuts are noticeably rare in Medieval artwork. False-edge attacks or diagonal upward cuts using the back are, for the most part, mechanically weaker. Few opportunities exist to use them where the forward edge would not be better employed by a simple turn of the wrist. Turning the wrist to align it with the stroke on an upward diagonal cut can turn it into a stronger true-edge attack.

Though they are weaker, such cuts can sometimes be quicker on exposed target areas. One back-edge blow can be made with a simple but quick upward or horizontal motion of the blade from the back guard. However, back-edge blows like this can actually knock a Medieval sword out of your hand. This is why such cuts were really only applicable with later Renaissance cut & thrust swords. These lighter weapons used compound-hilts and relied on the fingering grip. Even in Renaissance fence, in which swordsmanship was studied more scientifically, false-edge or back-edge attacks were applied sparingly and only as harassing cuts, not for lethal strikes. With lighter blades of the Renaissance they were much easier to employ, but were used only for debilitating cuts to the knee, wrist, and neck.

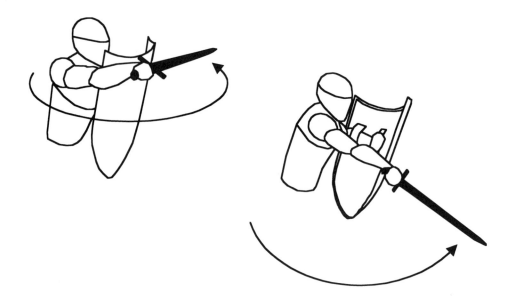

"Wrapping" the weapon up and around with the back edge is also mechanically weaker. A back or inward "wrap-around" motion with a sword typically cannot strike with the crucial edge placement or even sufficient power to cut properly. This kind of snapping, rotating wrist blow can be employed with a club or round stick, but it is very difficult to cut effectively with a blade in this way. There are only very limited applications of back-hand "reverse" strikes to the rear of an opponent's head or neck after stepping in. Nowhere in Medieval artwork is there evidence that such blows were widely used. To hit like this you must move so close to an opponent that he can easily smash his shield in your face or easily cut straight down toward your shin and ankle. Hitting like this, using the tip, is a popular technique among some practitioners. Yet it is really an artificial invention of a select group of modern stick-fighting enthusiasts using a specialized set of rules. Time spent training and test-cutting with real swords will quickly dissipate the illusion. Practitioners are strongly advised to attempt it with a real sword against a test target, such as a pumpkin or cardboard tube, and see how truly ineffectual and *ahistorical* it is.

140

Thrusting may have been a less common technique in the early Middle Ages because of the frequency of encountering mail or reinforced heavy leather as well as the protection offered by shields. Although neither mail nor leathers are invulnerable to thrusts, in most situations a thrust is certainly not as practical or effective as a cutting blow. But sword thrusts *were* known and widely recognized as useful and effective actions. Offensive thrusts were not simply an innovation of Renaissance methods. Sophisticated thrusting techniques had been in use since the time of the ancient Greeks and were widely employed by the Romans and their enemies. Thrusts have value in their range, angle of attack, speed, and penetrating power.

A straight face thrust from the middle stance delivered with a forward pass.

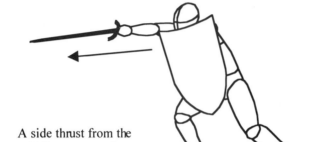

A side thrust from the middle stance made with a forward pass.

From the middle guard in particular a variety of thrusts can be delivered. Their main target is the face and throat. Thrusts can even be made under or around a shield to the abdomen. Thrusts can be quite effective with a forward passing step of the sword arm's side. This adds range as well as power to penetrate armor. One value of the deceptive middle guard lies in how cutting blows can be turned into thrusts and thrusts changed suddenly to cuts. Historical accounts of fighting describe assailants charging one another and jabbing several times with their points under each other's shields and into each other's arms and thighs until one was caught under the chin.

Such thrusts shown in historical artwork are also sometimes incorrectly assumed to be "back swings" using the false edge.

Quickly shifting between a thrust and a cut can
be effective, particularly against harder armors
or when the opponent has closed the range.

An upward thrust from the middle
guard under the adversary's shield.

From the back stance the weapon
can move to a point-on thrusting
position hidden behind the shield.
From here it can suddenly stab out.

From behind the shield it is difficult to
determine whether the sword is in a
back stance cutting position or has been
quickly shifted to a thrusting position in
transition to a middle guard. Similarly,
the middle guard can drop back behind
the shield to a lower back stance.

PARRYING WITH THE SHIELD & SWORD

Defending with the shield & sword is more than just parrying. It involves moving in relation to attacks and responding with counterstrikes. But before fighting with the sword & shield can be addressed, the fundamentals of parrying must be examined.

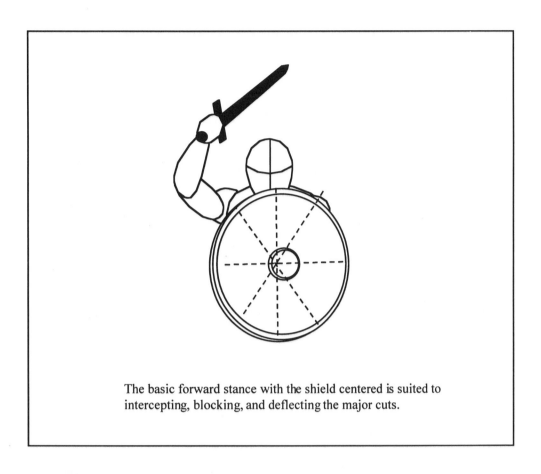

The basic forward stance with the shield centered is suited to intercepting, blocking, and deflecting the major cuts.

When a strike cannot be avoided, dodged, or evaded, a parry (direct block) is required. The general rule for parrying can be expressed as *deflect rather than block and evade rather than deflect*. Whether with a sword & shield, a single sword, or two weapons, the idea holds true.

Shield parries may be defined more loosely than those with a sword and can consist simply of high, middle, and low blocks. Because of the nature of the shield's size and balance, shield parries are applied predominately to the side on which the shield is carried (typically the left). Using the shield to parry to the opposite side (typically the right) takes additional time (movement) and may expose you. Blows to the right side are more often evaded, though the weapon may also parry them.

Fundamentally, using a shield to block with involves holding the tool between you and the attacking weapon. However, doing this while also trying to strike safely at the adversary requires additional elements. Parrying with a shield is merely a matter of blocking the attack from hitting the body or limbs by imposing the shield in the path of the blow. One core element of fighting with the sword & shield is to cause the opponent to overreact to an attack or commit himself to parrying an attack that is a deception. Either way the true attack may change its target or angle of intent to succeed.

143

Essentially there are three methods that can be discerned for shield parrying: *refusing* the parry, *greeting* the parry, and *striking* the parry. *Refusing* the parry means to simply let a strike fall upon the shield where it is. The idea is to allow the shield to do all the work with very little, if any, movement or action. Blows are received primarily on the face of the shield as it's held at the ready. This is accomplished by holding the shield in a passive, relaxed manner and properly controlling the fighting distance. Taking blows in this way can allow for a quick counterattack. It is also used when the swordsman is close in shield-to-shield with an opponent, and there is no room to maneuver. Often larger or heavier shields must rely on this method. *Greeting* the parry is a more common method of using any type shield and involves simply moving the shield to stop the blow. This action is invariably done while simultaneously delivering a counterattack. As the shield arm is moved to intercept, a step is taken either into the blow to close the distance or away from the blow to open a line of attack. *Striking* the parry is a means of actively using the shield to beat or smack an incoming blow. It requires a strong arm and a mobile shield. Usually the edge or the center umbo is used in a hitting manner intended to deflect or disrupt the attack. This action is used as preparation for one's own attack or counteraction. It can allow a quick counter against the attacker's extended weapon arm or exposed leg. This works ideally with smaller shields.

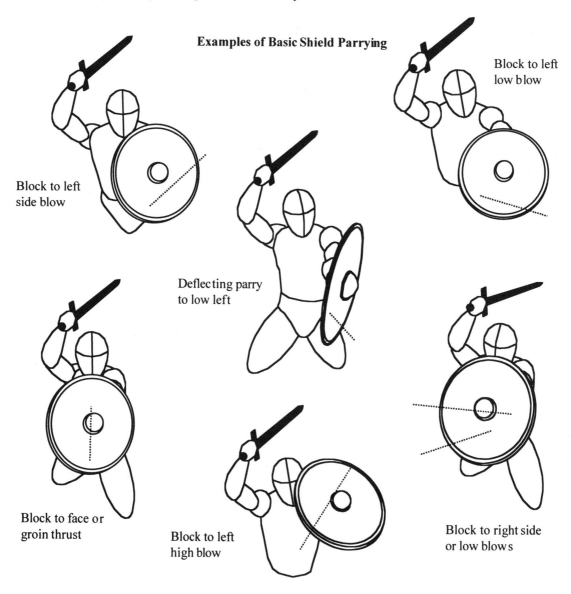

Examples of Basic Shield Parrying

Block to left side blow

Block to left low blow

Deflecting parry to low left

Block to face or groin thrust

Block to left high blow

Block to right side or low blows

Historical literature (as well as art) describes how Medieval shields were used to block with both their flat face *and* their edges. The flat surface of a shield naturally acts as its own area defense. But the edge of the shield is also used, not just the flat. A shield is not for "hiding behind," as is often portrayed. It should not be left stationary, hanging and unmoving (except against missile weapons). A shield should never be a "static" defense (once again, those who do not include lower-leg targets in their sparring and training will have difficulty grasping this fact because they habitually must fight in too close). Although it may end up doing so on certain parries, the shield should not be purposely held in front of the eyes where it blocks the user's vision. Also, just as the sword can recover its guard after striking or parrying, the shield is also normally returned to its central guarding position after blocking. Leaving it out will naturally offer an opening to the adversary.

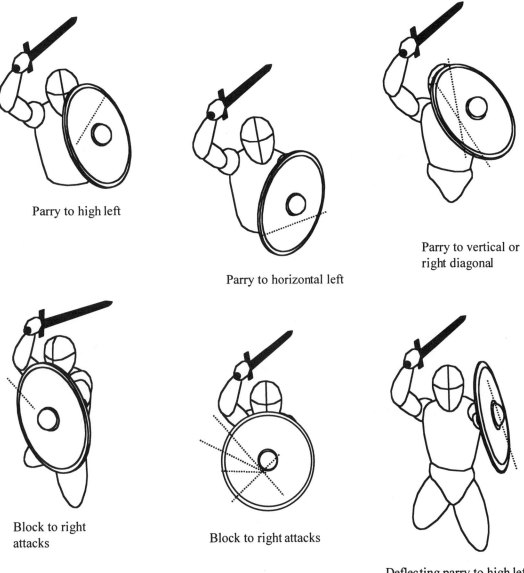

Parry to high left

Parry to horizontal left

Parry to vertical or right diagonal

Block to right attacks

Block to right attacks

Deflecting parry to high left

Parrying with the sword itself when fighting with sword & shield is something that is less common than popularly believed. It is far less necessary than simply obstructing and deflecting attacks with the shield or stepping to evade while you counterattack. There are very few occasions where it is preferable. The nature of parrying with the Medieval sword is covered in depth under the section on long-swords.

145

Although the Medieval sword's simple cross-guard is sufficient hand protection, it is so only when *not* intentionally used to block with. That is, you don't use it to intercept and receive a blow on the guard. Doing so is dangerous, and in the process you are likely to end up moving your hand into the path of an oncoming attack—especially if the opponent deliberately targets your grip! The correct way to parry attacks on the grip is not by attempting to use the guard alone, but by blocking with the flat of the blade in the middle (or preferably by moving the hilt and arm out of the way altogether). Failing to do this and trying to rely on the guard to block with is lazy and leads to hits on the hand (as well as misconceptions of how to properly handle a Medieval sword). Despite its prevalent dramatic use in movie swordfights, parrying with the sword's guard is not advisable (daggers, however, because they are agile and quick, *can* often use their guards against lighter weapons to bind and trap effectively).

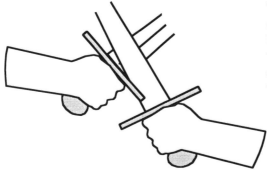

There is a considerable difference between closing to bind or knock the opposing weapon with the cross and actually trying to block blows with the guard.

The nature of "hack and slash" swordsmanship is such that the hand is really not *in the direct line of attack.* Although it might seem to be the case that with Medieval swords the hands are left very vulnerable, they are really no more open than any other part of the body—*until moved into danger or left exposed.* Even in the ferocious chaos of Medieval combat, the only blows that were likely to endanger the hands came from three places: those that occurred when combatants struck simultaneously, those that occurred as a hand struck a shield, and those that were intentionally aimed at the hand or "grip-line," the last of which can be defended against by the same manner of block or parry as that for attacks on other targets. Attacks to the hips in particular can also result in the defender "misparrying" and dropping his grip into the path of an oncoming strike, but this occurs more from inexperience than by accident.

A sure way of incurring blows to your hands is by not employing the blade to parry with and instead relying on trying to use the guard and greet attacks near the hilt.

In the Norse tale, *Njal's Saga*, a sword is described as striking the guard of another man's sword and then skipping off to slice through his wrist.

However, individuals doing various types of Medieval sword-sparring today may find their hands repeatedly being struck by accident (this is notoriously common among beginners). At first, they often attribute it to just their opponents' hitting them there, rather than to their own faulty attempts at blocking. Unskilled practitioners are well known for trying to parry with their guards instead of their blades. They instinctively and incorrectly move their hands (the "grip-line") into the path of oncoming blows. This more often than not results in strikes landing on or smacking into their fingers and knuckles. This can be witnessed especially in the case of horizontal blows to the belt-line and downward blows against the head or collar, where parrying with a sword can be more challenging at first. Once an individual learns to parry with his blade and not his grip, this problem soon ceases. The usual reaction in the beginning, though, is to condemn cross-guards as "insufficient." The reasoning here seems to go something along the lines of: "Later swords had compound guards only because those dim-witted warriors finally realized they could make better ones that offered more protection."

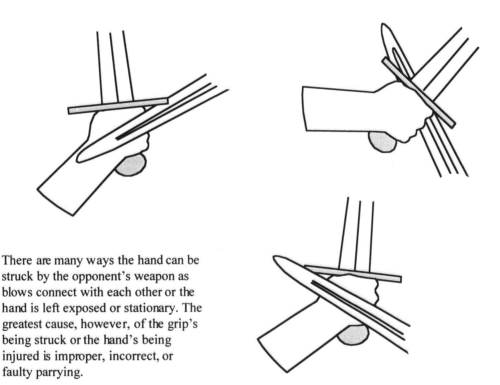

There are many ways the hand can be struck by the opponent's weapon as blows connect with each other or the hand is left exposed or stationary. The greatest cause, however, of the grip's being struck or the hand's being injured is improper, incorrect, or faulty parrying.

This, of course, is appallingly flawed reasoning and makes one ask why Medieval warriors would have put so much effort and ingenuity into armor design, yet left simple sword cross-guards pretty much "stagnant" for centuries. It also ignores the significant relationship of fingering and thrusting in guard design. This does not apply only to swords, either, but forces us to ask the same question with regard to axes, maces, flails, clubs, spears, and so on. Had their hands really been particularly vulnerable to injury because of poor cross-guards, we might wonder why Medieval warriors (as so many others before them) seemed to have gone so long before bothering to armor their hands. To many practitioners another reason that the grip seems to be so vulnerable and hit so often is the nature of much of the sparring being conducted today. Sparring rules and practices that outlaw attacks to the hands or grip of the shield arm even when such is left intentionally exposed by an opponent only encourage a misapplication of Medieval sword & shield techniques. When one fights under a rule structure that promotes excessively close fighting ranges and slamming hits rather than more realistic evading, deflecting, and countering, then the hand will naturally be hit more often.

To employ the shield properly against attacks, don't just move your shield toward a blow and "wait" for it. Bend the arm to smack back at the blow, using the flat for strikes farther out and the edge for closer blows. It may also be necessary to twist the body slightly into the block. Step out with the back leg as the shield blocks and your weapon counters, or step forward with the lead leg as the shield blocks and your weapon counters.

Whatever its shape, for a shield to parry or deflect, it really needs only to move in small outward or side motions from the elbow.

By deflecting with the shield's edge a blow may be stopped farther out. Keeping the shield out farther prevents it from stifling your actions or being knocked into your face. This also offers the chance that the attacker's sword might stick and its recovery be delayed, thereby leaving him vulnerable. This is also the manner in which a shield can be used offensively, which will be looked at in the section on fighting with the sword & shield.

By striking out with the shield as you parry, there is the possibility of knocking the adversary's hilt or grip with the shield. This can be a method of blocking in itself and could even cause the adversary to be disarmed, although that is unlikely. As described earlier, the angle between the extended ends of the guard and either the pommel or the blade can often act to prevent the knuckles from hitting the surface of a shield. The potential for the opponent's hand or grip to be struck by a sword is also somewhat misunderstood. This matter is addressed in detail in the chapter on long-swords.

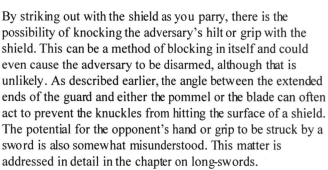

With the sword & shield, the shield assumes the role of naturally doing most of the blocking. But the sword, too, can be used to parry, particularly against blows on its own side. However, using a sword to parry is something to be avoided. It is not all that common an action to make (though this is not at all the case in theatrical and staged performance fighting). In fact, inconographical references to sword parries in Medieval artwork are exceedingly rare, as is their mention in literature from the time. It is easy to misinterpret positions of cutting, counterstriking, or preparing to cut as "parries." Parries with the sword were made to oppose an attacking blade only when absolutely necessary. Additionally, Medieval swords were certainly not "too slow" to make effective parries, quite the contrary. Intentionally and directly blocking with the weapon is simply inefficient—that's what the shield is for, so the weapon can be left to attack. A more effective defense is achieved by using the shield and simply avoiding and evading attacks. A quicker follow-up or counterattack can be made by the shield's meeting or deflecting blows or by your body's slipping away from the attack (without a shield or when using a long-sword in a two-hand grip, this is even more important). When possible, avoiding a deliberate sword parry allows for alternative, countering techniques and can also prevent unnecessary damage to the blade's edge. Parrying with a Medieval sword is addressed at length in the chapter on the long-sword.

Intentionally blocking with the sword horizontally, instead of parrying with the shield and countercutting, is foolish. Yet, this is typical of most all theatrical renditions of sword & shield combat. The action robs you of both threat and counterattack potential while ignoring the defense of the shield. It also endangers the hand and exposes the blade to unnecessary trauma. A skilled adversary will exploit such parries to strike the exposed hand and forearm or will feint high and strike low. It is only with the limitations inherent in fighting on horseback that parrying this way really becomes viable.

A warrior armed with a shield is no doubt safer than one armed with a sword alone. But it is important to avoid opening the shield up as you attack (this is typical in many amateur performance displays and Hollywood movie fights). There is no reason the shield must be pulled back or pulled away. Doing so defeats the whole reason for using the tool. Instead, the opposite is desired. The shield is pushed outward to strike, smack, or deflect the adversary's weapon or his own shield. This will be examined more closely in the section on fighting with sword & shield.

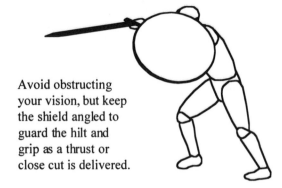

Avoid obstructing your vision, but keep the shield angled to guard the hilt and grip as a thrust or close cut is delivered.

In any parrying, the shield arm should not be made stiff or rigid, but should move naturally.

Raising the leg to avoid a low strike can be an effective means of defense without risking exposure by moving the shield. It can be applied in conjunction with either passing back or passing forward. The sword can also be brought forward to bind or close with the attacker's weapon before hitting again.

Just as the shield moves to block, your weapon can attack. A simple advancing step or a pass forward or pass back can be used to simultaneously bring the weapon forward and the shield back.

The kite shield offers superb coverage with little movement. Its extended length can parry low attacks at a safe distance without having to be lowered, thus exposing the head or shoulders.

A shield is a tool that functions superbly both for individual self-defense in single combat and under the confined and crowded conditions of group combat. In the massed armies of professional warriors intent on annihilating one another, those without shields (or heavy armor) would have a remote chance of survival under the intense barrages of spear, axe, and arrow. A common defense for groups of warriors was the "shield wall," called *skjalborg* by the Anglo-Saxons. The shield wall was a rank of frontline warriors on foot with their shields huddled close together to protect and overlap one another. Spears and axes protruded from it or were thrown from behind. It was an ideal defense by foot soldiers against cavalry. As with the similar method of the old Roman legions, it was highly effective provided it retained its static defense.

FALSE POSTURES, INFERIOR STANCES, AND BAD HABITS

Once the physical mechanics of cutting and parrying effectively are understood, the simplicity and effectiveness of the basic stances and guards make much sense. Yet there are many positions that by improper or inferior form violate the fundamental form, which is most efficient for free movement and action. Personal style is a matter of simply being free to use whatever works for you as long as it does not violate the basic concepts of attack and defense. Obviously, "style" will not be the same for everyone: different people have different physical builds and different levels of strength, quickness, and agility. Even individual weapons can themselves require a manner of use that is detrimental and self-defeating against another particular weapon (or armor). Some faults or flaws are a direct result of the limitations self-imposed by relying exclusively on one method of training or one set of preconceived sparring conditions. Other bad habits and misapplication of technique may be the result of a general ignorance of the nature of the weapons themselves. Of course, often we have no idea that our style may have deficiencies or even flaws until we encounter someone skillful enough to notice and exploit our personal idiosyncrasies.

Poor posture is often a result of insufficient instruction and understanding. Inexperienced fighters typically will bend their back and lean too far forward. Although this can "feel" aggressive and "ready," it robs them of reach and reaction time. There are minute split-second differences in evading and attacking between a straight posture and a bent one. Being able to both pull the torso back a few extra inches when evading and lean forward a few extra inches when striking can be crucial. If the body is already bent forward the ability to do either is severely hindered. If a stance leans too forward there is little more reach that can be gained when the need to do so arrives. If the body is already leaning forward when the need comes to instantly pull back, any movement loses time and results in just shifting to the proper straight position (from which it must often then move still farther back in avoiding a blow). But if the body is kept in a proper straight posture to begin with, then the opportunity for small, quick shifts forward or back can be much more effective. A straight posture will then make better use of associated footwork.

A stance that is too stiff lacks mobility and range. Too much movement is needed to act, and time is lost in the process. Both reach and speed are thereby reduced. In reacting to either openings or threats, a preliminary step must first be taken, during which the adversary can usually close or evade.

A stance that is too wide really adds nothing while diminishing mobility. The muscles are already extended and no further range (or speed) can be gained. However, in order to step at all, a preliminary move must first be made to close the gap. This loses time and can leave one open. Being slower to move, the lower legs are also more susceptible to attack. An unnecessarily wide stance should not be confused with briefly lowering one's hips to complete a parry or to cut low. Balance should not be overly placed on the back leg either, as this prevents rapid forward movement or easy side-stepping.

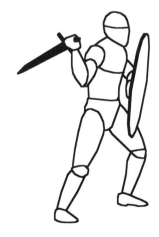

A stance that is too relaxed lacks readiness and reaction time. It is weaker and vulnerable without offering a counterthreat of its own. A timid or loose stance should not be confused with the presentation of a false opening ("invitation" to attack) or the misleading calm of a highly skilled warrior.

A stance that is too tight reduces range and mobility while increasing one's vulnerability. The shield's coverage is restricted, and defense of the lower legs is severely hampered, as is offensive potential against the adversary's own lower targets (those who do not include the lower leg as targets in their training or sparring will have difficulty grasping this fact because they must habitually fight too close). The shield must also move out to meet oncoming blows, thereby allowing your adversary a chance to alter trajectory. The sword arm is also inefficiently positioned. Before being able to deliver any strike the weapon must first make a small "preparatory" movement. This makes it have to travel in too large (and too slow) of an arc in order to successfully strike low. The hilt and grip are also in a position that unnecessarily exposes them to attack.

A slouching or forward-leaning stance is restrictive and leaves one vulnerable. Mobility is stifled, and this can telegraph intention to the opponent. Reach is already extended, and this limits range as well. Too many actions either fall short or waste time as the torso first straightens. It is instinctive to pull the body back first while the feet momentarily lag behind. This kind of posture is also a strain that delays movement by altering your balance. As with other poor stances, too much extra motion is required for even simple actions. A slouching stance should not be confused with briefly leaning in on a strike to ensure proper range. If the shield is held out too far, it, too, is slower and less maneuverable.

A back-leaning stance lacks balance and mobility. Although this form of stance is not unheard of in Asian martial arts, it is inappropriate for sword & shield application. The lead leg is highly vulnerable to attack and is outside the shield's coverage. Most of the body's weight ends up on the rear leg, placing undue strain on the legs. The stance limits freedom of movement (particularly in mass combat). Many strikes and parries are delayed because the legs must often make a preliminary step to close range. The shield is also hindered by this and cannot coordinate easily. The stance is also overly defensive in nature and relies too much on evasive motion, thereby limiting sword & shield combinations.

Although there is always a stylistic variety among fighters, it exists only within the parameters of the appropriate physical mechanics. When an adversary, because of inexperience or ignorance, noticeably deviates from this, you can exploit this as a vulnerability. Although any style or technique may have some chance at utility (no matter how remote), the idea is to use those techniques that have the greatest potential with the least limitations.

If an opponent holds his weapon cocked and ready on the shoulder to "snap out," his range is limited and he loses parry potential. This may be good for using a stick or a club, but *this is not how an edged sword is used to cut effectively.* Attacks are also limited to higher angles of attack. Against those fighting like this, throw attacks directly at their hands and wrists. Stay out farther and attack their lower legs. Keep distance and avoid fighting close in.

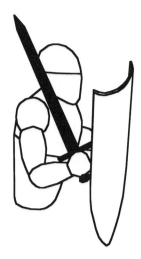

If an opponent holds his weapon too relaxed or with the shield pulled in too closely, his reaction time and counteractions will be slowed (too much extra movement to move from his guard position). The lower legs can also be hard to defend. Feints can create openings on an opponent who fights this way.

If an opponent holds his weapon too horizontally, he poses a reduced threat as well as opening more of his arm as a target. He is neither in a guarding nor a transitioning position and loses time and power in both offense and defense. Reaction time and momentum are the worst things to weaken as a result of improper form. In learning to fight well, the idea is to trim as much time off our actions as possible. You want to discard as much extraneous and unnecessary motion and inexefficeinct movement as you can. The idea is to refine the mechanics of our motions through practice repetitions in order to shave off as many split seconds of time lost as possible. The body must be taught to move naturally and react reflexively so that what is left is then smooth, fluid, and imperceptible in execution.

Holding the weapon with the point low behind can allow for a stronger blow, but it is much slower. The tip must travel along a much larger arc before the edge can cut. This is especially difficult with longer or heavier swords. It makes it nearly impossible to threaten, let alone strike the adversary's lower legs. It also exposes one's forearm and elbow while also diminishing the potential for striking low.

One of the most untenable positions is that with the grip rotated around and the blade resting statically on the shield and the sword tip pointing out. This position is often misconstrued from Medieval artwork showing what is apparently a simple left-to-right downward cut coming around from behind the shield. To use this as a guarding posture unnecessarily exposes the grip and forearm, obstructs your line of sight, and severely reduces the range of attacks that can be made. It also eliminates the ability to threaten or attack low targets. Most importantly, there is *no* attack that can be made from this stance that the sword must not *first* return around to the high guard in the process. It is a tremendous waste of time. A forward thrust from here has to be made with the wrist turned to the outside with the palm up, a very weak position that also inhibits raising the shield to parry. Parrying to the left with the sword itself is also not a useful option because that is what the shield is for. Further, a smacking attack or beat on the end of the weapon itself can easily cause the wrist to twist dangerously inward.

Holding the weapon with the point in front, angled downward and resting on the shield, is inferior and mechanically weaker. Although the position seems well defended, it offers no real improvement over the shield alone and even diminishes offense. There is no cut that the weapon can make without the tip's having to first turn back around. This position does little to allow an outward cut or a forward thrust. It also makes it nearly impossible to threaten the adversary or make low attacks. It unnecessarily exposes the forearm and grip, and the weakness of the position allows the tip to be knocked off or beaten to the side.

Holding the shield too far out or too open—although sometimes useful as an inviting feint or for striking with the shield edge—exposes far too much of the torso. It opens the leg to attack as well as more easily revealing when a passing step is being committed. It also requires more time to pull the shield back to defend on the other side.

Fighting with Sword & Shield

Now that you have an understanding of the fundamentals of moving, cutting, and parrying with a sword & shield, an overview of basic fighting techniques can be presented. But first it is important to understand that so much of swordsmanship just cannot be learned from books or even passed on verbally. It must be acquired personally and subjectively. It has been said that misunderstanding the basic mechanics of a weapon is the surest way of deluding oneself into misapplying techniques or inventing invalid ones. Enthusiasts today who sincerely seek skill must strive to ever examine their preconceptions even at the risk of bruising their egos. Acquiring knowledge (skill) often means risking one's self-esteem and reexamining assumptions. As with most all the techniques and concepts described in this book, knowing is only half, you must also do—and that can be achieved only through committed, long-term practice.

An interesting aspect of a sword is that, unlike many other ancient hand weapons, once you pick one up you can almost instinctively understand its use. Although the techniques and particulars of fighting with one require great practice and can even remain a mystery, a sword has an obvious function that most anyone can grasp intuitively. The speed with which new students can comprehend its basic application and learn its movements is a testament to both its profound simplicity and great potential.

Swordsmanship (and most fighting) has been described as a process of juxtaposing, of maneuvering for advantage. We act, react, and counterreact in symbiosis with the adversary. Yet, on a higher level of swordsmanship it has also been contrarily suggested that to strike or counterstrike is all the same. One can learn to move as if alone, and no opponent or target exists as a conscious object. This is very true . . . right up until an opponent strikes back.

There are only a handful of basic sword & shield techniques, but they must be practiced over and over to perfection. When applied with force, speed, and attitude (the proper timing and distance), they can be ferocious and formidable. Guards should be instinctive. They are not about just "getting into a position." Each is used smoothly and easily according to its inherent technical and tactical attitude. Each stance has attacks and parries that are best suited to it. The ability to execute them quickly and unpredictably is the heart of skill with the sword & shield. Conversely, the ability to anticipate and foresee the opponent's immediate action from his stance (or transitional position) is an equal part of higher understanding. Fighting with a sword & shield revolves around the fluid movement from one stance to another with the precise execution of techniques while you press forward, side shift, or draw back. The more obvious techniques as described here are sufficient for demonstrating the nature of the weapons and their fight. Understand, however, that stances, cuts, parries, and other actions cannot be looked at in isolation from the principles associated with them either tactically or psychologically. But these other concepts can only be addressed after examining the fundamentals of techniques.

156

Those who have not trained with a shield or faced a shield in free-sparring practice are apt to miss considerable aspects of the nature of its fight as presented here. Without direct physical experience, it is not easy to grasp just how easy it is to be fooled by the feints of an opponent's weapon or the deflecting hits of his shield and, as a result, to be struck in the head or lower leg.

It must also be pointed out that fighting (and training) with a wooden stick (or a mock padded weapon) is not identical to fighting with a sword. This is especially so with regard to the sword & shield. Hitting with a stick and cutting with a sword are not the same. Nor is the magnitude of the wounds and injuries they can cause hardly equivalent. Although there are many common elements in handling and the central physics involved, there are also crucial, fundamental differences. A Medieval sword is a singular weapon of the battlefield. At best a stick's impact will fracture bone and tear skin. A finely tempered sword splits bodies and can dismember even through armor. A stick can be useless against harder armors, whereas a sword can be designed to puncture them and the organs they protect. A sword needs to parry with its flat, slash with its edge, and properly follow through on the cut. A stick, though it can be a lethal weapon, need only lash out and make good bludgeoning contact. A sword is generally heavier, yet it can slice through the air more quickly and focus its force on a much smaller point. Stick fighting is a skill, but it is not swordsmanship. Those who study from this point of view alone miss a great deal. With a sharp real sword, trying to merely "smack-hit" rather than cut with the edge will quickly prove futile.

A sword's cut is not the simple slash of a long knife or slice of a machete. It is a strong, butchering, chopping blow. In weapon training, martial artists are fond of saying, "If you encounter a knife, expect to get cut." When it comes to Medieval fighting we could similarly say, *"If you encounter a sword & shield, expect to get killed."*

Shield & sword combat is not simply a matter of close-range whamming, bashing, and powering through. When used properly, a shield does not just hang; it is moved to hit the adversary's shield or even to knock the incoming weapon simultaneously as you launch a countercut. Obviously, motions such as ducking, sidestepping, and leaping forward or back can be employed as needed. Fighting effectively with a shield does not entail dancing about unnecessarily, but neither is it about just planting your feet and standing your ground.

By holding the shield too close to the body, maneuverability is lost. Although this can be more comfortable and places less stress on arm muscles, it is a passive method of shield use. It is more suitable for either mounted combat (where a maneuverable shield is virtually irrelevant) or for the massed, tight phalanx and shield-wall formations of the ancient Greeks and Romans (some Roman shields could even be locked together). In the case of the Roman method, one should remember the circumstances under which they developed this shield technique. It was not intended nor suited for single combat, but for the larger, well-drilled armies of ancient times. It was also inappropriate for mounted use or for individualistic warriors, such as those prevalent in the Middle Ages. Once the tactical limitations of the shield wall was recognized, it was used only for defense.

The value and effectiveness of a shield in archaic weapon combat can be established from a brief examination of the techniques for employing the round, kite, and heater forms. The reason shields existed for so long and were used so extensively in combination with swords is very simple: they were effective! Anyone who thinks the use of a shield in battle was somehow a hindrance or even "dishonorable" in single combat is foolish and sorely ignorant of its formidable historical effectiveness. As a tool of Medieval warfare in a skilled hand it could often be unassailable. It seems that the best tool for fighting an opponent equipped with a good shield was itself another shield.

From the high guard the fighter may easily feint with the weapon and then strike down horizontally to the hip or continue on to cut low to the legs. This basic attack can be made with a simultaneous parry or forward push of the shield. As your stance changes from a back to a high guard, a sudden feint can be most effective with this attack.

Similarly, from the high guard the weapon may cross over to the left and cut at the opponent's exposed forearm or head. But this action is dangerous because it also exposes your own arm and the shield must be lowered to allow the blow to pass. However, if the shield has to drop to block a low strike this action can be very effective. Feinting this action and actually cutting back to the right can also be effective.

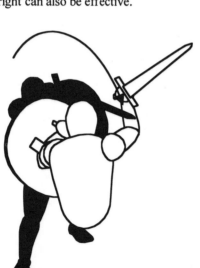

The sword arm can be a major target just as it extends to strike. If the shield and feet are not both moved in conjunction with a blow, the opponent may seize the opportunity and countercut to the arm with an action of his own.

As with a weapon, a shield is in a way an extension of the arm. It dramatically increases the ability of the forearm to block and the fist to hit. The shield is not held out flatly or kept stiffly back, but is held at a slight angle to freely intercept blows farther out. The sword & shield positions, although well defended, are offensive. The weapon is ready to strike out to cut or thrust, not just pulled in waiting to "whack" or receive blows. The weapon is raised high and not just placed to hang over the shoulder.

158

Those unfamiliar with the proper manipulation of a shield seldom seem to understand that a shield should not be wielded so that it blocks the user's field of vision. When properly handled, it hinders your sight actually very little. When this does occur it is because a fighter loses his awareness and proper sense of space. A poor fighter can even be made to use his own shield against himself in this way.

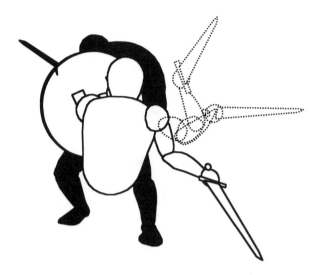

Unbanded, unrimmed shields without metal trim will cause a blade to cut into their side. This can cause an attacking blade to be momentarily trapped or stuck in the wood for a split second and in the process expose the attacker to a counterattack. Just as the attacker is trying to withdraw his weapon, he is vulnerable (especially his sword arm). Using an unrimmed shield in this manner may have even been an intentional tactic. Blocking an attack so that the opponent's blade caught in the shield's edge would allow you the chance just then to cut back at his extended arm.

If lifted too high or held aloft for too long in defense, the shield will block your line of sight, and you will lose the vital awareness of the opponent's weapon. The adversary will then either be waiting to strike when you lower the shield to see or will already be striking underneath it. He could also step in and knock the shield to create another opening to attack.

Leaving the blade out to the left with the point down in anticipation of a parry or to ward off the opponent is unwise. The position lacks strength to suddenly strike out, and reversing around to the right is slow and predictable against an experienced opponent. The forearm is also vulnerable, and the weapon can simply be beaten away at the point.

Those Medieval combat enthusiasts practicing only living-history *battle re-creation*, in which metal weapons are confined to half-speed strikes on limited body targets, will certainly not experience or understand the full range of fighting techniques or weapon use. Although highly valuable for many respected areas of historical authenticity and research, battle reenactment is *not* free-sparring. Its utility for replicating martial skills and fighting ability is seriously restrained. Much of what is presented here demands both contact-sparring and real cutting practice.

159

When facing a shield, the idea is to attack the unprotected areas of the opponent, but this is not easy. Targets must be exposed either by the adversary's own action or by provoking him to move his shield to defend another place. A shield defends well, but it does not defend everywhere. Moving to block one target from one attack can expose another to an attack from a different angle. The object, then, is to outfight an opponent's shield parries and counter sword blows in just this very way. But the act of striking can itself expose you to an instantaneous attack or an immediate follow-up attack after the adversary's parry. This is the character of the fight.

One of the most fundamental attacks: feinting high and striking low with pass forward. The attack suddenly changes its line and reverses down.

The converse of the above: feinting low and striking high with pass forward.

Passing back and striking the lower lead leg as the shield edge deflects the oncoming attack. Just as the adversary steps forward to attack, his lower legs can be vulnerable. The shield leg drops backward at the same time that the blade makes a diagonal downward cut. The edge of the shield is also shown here deflecting the adversary's crossing blow.

160

Most all the basic techniques and attack combinations can be equally employed from the high, back, or middle guards using a variety of shield types. To do so smoothly and quickly with both force and accuracy requires practice.

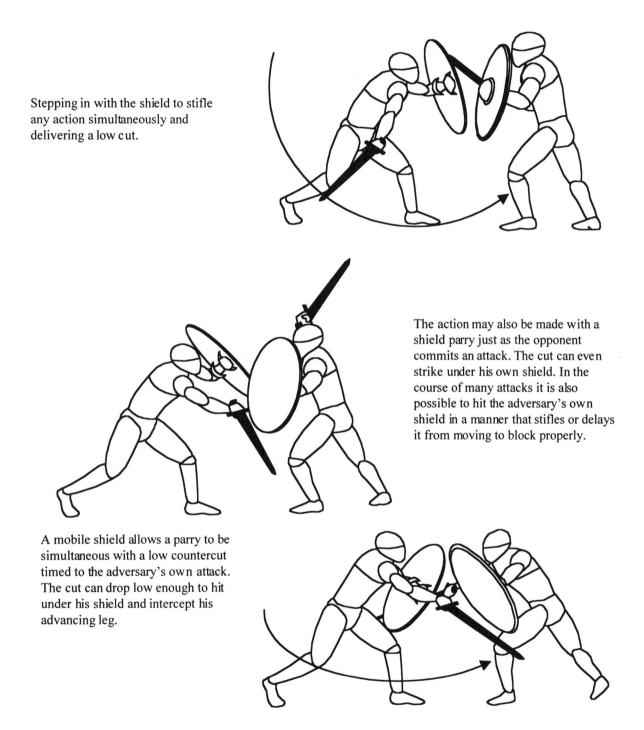

Stepping in with the shield to stifle any action simultaneously and delivering a low cut.

The action may also be made with a shield parry just as the opponent commits an attack. The cut can even strike under his own shield. In the course of many attacks it is also possible to hit the adversary's own shield in a manner that stifles or delays it from moving to block properly.

A mobile shield allows a parry to be simultaneous with a low countercut timed to the adversary's own attack. The cut can drop low enough to hit under his shield and intercept his advancing leg.

Fighting is not a matter of just stepping, parrying, and striking, but of simultaneously stepping while parrying and striking. The three actions are not separate but combined and instantaneous. Only by practicing the movements and actions in this manner until they are automatic can proper range be maintained and the adversary outfought with superior timing. It is in this way that the advantageous sword & shield combination can best be used.

A core element of fighting is to counterattack *in timing with the adversary's own action*. With any weapon, developing the essential perception to use the concept of counterfighting takes training and practice. With the sword & shield you move in to or out of the adversary's blow and countercut at him just as he exposes himself by his attack. This is accomplished with either a simultaneous block by the shield or an evading motion.

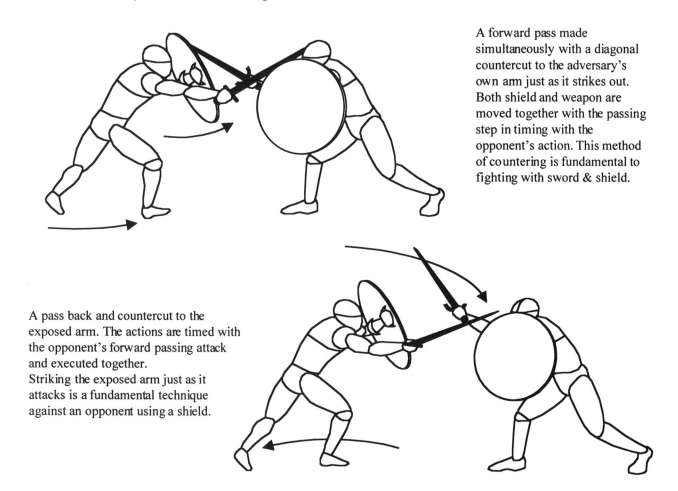

A forward pass made simultaneously with a diagonal countercut to the adversary's own arm just as it strikes out. Both shield and weapon are moved together with the passing step in timing with the opponent's action. This method of countering is fundamental to fighting with sword & shield.

A pass back and countercut to the exposed arm. The actions are timed with the opponent's forward passing attack and executed together.
Striking the exposed arm just as it attacks is a fundamental technique against an opponent using a shield.

Despite the fundamental and essential importance of timed counterattacks in most all forms of fighting, they are notoriously absent in virtually all choreographed theatrical fights and staged performance fights. Because of the very nature of such practices, realistic counterattacks are unsafe and too unpredictable for choreographed performers. Thus, they miss a significant and crucial element of the craft of swordsmanship.

From the middle guard, the shield is moved high and forward to intercept and stifle the attack while a rising left-to-right undercut is made with a forward pass. This is more difficult because it lacks power, but you can strike to the underside of the attacker's exposed arm or hit into his exposed torso. It may also recover around by following through to the left and cutting again from the right.

As with any weapon, familiarity *with* it is crucial in successfully fighting *against* it —in this case, this means practicing with another experienced shield user and someone practiced in specific Medieval shield-countering techniques. Martial artists and students of ancient weaponry who are inexperienced in this will be unable to easily handle the challenge of what a good shield presents. They just do not have any concept of its true capabilities when skillfully employed. You can't just kick at it—as well as being maneuverable, a shield has a yielding springiness and unexpected give. Trying will likely either break your foot or let the opponent chop it off.

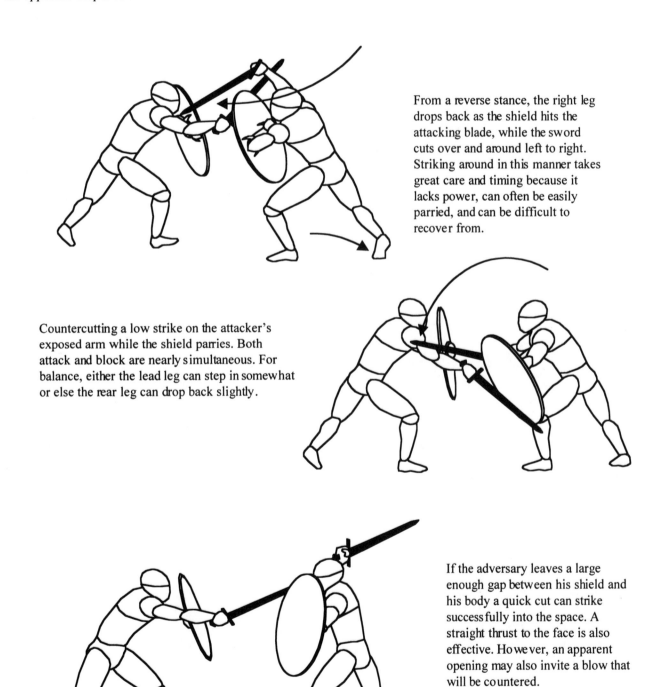

From a reverse stance, the right leg drops back as the shield hits the attacking blade, while the sword cuts over and around left to right. Striking around in this manner takes great care and timing because it lacks power, can often be easily parried, and can be difficult to recover from.

Countercutting a low strike on the attacker's exposed arm while the shield parries. Both attack and block are nearly simultaneous. For balance, either the lead leg can step in somewhat or else the rear leg can drop back slightly.

If the adversary leaves a large enough gap between his shield and his body a quick cut can strike successfully into the space. A straight thrust to the face is also effective. However, an apparent opening may also invite a blow that will be countered.

Because the Medieval sword is a straight, double-edged blade, much of its use is fairly obvious once you pick one up. But, gaining *real* proficiency and understanding of the weapon is something else entirely. This applies even more so to sword & shield use, the most common method of employing swords during the Middle Ages. There are very, very few secrets in any fighting. Much of it can be self-evident after years spent in training and free-sparring with skilled opponents. Over generations fundamental truths and subtle insights gleaned from real combat experiences were built up and then passed along. It is up to each modern student of the craft to learn them anew as best we can. As is often said, *you can know a hundred techniques, but you win with only one.*

A preemptive cut to the opponent's arm just before it is fully commited to a strike. The forearm and grip can often be vulnerable if the opponent focuses too much on defense with the shield alone. Such an attack can be executed by a forward or reverse pass or by just stepping and leaning in to the blow. It is particularly effective against stiffly standing or slow-to-move opponents.

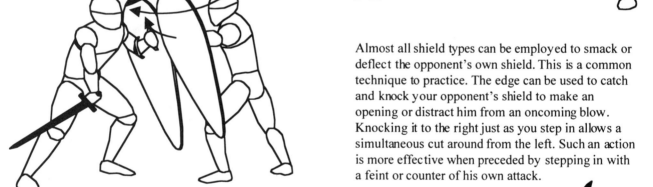

Almost all shield types can be employed to smack or deflect the opponent's own shield. This is a common technique to practice. The edge can be used to catch and knock your opponent's shield to make an opening or distract him from an oncoming blow. Knocking it to the right just as you step in allows a simultaneous cut around from the left. Such an action is more effective when preceded by stepping in with a feint or counter of his own attack.

Even with the best shield, the ankle and foot can be attacked in any stance. This target area can be made especially vulnerable after a high feint or deceptive low cut. It can also be used on those who extend their lead leg too far or who remain too stationary. A blow to this area travels down in a large arc and can have tremendous force. Even if not leading to an immediate kill, the result can incapacitate and permit a more lethal follow-up blow. Defending this target is best achieved by nimble footwork, counterthreat attacks, and proper distance to inhibit the adversary from freely striking there. However, attacking this area outright without preparatory action is dangerous because it can too easily expose the arm to a countercut.

When closing in, whether intentionally or not, don't stand shield-to-shield, face-to-face and bang away in the hope of hitting without getting struck. There are a variety of offensive and defensive movements for close fighting with a shield & sword. Care must be given to recovering to a more controllable distance and fighting stance. Pushing the shield in against the opponent to obstruct his weapon and vision before suddenly striking can be useful. The rear leg can drop back and give space for the sword to cut down low, or the lead leg can step in even closer. The sword can even be brought into position to stab under, around, or over the shield. The hilt can even be employed to strike with and the sword itself used to block. Reverse blows and false-edge cuts are very useful here as well. Hitting with the shield itself is also very effective. When close in, extra attention must also be paid to the lower legs, ankles, and feet. A simple downward blow that is impossible to block often can be made.

In close, there are a variety of techniques for whipping your sword around and striking or even cutting with the back edge to the rear of your adversary's head and neck or behind to his kidney area.

By controlling the distance and not standing face-to-face, the more mobile fighter can take advantage of his opponent's keeping his shield in too much and his feet too close together.

As a strike is made around the opponent's shield, care must be made to not allow him to do the same either high or low. This can best be achieved by attacks coordinated with a mobile shield (whatever its design or shape) and proper footwork.

Ignoring the lower legs can be fatal when the adversary has closed in. Simply pushing with the shield is insufficient. A skilled opponent can cut down and around to the thigh, knee, calf, or even ankle. The hips, waist, side, and lower back can also be struck with certain blows. High attacks may strike the neck, the back of the head, or shoulder. By maintaining agile footwork and a mobile shield, obstruction of your view can be minimized and the freedom of your sword to make cuts can be better ensured.

Thrusts should not be overlooked when the opponent has closed to shield-contact range. A stab can be made around or over and down behind his shield. What must be avoided is either a constant forward push of the shield, which the opponent can sidestep, or the habit of leaving the sword raised high where the grip or arm can be attacked.

The shield must not be left statically close to the body, but should be used to beat and block the opponent's own weapon and shield out of the way. The can be done just as he attacks, just before you attack, or just as you attack.

Reverse cuts with the back of the blade or false edge can be employed but are much less effective than is popularly believed. Concentrating on high back-edge attacks also ignores the vulnerability to the lower legs, which can be out of sight and left unguarded. Again, stepping out or off to the side can immediately open the adversary to a low cut without exposing you to attack.

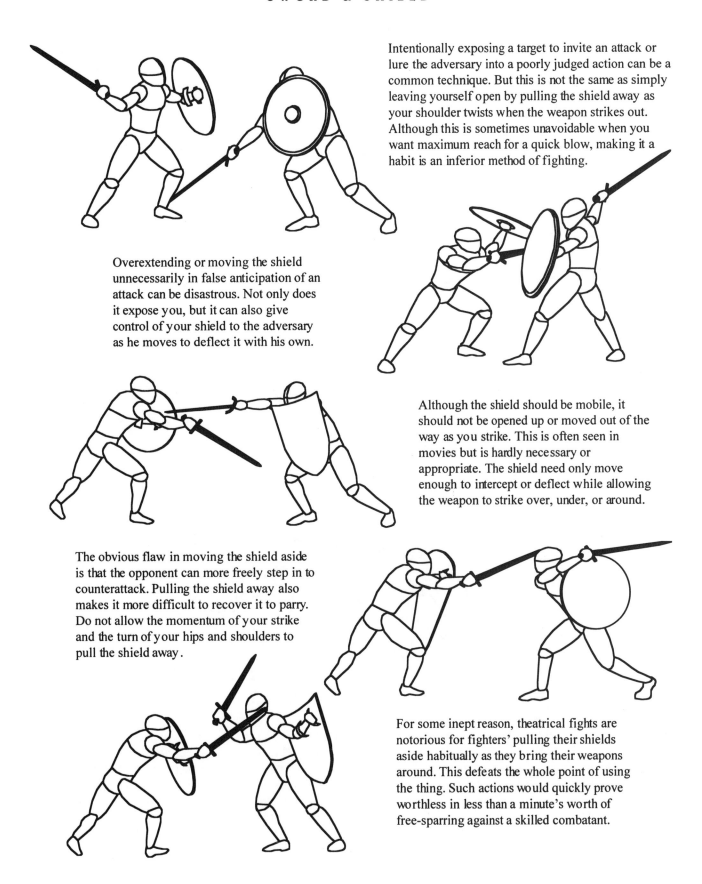

Intentionally exposing a target to invite an attack or lure the adversary into a poorly judged action can be a common technique. But this is not the same as simply leaving yourself open by pulling the shield away as your shoulder twists when the weapon strikes out. Although this is sometimes unavoidable when you want maximum reach for a quick blow, making it a habit is an inferior method of fighting.

Overextending or moving the shield unnecessarily in false anticipation of an attack can be disastrous. Not only does it expose you, but it can also give control of your shield to the adversary as he moves to deflect it with his own.

Although the shield should be mobile, it should not be opened up or moved out of the way as you strike. This is often seen in movies but is hardly necessary or appropriate. The shield need only move enough to intercept or deflect while allowing the weapon to strike over, under, or around.

The obvious flaw in moving the shield aside is that the opponent can more freely step in to counterattack. Pulling the shield away also makes it more difficult to recover it to parry. Do not allow the momentum of your strike and the turn of your hips and shoulders to pull the shield away.

For some inept reason, theatrical fights are notorious for fighters' pulling their shields aside habitually as they bring their weapons around. This defeats the whole point of using the thing. Such actions would quickly prove worthless in less than a minute's worth of free-sparring against a skilled combatant.

Again, an inflexible stance lacks agility and versatility against an opponent who understands distance, who can deceptively cut low and high, and who refuses to fight shield-to-shield. By comparison, the rigid, less mobile fighter has far fewer offensive options or defensive techniques at his disposal and can be outfought.

At the other extreme, an opponent who dances around, darts and weaves unnecessarily, and stays too low also loses effectiveness. Once he enters the range of a ready adversary or throws himself off balance, he can be defeated by basic techniques.

Range is a crucial matter in striking. Staged or choreographed fighting and performances by nature routinely follow a "safe distance" by which blows that are not properly blocked or evaded will still miss. This makes sense for theatrics, but it does not serve for methods of contact-sparring. An actual strike is delivered with the intention of connecting and hitting. Obviously this is how real weapons did damage. But even in safe modern practice and training, blows must have the proper range. In drills and exercises techniques can reasonably be controlled for power and aim, but in sparring they should not be thrown "short" or "pulled." Otherwise, proper range cannot be learned, and the vital sense of distance cannot be developed. More profoundly, a false, artificial range affects the timing and footwork of all attacks and parries.

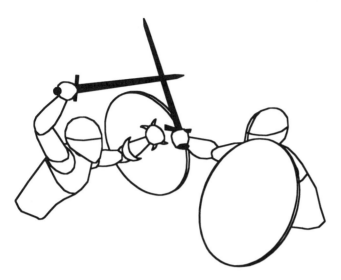

Striking with the shield is an area that is seldom practiced by enthusiasts today because of the inherent danger in the techniques. However, such actions as smashing with the umbo or face and hitting with the edge were clearly fundamental aspects of fighting with a sword & shield. Straps on shields were even arranged so that a shield could be held in ways to make this easier. The side of the shield could be used to smack or strike the opponent's hilt, hand, or forearm just as he strikes. This could be done in conjunction with a counterattack, as a form of parry, or as a preliminary action before cutting.

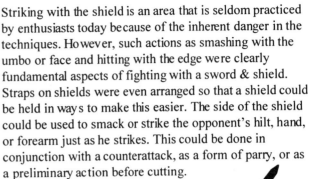

Pushing out with the bottom edge of the shield can enable you to quickly strike to the face or head just above or to the side of the adversary's own shield. Such a move can be applied as a counterstrike or intercepting stop-hit. The force of such a blow is enough to break bone, to render the adversary unconscious, or, if it lands against a helmet, to rattle him enough to let a decisive strike follow.

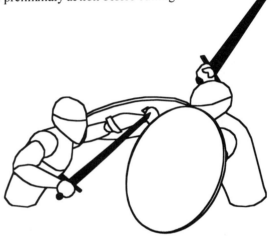

Hitting with the shield, or a "shield rush," is well suited to a forward pass of the shield leg or else quick stepping in with a sudden extension of the shield arm. The face of the shield can be slammed into an opponent's head or grip/hilt, or even against his own shield to knock it back into him.

A downward blow with the edge of the shield can also be made against the adversary's thigh or knee as he passes forward and you step in to receive him. With padded contact-sparring shields and sufficient safety equipment, shield strikes can indeed be practiced during free-sparring. Actions can be made with just enough force to cause the desired effect without doing harm to the other person. Keep in mind that a shield strike should be made so that if it misses or is deflected you do not leave yourself wide open or ill positioned.

169

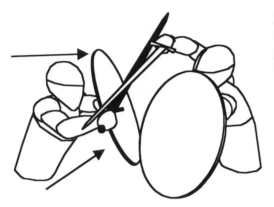

From the middle guard, the opponent can be closed with and his weapon bound up by either a push of the shield or a direct parry by the sword. It is also possible to thrust at an opponent's face if he does not raise his shield.

From this position your shield can instantly push in, continuing to stifle your opponent's weapon and preventing him from cutting around, down, or over. As this happens, your own blade can slip behind his shield or even strike all the way back down to his shin.

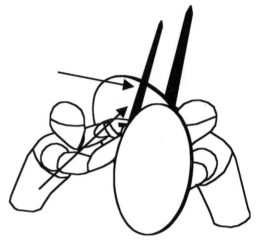

One of the most common techniques is to step in as the opponent cuts low or feints a high-low strike. Your shield closes and lowers just before he is close enough to connect. Your weapon comes in to strike at his arm, exposed shoulder, or head. Your shield can strike to the left to continue deflecting his weapon or hit to the right and push open his shield.

Although facing a left-handed shield user can be unfamiliar and disconcerting, do not overreact. The same fundamentals of fighting still apply. Because the opponent will strike from your right and defend better to your left, you can wait for his arm to be exposed and also strike to his left where his weapon does not defend as well. With a little practice, left-handed opponents will present no greater obstacle than right-handed ones.

170

Shields should be used offensively in sparring whenever possible (what is now known as a *shield strike* or a *shield rush*), though great care should be taken in including this as an allowable condition today. Well-padded contact-sparring shields offer one means of doing this, as do some wooden ones when full plate armor is worn.

Replica shield designs for training or sparring should not be so light as to allow for oversized, historically unrealistic ones. Second, they cannot be made of too thick or too heavy a material or they will be unsafe. A maximum 1/4-inch plywood is suggested. This should be covered in 1/2 inch of *firm* foam, *front and back,* and then with foam on the edges as well.

The shield & sword has another aspect of how it can be employed. It can be used to successfully attack by closing in with a slamming push, placing the blade behind the opponent's shield, and slicing across his face, neck, arms, or chest. This kind of hit-and-draw technique can be employed in a number of ways. A running charge or a passing step can be used to engage, followed by a side step or reverse pass to recover.

The kite shield has a number of advantages. Depending on the strap arrangement and grip, it can be thrown out so that its bottom end can strike. This can be thrown against the opponent's thigh, knee, or shin or at the opponent's shield to beat or knock it.

The historical method of employing shields and swords described here stands in stark contrast to the typical manner of static shield use witnessed in a number of popular Medieval role-playing organizations and historical re-creation groups. In an effort to reproduce "knightly tournament" fighting, numerous groups have contrived rules with restricted target areas to not only favor extralarge shields and shorter swords, but also to encourage severely restrained footwork and cutting angles. Such forms of idiosyncratic, stylistic bashing are invariably only a limited and distorted version of what Medieval shield & sword fighting actually was and can be. Those practitioners who spar under limited rules using toe-to-toe styles of fighting without any lower-leg hits will have an artificial and misunderstood sense of shield use and coordinated weapon strikes (this is addressed in detail in the appendixes). Similarly, experience that is limited to semi-contact practice with blunt weapons unable to make realistic hits can also create misleading impressions.

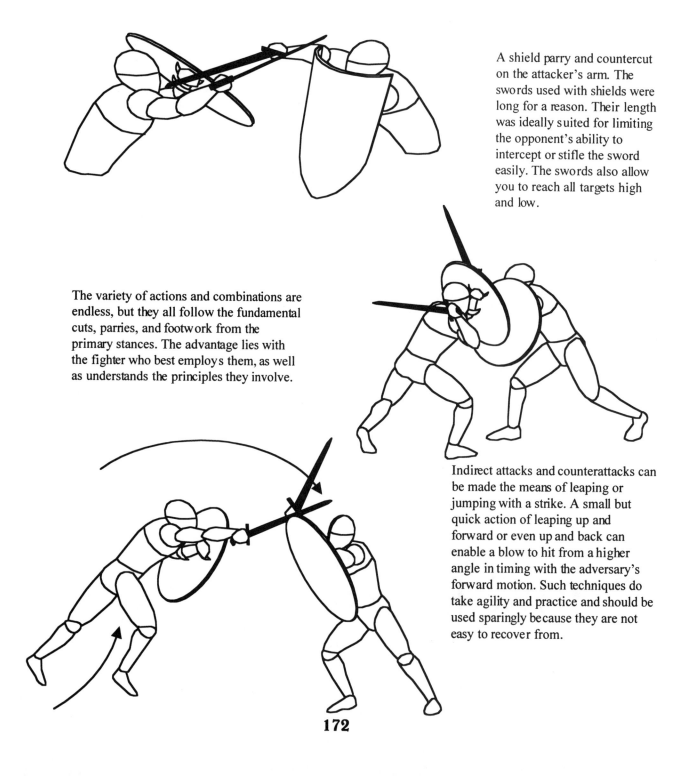

A shield parry and countercut on the attacker's arm. The swords used with shields were long for a reason. Their length was ideally suited for limiting the opponent's ability to intercept or stifle the sword easily. The swords also allow you to reach all targets high and low.

The variety of actions and combinations are endless, but they all follow the fundamental cuts, parries, and footwork from the primary stances. The advantage lies with the fighter who best employs them, as well as understands the principles they involve.

Indirect attacks and counterattacks can be made the means of leaping or jumping with a strike. A small but quick action of leaping up and forward or even up and back can enable a blow to hit from a higher angle in timing with the adversary's forward motion. Such techniques do take agility and practice and should be used sparingly because they are not easy to recover from.

Because single attacks rarely succeed, attacks should be delivered in combination. After any attack, parry, or other technique, either you or the opponent may continue to press and close. The ability to follow up with a shield hit or quickly cut both low and high can be indispensable. Seek to catch the opponent in an awkward transitional position between guarding and striking.

There are also several ways of employing the sword's cross-guard in hooking the opponent's shield and pulling it open.

Each fighter may repeatedly rain blows upon his adversary as they both manage to parry. The fighter who can more effectively outtime and outrange his adversary with steps and feints and efficient shield work will triumph.

Remember that real Medieval swords, as with so many other Medieval arms, were sturdy weapons with thick, flexible blades slanting to fine edges. They were not crude or flimsy. They were durable steel weapons capable of withstanding the blows of other finely tempered blades. They were designed with the understanding in mind that armor of many types was prevalent and had to be defeated. The relationship of arms to armor is an ancient one that cannot be discounted or ignored. European armors in particular were tough and highly sophisticated. Medieval weaponry was practiced with almost constant regard to the armor (typically mail) that would be encountered. Not all fighting in the Middle Ages revolved directly around metal armor, and its use is by no means exclusive to temperate regions or northern climes. Personal defense for Medieval warriors was certainly not based on wearing armor alone, but those who could afford metal armor used it. Naturally, the methods and techniques of the Medieval sword & shield work even better against *unarmored* opponents. Many people training in martial arts weaponry today do not have a realistic appreciation for the way in which armor can fundamentally alter the nature of fighting or even the usefulness of a particular weapon. There are many fighting arts that developed in tropical or subtropical regions or that were based on farming tools that never had to take much armor into account in either weapon design or application.

The much smaller, more triangular version of the "heater" shield was used something like a footman's buckler. But by having arm straps it was suited to mounted combat as well. Smaller shields allow cuts and thrusts to be delivered from all around them without losing protection. They can be held out for defense at the same time attacks are thrown out above or below them. Such small shields were better suited to fighting in plate armor and also allowed knights to get in closer to their adversaries to stab at them. Eventually, plate armor became tough enough that a shield could be discarded in favor of using both hands on a longer sword that could make stronger blows yet still allow the second hand to reach out to grapple.

The small heater is used with the same basic actions as its larger brother, but the actions resemble those of the buckler.

Small heaters were popular with mounted fighters and were easy to hang from the shoulder or belt when two hands were required on a weapon. Small heaters at first encountered the older shields still being used, but eventually were themselves more numerous.

With a small, hand-held shield, a strong grip is needed to parry the hard blows of a sword. Thrusts can be parried with a sweeping motion using the face of the shield. Cuts can be parried by opposing with the edge. Because of its size, this shield is quick and makes leading with either leg forward possible, thereby making the shield very versatile. But its size is also its weakness as it offers less protection, and without practice it is easy to misparry and be struck on the arm. The Medieval use of the small buckler is a much underrated, though very effective, means of sword combat. Although its use in the Middle Ages differed from that of the Renaissance it did not do so significantly, and so its study will be left outside of the scope of this work. Primarily it was differences between the swords used that distinguished the use of the Medieval buckler from the Renaissance method.

There are ancient martial traditions of India and Indonesia that are still practiced today using quite similar sword & buckler combinations. Combatants use both blunt steel and wooden weapons, wear protection on their shins and forearms, and even employ footwork not dissimilar to that of Renaissance methods. Such similarities in other arts further emphasize for Medieval combat enthusiasts the true nature of historical shield use.

No type of sword or Medieval or Renaissance weapon (excluding projectiles) offers superiority in itself. If this were not so, there would not have been such a great variety of swords and weapons.

No examination of the general techniques of the sword & shield would be complete without some reference to the range of other weapon combinations it faced, specifically the axe and shield, spear and shield, and long-axe. They can be handled with surprising agility and speed and their blow can have tremendous power. They could easily cut through mail and helmets and in two hands even split unrimmed shields. For speed, their blades were fairly thin and slender yet thickened at the edge to improve their devastating blow. Some even had specially hardened edges.

Although they were used essentially to make chopping blows, axes were capable of a variety of techniques. Medieval war axes were quite versatile. They could be used to hook, trap, bind, and disarm, and some could even stab. Unlike our modern tree-chopping versions, war axes were quite light and agile, weighing on average 2 1/2 pounds.

One of the major elements of fighting an axe is that the weapon has reach not just in distance but in depth. A blow can often reach behind a parry or around a shield to connect.

Compared with swords, however, axes have far less striking area, are not easy to parry with, and cannot slice or thrust. But, then again, several types could also be thrown quite effectively. There were short-handled horsemen's axes and long-handled footmen's axes. Many later axes also had backs or tips with spikes or hammer ends, making them even deadlier on backswings and hooking moves.

The swing of an axe blow has great inertia, and this can be used to bring the weapon around again should it miss or the initial strike only be a feint.

As with a sword, the axe is used in combination with coordinated shield actions. Here the shield is thrown out with the edge pushing the opponent's shield back and opening a line of attack to the leg. The push of the shield and the motion of the axe are executed in a quick "one, two" movement.

With a sword & shield there are particular techniques and moves for fighting against an axe. Presented here are only a few of the more basic techniques.

The axe was among the most common weapons on the Medieval battlefield. It was the principal weapon of the Anglo-Saxons and a favorite of the Vikings. The Norse were so fond of their *skeggøx* ("bearded") and *breidøx* (broad) battle-axes that they named them as they did their swords. The French people even gained their name from the *francisca,* the feared weapon of the Franks. No Medieval warrior would have been considered skilled without understanding the virtues of the axe whether gripped in two hands or used with a shield.

Just as with fighting a sword & shield, the axe can be countercut as the opponent's arm is exposed in attacking. The sword's greater maneuverability and agility offer a distinct advantage over the axe in this regard.

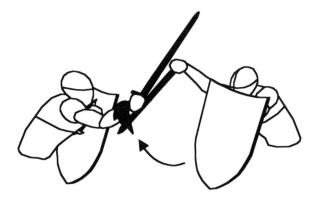

The axe does have its own unique techniques and can be used to hook the arm. This can be done with an upward intercepting motion or, after the shield has parried an attack, with a sideways downward one.

One of the more basic techniques is to hook the adversary's shield momentarily and draw it down and forward. As his shield is pulled, the opponent's reaction is to resist and not to unhook it to attack with his own weapon. This can be followed up with a quick deflecting smack of your own shield to move it off as the axe then strikes a blow. The pull can also suddenly be let off, and as his shield snaps back, a low strike may be made to the legs.

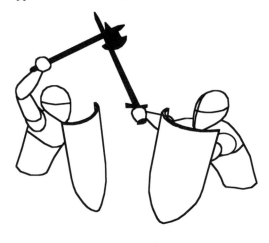

Even though the axe is not as practical in some ways as a sword, it can still be useful in more ways than just as a chopping weapon. The grip could be shortened by choking up on the shaft and shortening the range. Used close-in, the blade could simply be jammed or shoved into the opponent's face or neck.

The axe's ability to hook is most useful in catching swords in a parry-like action. This can also be employed as a trapping bind after closing in. However, hooking like this works both ways: the sword can catch onto the axe blade and then more quickly disengage to strike elsewhere.

Fighting with an axe and shield was widespread, but by the later Middle Ages swords had increased in number until they were quite common among warriors of all classes and ranks. Axes had originally been weapons primarily of the common warrior, but were to gain popularity with knights. Eventually they fell out of common use as warfare gave way to mass employment of various pole-arms and use of armor began to diminish. Far more could be said of the use of the axe and shield or of the single long-axe, but this will suffice.

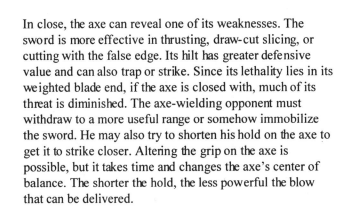

Even if the axe blow misses or falls past a target, the blade head can be used to hook and pull the leg. If not causing a serious wound in itself, it can allow for a more effective follow-up action.

In close, the axe can reveal one of its weaknesses. The sword is more effective in thrusting, draw-cut slicing, or cutting with the false edge. Its hilt has greater defensive value and can also trap or strike. Since its lethality lies in its weighted blade end, if the axe is closed with, much of its threat is diminished. The axe-wielding opponent must withdraw to a more useful range or somehow immobilize the sword. He may also try to shorten his hold on the axe to get it to strike closer. Altering the grip on the axe is possible, but it takes time and changes the axe's center of balance. The shorter the hold, the less powerful the blow that can be delivered.

A long-axe in two hands can be a formidable weapon that could even cut deep into the face of a shield and the arm behind it. Its reach is considerable, as is its speed, but it lacks versatility and defense. A proper combination of shield blocking and sword striking can defeat it. In close it is also vulnerable. In the Norse tale, *Njal's Saga*, one man is described as slapping a descending axe blow with his free hand while striking with his sword in the other.

Although this is certainly not an examination of all Medieval weaponry, some brief mention must be made of those swords and shields regularly encountered. But we must avoid making too many generalities about the use of Medieval weaponry: a whole book could be written on the use of weapons other than the sword. There was a wide range of other weapon combinations that might be employed together by Medieval warriors, including spear and axe, dagger and axe, or axe and mace.

The war hammer (known by a variety of names) functions similarly to the axe. However, it was a secondary weapon. Unlike axes, war hammers were devised primarily to fight plate armor and existed in both single- and two-hand versions from about the early or mid-1200s. Their blows could make horrendous injuries and were effective in crushing and puncturing plate. Many were all metal; others were wood with metal hands. The longer two-handed form, known as a *pole-axe* ("poll" axe), was later a weapon of great popularity and effectiveness. (Although it was a significant weapon of the later Middle Ages and early Renaissance, I have omitted it because it is outside my area of personal study.)

The mace, on the other hand, was an ancient weapon based on the simple club that found renewed value against heavy armors. Many styles were in use, often with studded or spiked heads. It was also the secondary tournament weapon for knights. Many accounts describe the ferocious power of hammers and maces crushing shields and breaking bones and denting and crushing armor. Because of their weighted ends, they were each wielded somewhat differently than swords. Again, the study of these weapons lies outside the focus of this book.

Another weapon encountered was the fearsome flail. The flail was much less common in the later Middle Ages. It was adapted from agricultural tools, but it had tremendous power. It was used to bash and tear armor and break bones with its tremendous concussive force. As a flexible weapon, it was quite fast and agile. Its weighted metal end (often with small spikes) could deliver great blows through the twirl of its whiplike chain. A variety of different sizes of flails were devised for both foot and mounted combat. Some had cylindrical weights or round balls and others just loose chains.

The flail was effective against plate armor as well as more lightly armored fighters. Powerful blows can be made with a deceptive whirling motion or just a quick whipping action. It has the unique capacity to strike around, over, and behind shields and attempts to block. This can make fighting them difficult. Although it also has the capacity to wrap around a blade, this does not happen as much as is often assumed. A chain is fairly heavy and not nearly as flexible as rope. It functions differently and a thin steel sword blade can usually slip off or pull out when the chain wraps it. The flail itself can more easily become trapped than can the sword.

The flail is very much an offensive weapon and lacks versatility. If its swing can be outtimed and its range interrupted, its threat can be neutralized. Once in close its usefulness diminishes considerably. A flail can't be just swung around; it takes practice to become adept with it and not leave yourself vulnerable as you attack. Students today can train with a variety of safe versions devised from materials ranging from plastic garden chain and rubber balls to foam-covered rope and padded tennis balls. There are a few quality replica flails available and many that are terribly inaccurate. Great care should be taken when practicing with any modern reproduction. If handled improperly, it can injure the user by bouncing off or swinging around to strike him.

CHAPTER TEN

The Long-Sword

THE LONG-SWORD

Presented here as a guide for modern students are the general concepts and fundamental techniques of the long-sword (both obvious and subtle) distilled from the historical manuals, as well as derived from years of hands-on research and personal study with actual weapons. This is intended simply as an introductory outline of the nature of the long-sword and its handling. No one historical master's style is really available to us whole or entirely complete. It is thus somewhat foolish for modern practitioners to try to "re-create" a fraction of a method interpreted from their texts (which means different readers will also argue interpretation instead of training to acquire genuine skill and understanding). Rather than risk missing the big picture, we can instead try to synthesize historical skills and ideas into a simple and coherent overview to aid those training in the historical art to apply as appropriate in their own weapon sparring.

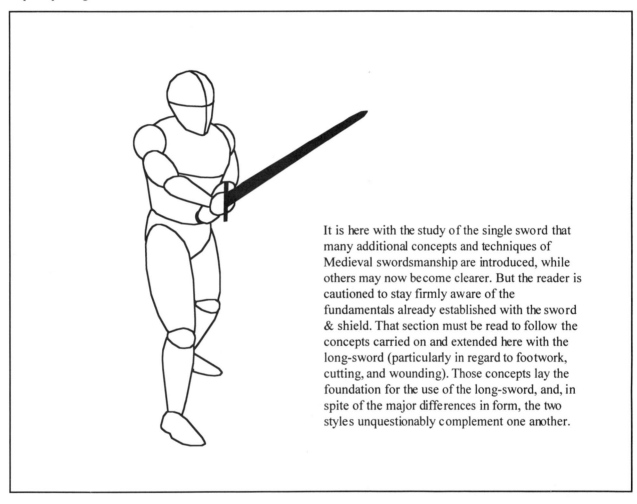

It is here with the study of the single sword that many additional concepts and techniques of Medieval swordsmanship are introduced, while others may now become clearer. But the reader is cautioned to stay firmly aware of the fundamentals already established with the sword & shield. That section must be read to follow the concepts carried on and extended here with the long-sword (particularly in regard to footwork, cutting, and wounding). Those concepts lay the foundation for the use of the long-sword, and, in spite of the major differences in form, the two styles unquestionably complement one another.

Historical terminology in any area of research is often subject to revision. The descriptions of key techniques and the terms used here are not definitively those of all Medieval long-swords or great-swords. They represent only the fundamental stances, attacks, parries, and concepts usable by a single, long, Medieval sword. Through both reference and deference to surviving German and Italian works, we can come to the understanding that, for centuries, sophisticated and effective methods had been well worked out and systematically taught. They offer us the basics for a highly developed system of employing various types of Medieval long-swords. Though not nearly as much material from English, Spanish, French, Dutch, or other regional sources on long-swords survive, that which we do have offers a strong foundation for understanding the nature of this form of Medieval swordsmanship. But exclusive reliance on modern interpretation of historical German and Italian manuals is not enough, and it is no great difficulty to extrapolate further mechanics as a result of committed training with replica swords and intensive mock fighting. The many reasons for this will become clearer as the chapter unfolds.

The Medieval European long-sword is a familiar and ubiquitous weapon, but one surrounded by a great deal of myth and misconception. It is seen in countless adventure films and fantasy settings such as *Highlander, Braveheart,* and *Conan.* Although not often realized, the use of a longer blade gripped in two hands was actually not all that common during the Medieval period. Fighting sword & shield (with a shorter, single-hand blade) was by far the norm. A long-sword style only really became practicable during the 1300s and 1400s when reinforced mail allowed for the discarding of a shield and full, articulated plate armor later became common for foot combat. There are only sporadic accounts of such weapons being employed prior to this.

A variety of types fit the family of Medieval "long-swords." Although they cover the war-sword and great-sword of 1200–1350, the spadone, the *Bidenhänder* of 1300–1400, and bastard-sword of 1400–1500, each has its own subtle characteristics. All are wielded and handled in the same general manner but with particular differences among them, depending on blade length, shape, and handle/grip configuration.

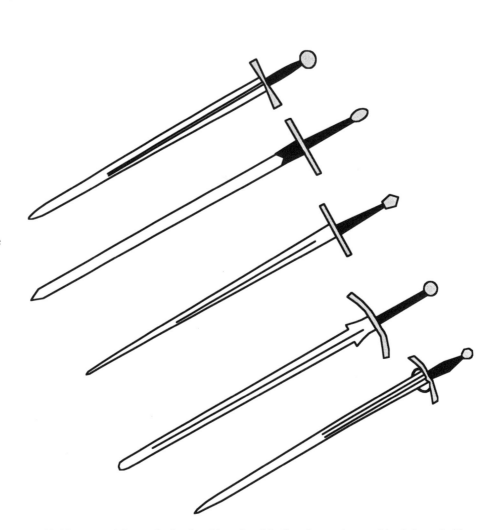

Though it can be argued that the shield & sword forms the basis of learning Medieval swordsmanship, it is probably true that it is the techniques of the single long-sword that provides a better foundation for concepts and principles. Using a shield gives a certain sense of "cocking the weapon back into a firing position," while waiting for an opportunity to strike; just being behind a shield produces something of a "guarding attitude." One readies to receive a blow or push and knock forward (which is also somewhat true when using a weapon in each hand). By contrast, when both the hands hold a sword, the feel is more symmetrical. Blocking and attacking become more intertwined because the user must focus on both. Doing so naturally leads to both countercutting techniques and an evasive style. This does not argue that any method or form is better or "superior" to any other. Each relies on its own physical mechanics and merits.

The various concepts and principles previously covered have direct bearing upon the study of the long-sword, but to avoid redundancy they will not be repeated verbatim in this section. When studying the long-sword, constant reference needs to be made back to the fundamentals of shield & sword, specifically with regard to the basic essentials of posture, stepping, passing, cutting, and parrying.

When swung with both hands long-swords are capable of delivering tremendous and devastating wounds. Used in this manner they have a well-rounded and symmetrical offense and defense. The lighter blades can make use of numerous thrusts and maneuvers, allowing the second hand to be employed in helping guide the weapon or in grabbing the adversary.

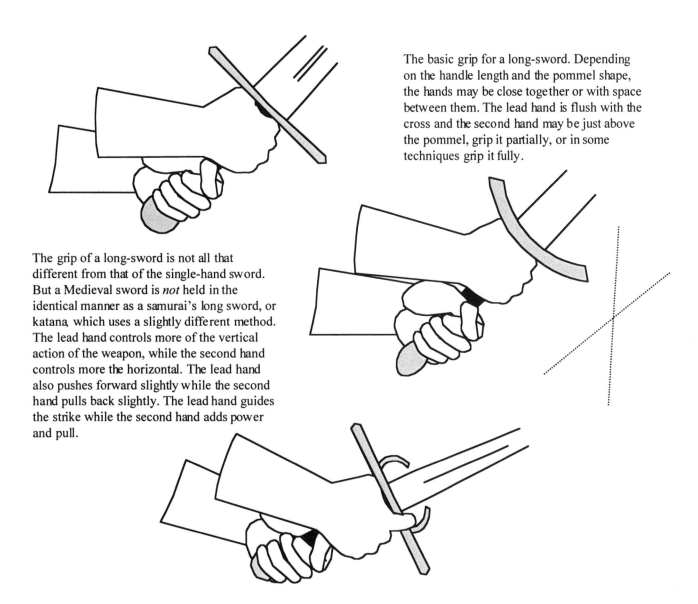

The basic grip for a long-sword. Depending on the handle length and the pommel shape, the hands may be close together or with space between them. The lead hand is flush with the cross and the second hand may be just above the pommel, grip it partially, or in some techniques grip it fully.

The grip of a long-sword is not all that different from that of the single-hand sword. But a Medieval sword is *not* held in the identical manner as a samurai's long sword, or katana, which uses a slightly different method. The lead hand controls more of the vertical action of the weapon, while the second hand controls more the horizontal. The lead hand also pushes forward slightly while the second hand pulls back slightly. The lead hand guides the strike while the second hand adds power and pull.

During the mid- to late 1400s swords of all lengths began to have guards with various protective rings and bars on their hilts. The addition of these extra bars and guards was a result of a new method of gripping, which came into use as a result of the need for increased thrusting attacks. As mentioned previously, improved point control for stabbing into armor gaps was gained by wrapping the index finger around the cross-guard. Gripping in this manner required more protection for the exposed fingers and necessitated the development of the compound or close-hilt. The close-hilt offered superb hand protection and was used on many bastard-swords, even Renaissance two-handers. Later, improved close-hilts became the swept-hilt found on most Renaissance swords. Despite changing to meet the need for bashing and stabbing at plate armor, a sword still needed to be able to cut effectively at lightly armored opponents. But improved armor also meant that a shield for defense was not quite as mandatory for a knight or man-at-arms. This freed the second hand for the necessity of using a longer blade (or for grabbing at the opponent). Using both hands on a weapon allowed for a stronger blow against more heavily armored combatants.

When gripped, a bastard-sword's "waisted" shape, with its wider center tapering toward the pommel, allows better control however held. It can also be used with the technique of "pommeling," in which its rounded or plum-shaped pommel is partially held in the palm of the second hand. This allows for powerful thrusts into heavy armors.

Interestingly, a waisted grip allows the hand to hold it not only above and below the half-grip, but also directly in the middle at its widened belt. This gives a secure and comfortable hold in the palm, while also extending the weapon's reach. A waisted grip also makes "slipping" easier to do.

In many stances (such as the left back and hanging guards) the grip needs to remain supple, not tight, because the second hand often must loosen and open up to allow the wrist to properly bend or the hand to hold on to the pommel. With longer pommels (such as on many bastard-swords and the spadone, this is less of a problem because the second hand can more easily grip them in this way). This is something many students have difficulty with and is not easy to describe in words and pictures alone. Understanding of it comes with practice.

Many people expect that the average Medieval long-sword should have a handle 14, 16, or even 18 inches long. Some enthusiasts are used to using extralong grips with their sticks and foam swords. Novices sometimes feel that the wider space between their hands allows them to gain better leverage and torque. They also think it gives them a reach advantage over those with shorter grips. Many stage-combat blades are also intentionally given extralong handles to allow their weight to be maneuvered around in wide, flashy actions. However, all this ignores the actual historical weapons whose own handles are only 8, 9, or 10 inches long. Certainly, true two-handed swords of the Renaissance had huge handles of 16 or 18 inches to match their huge blades, but Medieval war-swords, bastard-swords, spadones, etc., only had handles of roughly 8 to 10 inches (not counting pommels). Great-swords themselves even had handles that ranged from only 9 to 15 inches. A long-sword had a handle optimally designed for maneuvering its blade around its center of balance to effectively wound an opponent. We know this from examining the actual weapons, from the illustrations in historical manuals, and from modern practice with accurate replicas. Practicing to hit with a stick or swinging blunt props against one another is not the same as using a sword to cut and slice.

A long-sword's handle length was not excessive. It was ideal for employing two hands to cut strongly and quickly. An extralong handle can actually be a hindrance. It gets in the way of the forearm of the leading hand and prevents quick rotation of the blade on many cuts and parries.

184

This a general look at the fundamentals of the Medieval long-sword, and by no means does it offer an extensive examination of all concepts and techniques presented in the many historical manuals. Although most of the German and Italian terms from the early 1300s to early 1500s apply more to the use of great-swords, their basic concepts are those derived from most, if not all, Medieval long-swords or war-swords. The Germans masters had a rich store of terminology to describe the techniques, actions, and concepts of their fighting systems. *Kunst des Fechtens*, the German art of fighting, consisted primarily of the arts of the *Langenschwert,* or long-sword, the *Messer* (a sort of "two-handed falchion"), and *Ringenkunst* (wrestling). Unarmored combat was known as *Blossfechten*. Combat in plate armor was known as *Harnischfechten* (harness fighting). Fighting on foot was also distinguished from *Rossfechten* (mounted combat).

As clarified previously there is a significant but subtle difference between the handling and action of wider, flatter, parallel-edged Medieval swords (in this case, war-swords and great-swords) and the narrower, thicker, tapering kinds (like many bastard-swords). The later, more rigid, diamond- or hexagonal-shaped blade (such as the Italian spadone) is designed for fighting plate armor, and although it does not cut as strongly as the earlier type, it can thrust superbly and is noticeably more agile in the transition from offense to defense. Each type does follow the same basic mechanics of use, and each type is shown used in Italian and German manuals. In plate armor fighting, the tapered and sharply pointed spadone blade was a versatile weapon that could be used like a short staff, like a club or spear, and to hook and trap with its guard.

The difference between these two blade forms is significant and once more underscores the distinction between the manner of using a Japanese katana and a long Medieval sword. The tapering Medieval sword form has a different center of balance and is often a lighter blade. Its point of percussion is located farther down the blade, and its slender, sharp point is capable of making quick, accurate, and strong thrusts. The earlier form can make a somewhat greater variety of strikes and delivers more effective cuts overall. But the later is more agile and easier to guard and parry with. It can also more easily employ its versatile hilt in binding, trapping, and striking. Its proper techniques and style of use are rarely depicted with any accuracy in movies and television fights.

STANCES, GUARDS, AND POSTURES

The brutal style of the Medieval long-sword is one of power and practical efficiency, but one with an artistry all its own. Methodical and practical methods for skillfully using the weapon were practiced for centuries and have survived for us in some of the manuals from the era. Indeed, an entire book could be written alone on the use of European war-swords, great-swords, and two-handers.

Historical names for the long-sword's major stances or guards and their many variations are somewhat convoluted. Not all the masters taught set stances or guards either, just obvious positions for striking. Rather than using all the numerous German, Italian, or Old English terms, we will instead resort when possible to modern approximations descriptive of their intent and general use. For purposes here, rather than a separate in-depth dissertation or analysis of the manuals, this approach will be sufficient for presenting their concepts and underlying mechanics. In the future, more reliable scholarship currently under way by numerous parties will surely provide additional clarification and understanding. The reader is strongly encouraged to research further. There is still tremendous knowledge awaiting those pursuing historical fencing today.

The Five Primary Positions

Middle guard

High guard

Low guard

Hanging guard

Back guard

For the Medieval long-sword there essentially are 14 recognizable and legitimate fighting postures overall (*Leger* or position in German). They are all guards or "wards" from which to launch an attack or parry. Of these, five can be considered "primary" guards, and nine can be considered "secondary" guards or transitional stances. The primary guards are major stances with the greatest application and the most frequent employment. Many of the German masters recognized only the first four of these as having the greatest utility. The secondary ones are parry positions used either for recovery to another guard or for a particular attack or parry.

There appears to have been considerable variety in the stances among the various masters and schools as well as the names they gave them. But whether the arms are slightly extended or slightly pulled back, the hilt or point held higher or lower, they all followed the same basic physical mechanics optimized for cutting and parrying with the weapon from these positions.

Application of the various stances in cutting and parrying will be covered later. Making clear and concise sense of the cuts, thrusts, and parries that each stance can perform to a novice student while also giving them historical reference to experienced scholars is challenging. Occasionally, interpretation of material described in historical texts must defer to the practical insights resulting from physically handling the weapons with other skilled practitioners. At their core the stances for the long-sword are simply ideal positions from which to attack and defend. They are those postures that, because of the nature of the weapon and the physical mechanics of the human body, are best suited to employing the techniques of the weapon. They are better to assume than being in "no stance" or in some arbitrary position and hoping it makes sense or isn't self-defeating.

The essential positioning for each stance is the same with the obvious movement of the arms, the location of the sword's hilt and point, and any shift of the leading leg. Each stance conveys its own attitude and has both a tactical and technical context for employing moves and actions. In some stances the degree of bend in the knees and at the waist can slightly alter to accommodate this change in positioning. The body may lean forward more, or the arrangement of the feet may be a step closer together or a step farther apart.

Of the five *primary* stances all but the back guard can lead with either the right or left leg forward. For a right-handed swordsman, a right leg stance can be called a *forward* stance; a left-leg lead would then be a *back* (or reverse) stance. The opposite applies for a left-handed swordsman. The dual nature of these five guards is another reason of their importance.

Of the five primary guards, the low, middle, and high are *center* stances in that the weapon is held in the center. They have no "left" or "right" positions and are equally viable leading with either leg. The three *center* guards, low, middle, and high, allow you to freely move to any of the others, as well as make virtually any cut, parry, or thrust. The hanging guard also does, but to a slightly lesser degree.

The nine secondary guards are not fighting postures in the same sense as the major five for engaging an opponent. Their positions do not lend themselves to easily delivering the major cuts or making the major parries as easily. Instead, they are more transitional positions from which to either make a parry or pass through on the recovery to another parry or a cut. They are not as well rounded, symmetrical, or nearly as versatile. They are much more specific and particular in their application and this is their very value.

The hanging guard, back guard, close guard, and inside guard each have right and left positions. However, they are not identical in their utility, and there are several differences between the left and right stances of each. A right-handed swordsman can employ right stances better than left, and the opposite is true for a left-handed swordsman. Although techniques must be practiced to be effective with either leg forward, those stances from the left are less versatile for a right-hander (and vice versa) because of the physical mechanics involved. This will become clearer later on.

Although the Medieval masters worked out numerous guards and fighting postures best suited to handing the weapon in offense or defense, there is certainly nothing to compel a swordsmen to use every one. By virtue of their build and natural gifts, different swordsmen may find more or fewer necessary than another with different personal attributes. In the later English systems of the cut-and-thrust sword in the 1500s, the hanging guard was sometimes known as the *guardant ward*, the high as *open ward*, the middle as *close ward*, and the low as the *variable ward*.

As the basis of fighting, what the various postures really say about the use of the long-sword in Europe during the Middle Ages is that it was vigorous and evolving and by no means uniform or primitive. Many styles and many schools in different kingdoms and regions were constantly developing, experimenting, refining, and improving as the weapons and armor changed over the generations.

188

The middle posture of the long-sword is equivalent to the middle guard of the sword & shield, but with the single sword is far more versatile and powerful. It was called *Pflug* or (plow) in the German schools for its resemblance to the position of plowing behind a yoke. The Italians called it *corona* (crown) since it was the foundation of all other stances, and as such offered key guidance. As with all stances, the position should be relaxed and flexible, not stiff or fixed. The feet should remain nimble, and the knees should be slightly bent. The back must be relatively straight and not leaning too far forward, and the shoulders should also not be tense. The arms extend out from the body with some bend in the elbows. The weapon is held in the center at a 45-degree position aimed approximately at the opponent's throat or face (regardless of his height). It must not be held either stiffly or wobbly. The hilt should point out from the lower abdomen, not from the stomach or the groin. The elbows should be slightly bent and neither touching against the body nor pointing outward too far. In this way there is freedom of movement to parry or thrust. The grip must be firm yet relaxed. If the hands hold on too tightly the shoulders will actually soon tense up. The middle stance offers the greatest number of possible parries but can easily make almost all cuts and transitions to other stances. By its nature, it is neutral, threatening, and guarding equally. The middle guard is the most important and the most natural posture.

Right leg leading

Right leg leading

Left leg leading

Left leg leading

Right leg leading

Right leg
leading

The high guard is also equivalent to the high stance of the sword & shield, but with the single sword is again much more versatile and powerful. The Italians called the high stance a *hawke* guard (*posta de falcone*), and to the English it was known as the *haukse bill* (as if "striking down like a bird of prey"). German schools usually referred to it as *vom Dach* (from the roof) or even *Oberhut* (upper guard). The weapon is held above the head at a 45-degree angle. This allows for the shoulders and arms to pull it down to strike with maximum force and speed. The pommel should be just above the forehead and be visible in your peripheral vision. The blade should not tilt back horizontally or be held down behind the head (this is reserved for cutting motion not stationary readying). Leading with either leg, the high stance can make powerful and quick cuts vertically or diagonally as well as suddenly swooping down to strike horizontally or low. Although it somewhat exposes the body to attack (or invites it in to be countered) it is the most threatening stance and one that offers no parry. It can be particularly effective on the counterattack with a reverse pass. Cuts from the high position can recover around and return back or drop to any of the other stances.

Right leg
leading

Left leg
leading

Right leg
leading

Left leg
leading

In the German schools the low guard was called *Alber* (the fool's guard, because apparently it was thought foolish to rely only on defense). Depending on placement of the blade, this low position may have been known to the Italians as a *boar's tooth* guard (in the sense of thrusting up) or the *porta ferrea,* ("iron door," in the sense of "shutting the enemy out," perhaps?). German schools also sometimes called it *Eiserne Pforte* (iron gate*)*. The low guard is itself a parry position for strikes to the lower legs and thighs. The low guard does have substantial value in inviting attacks that can be countered with a thrust, rising cut, or shift to a hanging guard. As well as conveying a lure to the enemy, it also allows the arms to rest.

Right leg leading.

The low guard is clearly a more defensive posture because its immediate threat is in either a straight rising thrust or in its potential to lift and cut around with great force. The large arc that a cut from the low position travels can make it powerful despite the space it must travel through in the process. The low guard can easily lift to the middle or high guards and instantly rise to assume the hanging or inside postures. It can also become either the left or right close guard or move with a passing step to adopt a right or left back guard. After following through and before recovering, many cuts end in essentially what is the low guard position. But the low guard's very value in protecting the legs, threatening thrusts, and making wide cuts is completely lost if students are not proficient in parrying low, stabbing from underneath, or using the hanging guard. As with so many of the other fighting stances of the long-sword, each depends for much of its worth not just on what attacks and parries it can execute, but on how it does them in conjunction with the other stances. Italian Masters also write of "full" and "half" iron door positions, depending on which leg is forward and whether the weapon is to the left or right of it.

Left leg leading.

The back guard was called a *tail* guard by the Italians and *Schrankhut* by German masters. It is an often underappreciated and underused position by modern students. It is a powerful stance that can make deceptive strikes and countercuts. Similar to the back stance with the sword & shield, it pulls the weapon away from the opponent while threatening a counterattack. The back stance is an intercepting posture, and its apparent exposure seems to entice the opponent to attack. But it can deliver several strong cuts from angles difficult to parry. However, there are both right and left versions of the tail stance. The right-side stance places the weapon on the right side but leads with the left leg forward. The left stance places the weapon on the left side but leads with the right leg. The reverse stance (leading with the opposite leg) is the more effective. For a right-handed swordsman, this is with the right arm furthest back and the left arm crossing over. The opposite stance (weapon on the left side, for a right-hander) requires that the arms cross over each other, and this awkwardness does not allow the weapon to strike as freely or the body to move as easily.

Right back stance left leading leg.

Left back stance leading with right leg.

For a right-hander, the right back stance with left-leg lead has greater utility.

A strong upward cut can be delivered from the back guard with a forward pass of the rear leg. A reverse pass with the lead leg dropping back as the weapon is brought forward and up is also a very effective time attack. Each of these can strike to the lower legs, abdomen, groin, inner thigh, or forearms. From this position the blade can also be lifted up to cut forcefully around to a right-to-left downward diagonal or vertical cut and even brought around to cut left to right. These cuts can also be executed with a forward pass. Just as cuts from the high guard pass through or end in the back guard these cuts pass momentarily through the high guard as they are delivered. Assuming the back guard requires a reverse stance, either the lead leg must step back or the rear leg step forward. This position turns the shoulders and hips just slightly as the point is aimed back. Again, the sword should be held at a 45-degree angle with the tip aimed behind and somewhat to the side, not horizontally or pointing down at the ground. The hilt is just below the waist, and the edge should turn to face outward, as if when brought around it is already "aimed" at the opponent. This positioning allows the weapon the easiest and smoothest motion in any cut so that the hips and shoulders can turn to maximize its force and follow through to recover. The menacing utility of the tail guard cannot be understood without practice, and the upward cuts and counterattacks so effective from this posture are particularly difficult to master. It is not an easy stance to strike from but, once learned, can be among the most formidable to employ.

The hanging guard is an important and very versatile long-sword posture. It is also one that is confused and misunderstood more than any other. It was called the *Ochs* (ox) stance in the German schools (for resemblance of the point to the sloping horns of an ox). The Italians knew it as the women's (*posta di donna*) or *queen's* guard (possibly because next to the crown guard it is the most useful). In the hanging guard the hilt is raised to head level and the point of the sword "hangs" down. The standard position lifts the hilt high enough to parry attacks to the head. The blade is angled so that blows are intercepted with the flat and the edge is aimed at the opponent so that no motion is lost in turning it as a cut is made. The position forms something of a "right triangle" with the shoulder parallel to the ground and the forearm more perpendicular. Either the point or the hilt can be lowered to parry as necessary, depending upon the angle of the attack. The side the sword points to determines whether it is a right or left stance.

Right hanging stance.

Left hanging stance.

Both stances may lead with either leg forward but are optimally employed leading with the leg on same side. As a pass forward or pass back is executed, the stance shifts to the other leg. This allows cuts to be delivered or closing techniques to be initiated.

193

Although the *Hengen* (hanging guards) may at first glimpse appear to be open and vulnerable this is not the case. Cuts or thrusts to either side or directly downward may be instantly parried with a small motion of the hips and torso. By simply turning and raising the point it can assume the inside guard. By lowering the hilt to the hips it can easily become the close guard. The posture of the hanging guard itself is one that is immediately a form of parry and a form of cut. The posture allows striking diagonally upward, parrying in, or meeting outward and closing with the opponent's weapon.

One possible variation holds the hilt back more and turns the lead shoulder forward more.

It is by its nature a very responsive, countering posture. It is also uniquely positioned to countercut by bringing the blade up and around to strike diagonally from the opposite side in one swift motion. This is particularly effective with a timed pass forward or back. It is not an easy stance to learn and takes considerable practice to not only cut and parry from, but also to thrust and shift from. The hanging guard is also well suited to entering and slicing or binding at close range. Its weakness is that when the you close, the hilt or arm can easily be seized. Another weakness of the hanging guard is its potential for the opponent's forcing or twisting the weapon off guard. This is a dangerous technique that can be learned well to disarm or bind up the opponent by entering to close range. The hanging guard is a versatile and important stance, but it loses effectiveness if a swordsman is not practiced at rising cuts or using the close and inside guards. The hanging guard is also very similar to the inside guard, yet each is distinct and has separate application.

Another variation holds the hilt at chest level and aims the point more forward than to the right. Still another allows the weapon to parry over the shoulder and behind the back by twisting away from the incoming blow.

There are both right and left hanging guards, and each can lead with either leg. However, the stance opposite that of the lead hand has hazards. For a right-handed swordsman the left version has the inherent problem of the grips crossing into the "weak hold"; rather, the arms must twist over one another. Avoid crossing the arms like this as much as possible, as it leads to weaker cuts and parries and can allow the weapon to be more easily bound up or beat away. Application of the hanging guard in cutting and entering will be covered later.

194

The inside stance is called the *window* (*finestra*) guard by some Italian masters (perhaps because of its resemblance to peeking carefully out of a window). One German term for it was apparently *Hangetorte* (hanging point) and possibly even *Wechsel* (change). Although very similar to the hanging guard, it is much more likely that dei Liberi's true window guard is this position and not the hanging point of the German schools as some researchers now contend. The inside guard can be instantly adopted from either the high, middle, hanging, low, or close postures. The position is with the blade raised horizontally (edges sideways) with the hilt pulled in near the head and the point directed toward the opponent's face (on those swords suited for it the pommel can also be gripped). The utility of the inside guard lies in its warding off the adversary with its pointed threat as well as defending the head from attacks to the side. It is a position to thrust or parry from rather than cut. A side parry can be made by slightly lifting or pushing out the blade from the hilt. The inside guard holds danger for a swordsman in that when struck forcefully the two-edged sword with wide cross-guard can be slammed against the head if a blow is not properly parried or evaded. It takes care and practice to prevent this. By dropping the point down on the same side, the swordsman can perform a low parry.

Left inside stance.

The inside guard uses a reverse stance leading with the opposite leg and the body turned slightly inward. There are both right and left inside stances; however, the posture is more effective on the *opposite* side of the leading hand. For a right-hander, using the right inside stance slightly does cross the wrists, but this is not as much of a factor in this case. Variations of the window guard may place the hilt lower and farther back with the blade tilting upward.

Right inside stance.

Variations holding the hilt lower or higher.

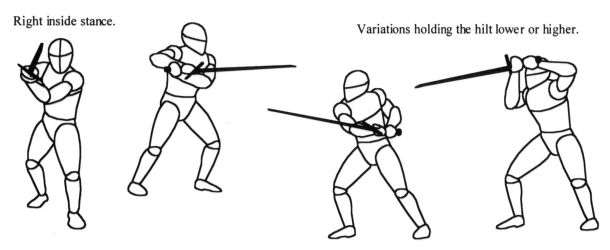

The inside and the hanging guards have a strong relationship. Indeed, the inside guard can be assumed from the hanging guard by merely turning the point of the sword forward toward the opponent and pulling the hilt back slightly. Conversely, the hanging guard can be assumed from the inside guard by turning the point of the sword down away and bringing the hilt forward some. The inside guard, however, turns the body more sideways than the hanging in order to pull the hilt back and aim the point straighter out. Apparently not all schools recognized the two as distinct, but rather as the same guard with a slight turn of the blade. This likely was dependent on the type of long-sword used, since an agile spadone with its narrow, piercing point can make far more use of the inside guard, whereas larger great-swords are adept at using the hanging guards for many techniques. This is a significant difference. Many historical drawings are quite unclear as to whether they are in ox or window guards and even as to whether the guards are being used for simply guarding or for parrying, thrusting, or even cutting upward diagonally. Alas, such is the nature of the craft.

The close guard is itself a ready position that is also a parry. The stance directly blocks horizontal or diagonal cuts to the difficult belt-line or hip area. This is its primary value. The hilt is held down low, close against the hip and below the waist. The body also turns slightly while the knees bend more. It can lead with either leg, but naturally the side opposite the lead arm has somewhat more utility. The posture can easily be assumed from the middle or high guards by lowering the hilt off to the side and from the hanging and close guards by simply dropping down the hilt while keeping the point outward. From the close guard a powerful upward thrust can be issued. With a pass or large step out it can stab in low to the abdomen or groin (and under an opponent's guard) or high to the face and neck. Since the weapon is held close by the hips, as a pass forward or back is made the hilt naturally comes out and can fall right back on the opposite side, thereby changing from a left to a right close guard with ease. This stance also has the virtue of pulling the weapon away from the opponent to prevent his playing off it, binding it up, or entering to seize the hilt or to grapple. Other parries can also be executed from this defensive, warding stance. The close guard can easily drop to the low guard to block leg attacks or push out and over to parry the opposite side. As well as lifting to adopt an inside, hanging, middle, or high stance, this guard can turn the point around to become the back guard.

Right close stance.

For a right-hander, using the right close stance does cross the wrists slightly, but in this posture it is not as significant.

Left close stance.

Like the inside guard, the close stance does not initiate cuts in itself, but they can result from the execution of other cuts as they end or recover to this posture.

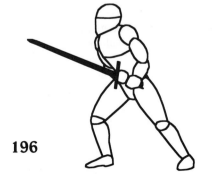

Another lowers the hilt and the point while turning the guard.

196

The long guard, short guard, and side guard are really just variations of the middle and high guards. Of the nine secondary guards, these three are *lesser* postures and are not quite as serviceable. Like the three primary "center" guards, they can also be utilized in right- or left-leg stances, and the weapon is basically held in the middle.

The long guard (*posta longa*) is a defensive thrusting position ideal for stabbing attacks or stop-thrusts. German schools may have called it *Langortt* or *langer Ort* (long point). There are several variations (such as the "two-horned" or "two-cornered" guard), where the blade is held at face level rather than chest or where the second hand is turned around (a *reverse grip*) to enable a stronger thrust and to allow certain binding techniques. The long-guard is useful in warding off an attacker attempting to enter close range. But it also is somewhat weaker because the point can be beaten aside and any other action considered requires the weapon to recover to another guard in the process.

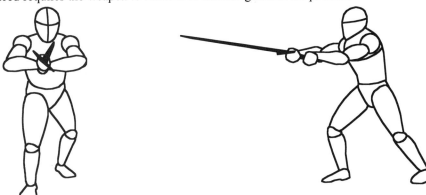

Long guard.

The short guard (*posta breve*) is an "entering" or close-range posture for both parrying and preparing to slice, hit, or bind. It has limited application in that it is vulnerable to thrusts and is not favorable for side and low parries. The side guard is a high guard lowered to just above the shoulder. It can be seen frequently in Medieval artwork. It can be in either a right or left posture leading with either leg. It is useful as a transitional posture and, when space does not permit, an actual high guard. Although it is not that different from a high guard, it can only cut easily on one side at a time. In some illustrations, the side guard is held angled more behind the head in what almost appears as a sword version of a baseball batting stance. Different schools and masters likely had variations for many of the stances. One form of the low guard even consisted of the blade's being held to the outside of the lead leg or tilted on an angle in something of almost a "low hanging guard." The Bolognese Master Fillipo Vadi told of other guards, including an "archer" guard (*sagittaria*), a "guard of the cross," and a "frontal guard." He also wrote of special guards for the long-sword used with full plate armor, such as the high and low "serpent" guards (*serpentino*), the leopard laid-back tail, and the guard of the serene leopard (*posta del leopardo sereno*).

The short guard is in some ways a variation of close guard with the hilt centered and closer in to the body.

The side guard in a right-leg stance.

Although lingering in a static posture can be as bad as constant bouncing and dancing about, there is value in patiently waiting to strike instantly at the moment the adversary shows an opening. This takes considerable practice to understand. Conversely, rapid, smooth shifting from stance to stance as the distance is altered and techniques are performed is the means by which these postures are employed.

But practicing fighting with the long-sword is obviously much more than getting into one of the stances and swiping at an opponent. It is more than just striking and parrying and striking and parrying. There is stepping footwork and cutting actions to use at various ranges and numerous ways of countering and deflecting attacks with blade or guard. There are a great number of thrusting and clubbing moves and a multitude of techniques for closing or "entering" with the opponent and seizing his blade or arm. It goes without saying, then, that the art of the long-sword is far more than "hacking and slashing." Additionally, in the crowded confines of mass battle, the middle guard, hanging guard, and inside guard are far more appropriate and easier to use than those that require more room for their sweeping motions and powerful cuts.

Hollywood theatrical swordfights and displays arranged by stunt actors and stage-combat performers typically present a form of Medieval long-swordfighting that only bears superficial resemblance to the nature of the historical craft. The attacks are fairly basic ones made with large, obvious motions too short to actually connect. Little or no attempt is made at deception or maneuvering, and parries are exaggerated and usually made too far out. Virtually no cuts and few parries are ever made to the lower legs. Often they incorporate inappropriate elements derived from modern saber sport-fencing or just improvised "barbarian" techniques. When they are used, close-range actions and techniques are regularly unrealistic and awkward, rather than pragmatic and obvious. The example set by these choreographed fights, although entertaining, should never be taken as representatuve of the correct historical use of these tools of war. Writing in 1389, the German master Doebringer made similar criticism of those who taught flashy but impractical techniques at the time, calling them *Leichmeistere* (dance-masters). Those masters who taught flowery, ineffective swordsmanship were also sometimes referred to as *Gaukler* (jugglers or acrobats). Similar remarks have been expressed about some styles of modern Asian martial arts. We also know during the later 1500s and 1600s in Germany there were itinerant swordsmen performers known as *Klopffechter* (clown fighters). It would seem that this tradition continues in some ways today.

It has been pointed out that weapon combat is really too intense, too unpredictable to be reduced to static, preconceived patterns. With Medieval swordsmanship (and fighting with other weaponry) there is no emphasis on a preset model or formalized movements. There is no preservation of minor differences or focus on minutiae to differentiate among schools or teachers. Following no preserved model, it is not any art itself that is primary, but rather the individual's personal expression of technique. Artfully displayed or not, the fighting method consists of brutal, utilitarian actions.

These 14 stances can be practiced as a sequence of moves. Each posture can be assumed one after the other by passing forward with the rear leg or passing back with the lead. Repeated practice of this routine can help familiarize a student with the flow and transition among them. The sequence can be altered infinitely with one stance changing instantly to one of the others. Naturally, due to the mechanics of each posture and depending upon which leg is leading (either a forward or a back stance), not all of them can smoothly shift to every other. Many must pass through another posture first. After practicing quickly and easily changing stances, the cuts and parries possible from each can then be incorporated into improvised routines. This can continue until the many moves and actions are familiar and ingrained. Yet, keep in mind that it is very difficult to display in two-dimensional drawings alone the fluid motions and changing balance necessary to properly move and step with cuts, thrusts, and parries while shifting between postures.

It is important to neither neglect correct fighting postures nor be obsessed with them. However, without the foundation of correct stances, your footwork and movement will be off. Without correct footwork and movement your cuts and parries will be weak. Without proper cuts and parries, your techniques will be ineffective. Without effective techniques your attacks and defense will be inferior. Without them you will be in peril.

It has been said that to do a wrong thing well is not a virtue. The more a postulated technique conflicts with previous experience, the more complete must be the demonstrated example to justify its dismissal or use. A slight alteration of the basic form of a stance or its improper application can render it impotent and make the swordsman vulnerable. As with the sword & shield, many practitioners today will try to use the long-sword in theatrical postures or end up in incorrect positions and fanciful "non-stances." Sometimes they can get by with this under the particular set of sparring guidelines they adhere to or because no one of greater knowledge has yet exploited their flaws and weaknesses. At other times, poorly assumed stances are only a result of a lack of study. There are so many ways to do things wrong, yet many of these habits and errors are obvious and easy to correct. Either way, there are a multitude of common mistakes to avoid, and a skilled adversary will be ever alert to spot openings and take advantage of mistakes.

Holding the arms out too far in the high guard can easily result in their being easily cut, as well as the hands.

Standing with the weapon poised too far back loses valuable time in striking or countering.

A posture that is too energetic and animated is inefficient and can result in techniques and actions being distorted.

A posture that is too relaxed saps the weapon's speed and strength, as well as robbing you of reaction time and response options.

Keeping the weapon in any position where it is not immediately able to strike out cleanly, make a direct parry, or apply an entering technique (close action) is flawed. If it does not directly result in the adversary's attacking successfully, it will invoke a preparatory action by him that will.

Leaning too far forward in any stance wastes motion and exposes you unnecessarily.

A point that is too low in the middle posture detracts severely from cutting and parrying options and allows the opponent to "attack the the blade." It offers a decent and very obvious thrust, but nothing else.

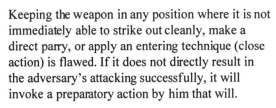

If the arms are too relaxed in the low stance, your ability to do anything from it is considerably weakened while you unnecessarily invite danger.

Keeping the hilt out too far in the inside guard completely defeats its whole value.

A point that is too low or too vertical in the hanging guard removes its blocking potential and weakens it greatly. Cutting power is lost, and the blade can be forced into the "weak grip." A blade that is too horizontal is open to attack.

199

The postures that are best are those that are the natural result of the physical motions of preparing to strike or following through with a strike, and these are surely the origin of the long-sword stances. Medieval German fighting manuals and other manuscripts show many stances and movements equivalent to ones recognizable as standard in traditional Japanese kenjutsu. There are certain practical positions for both offense and defense that are universal for using any long-sword, and beyond any doubt, these were used to the utmost in Medieval Europe. Naturally, since European and Asian warriors used different swords and faced different armors, the basic movements themselves are not exclusive to one method. Neither system of swordsmanship should really be viewed as somehow referring to or legitimizing the other. Each developed, evolved, and existed independently. Some commonalities between the two are only natural. There was even an obscure form of Chinese "two-handed sword" first developed around 250 B.C., but it was apparently not that different in composition or handling from its one-handed versions. Nor did it become a specialized a weapon as the Japanese or Medieval ones did. There were also forms of Filipino and Indian long-stick methods. There is something of the belief that because European methods of Medieval swordsmanship fell out of use or changed to the point that they were unrecognizable over time, they may not have been as refined or formalized as those practiced in kenjutsu. This contention is factually untenable.

Although there are major similarities between how a Japanese katana (with its shorter, single-edged, curved blade) is used and how a longer, straight, two-edged-blade Medieval war-sword (particularly the narrower, tapering form) is used, there are also fundamental as well as subtle differences between them. These are most significant to those who have carefully studied with each in test-cutting practice and free-sparring. The manner in which the long-sword or great-sword transitions among cuts, parries, and thrusts is not identical, nor is the grip, or even the attitude of handling the two weapons. Each has its own unique center of balance and agility. The katana's edge, being curved, meets its target at a better angle to make an efficient, continual slice as it cuts, and emphasis is typically placed on using the first few inches of blade. The straight Medieval blade cuts with a chopping motion of its second quarter, and although it cannot be used for as many drawing slices as curved ones, it can be excellent for thrusting. The large cross-guard also enables a wider range of binding and counterparrying options. To unfairly force too many similarities between the two sword forms and their corresponding methods does a disservice to each.

Also, in contrast to the powerful slicing slash of a curved, single-edged, Japanese katana, Medieval long-swords were made for hacking, shearing cuts delivered primarily from the elbow and shoulder. It is a mistake to think that a straight, double-edged sword with a cross-guard and pommel is handled liked a samurai's katana despite obvious common elements between the European and Japanese stances and cuts. Instead it strikes more with the first 8 to 10 inches of blade and has two edges to work with (it can "reverse cut" up or cut back). Also, a Medieval sword's simple cross-guard (or cruciform-hilt) is intended not so much to protect the hand from incoming blows, but to allow the blade to bind and lock up another weapon and then quickly slip off (it does also offer some protection from hitting into an opposing blade). Additionally, it protects the hand from slamming into an opponent's shield —which is moved to greet and smack attacks, not left just hanging (contrary to myth, a Medieval shield was far too strong to simply cut through with a few blows).

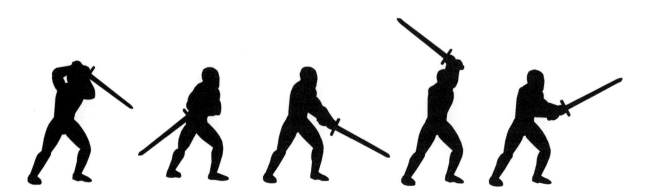

CUTTING WITH THE LONG-SWORD

The targets for the long-sword, as with any weapon, are those of opportunity: anything that can be struck effectively. Attacks to upper targets are preferable since wounds to the head, arms, and torso can be immediately incapacitating or fatal. But attacks to the lower legs and the hands often have the greatest likelihood of success. The arms and head are the primary targets followed by the legs. Cuts to the arms are among the most common and immediately effective. The same applies to the head, but if an attack there falls short or is defeated, the collar or shoulders can often be struck lethally. The body is less easily hit, but the midsection and groin can be reached on many attacks. Cuts to the soft abdomen are preferable to the rib cage or hipbones. The thighs and the lower legs and knees (as previously explained) are especially vulnerable. Thrusts are obviously made to the face and abdomen, as well as to the neck and groin. One target that is often quite vulnerable and notoriously exposed in novices (and among many experienced fighters) is the hands. You can't hold your weapon if you have no fingers. The hands or grip can be attacked purposely in a wide range of stances. The hands are persistently and regularly overlooked or outlawed as a target in most practices and sparring sessions by enthusiasts today. This is unfortunate. There are many methods of safely including this important target, and in the end its inclusion will substantially improve skill and understanding.

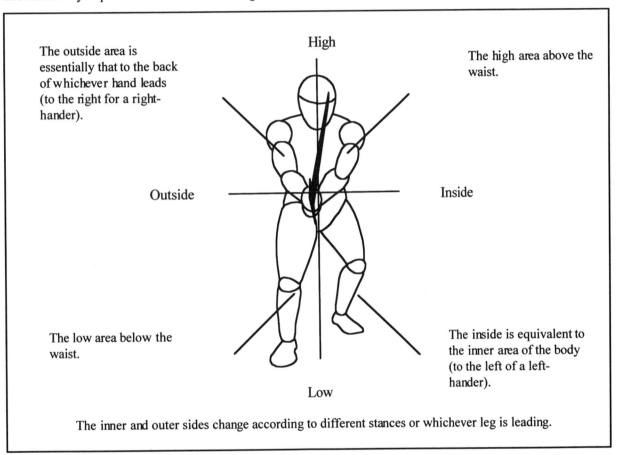

The outside area is essentially that to the back of whichever hand leads (to the right for a right-hander).

High

The high area above the waist.

Outside

Inside

The low area below the waist.

Low

The inside is equivalent to the inner area of the body (to the left of a left-hander).

The inner and outer sides change according to different stances or whichever leg is leading.

Once again, there are only eight simple angles of cutting: three downward (*Oberhau*) cuts, three upward (*Unterhau*) cuts, and two side cuts. The three downward cuts are vertical straight down and diagonal left or right. They cut from head or collar down to waist or hip. The three upward cuts are diagonal left or right and a back cut straight up (which is difficult and less useful). They cut from either thigh or waist up to collar or head. Thrusts are made either high or low and either left or right. They may be above or below the adversary's grip line (or waist) and either to the left or right of the guard (or center line). Thrusts had no reason in the Middle Ages to be defined or organized, as they later would be with Renaissance swords. But some German Masters did distinguish those that were made *obere Ansetzen* (over or above the guard) and *untere Ansetzen* (under or below the guard).

This is a general look at the fundamentals of the Medieval long-sword; however, because of the need for brevity, it by no means offers an extensive examination of all concepts and techniques presented in the many historical manuals. Although an understanding of Medieval swordsmanship is not limited solely to studying the historical masters, it certainly can't be properly understood *without* studying them either. Students practicing today who say, "I learned everything I know from only historical manuals," likely know about as much as those students who have never seen them.

Although many of the German and Italian terms from the early 1300s to early 1500s apply more to the use of great-swords, their basic concepts are those derived from Medieval long-swords or war-swords. The German masters had a rich store of terminology to describe the techniques, actions, and concepts of their fighting systems. *Kunst des Fechtens*, the German art of fighting, consisted primarily of the arts of the *Langenschwert* (long-sword), the *Messer* (a sort of "two-handed falchion"), and *Ringenkunst* (wrestling). Unarmored combat was known as *blossfechten*. Combat in plate armor was known as *Harnischfechten* (harness fighting). Fighting on foot was also distinguished from *Rossfechten,* or mounted combat. Similar distinctions appear to have been made in Italy and elsewhere in Europe.

The Lines of Attack against the Major Fighting Postures

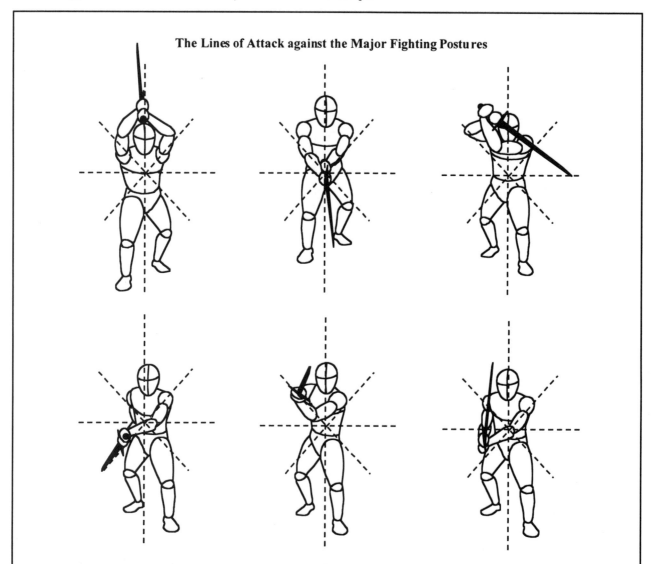

As with the sword & shield, depending on the stance of the opponent, certain target areas are more defended or more exposed than others. Different parts of the body are ideal targets for lethal or instantly disabling wounds, while other areas may only injure and not incapacitate. Each particular stance may expose or invite attacks more so or less so to the head, arms or legs, or to the body. Protecting different areas is part of a stance's value; exposing them is part of its danger, but also equally a part of its deception.

Basic cuts, parries, and footwork with the long-sword must be covered before more complex and significant techniques can be examined. Cutting with the long-sword is not a complicated matter. The actions are fairly obvious once the basic physical motions of bringing the weapon around, or up and down, or down and up, with force, speed, and aim are understood. With a longer blade held in both hands the same elements of focus, follow-through, and recovery already described under the sword & shield apply even more so. Without the shield, the body's motion is freer to move behind the force of cuts in adding power or in stepping in to and out of the adversary's actions.

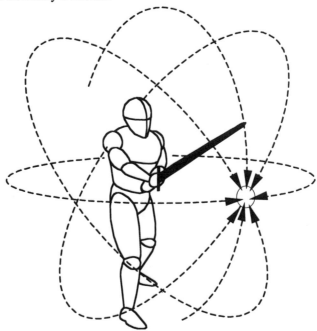

Eight basic cuts can be delivered with the long-sword that can strike to the adversary's head, torso, or limbs. But each stance has specific cuts that can be made either high or low from either right or left angles.

Early on, the German schools recognized three major forms of cut: *Oberhau* (over cuts), downward diagonal or vertical; *Unterhau* (under cuts), upward or rising; and *Zwerchhau* or *Mittelha* (cross cuts), horizontal right-to-left and horizontal left-to-right. Diagonal cuts were *Zornhau*, and vertical were *Scheitelhau*. In later Italian Renaissance schools of fence these were known as *squalembrato* and *tondo*. Side cuts were *traverse*, and vertical cuts were *fendente*.

The Medieval German schools relied on a handful of old masters for the majority of their teachings. In simplest terms, not all the schools or masters agreed or interpreted the older traditions in the same manner, and in some areas there are significant disagreements among them. Perhaps not until the later introduction of the Italian rapier methods during the Renaissance did they begin to study differently. There were also several names for other specific individual cuts to forearms, neck, or legs with either the forward or back edge. Some of these were *Schielhau* (the "squinting cut"), *Streithau* (the "battle cut"), *Vater Streich* (the "father strike"), and a *Scheitelhau* ("scalp cut"). Variations included others such as *Krumphau* and *Zornhau*. Draw-cuts and slicing pulls were usually known as *Schnitt*. But all this only just begins to address these major cuts or describe their tactical application.

An obscure English great-sword text of the 1200s describes what is obviously a sophisticated means of employing the weapon. Although its archaic language is difficult to interpret, it concerns itself with what are evidently various combinations and counterattacks delivered from numerous guards. In quite practical terms the text refers to enigmatic yet familiar actions such as ye *double rowndes, rakes, haukse,* and *halfe haukes*. It talks of *smyting strokes* and of striking with *"a sprynge of ye foote."* It describes various footwork, or *steppes,* such as the *cockstep, grete steppe,* and *backsteppe.* Interestingly, it also gives some instruction in *verse form,* a not uncommon means of learning subjects at the time.

A cut can be made with nearly any sharpened portion of the weapon. Ideally, the cut is made with the portion of the blade where the force can be maximized. This precise location varies from sword to sword, but with a straight Medieval long-sword blade it is approximately 6 to 10 inches down from the point. The blade's length and width are determining factors in this, along with the weapon's overall balance and weight. Cuts made nearer the hilt are less powerful because the weapon has a shorter arc to travel in and cannot generate as much momentum. On a straight blade, cuts made with the first inch or two of the point can have great velocity, but the tip (usually being more slender) can just slice off or cut across of the target instead of biting into it. This is truer of swords of the spadone variety.

Strong downward and rising diagonal, vertical, and horizontal cuts can all be delivered from the high guard.

A variety of deceptive rising and downward diagonal, horizontal, and vertical cuts can all be executed by the tail guards.

Several rising or downward diagonal and horizontal cuts can be made in the hanging guards.

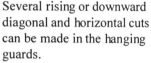

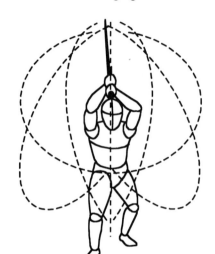

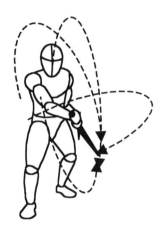

Whether cutting vertically or diagonally the weapon follows the same general arcing path as it slices and recovers.

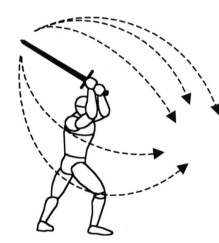

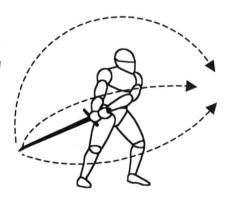

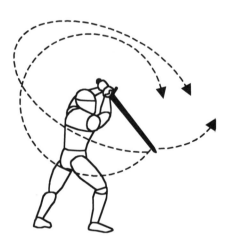

As cuts are made, whether they connect, are blocked, or pass by, the weapon must recover to strike again, or to parry, or to resume a guarding posture. In the Renaissance Schools of Defence the various sword cuts became much more defined and were given specific names for reasons dealing more with the change to more agile blades, which involved quicker transitions between cuts and thrusts.

A sword strike is not a "tap"; it is a *cut*. It is a forceful blow with the blade's edge. Sword cuts can't be just light downward and forward slaps from the forearms. They must be quickly raised up and then quickly brought down with force using the full arm (or vice versa for rising cuts). The cuts follow through and flow around in a large arcing motion. These are sometimes referred to now as *molinets* or "windmills" (although this is not a Medieval term), as was the German *Zucken* and perhaps the English *rownde*. This arcing motion allows the cuts to generate momentum and to threaten other targets. The blade is pulled back to swing around from the other side or to lift right back again with force. The point can drop and the hilt be raised to bring the blade around in a quick downward cut or to push it forward and raise it for a lifting cut. This following through can be employed to deliver combination attacks or to deceive the range by altering the distance with steps and arm extension. Remember, the sword can strike from the full shoulders in a powerful action or from the arms (half-arm) in somewhat weaker but faster motions or even by the wrist with weak but quick actions. Cuts from the shoulder (the full arm) are strongest and therefore primary (a requirement against armors), but all three are used. By altering cuts and techniques between shoulder, arm, and wrist motions, distance can be manipulated and the adversary deceived. Most cuts are from the shoulder or arms; wrist-delivered attacks are seldom decisive and are used for little other than quick, short slices.

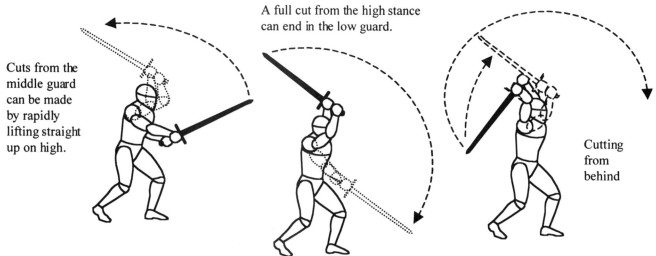

Cuts from the middle guard can be made by rapidly lifting straight up on high.

A full cut from the high stance can end in the low guard.

Cutting from behind

For the most basic cut the blade is lifted straight up and brought down vertically or diagonally from the left or from the right. This way the opponent cannot be certain in that instant of attack which side or "line" of attack it will strike. In this way the cut can be deceptive, with subtle or blatant misdirecting motion. A skilled fighter can change his line of attack more than once as he strikes and can do so several times in combination attacks. The use of feints to open up potential targets and *falsing* (or fake cuts that set up another angle of attack or that turn into thrusts) is fundamental to the long-sword, and related more to the change to more agile blades involving quicker transitions between cuts and thrusts. Pulling the weapon fully up and back (to almost 45-degrees) on some cuts allows it to generate greater power in the cut. This position, although fleeting, is also slower and more vulnerable. It's important to realize that while the sword can be moved behind the body in this way, it is not itself any "stance," but rather a transitory position the weapon may traverse while either striking or being brought around to the other side.

The back stance can cut around to become the middle or even the low guard.

By pulling the point up and back while pushing out and turning with the hilt, the middle guard can deceptively cut diagonally upward in a quick, short motion. Although this cut takes considerable practice and is not strong, it can be one of the most useful.

Both horizontal and vertical cuts have less power than do those delivered on an angle (roughly 45 degrees). This is because with the angled cuts the entire body may more easily be employed behind the blow in following through by twisting the hips and shoulders. To add power with vertical cuts straight down or horizontal cuts the body can only move forward or make a side-step with the rear leg. Also, the arc that the weapon travels in is much shorter. A downward vertical cut must avoid striking the ground (or your own knee), and a horizontal strike, rather than being itself thrown, tends to want to pull. Although they are still quite effective, this makes them less powerful than diagonal cuts.

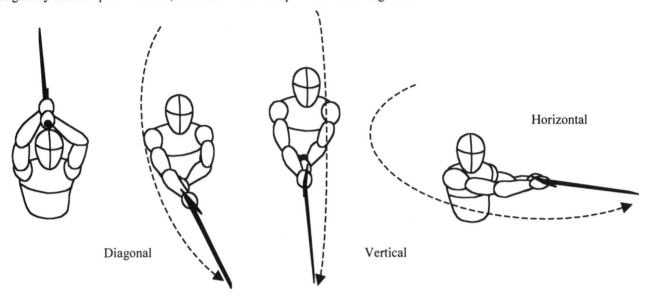

Diagonal

Vertical

Horizontal

With a straight blade, horizontal cuts are also somewhat less useful and less powerful because of the physical mechanics of the motion. With diagonal cuts the blade strikes at a 45-degree angle and the hips and shoulders can twist into the motion to add power and follow-through. The body's natural manner of moving lends itself to pushing out and then pulling in with the arms as the feet step forward or back. With a sideways or horizontal cut, this does not occur. Instead, the blade must meet its target at a more direct angle, and for power the body must turn in to the blow while the lead foot must step out. There is less ability for the body to get behind the blow or for the arms and shoulders to maximize its energy. Still, horizontal cuts can be just as useful and can be employed advantageously from the high or hanging guards, particularly after parrying. They are effective at decapitating, striking the forearms, and hitting deeply into the waist or abdomen.

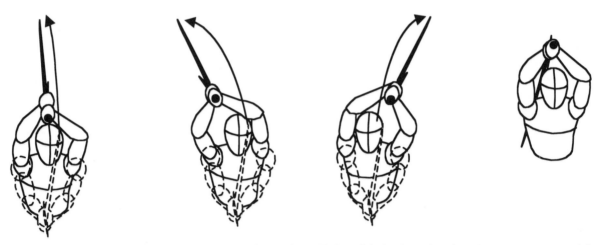

As the blade is lifted to strike from the middle stance, it may be pulled straight back so that the adversary cannot anticipate its angle of attack. It may also be pulled back to the left or right, which allows it to generate somewhat greater power in the cut by virtue of the motion of twisting of the body and shoulders. If it is done quickly enough, this movement will not alert the opponent to its line of attack. This can also be done intentionally as a false attack that suddenly shifts around to cut from the opposite side. Lifting the weapon all the way back until it is at a 45-degree angle *behind* the back does makes the most powerful cut possible, but be aware that it is slower, is less able to adjust its line of attack, and warns the opponent of its arrival. To strike with the edge, the sword cannot just be swung from side to side horizontally around the head. It must be brought back by the arms and shoulders before descending.

206

After cutting down left to right from a right-leg stance, the blade ends up outside the leg in a semi-low guard, or what the Italian master dei Liberi called the guard of "half iron door." After cutting down right to left from a right-leg stance the blade ends up on the inside of the leg in another semi-low guard, or what dei Liberi called the "iron door" guard. In either case, the weapon can follow thorough and be brought around to strike again or recover, or the hilt is turned so the lead edge then faces the adversary in a proper back guard. This simple motion of cutting and following through (up) or down to the back guard is fundamental and vital to proficiency. Its opposite is the rising diagonal cut (left to right or right to left) that either comes fully around, reverses and strikes back again, or assumes a high guard.

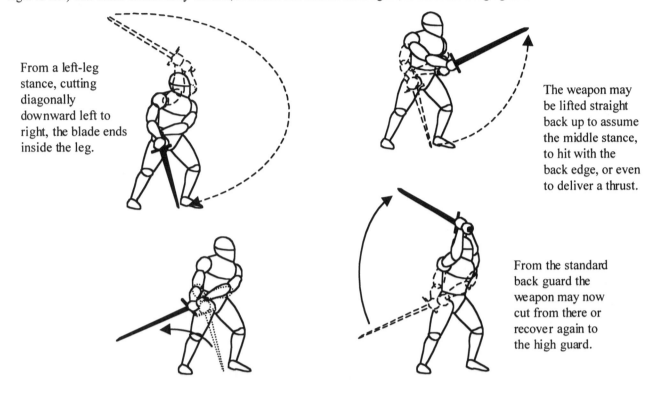

From a left-leg stance, cutting diagonally downward left to right, the blade ends inside the leg.

The weapon may be lifted straight back up to assume the middle stance, to hit with the back edge, or even to deliver a thrust.

From the standard back guard the weapon may now cut from there or recover again to the high guard.

Alternatively, to follow through and cut again or to recover to another guard, the weapon must be turned into the back posture by simply rolling the hilt over. This action must, naturally, be done very quickly.

Whatever side the long-sword is placed on, shift to lead with the opposite leg. Hence, with the weapon on the left side, a right stance will be used; with the weapon on the right side, a left stance will be used. In this way, the leading leg will never hinder the delivery of a cut and instead will position you to make a pass forward or back with each blow and allow the hips to properly twist with it. However, this is *not* a hard-and-fast rule, only a general one, as there are plenty of times in which the lead arm and lead leg can easily be the same (such as with the hanging guard and in the "center stances" of middle, low, high, long, short, and side).

For a right-handed swordsman when leading with the right leg, leading cuts from right to left can be delivered with a forward step or a pass back. Cuts from left to right can be delivered with either a forward step, a pass forward of the rear (left) leg, or a pass back of the lead (right) leg.

For a right-handed swordsman when leading with the left leg, cuts from left to right can be delivered with a forward step. Cuts from right to left can be delivered with either a forward step, a pass forward of the rear (right) leg, or a pass back of the lead (left) leg.

When passing, the body turns and the leg moves just as the cut is delivered. The action must be simultaneous to maximize speed and power without alerting the opponent.

To strike the opponent strongly is the goal; to hit him inadvertently, fortuitously, or accidentally because he ran into your blade is not. It is far better to hit by intention and purpose. Additionally, although Medieval swords were certainly sharp, just bumping against the edge of the opponent's sword or being knocked into the blade as you strike is not the same as being cut forcibly by the weapon. When armor is factored into this (as it typically was), such incidents are negligible. To wound or be wounded with a Medieval sword, a good solid chop, slice, or stab is required. It is one thing to be struck by a blow and quite another to simply be knocked into or brush against a stationary sword while you cleave its owner. Inexperienced practitioners are well known to just leave their weapon out in front of them, expecting it to fight for them while they are being cut elsewhere.

Rising cuts from the back guard are among the most difficult to perform but also among the most important to include in your repertoire.

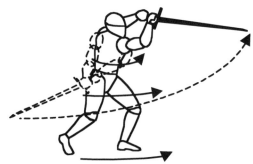

The cut is executed not by simply swinging around the point in a big arc, but rather by pushing out with the hilt and slicing upward diagonally with the edge following. The body must turn into the cut, and the feet must also move into the motion (either by stepping out or passing). To actually throw the cut with force and accuracy, considerable practice is required for the proper motion and focus.

This cut can be extremely effective in countering numerous attacks and easily strikes into the opponent's grip, forearm, abdomen, inner thigh, or shin.

Recovery is important with this cut. Follow-through brings the blade up where it must immediately recover by turning the hilt and bringing back the point. From here the sword is in essentially a high guard and can now strike again.

The German masters reference the division of the long-sword into two portions: the *Stark*, or stronger section from middle to hilt, and the *Schwech,* or weaker section from middle to point. This is based on the understanding that the closer to the hilt or grip, the more strength and control can be employed in resisting or pushing. The farther toward the tip, there is less strength and control—but there is much greater speed, maneuverability, and deception. This idea was taken even further in the Renaissance methods of rapier fence.

There is considerable crossover that has been detected between German and Italian fencing during the Medieval Ages as well as the Renaissance. Although probable elsewhere in Europe, how much this applies to other regions and kingdoms is less documented and open to speculation. Similarly, both historians and re-creationists often will try to draw too distinct a line between the sword forms of the late Medieval and early Renaissance periods. The progression of changes was a gradual process and is not that easy to trace. Before turning into distinct civilian forms, swords very similar to Medieval ones continued to find use in combating battlefield armor well into the 1600s.

Cutting from the hanging guards is also difficult to perform as these guards are by nature more countering actions than direct attacks. The position is ideal for both parrying and closing in to bind, trap, or deflect, but strikes are limited to only a few slices and cuts.

The weakest cut is the most direct. A forward step is taken while the blade simply lifts up and pushes out to slice the opponent's forearms or face. This can be most effective after having parried or entered close.

The strongest cut is accomplished by pulling the blade back and around behind the head to strike from the opposite shoulder. This is most effective upon initially parrying or closing in to greet the adversary's weapon.

Another cut that can be executed directly after parrying from the hanging guard is simply slicing across the opponent's forearms. With a forward step, the blade is quickly pushed against them and then drawn back across.

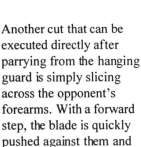

The hanging guard can pull up and back to cut from the high position. The blade is brought around in a short arc by quickly turning and lowering the hilt.

The hanging guard has great versatility and utility and should probably be practiced with more effort than any other. It can be used to thrust to the adversary's face and neck, to slip between his arms and cut, and for many binding and trapping actions closer in, which will be examined later. From a high thrusting move the hanging guard can easily pass forward and lower to the inside (window) guard and from there drop down to parry or thrust from the close guard. This is but one example of the many possibilities for the integration and coordination of the various postures.

From the high guard again, a shorter, closer cut can be made with the middle portion of the blade. This can end in a near-close guard. The close guard can easily thrust forward with a passing step.

By having the weapon pulled back just prior to thrusting, much more power can be generated for a stabbing attack. This can be crucial in thrusting effectively into mail or leather or just flesh and bone.

There are innumerable combinations of the basic eight cuts from the 14 general stances, and not all of these can possibly be illustrated. Only the motions of a very few fundamental ones have been described here.

When cutting low from the opposite of the leading hand the wrists must cross. With a right-handed grip this occurs when cutting underneath from the left back side and the left side hanging posture. In trying to grip this way, the wrists will be twisted, and this is not good. The weapon can rarely be brought out smoothly or quickly enough to have sufficient force or good edge angle. Avoid allowing your arms to become crossed over. In the hanging guard especially the arms can become tangled. Careful practice in flowing in to and out of parries, cuts, and binds with the hanging guard is necessary to learn this.

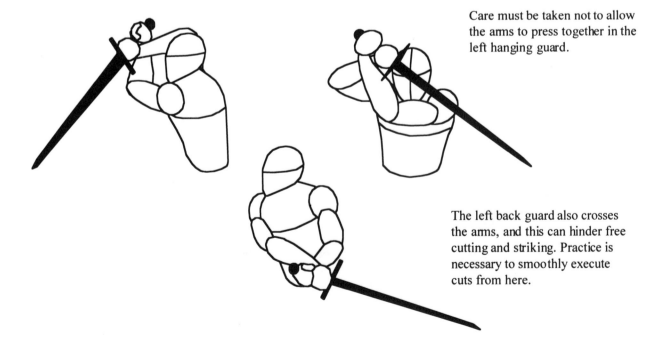

Care must be taken not to allow the arms to press together in the left hanging guard.

The left back guard also crosses the arms, and this can hinder free cutting and striking. Practice is necessary to smoothly execute cuts from here.

PARRYING

Defense with the sword, or the opposition blocking of attacks, is a much misunderstood aspect of using the weapon (almost as much so as cutting itself). Parries need not be made with nearly as wide or large a motion as customarily seen in movies and staged performances. The large, solid, familiar movements of blade banging on blade are unrealistic and hardly portray the weapon's true capabilities. With skill and confidence, a parry is made with a simpler movement. In any parrying the goal is to not move in such a large motion that another target or angle of attack is exposed in the process. The essence of most all swordsmanship has been expressed as *parry and riposte*; that is, block and attack or deflect and counterattack. But remember that *evasion*, or dodging attacks, is the ideal form of parry. If an attack can be made to miss, there's no need to expend effort and motion in parrying it.

It is vital to realize that parries with a Medieval sword are made with the *flat* of the blade and *not* the edge (or the back, as with Japanese swords and other single-edged blades). It is astounding how often this basic fact of swordsmanship is violated or ignored. Virtually every example of sword fighting in film, television, stage, and even live-action shows has the combatants blocking directly with their *edges*. This is incorrect and fundamentally wrong. Edges need to be kept sharp and free of nicks or gouges. Edges are too fine to be intentionally placed in the path of oncoming strikes. In fact, good swords are designed with this in mind. A blade's flexibility, after all, is in its side-to-side motion, and obviously it cannot flex correctly when hit from the edge side.

Parry with the flat of
a Medieval sword,
not its edge.

Whether a sword has a keen, hard-tempered edge or duller, softer one, parrying edge to edge will quickly trash it. Doing so will also likely break a blade far sooner than not. Parrying with the stronger, flexible flat side of the blade is not difficult (especially when correctly taught from the onset). It requires only a slight turn of the wrist to accomplish and no serious change of technique. Though a parry may be made with the edge when completely unavoidable, it is not a proper or smart action to take normally. Sometimes in the heat of battle, there is no choice, but the weapon was not intended to be used that way, and it should not be your practice to deliberately do so.

When beating or knocking with the weapon, such blows may be done edge on flat or, less effectively, flat against flat.

The motion of blocking with the flat of the blade actually allows a more effective counter or return attack. The action lines up the edge in a position better able to cut than if the wrist had to be first turned away from the parry in order to strike. It is perhaps the lack of a truly discernable edge on many forms of sparring weapons (e.g., round sticks, bamboo shinais, foam "boffers") that may affect the parrying habits of some practitioners so that use of the flat rather than the edge is unfamiliar. Most stage-combat or theatrical swords are also extra thick and heavy, making them seem quite capable of holding up under edge blocking. Of course, these weapons were *never* intended to cut with, let alone be handled by true swordsmen. How could a dented, nicked, and chewed-up edge on a real blade possibly cut effectively? Because cheap imitation swords often have a weak, wobbly blade, they confuse novices, who cannot see how a substantial parry could be made using the flat. Parrying with the edge may be far easier for those with a weak wrist or inexperience since the wrist and forearm can seem to line up better this way to resist the force of a blow, but it is still unsuitable, incorrect, and self-defeating.

The ability to use the sword to defend by blocking attacks in a way that does not diminish offensive capacity is one of the many virtues of the weapon. Other weapons, such as axes, spears, or clubs, lose some of their threat potential if their haft or shaft is employed defensively. Yet parries with the Medieval sword were rarely defined in exact terms. They were described more as basic defensive reactions rather than sword placement, and the idea was to move to evade and countercut rather than block. Although with the long-sword there are some superficial similarities in the basic motions to those parries used in the sport of modern saber fencing and its ancestors, they are not equivalent.

There are eight fundamental blocking actions, but only four real parries with the long-sword. These eight defensive actions are sufficient for defending against all attacks, whether thrusts or cuts. They consist of both left and right parries to high attacks above the waist, to low attacks below the waist, and to the hips or waist. Of the eight blocks, two are the inside postures, and two are the hanging guards (or hanging parries). The remaining four are true parries to high or low attacks.

The middle guard allows all parries to be made. The side parries are performed by moving the sword over, the waist or middle parries are made by moving the weapon back and down to the inside position, and the low parries are made by dropping it down to the low position and then over. The two hanging parries are executed by raising the hilt up and lowering the point to assume the hanging guards.

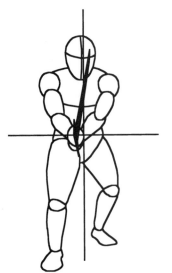

As with attacks, all parries fall into one of the four areas: high outside, high inside, low outside, and low inside. They require no further elaboration. There was no effort to categorize parries with the Medieval sword into the areas associated with Renaissance and later methods of fencing (*sixte, tierce, quarter, prime, octave, seconde, septime,* and *quinte*).

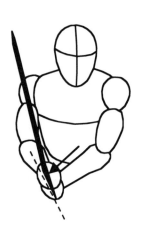

When performed incorrectly, the grip is improperly moved directly into the path of a cut angled toward the waist or hips or even the hands themselves.

In parrying, the angle that the blade meets the oncoming attack must be such that it will not skid off and hit against your own grip or elsewhere. Novice fighters are notorious for getting their hands struck (either by misparrying or not parrying at all). Additionally, one cannot make too wide a motion or stretch out too far to meet a blow or the parry will be weak or the opponent will alter the line of the attack to bypass your defense. Overparrying results in poor recovery, thus preventing your counterstrike, or it creates an opening for the opponent to attack further. When a parry is made, sufficient pressure must be used to actually sustain the block. Novices often make the mistake of just moving their weapon into the line of the attack, expecting the mass of the sword to block for them. This results in the parry turning into a hitting blow against their own blade, disturbing recovery and offering the attacker yet another opening. Parrying is most effective when you move to meet the blow by stepping in to or out of it rather than just throwing your arm and weapon at it.

Since certain attacks can be stopped by only one particular parry and others can be blocked by two or more, which one to choose is a matter of three things: (1) the type of the attack (cut or thrust, high or low, inside or outside); (2) how quickly you can respond; and (3) your intended action immediately following recovery (i.e., a counterattack or another parry). It goes without saying that the decision must be made in an instant. The nature of swordsmanship is such that evading and counterstriking is often more useful than direct parrying followed by separate attacking.

Simple side parries to the left and right can be employed equally well against vertical *or* horizontal cuts. Whether the attack is directed toward the head, collar, shoulder, arm, grip, or side, it may still be blocked with the *same* basic motion. This is the subtle power of the side parry and one that seldom seems to be fully appreciated.

The middle parries are the most useful because they defend against diagonal, vertical, and horizontal cuts, as well as straight thrusts.

Right-side (high outside) parries against various lines of attack.

Left-side parries (or high inside).

In any parrying, the arm naturally should not be rigid or fully extended, or the block will be weak. The grip should also not be too loose or too tight. For most parries, rather than move the whole weapon over or out to meet the attack in a wide action, only the blade and tip need move while the hilt remains more or less in the same position. If the hilt moved in too large a manner, the opponent can strike around it or even strike the weapon in such a way as to make proper recovery impossible. Overparrying is one of the most basic mistakes that a swordsman can make or that an opponent can be lured into making.

A common mistake in side parries against vertical or diagonal cuts is to only turn the hilt outward or to only turn the point inward. In each case, the force of a blow can push the blade aside or downward and still hit the body. Parrying like this is insufficient and merely opens the arm, shoulder, and collar to the blow.

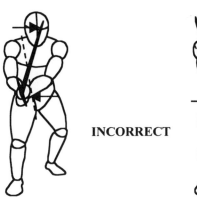

INCORRECT

Neither of these incorrect parries really allows the weapon to recovery quickly enough to cut back or parry again.

Another common mistake in parrying is to just move the point outward or to move the hilt inward. This is also insufficient and cannot properly block the force of a blow. Diagonal and horizontal cuts can skip right past the weapon to strike the side or hips and vertical cuts can skip down to strike virtually anywhere on the torso, head, or arms.

Cutting back immediately from a side parry.

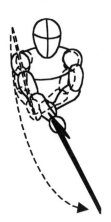

Ideally, a side parry can be performed in such a manner that the very motion of moving the blade outward aligns it so that it can then cut right back at the opponent, using the very momentum of the parry itself along with a a forward step, side-step, or even a passing step. Accomplishing this takes great practice to develop the required reflex and muscle.

213

Parries to protect the lower legs are crucial to master. Attacks to the lower thighs, knees, shins, and ankles are blocked by the *same* simple action of quickly dropping the weapon to the low guard and moving it over. The reflex of being able to drop the blade down and over left or right must be tirelessly practiced. A common attack can be to feint low and then strike high as the opponent presumptuously drops his blade to parry an expected leg cut.

To parry low the blade simply drops straight down to the center, and then both hilt and point move to the side. The point must naturally move out farther to actually block. Too short or too soft a movement will be insufficient, and the blow can knock the parry back.

Low right parry (low outside).

Low left parry (low inside).

After parrying low from this position an immediate diagonal upward cut or thrust can be made. A quick recovery may also be made to the middle position. Just as easily the weapon may remain in the low guard, rise to a hanging guard, or pull back to one of the many others, depending on need.

Most often students will be struck when trying to parry high when they should have parried low or parrying low when they should have parried high. But the ability to block attacks to the lower legs and then recover to strike back or parry elsewhere is something many practitioners are now deficient in because of the rule structure under which they spar. (This is addressed at length in the appendixes.)

Dropping the blade prematurely will cause a misparry and allow the adversary to cut down across the grip or forearms.

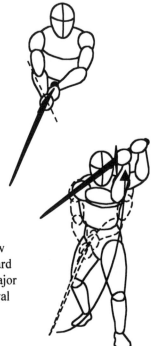

The action of lifting from a low parry directly to a hanging guard (or vice versa) is one of the major components of using a Medieval long-sword and should also be practiced to proficiency.

The most fundamental and crucial error of parrying low is to bring the weapon *around* instead of straight down and then over. Bringing it around (as if to first parry to the side before realizing a low one is necessary) actually helps to pull the attack into the leg. A parry attempted this way will come from *behind* the strike rather than intercept in front of it. A common tactic is trying to induce an adversary to make this mistake by deceiving or "forcing the parry." A high- or midlevel attack is first feigned before a low cut is made.

The hanging guards are also hanging parries. By the nature of its use, the hanging guard (more so than any other) is an active, energetic posture, not static and expectant. It is used either by suddenly and quickly adopting the posture just as the opponent strikes or by assuming the stance and moving in to the opponent's strike. Apparently, for some reason the hanging posture was also sometimes called the "woman's parry."

The hanging parry can defend well against vertical and diagonal cuts while allowing an immediate return cut to be made. Against horizontal and midlevel waist cuts, it has less applicability and must be turned and lowered to parry, thereby diminishing its possible counterattack. The action of quickly performing a hanging parry (or assuming the hanging guard) from the middle stance must be tirelessly practiced until it can be a fluid and instantaneous response. Hold the weapon at a 45-degree angle to allow blows to slide off. Most important is to receive the opponent's attack on the flat of the weapon and not the edge. Parrying with a sharp edge does not let it "bite" into an attacking weapon as some believe.

Hanging guard parrying right (high outside).

Hanging guard parrying left (high inside).

Parrying is nearly always done in conjunction with footwork. Generally, one can step to the side against vertical cuts, step back to let lateral cuts pass, or step in to stifle or preempt either. This is especially true with the hanging parries.

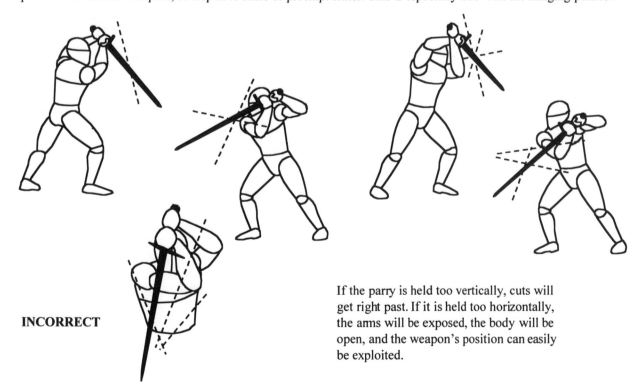

INCORRECT

If the parry is held too vertically, cuts will get right past. If it is held too horizontally, the arms will be exposed, the body will be open, and the weapon's position can easily be exploited.

To quickly execute a hanging guard or parry from the middle stance, the weapon is brought up and turned to the side by first slightly dropping the point. From the high guard the weapon need only be brought forward and the point rotated around and down.

The hanging guard has left and right versions, yet each can parry to either side by turning the body into the path of the cut and raising or lowering the weapon as necessary. Doing this, of course, can turn the parry into an inside or close guard in the process.

Two dangers of parrying in the hanging guard are exposing the hands to attack (especially if the weapon is held too far forward) and the exposure of the midsection to thrusts and waist cuts. Keeping the weapon raised at the correct angle and the point out far enough to threaten a thrust can prevent these problems. But if overextended forward, it can be exploited by the opponent.

It was only with the lighter thrusting swords of the Renaissance that the action of deflecting or parrying an attacking blade before making a separate counterattack became "doctrine." The tips of slender thrusting swords can be intercepted and deflected at the same time a counterthrust is executed. With a wider, somewhat heavier cutting sword, using an arcing cut of considerable momentum, such actions are certainly possible, but just inefficient. Far more practical is a timed evading motion in to or out of the adversary's action in order to make a countercut. But direct parrying does, of course, allow the use of entering techniques such as for closing to trap or bind the opponent's weapon with your hilt. Also, it was not until later Renaissance methods of using slender thrusting rapiers that using the edge to parry with became a viable technique against certain attacks.

The close guard is ideally suited to parrying those middle attacks to the hips and waist or "belt line" and is likely the origin of the posture. The utility of threatening or executing an immediate thrust after parrying attacks to the waist gives the stance its value (when performed with a wide, lunging forward step, stabbing this way can be quite effective). Due to the typically indeterminate intention of incoming strikes there, middle attacks to the waist/hips are notoriously difficult to parry. Attacks can come in directly to the grip at hilt level. Such strikes can change from torso or thigh cuts or anywhere in between with only a quick and subtle motion. It is not easy to perceive exactly where they are aimed (in fact, on inexperienced fighters the hand is a fairly easy target for this very reason). Dropping the blade too low can result in taking a hit in the forearm or hand, while blocking too high can leave you open on the hip, thigh, or groin.

If you attempt to block a midlevel attack by a low parry, the strike will hit the hands or forearms if it is not pulled in under the blade. If you attempt to block a midlevel attack by a side parry, it again will hit the hands or simply miss and let the strike succeed. Ideally, such attacks should be evaded by passing back and countercutting. They can also be defeated by moving forward to close the distance and using a side parry. Alternatively, dropping down to the close guard allows a solid defense against middle attacks without putting the grip into the path of the cut or hindering the ability to instantly turn the close guard into a low parry by dropping it down or a side parry by pushing out. If desired, the close guard can also easily shift to a middle or high stance to deliver a cut after it parries.

Close guard parries right and left.

Often novices fail to block middle attacks at all and simply leave their hands right there to be hit. Their instinct is to move their fists (the hilt) into the path of the attack instead of properly moving the weapon to intercept. The best method for defending the hips and belt line (as with most swordsmanship) involves some turning, some stepping, some leaning, and only then some parrying.

The inside guard, although not a parrying position, does have defensive capability in blocking certain cuts. However, a strong blow can knock the guard into you (at the head, face, neck, or collar). Care should be taken not to turn the guard sideways (horizontally) or to keep the hilt too close to the side of the head. By pushing out with both the point and hilt, the inside guard can receive high cuts without wavering. But high feints followed by middle or low cuts reveal the weakness of this stance for parrying.

Another defensive failing of the inside guard is that beating attacks can be used to knock the point off and open up a line of attack. Binding or pressuring the blade can also force it back into a hanging posture where it can become entangled or seized. The weapon must be wielded in a supple and flexible stance to prevent this.

Both the close and inside guards are well suited to a sword with a longer handle and longer blade. Although they are not as strong against side parries, they are able to recover quickly and attack with thrusts or shorter blows. Their value also lies in offering transitional warding postures prior to recovering to a stronger cutting or parrying position (high, middle, hanging, back).

The short guard is also a form of parry, but it is only a center variation of the inside guard. It can be useful when an attack is made at closer distances or as a parry while you step in close against an opponent. Its drawback is that by pulling the weapon in close it waits to intercept an attack, thereby allowing it to alter its angle before connecting. This is particularly so with thrusts, which can quickly change their line of attack to "disengaged" left or right.

Noticeably absent from the previous eight parries is a "horizontal block." This is a familiar and almost instinctive parry, but one fraught with serious flaws and vulnerabilities. It is more or less the "Hollywood" parry, taught as standard defense in virtually all theatrical fighting and stage combat as a universal blocking action. Although it is suited for the safety requirements of pretend swordplay and ever present in movie sword fights and other performances, it is ill-advised and self-defeating for swordsmanship. Such a parry can result when the warrior is caught off guard or when he is unable to respond more effectively, but it is actually a weak and crude action. It almost immediately puts the blade's edge in the path of the attacking blade, thereby ensuring its damage and possibly causing it to break. Recovering to another fighting posture from this horizontal parry also delays you from more efficient movements. The motion requires the point be withdrawn off the opponent and brought around sideways, thereby significantly reducing the threat of a thrust and the range of other possible options. To cut back after parrying like this, the weapon must traverse all the way back around to generate momentum or else try to cut forward with much less power. The hanging guard is the proper employment of a parry to defend in this way and has far greater potential for counterattacking. The horizontal parry offers nothing that the hanging and side parries cannot themselves already do better without withdrawing the weapon from more versatile postures. Offering the horizontal Hollywood parry to a skilled swordsman's attack can be suicidal.

The horizontal parry's idealized form is seen as that of protecting from all high attacks with a wide obstruction.

The reality is that attacks can easily fall on or purposely target the hands (it is very unlikely the handle itself can be used to block). The forearms are also vulnerable in the same way, and cuts can easily angle in to strike below and under this parry. This is a very easy way of striking novices who use it. And, as mentioned earlier, relying on the cross-guard to block with is foolhardy.

If the weapon is held with the point raised, this does little but expose the hands and forearms without offering protection to the torso. Only when the warrior has entered to close range is this effective.

It is important to point out that parrying techniques that may work fine in stick-fighting or padded contact-sparring are not *entirely* equivalent to those used with real swords. Parrying with a real sword is simply different (not necessarily harder). A thin piece of sharp metal behaves differently than do wooden sticks or foam-covered rods. Blows of metal on metal can skip or deflect off, redirecting themselves rather than having their momentum stopped. The difference follows even to the use of thick, blunt theatrical swords. This can be fully appreciated through practice parrying with accurate replicas of medieval swords. Of course, almost any strong opposition against a sharp edge can cause it to deflect enough that it will not cut well.

FIGHTING WITH THE LONG-SWORD

The art of single long-sword against single long-sword is among the most exciting and rousing of Medieval fighting skills and historical fencing. It is likely the most popular area of study for enthusiasts of Medieval combat or arms and armor. Having established many of the central and rudimentary concepts in the section on fighting with the sword & shield, it is not necessary to reiterate them here. But just how to go about using these actions and ideas with various tactical concepts, including close-range entering techniques, brings us finally to fighting with the long-sword. It goes without saying that techniques, whether attacks, parries, or close-in actions, can be performed in motion timed with the adversary's actions. They can be performed as simple advancing or receding steps or with forward and back passes. Attacks can be made from direct inaction, with preparatory action and combined actions, or in counteraction. Cuts and thrusts can be made high or low, left or right, with lead edge or back edge. These actions are employed in conjunction with the principles of timing, distance, perception, and technique.

There are innumerable combinations of basic cuts, thrusts, parries, beats, binds, and feints applied with stepping and closing actions. It is not possible to illustrate them all, even the most basic ones. Instead, we will concentrate on a few of the more obvious techniques that express the nature of the weapon and its attitude.

The range in which to engage the opponent with a long-sword is a matter of judgment and circumstances. Ideally, it is that which allows a strong cut to be delivered by a simple step or pass.

Feeling confident and mentally centered with your weapon is nothing metaphysical. It is a matter of intuitively knowing the feel of a blade balanced, weighted, and comfortably fitted to your physical attributes and natural style. This familiarity comes about only through long practice.

Just as for learning and practicing the fundamental stances, there are innumerable drills that can be devised for sequences of striking and parrying, closing and binding, and stepping and evading. The drills can be practiced at slow and full speed, both with a partner and alone in individual practice. Most important is the ability to deliver a variety of strong, quick cuts and thrusts with mobility. Because they can be constructed from the practical application of techniques and actions learned in free-sparring, there is no need to offer examples here.

A useful sword training tool is a simple wooden stick. An ordinary 1 1/4-inch oak dowel available at most hardware stores makes an excellent substitute that can be used for exercises and safe drills. Even without a hilt or edge, a good, solid stick is a weapon in its own right. Although very useful for practice, such sticks are not really suitable for free-sparring. Many fine-quality wooden swords are also becoming available now from specialty craftsmen. These wooden swords are the Medieval equivalent to the Japanese *bokken* used in kenjutsu and can be ideal for students. Bokkens themselves however, have a different shape, balance, and feel that is not suited to Medieval sword practice. In the end, though, it is through the process of actually trying to cut a test target with a real sharpened blade that understanding is properly gained of the motions required to do so and the positions you end up in afterward.

The grand *Fechtmeister* Liechtenauer divided sword combat into two separate phases. The phase where the swordsmen are coming to distance and have their weapons make contact was referred to as *Zufechten*. Once swords have crossed and the distance has been closed, the fight enters what the Germans called *Handarbeit* (handwork) or *Krieg* (war).

The engaged position with the swords crossed was called *Anbinden* in the German systems of long-sword (*Langenschwert*) and later the huge two-handers (*Dopplehänder/Bidenhänder*). Although this can occur in the course of fighting, this position is artificial to begin combat in. No one in his right mind should approach an opponent and allow him to be so close that the blades cross from the start.

Each stance has its own attitude and tactical context. Each offers certain offensive and defensive options and advertises this to an opponent.

Whatever combination you are faced with, there are multiple options of how to respond. The opponent may adopt the same stance or oppose you with a contrary posture.

Changing stances communicates something. It may reveal aggressiveness, defensiveness, neutrality, or apprehension; or it may offer an opportunity to strike.

Remember, stances cannot be separated from the footwork employed with them (or the cuts used by them).

It is not possible to convey in drawings alone all the many tactical possibilities and the infinite combinations of cuts, thrusts, and other techniques along with their associated stepping and countertiming. To illustrate examples of various simple techniques and concepts a collage of cuts and thrusts against attacks (both left and right) from a variety of stances are depicted on the following pages.

If the high guard is held too close to the opponent, it is vulnerable to a direct thrust to the face. As the arms are brought down to strike they can also knock against the back edge of the opponent's weapon.

The back guard is ideal for intercepting an attack. It is difficult for the opponent to judge the distance or the angle it will strike from.

A counterattack against the opponent's grip just as he strikes or just before he strikes can be very effective and difficult to prevent. It is especially effective against a slower opponent or one who keeps his hilt too far forward.

To be able to judge the distance and timing such that the opponent can be made to miss by mere inches is a hallmark of a fighter of great skill. The adversary can be counterattacked instantly after his own cut misses. Just as he strikes, you can move out of range with a pass back and then in again with a forward pass to strike.

One of the most fundamental attacks is to feint high and strike low. It is most effective with a cut from the full shoulder, followed by a shorter, quicker one from the arm.

The opposite is to feint low and strike high. The low strike can be a short motion from the arms, whereas the high cut may be either from the arms or shoulder.

There were four ways in German schools for when an attack could be made: *von fechten* (attacking before), *gleich fechten* (attacking at the same time), and *in des fechten* (attacking in the middle of the adversary's attack), and *nachreissen* (attacking after). *Nachreissen* was a fundamental tenet of Medieval German swordsmanship in which rather than taking the offensive the opponent was invited to attack first and then counterattacked either in the middle of a cut or just after his cut missed. This is the familiar idea of the timed countercut. The German grandmaster Liechtenauer called these prized techniques *Meisterhau* (master cuts). These are techniques in which the swordsman strikes so that his sword deflects the incoming blow while simultaneously hitting the opponent. However, Liechtenauer taught that a superior swordsman seeks the initiative by going on the offensive. If an adversary attacks first, the swordsman responds with the *Nach*, or defensive principle. The offensive principle was called *Vor*. Passively accepting attacks by merely parrying blows without responding is inferior and will result in defeat. The German masters also expressed the idea of *Stuck und Bruch* (technique and counter). This is the concept that every technique has a counter and every counter a technique.

A counterthrust can be made by pulling away with a pass back as you extend the arms in to the oncoming opponent. The reverse, passing forward in to the adversary, can also be effective.

A counterthrust against a cut. This is the classic use of a thrusting attack's directness and reach. The motion of cutting can make the opponent vulnerable until he recovers or renews his attack. The best way to avoid counterthrusts is to step in closer with your cut, make a preparatory action before you cut, or wait to countercut instead.

A countercut timed to the adversary's attack by passing forward or back. Such fundamental attacks may be made high or low from most any posture. Often the closest target is the adversary's extended arm, exposed shoulder, or undefended lower legs.

Countercutting also involves the idea of *Überlauffen* (overrunning). This consists of trying to outreach the adversary as he attacks by striking his closer targets. When he strikes high you cut low; when he strikes low you cut high. As he cuts toward your leg you cut his extended hand or arm. As he strikes toward your head you cut his advancing leg. As he strikes your midsection you come down across his shoulders or head.

Many actions and techniques work on both sides equally well, left or right. Others are defined by whether they are delivered from right-or-left stances or by which leg is leading at the time. Many actions and techniques require a pass forward or back as they are executed, whereas some may need only a small step by one or the other foot. This should be well researched by practical drilling.

A strike may be made from below just as the opponent lifts his weapon or as it comes around from another action. Waiting until the weapon is just in front of his face can allow the vulnerable grip or forearms to be struck with ease.

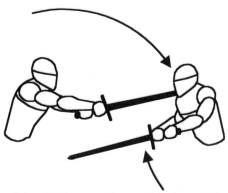

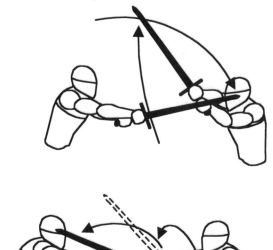

Another of the simplest attacks is to block or deflect a direct thrust with a small side parry movement and immediately extend the arms to slice or chop the adversary's extended arms. A forward step may be made to increase the range.

Cutting by striking down vertically on the blade just as the adversary strikes diagonally.

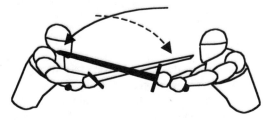

Cutting by striking down diagonally on the blade just as the adversary strikes vertically.

Deflecting a blow, as opposed to blocking it, is a means of beating an attack off as you make your own attack, knocking the incoming weapon aside simultaneously with launching your own. This can be a difficult but highly useful action to perform. As the adversary cuts downward either vertically or horizontally, you strike with a sideways motion to intercept his cut in the middle of the blow. As your weapon pushes his to the side, you then reverse your blow by turning the edge and swinging back to hit. Such deflecting cuts must be instantaneous and smooth. If your strike is poorly timed, you will get hit or miss with the countercut. Similarly, you may even strike a strong diagonal cut in this same way that deflects your opponent's blade by your own hits.

One of the Medieval German fighting guilds was the "Luxbrueder" or "Brotherhood of St. Luke." Similar to later English schools of defence, they were headed by four adepts and a captain. There was also the successful *Marxbrüder*, or *Brotherhood of St. Mark*, a group of masters who at one time organized and regulated the tea rotherho, as well as others, lasted well into the Renaissance. Examples of the blunt training blades as seen in their manuals still survive. Reportedly, some guilds even used armored gloves in practice (which is not at all surprising).

As the opponent is enticed into cutting or thrusting, his attack can be countered with a well-timed sidestep and simultaneous counterattack to deflect his thrust or parry his cut. This was known as *Absetzen* (setting aside). However, the word was also used to signify various techniques for countering or parrying cuts and thrusts, such as a type of trapping move where the sword is hooked over the opponent's and forced downward. It can also mean a simple parry, generally followed by a thrust.

One of the simplest cuts can often be made with just a forward push of the blade while still maintaining contact or opposition with the adversary's blade. Such action can be applied after having moved in to lessen the distance or after the adversary tries to close in.

If the opponent is too close, a simple stab to the face can be most effective. This occurs frequently against novices, who, in their concern for defending against the many cuts, forget to maintain range.

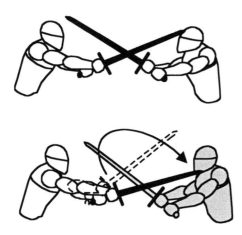

Another basic movement when blades are crossed is to "cut over." As the weapon is lifted to strike on one side, it instead comes down on the other by crossing over the opponent's point. The short motion to which the weapon is limited does restrict the power and effectiveness of this action.

A similar action quickly slides or glides down with a pressuring motion against the opponent's blade and then slices across his forearms or even his neck. A forward step or push can pull his weapon off and, as he resists, he will actually permit your use of the technique.

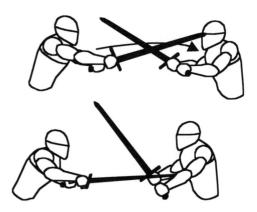

Similarly, simple slices or chops to the hand and forearm can be made when the adversary allows you to be too close.

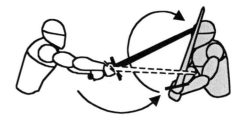

The opposite of the cutover is a "disengage," in which the weapon drops under the opponent's guard to strike to the other side. This is more effective when the initial attack provokes a parry or when using thrusts. As with the cutover, attacks from here are not strong.

Disengages, or countering or blade evasions similar to those now familiar in modern fencing, were also taught in the Medieval German fighting guilds. When the adversary attempts to cross blades, the sword is dropped under and an attack is made on the other side of their guard. This can be either a circular movement with the point or an evasive cutting motion with the blade.

There are many basic actions and techniques that can be employed to force the opponent's weapon away before you strike or to lure him into creating an opening you can attack. There are also many fundamental mistakes that, if committed, a skillful adversary will easily exploit.

If an opponent engages too closely, there are a multitude of offensive techniques that can immediately be applied against him, such as thrusts to the face, slices to the arms, and cuts to the hands.

If an opponent engages too horizontally, he will lack offensive options and his threat will be limited. His point can also be beaten aside or bound up. Ward against thrusts and target his grip and forearms.

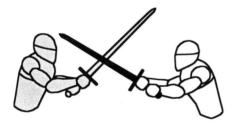

If an opponent engages too vertically, his weapon loses potential and he will be vulnerable to thrusts as well as having to delay his responses to attacks. His own attacks will also have a minute delay as his weapon moves to generate momentum. Use feints and combination attacks to overwhelm an opponent employing his weapon too vertically.

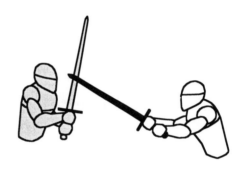

The "beat" is a fundamental technique to virtually all weapon arts and was a well-developed move in later Renaissance systems. The attacking sword makes a harassing or preparatory strike against the opponent's weapon. A beat can be taken to knock the opponent's blade away, push the point off, and provoke a response or to startle an opponent into action. With the long-sword a beat can take several forms. It is not a very sophisticated action, just a natural motion usually on the flat of the opposing weapon. There can be a quick, short, sideways beat using the end of the sword against the opponent's extended point. A stronger beat can be made upward from under the adversary's weapon to knock it away before then cutting down or thrusting in. This beat may also take the form of "attacking the blade" in which a blow is deliberately aimed at the weapon to strike it down forcefully or smack it hard enough to prevent your opponent's recovering before you follow with a cut or thrust. Last, there can be a slow pressing beat that lingers against the opponent's weapon before pushing it forcefully aside as you step in closer.

Striking down or to the side.

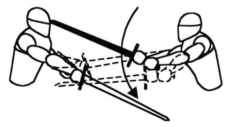

Striking off from underneath.

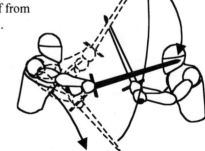

Beats, binds, and other attacks on the blade should be used with care. They seldom succeed against a skilled swordsman, who will avoid them and cut at openings created by the attempt.

225

The hanging guard used as both attack posture and parrying posture. This engagement is really no different than if each fighter were in a middle guard.

Techniques were closely guarded by masters and not readily disclosed. The German schools of swordsmanship taught that there were three principle actions called *Drey Wunder* (the "three wonders). These were the thrust, the cut, and *Schnitt* (a slicing or drawing cut). They taught that the thrust naturally was used primarily at longer range, the cut at medium range, and the slice more at closer range.

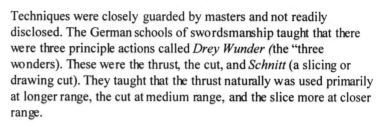

Using a hanging parry right while passing forward to the left. Stepping diagonally forward in this way allows for a follow-up cut from the side to the opponent's exposed shoulders, arms, or legs.

The hanging guard delivering a rising cut to the midsection. This could be accomplished as a direct attack with a forward pass or a countercut with a pass back.

A rising cut to the exposed arms of an opponent cutting downward from the high guard. This type of highly effective cut can be delivered from the hanging guard, back guard, or even the middle guard. As with virtually all other counterattacks, timing and proper distance combined with stepping are vital.

A hanging parry against any number of high cuts can immediately lift up and around to cut from the same side. It is effective with a step in but can also be used with a pass backward. This is one of its primary virtues, and such cuts should be practiced well.

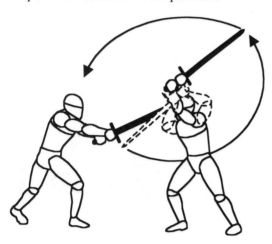

Cutting under with a slicing motion from the hanging guard is another value of the posture. Cuts may be made underneath the attacker's weapon and hilt by stepping or passing forward. They can be delivered to the groin, inner thigh, abdomen, or forearms. These are difficult cuts and require strong motions. They are more slicing than chopping moves and can be ineffective against armor. However, they can also be made with a hitting motion in order to just knock the opponent.

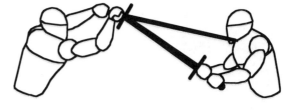

Another view of the hanging parry.

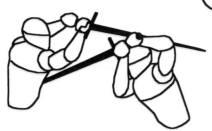

By dropping under and moving forward, the same cut can be applied without a parry being necessary.

Side cuts can also be initiated from the hanging guard. They can be made with a forward motion against the neck or head.

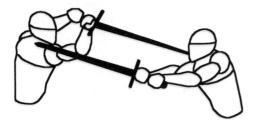

With evasive movements and steps, thrusts can effectively be delivered as well.

One weakness of the hanging stance (and also the inside stance) is exploited by forcefully beating the point off to the inside so that the opponent's wrists are twisted. The awkwardness caused by this prevents him from parrying or attacking and delays his recovery. Beats against the hanging guard in this manner should be followed up quickly with an attack to the opposite side.

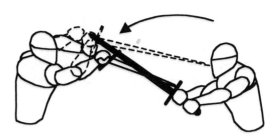

Single-hand techniques with the long-sword can be quite deceptive as they are suddenly "whipped" out. They unexpectedly increase the range of a blow. But unless you have a strong hand, they can hit on a poor angle as well as upset your recovery. One-hand reaching attacks are most useful from the high and back guards. Cuts from the left-side back stance in particular can often actually be more effective with the long-sword held in one hand.

Slipping in to the outside of a hanging or inside stance with a thrust.

Knowing when to take advantage of the opponent's misjudging the distance or overextending himself is something learned only by experience.

The side guard can allow a blow to be struck when the opponent is too close or too quick. It pulls the weapon away, thereby preventing the opponent from employing binds or close-in trapping actions against it. By using proper footwork you can bring the weapon back in against him, adopt a defensive posture, or ready a counterblow. As with so many other postures, without using effective footwork all it does is remove your defense and open yourself to your opponent.

As mentioned in the section on parrying, if the weapon is brought outward and then down against low attacks, it will not only fail to block but also help to bring the opponent's weapon in. The correct defense is to drop the weapon down and over.

Hanging guard against hanging guard allows for a wide range of attacks and technique combinations. For the most part, the goal is to keep your weapon where it can evenly turn to parry inside (left) or lift to parry outside (right). This means keeping the point more or less centered. The utility of the stance allows cuts under, over, and around, and numerous binding and trapping actions. Therefore, don't become fixed in either a defensive parrying mode or an anxious countering attitude.

Stepping out and pushing the blade into the opponent as he advances. Again, this can be executed from the middle, back right, hanging, or even high guard.

Stepping in with the close guard to parry and thrust.

Stepping in preemptively to thrust with the close guard.

A classic countercut timed with the opponent's motion so that the blow strikes as his attack passes by. This is another fundamental concept that can be applied in numerous variations. One name for such moves of evading the opponent's blade as you strike was *Durchwechseln* (changing through).

Using the inside guard to parry a rising cut before stepping in to thrust.

Short drawing cuts known as both *Abschneiden* (cutting aside) and *Schnitt* (slice) in the German schools can be used at closer distances against the opponent's forearms and hands. They can be made with both the lead and the back edges.

Cuts against the forearms can be made just as the opponent brings his weapon down or as he is in the process of raising it up. These strikes can be made by lifting the blade from the middle guard or lowering from the high guard. These were known as "pressing the hands."

If the opponent has the same intention or is too close to allow other actions, the swords can end up in a crossed or locked position. However, this occurs with far less frequency than is commonly depicted in theatrical swordfights. The situation is usually fleeting as one or the other fighter will disengage to cut elsewhere or lift off to attempt a close-in technique against the arms or hilt.

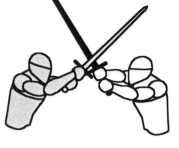

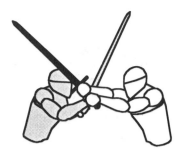

Disengaging to strike with the guard to the face by pushing forward.

Hitting with the pommel as the opponent pulls back.

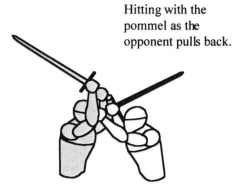

The familiar movie fight scene of swordsmen locked close together pressing blade against blade is sheer nonsense. Such actions occur for only brief instances and are countered by the most simple disengages and a variety of beating, striking, or seizing techniques. There is absolutely no reason to lock together with an opponent for prolonged dramatic moments of pushing back each other's sword. It serves no purpose in either real fighting or serious, realistic sparring. Such fanciful actions take the place of the more brutal and efficient techniques that are actually used. Who knows what they think they are trying to accomplish, but it usually ends up in some ridiculous shoving or spinning motion. The close-in moves typically portrayed in such fights are far different from the many close-range techniques available to the long-sword. When you are actually trying to hit your opponent (in safe sparring bouts), there are several mechanical and technical differences other than the artificial pauses for slapstick or improbable moves of most stage-combat routines.

According to at least one *Fechtmeister,* attacks made while maintaining constant pressure on the opposing blade were known as *am Schwert* (on the sword). Contact is kept throughout the course of the attack without disengaging, in a sticking, binding manner. This is also known as the *Winden* (winding or turning). This is a form of gliding attack that slides along the opponent's blade and thereby keeps a distracting and controlling pressure just before lifting off to slice or cut. Fighting close allows the opportunity for striking with the pommel or guard, or binding with the guard. It also allows for grappling and grabbing actions. There were many close-in techniques for "wrestling at the sword" (*am Schwert*). Most involved throws or grappling and disarming moves known as "swordtaking" (*Schwertnemen.*)

A pommel strike made while passing forward and grabbing the opponent's sword handle in the middle. Before hitting, your blade must maintain opposition as you close in.

Closing in and punching to the face. Contact is maintained with the opponent's blade as you advance, thereby pushing and binding it up so he cannot strike or evade.

There are dozens of entering techniques called *gopostreta* (body contact) by Italian Masters for fighting close in at seizing/grappling range (in the later English systems of cut & thrust sword in the 1500s, these were known as *gryps*). All of these essentially are based on a handful of key actions: reaching out to grab the opponent's hilt or arm; striking with the pommel or guard; slipping the blade against or between his forearms; using the second hand to hold the blade while binding, striking, or slicing; and, of course, tripping and kicking. Correspondingly, a good number of illustrations and paintings of Medieval combat show considerable grappling and grabbing as blows are struck and thrusts made. Many manuals on the long-sword even go into great detail on these important actions. Yet today, for safety, touching an opponent in like manner is commonly avoided in most re-creational practice. This results in deficiencies that students must overcome through more realistic martial training. Considering that these close-in techniques make up at least a good third of all those in the historical manuals, it is remarkable how often they are ignored by practitioners. It also brings great skepticism to mind when, after more than 200 years of ignoring the vital element of close-range infighting, some modern sport-fencers can somehow presume they understand something of the historical skill of using Medieval and Renaissance cutting blades.

One of the most basic seizing moves: step in and reach out to grab the opponent's wrist while blocking his weapon.

Once close distance has been reached and the weapons are opposing one another locked together, even if only for an instant, it is so easy to end up on the ground wrestling whether you want to or not. Wrestling or grappling moves were therefore included in the curriculum of every master and school (but are not included here). They were sometimes known as *Unterhalten* (holding down) in the German systems of fighting. Close-range techniques tend to favor the stronger, larger fighter and work to the detriment of a smaller or weaker swordsman; though such entering or infighting techniques have great value, they are much less applicable under conditions of fighting multiple opponents. In those instances when you are outnumbered, staying mobile and free to move or cut in any direction greatly outweighs their utility.

Another fundamental action is the bind. There are a variety of ways to employ binding movements to force the opponent's weapon off, knock the point away, or press him into pulling it back. All of these result in either an opening to attack or a delay in the adversary's ability to react, recover, or attack.

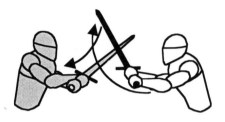

Immediately after you step in to make blade contact with the opponent's weapon a push against his weaker point (*Schwech*) by your stronger middle (*Stark*) is followed by an instantaneous slash on his head, face, or arms. This should be executed as one quick, smooth movement.

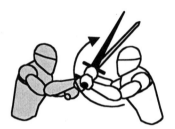 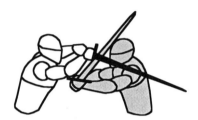

Other binds are possible using the cross-guard to smack his blade aside as you close in or as he advances to strike or close. These may be used prior to any number of close-range techniques such as slices or blows by the hilt. Again, such actions are not the same as the unnecessary locking up of the swords so often depicted in movies and television.

Knocking the opponent's weapon away with the cross-guard before hitting.

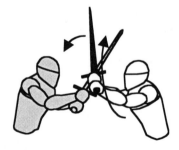

With the long-sword much more so than with a single-hand weapon, the cross-guard is useful for binding techniques. When a blocking action or trapping parry is executed, the opponent's blade may glide down against the guard or your own blade can be raised to meet it. At this point a twist of the sword will release it from the guard and free the weapon for an instant counterstroke or recovery (of course, this works both ways). A wide range of moves using the cross-guard can also be done to hook the arms, legs, or neck.

Close-distance fighting demands that you be extra quick and alert to the short, intense beats, binds, hooking actions, and grabbing that precede blows, disarms, and even takedowns. If you are not comfortable at such ranges whether because of size, strength, speed, inexperience, or personal preference, avoid it by being able to successfully keep the fight at other longer ranges.

Instead of strength alone, disarms and grabs often utilize the adversary's own force and motion against his. This use of leverage can involve shifting stances while lowering and twisting one's hips.

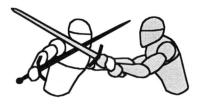

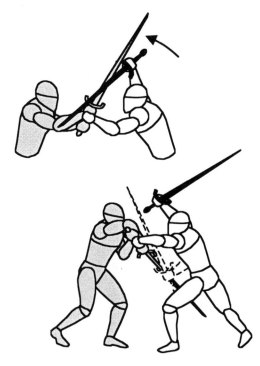

When his weapon is grabbed, an opponent will typically focus on nothing other than the item in his hand that is being taken. It is part of human nature for people to freeze momentarily as their mind centers on holding their weapon rather than realizing that they should be moving or counterseizing or performing some action other than just resisting by strength alone. In this split second or so of indecision and hesitation they can be struck or be disarmed (and then struck). There are many ways of grabbing the hilt and momentarily trapping the opponent's blade. One method used by an armored fighter employs the second hand to close around the opponent's weapon, trapping it flat between the body and under the arm. The hand can then quickly reach out to grab the opponent's cross-guard.

By closing in with pressure from your sword, a grab can be executed to his hilt. Pushing his weapon down while twisting the hilt up forces his arms into a weak and helpless position. From here you can lift off to strike or even disarm him or take him to the ground.

Closing in to grab the wrist while applying blade pressure can twist the opponent's grip into a weak palm-up position. He is left momentarily vulnerable to a draw-cut, pommel strike, or other blow.

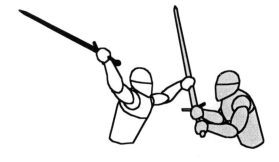

With gauntlets, even the blade can be grabbed. This changes things significantly.

To quickly allow both the hilt and tip to be better employed, stances such as the hanging and inside guards are used more often at close range. These allow the weapon to remain point down and pommel up so that the cross-guard can then be used to block, trap, and push while strikes can be made with the pommel. For greater stabbing power, a grip can be used whereby the pommel is grasped in the second hand's palm to more easily add force to stabs. The middle guard also is very useful at close range, but it does expose the hilt for the opponent to seize.

233

When used with armored gloves or gauntlets, the blade itself can be gripped by the hand. This allows for a wide range of offensive and defensive actions. These techniques were known as *Halbschwert* (half-sword). Italian schools might have called them false-point blows. A wide range of such techniques were done usually by placing the left hand on the midpoint of the blade, as with gripping the long ricasso on two-handed swords. Using the left hand to hold the blade allows the right to grip more strongly near the hilt but some using the right hand could hold the pommel in the left. These moves are suited to plate armor fighting when gauntlets are employed and cuts are less effective against the opponent, but the *Fechtbuchs* show them practiced by unarmored students.

Parrying with the guard and deflecting.

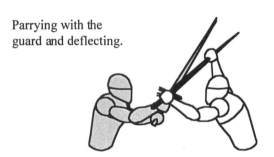

Controlling the point in thrusting while parrying.

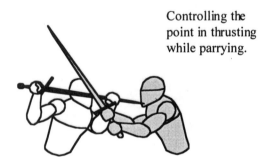

One half-sword technique used against a vertical downward cut consisted of catching the incoming blow on the portion of the blade between the hands and then delivering a thrust to the opponent's face or underarm. This type of parry with the sword held point forward over the head was called the *Kron* (crown). Another blow might be made by holding the sword blade itself with both hands and striking clublike with the pommel or guard. Once term for this is *Mordschlag* (death blow). However, it was a rare action and used typically only against heavily armored opponents or when the blade's edge was not cutting well. Most obvious is that once this blow is parried the guard can be hooked by the adversary's weapon to disarm you with a simple pull (this has not stopped it from being included in numerous theatrical swordfights).

Knocking the opponent's weapon aside and striking with the pommel.

Using a reverse grip on the ricasso to deliver a thrust.

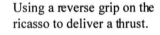

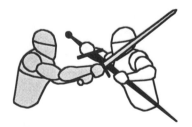

Parrying and deflecting with a half-sword technique. For reference these are shown here against middle stances and downward cuts, but they can be used against many high attacks and even a few low attacks.

The examples here have illustrated some of the most basic and obvious techniques of close fighting. The historical manuals, of course, show many, many more. Yet the historical manuals, as stated before, are hardly complete or offer comprehensive instruction themselves. There are indications that some of both the simpler and more subtle fighting techniques are not represented. This may very well be due to some having been intentionally left out as too ordinary and commonly known, while other more sophisticated ones were too difficult to draw or explain (or perhaps were even kept secret).

Coming in close to grapple was also necessary when a sword broke. There should be no misunderstanding that swords could break in battle. There certainly are plenty of accounts of it happening. Distal-tip sword points are thinner, and these will break more often. The breaking of swords was apparently something to expect and even accepted as inevitable. To most of today's practitioners, who rarely use a metal blade against another one (and certainly never sharpened blades), the breaking of a sword other than theatrical versions is fairly uncommon.

The body itself can be used to good effect. Although these techniques are very natural, most practitioners must spend more time avoiding body contact for safety's sake than learning how to use their momentum and weight effectively. At close distance, a simple turn of the hips and shoulders can often push hard enough against the opponent to unbalance him or disrupt his action. Simply slamming with the shoulder as you step in is itself a strong technique, especially in armor. Stomping down on the opponent's foot can also be very useful. Not only can it distract or injure him, it can also hinder his movement.

There are many techniques for twisting a foe's weapon by slipping an arm in between his. Having closed in and parried the opponent's sword, it is possible to wrap your arm around his grip or forearms, thereby immobilizing his weapon. Lowering your knees and leaning back puts your body weight into the action. This can pull his weapon down further. Your own sword is free to strike a blow or deliver a lethal cut. There are many instances where this technique is applicable by simply taking another step in closer. Again, stepping on the opponent's foot whenever you are close can be useful.

Kicking is obviously a useful action when appropriate. The historical manuals show "front" kicks to the groin, knees, and stomach. Again, this is an area not often practiced today by enthusiasts but one very much worth exploring. Typically, the kicks are shown being used in moving closer. A stopping kick can be delivered with a forward pass or a large advancing step. Kicks can also be used as feints. But beware: unlike what is shown in the movies, feet are seldom faster than blades, and swords that can parry other sword attacks can more than defend against feet. It is quite easy to kick out right into a sharp edge. If you kick at a skilled swordsman, be ready to lose your foot. Low kicks and leg sweeps are often more useful than body kicks.

A disarmed fighter is by no means defenseless. Although the techniques of unarmed fighting are well outside the scope of this book, the relationship between weapons and grappling/wresting moves, as well as punching and kicking, has always been seen very close indeed. This is expressed throughout the historical manuals and is evident in any martial art. The bottom line is not to think any differently when your weapon is lost or discarded than when you are armed and fighting. The same principles (e.g., timing, distance, perception) apply, and the same motions and movements can be used to flee or to enter and neutralize the opponent's weapon. All hype and myth of unarmed skills aside, the obvious difference between armed and unarmed is that without a weapon we clearly have less defensive capacity and much less offensive threat.

The great master Talhoffer included many moves for grappling and taking down an opponent after having closed with him. Among other weapons, his work is usually illustrated with descriptions of several techniques for dagger and pole-axe fighting. Talhoffer reveals in his instructions a grip using the thumb around the ricasso, as well as familiar grips using the left hand to grab the bottom of the pommel as an aid in lifting to thrust. Talhoffer shows the use of the great-sword's cross-guard in binding, hitting, pulling, trapping, and other actions around the opponent's blade, as well as, uniquely, against his grip, forearms, neck, and even legs. He also shows such unusual moves as how the opponent's blade might be grabbed in the middle and how strong close-in parries can be made by shifting a hand to hold your own blade in the middle *(Halbschwert)*. Additionally, he shows the use of "reverse" grips to allow the point to be used suddenly or to allow for a stronger thrust.

The seldom used "guard of wrath" or *Zornhut* (rage guard). This is a vulnerable posture but one that allows the most instinctive and powerful blow *(Zornhau)*.

Posture is crucial. Attempting any cut, particularly low cuts, by leaning too far forward or fighting too low (with knees too bent) restricts proper motion and cutting angle. It also exposes you to counterattack, limits mobility, and delays recovery.

Two examples of parrying out and grabbing the hilt. This can be applied with the point up in a basic side parry motion or with the point down in a hanging position. The first is better suited to thrusting immediately to the chest or face or making simple high slices. The second is suited only to thrusting underneath unless the weapon is brought back and around to strike with more power.

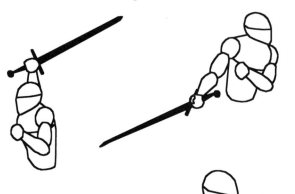

Examples of using one-hand grips. This is more practical than is commonly realized and could be necessary when the swordsman is injured or facing certain weapon combinations.

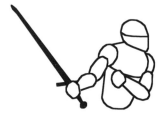

In certain instances, such as against heavy armor, a reverse grip can be used to deliver stronger stabs.

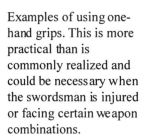

There are numerous techniques in the manuals that are routinely misunderstood and misapplied by stage combat choreographers and theatrical combatants because they do not freely practice them in an adversarial tactical context —*against someone actively opposing and earnestly trying to counter them.* Simply "working them out" in slow motion and speculating on their assumed application is hardly sufficient. What is demanded is to first practice techniques alone with a real weapon and then again with a mock one in safe contact-sparring.

In attacking, a strike may be made that, if it does not itself connect, will force the adversary to either evade or parry. Striking continues with combinations of two, three, or four attacks, each causing expected responses or openings that can be exploited and attacked. This is elemental. Each technique, whether thrust, cut, parry, or other blow, prepares for another. Changing the rhythm of strikes may abruptly break the adversary's sense of timing, and the momentary distraction caused can be exploited. This is a subtle but powerful idea that should be studied well.

German fighting guilds also knew the technique of "throwing the point," or making a false cut that suddenly and deceptively turns into a forward thrust. The notion that thrusting techniques in Western swordsmanship began only in the later Renaissance period is a complete myth. Thrusts were used since ancient times, and many Medieval swords are capable of quick and agile stabbing attacks. Using two hands on a long-sword even allows considerable point control and greater thrusting power. While thrusting with a long-sword is not nearly as agile, quick, or deceptive as what would later be developed for the rapier, anyone who has handled one extensively is aware of how versatile its point attacks can be.

Stepping in suddenly with the sword held in either the short or close guards can intercept an opponent's attack. A slicing cut can then be made or any number of close-in techniques employed. This move can also be used as you parry to slam your shoulder into the adversary, thereby knocking him back or off balance.

Stepping forward to greet and stifle an attack before it fully extends is always possible. Such action is not just putting your weapon into the path of the opponent's or trying to catch his blow on your guard. It is about unexpectedly intercepting the attack and following up with your own. This requires moving into the adversary's motion and upsetting his timing and momentum. Defending against this requires simply stepping away quickly.

Avoiding a thrust by a traversing pass with a low cut.

The reconstruction of these historical skills today has its own character, but real Medieval swordsmanship wasn't pretty. Although its movements and actions surely have an aesthetic quality, it didn't have rules or really any concerns other than killing an enemy. Yes, there are specific techniques; yes, there are principles that were (and still can be) devised into a martial "system," but was it truly an "art" at the time? Some consider this question open to debate. It has been said that only when a philosophy is added to a fighting method does it then become a martial *art*. However, there is no doubt that the historical Masters clearly thought it was.

THE LONG-SWORD AGAINST THE SWORD AND SHIELD

Whether faced with another long-sword, a sword & shield, or a pole-arm, the techniques for the long-sword are fundamental and work equally well against any weapon combination. Historically, as plate armor improved and became more common, shield sizes decreased. Longer swords for use in both hands became much more popular while single-hand ones became much better at thrusting. But before, during, and even after these changes, the familiar sword & shield style of fighting encountered the single long-sword in combat. Two weapons are often better than one, and the sword & shield combination is highly effective, as has been shown. It presents considerable problems for the long-sword. At first look it would seem the long-sword is no match for the sword & shield's advantages. Yet, because the long-sword did, in fact, become well known and highly developed, there must have been significant reasons for this. Examination of this fight is therefore very important. Neither can be seen as "superior" or "inferior." Each existed in its own context on the battlefield and in single combat, in tourney, and in judicial duel. The nature of the fight depends as much on the skill and attitude of the men using the weapons and the armor they wear as on the circumstances and situation.

Nothing teaches better than having to apply techniques and principles in less than "ideal conditions." This applies whether cutting, thrusting, hitting, or entering to trap and grapple. It's sad that despite the wealth of knowledge contained in historical manuals, enthusiasts around the world can remain unaware of even basic elements until they finally see it in a movie or on a TV show (for instance, many seemed completely unaware of rising cuts or the vulnerability of the lower legs until they saw it in *Braveheart*!). Even then, what they "learn" is usually a mistake or an illusion. One of the best means for learning the important concepts of controlling range in a fight and developing a keen sense of countertiming is to spar with *dissimilar* weapons. That is, to train against weapons of differing lengths (sword versus dagger, long-sword versus sword, long-sword versus pole-arm, long-sword versus two-handed, pole-arm versus two-handed, etc.).

We will look briefly at the general nature of the fight between sword & shield and long-sword with regard only to the fundamental techniques that can be employed rather than specific conditions under which it might occur. The fighting distance between long-sword and sword & shield is essentially one of equivalence. The most obvious difference is that for the long-sword there is no central weapon to attack or overcome. Instead, there is a serious barrier blocking targets. For the shield, the main difference is the very lack of another opposing barrier. However, there is the long-sword's reach and symmetrical offense to deal with. From a strictly mechanical point of view, the characteristics of the shield & sword have the advantage. But, of course, fighting is not a matter of mechanics only.

The shield's major value, other than blocking targets from attack and preventing them from even being threatened, is offensive. Rather than waiting to parry an attack, the shield can close in to stifle, disrupt, or hinder the long-sword's movement by hitting against its grip or intercepting its path near the hilt. The shield user can stay at a safe distance while bringing his sword into use. Binding the sword in this way is followed with a cut to any exposed target.

Passing forward to even closer range can be executed with a direct cut and simultaneous hit with the face of the shield (whether the opponent attacks or parries or not).

The shield can be used to close lines of attack to the long-sword and also to strike with should the bearer of the long-sword lower his guard in an effort to attack. By stepping in to and out of his cuts, the shield user can control the distance to his advantage, all the while readying his own weapon to strike.

By keeping proper distance, the shield user will be able to maintain visibility so that the longer weapon cannot cut under or around. As the opponent tries to do so, he will expose his arm or hands to attack as well as offer opportunities to step in and bind himself up with the shield.

The long-sword's postures must be employed with greater care because the shield user can make attacks and movements in safety that an opponent armed with a single weapon cannot.

The sword & shield has greater versatility in that one implement defends while the other one attacks. This offensive-defensive combination limits the ability of a single weapon alone to provoke openings or exploit gaps in actions.

Just as the opponent strikes the shield, the shield user steps in with the shield raised and brings the sword out from the middle guard to cut across the long-sword user's arms.

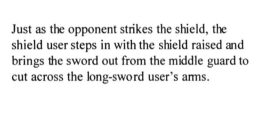

A similar action can be made to the side by bringing the face of the shield out to deflect the cut while the sword strikes from the right.

Regardless of the angle or direction of the cut, the shield user can simultaneously parry with the shield and countercut with his weapon. This can be done defensively as the opponent himself attacks, or it can be done offensively before he makes his own attack.

Against an opponent armed with a shield, once more the major countertechnique is to cut at the user's exposed arm as it comes out to strike. This can be very effective from the high and middle guards. As always, caution, patience, and careful timing are required. The most useful countercut is a vertical or diagonal downward strike, but rising cuts can sometimes be employed.

The key to countering the shield is to maintain a range better suited to the long-sword's preferred cutting distance and not allow the shield to get close enough to be employed offensively. This can require considerable footwork or movement in side-stepping, passing, retreating, lunging, and even hopping about.

Thrusts are somewhat less useful: if they miss, skip-off, or are deflected, the shield user can usually step right in to strike. However, combined with false attacks, thrusts can get in right over the shield and sometimes even under it.

What is to be avoided is close-in contact where the shield has the advantage. The shield can hit and block and beat while its companion weapon strikes from any number of angles. Here the long-sword is hindered by its length and the lack of the shield user's exposed targets. It is possible, though, to use the second hand to grab the shield user's grip or hilt should his weapon be parried. When this occurs it is important to step out and gain distance before the shield is used to hit with. One of the easiest targets when close in is to strike directly down to the feet, ankles, or shins. Also, be wary, whenever you are in close, of an opponent's dropping his sword and pulling out a dagger.

An opponent with a shield can close in and often outfight a longer single weapon by binding it with blocks while striking around it. Taking out an attacker's leg prior to his closing the distance is one effective countertechnique for this.

Lashing out with one-hand strikes can also be very useful against a shield.

One of the more effective shield-countering techniques is simply to strike high and cut low. As the shield fighter raises his weapon in defense he can expose his legs and block his own vision. Care should be taken to maintain good distance. A skilled shield user will take a step back or even step in to stifle such an attack with his shield. Another danger in this is that if the shield user does not react to the feint, he can strike down to countercut the arm of the long-sword user.

THE LONG-SWORD AGAINST POLE-ARMS

Pole-arms were the primary weapon of foot soldiers in Medieval and Renaissance times. The "fight" of pole-arm against the single sword is very probably the most challenging that any swordsman can face. Even in the hands of a novice such weapons can have a tremendous advantage in reach and can be very quick. No swordsman can really hope to be fully versed in the long-sword without training against pole-arms. As covered previously with regard to the sword & shield, there is a reason long-shafted weapons were so common and popular: they were deadly instruments that were relatively easy to use (especially in groups). Spears of all types were extremely common, and even a long lance could easily be cut down for easier use on foot or a wooden staff employed as a pole-arm. Still, if the pole-arm fighter is not trained well or is himself ignorant of the sword, he will lose to a skilled swordsman. Although this book can only examine Medieval pole-arms briefly in reference to the long-sword and does not describe their use in detail, weapons such as *glaives*, *halberds*, *guisarmes*, *bardiches*, *bills*, and *pikes* are worthy of dedicated study on their own.

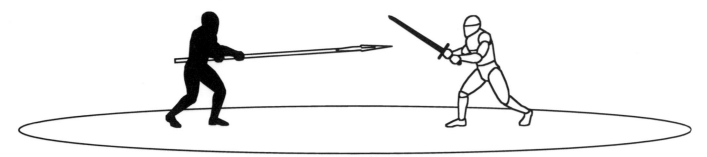

Because pole-arms can have such tremendous advantages over single swords, there is really not much that can be said of fighting them except *practice* (and perhaps consider using a shield). However, we must look at some specifics of facing *and* defeating pole-arms with the long-sword. Those students of Medieval swordsmanship who have never drilled intensely with or experienced free-sparring against a skilled pole-arm fighter should rectify this gap in their learning as soon as possible.

The hands or grip of the swordsman is a prime target that is difficult to defend; many modern students don't know how to defend this target.

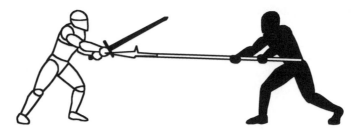

Another advantage of spears and shafted weapons is that, like axes, they are fairly easy to use with little instruction, whereas a sword requires *swordsmanship* to be used properly (which is precisely why the craft of fencing came about). When armies of those times suffered severe casualties, they simply could not wait until newly levied troops were trained as swordsmen. Besides, swords were expensive, but pole-arms could often be adapted from common agricultural tools.

The high guard easily exposes the body, legs, and face to attack. It is very hard to pull the weapon down in time to deliver a blow to the shaft.

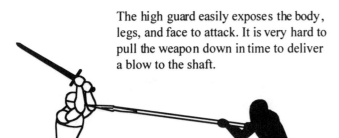

Pole-arms can attack over or under the guard. Trying to match their superior reach and thrusting speed by lowering the sword horizontally is also a common mistake.

There is danger in allowing the pole-arm to get too close before acting to close the distance or step out of range. As with most concepts in fighting, it is a matter of careful judgment and timing. Simply backing up will do nothing and just stepping forward will get you impaled.

Defense with a pole-weapon relies on opposition blocks and deflecting parries within the same four areas as a sword (inside-high, outside-high, inside-low, outside-low). Attacks come in the form of straight and angled thrusts and straight and crossing blows. Additionally, pole-weapons can be fought with, or against, using the same concepts of feints, beats, disengages, glides, grabs, or binds. The major difference is one of reach and timing. In comparison with the use of a sword against another sword, the fight against a pole-arm is one of altered distance and movement.

A disengage by the spear. The weapon comes in with great speed and makes a small circular drop under the guard before a parry can be made. Double-disengages can also be executed to first feint on one side and then the other. These attacks can be made to the face, throat, chest, abdomen, or groin. These are among the weapon's primary techniques.

Pole-arms can also employ beats and binds quite well against the sword. The shaft or head pressures the blade, forcing it to the side. As the swordsman resists, the weapon cuts back or thrusts suddenly forward. Blows can also be made against the sword with sideways, upward, or downward strikes to knock it away or move it aside before thrusting.

The brutal speed of a pole-weapon's thrust and its formidable ability to feint and disengage are often underestimated. This can lead to ruin. A skillful practitioner (although reasonably uncommon) can be as effective as even an expert swordsman and sometimes more so.

Another dangerous spear technique is a deliberate attack made to provoke a parry from the sword. This can then be disengaged to thrust at the opening created. These can be done to the left or right as simple high-low feints or low-high feints.

Feints are one of the most effective actions to use with a pole-arm. Both thrusts and cuts can be faked to harass or distract the swordsman. Additionally, even when real attacks are opposed and blocked by the sword, a pole-arm's inertia and strength can sometimes overwhelm a parry and get through.

Pole-weapons can make wide, sweeping strikes and circular thrusts that are deceptive in their difficulty to intercept or block. Their users can often recover from misses and failed attacks in safety and immediately renew their attempts. A pole-weapon's ability to alter its range easily by shifting and sliding the grip is one more of its assets. Another lies in the unpredictability of its quickly moving tip (although this varies with the type of blade or point it may have). Those pole-arms with hooked or beaked blade heads offer additional problems as well as opportunities. These blades can trap, pull, push, and hook a sword with considerable force. Of course, this can work both ways; a pole-arm may be locked and forced down or held long enough to be grabbed and closed in on. Also, the possibility that a pole-arm fighter may let go of his weapon with one (or both) hands and draw a dagger or short-sword must not be overlooked. A swordsman ignorantly rushing in can fall victim to this tactic. **243**

When necessary, pole-weapons can always have their points pulled away and used to parry with the shaft or point to keep the sword away.

Although less common with heavier pole-arms, staffs and other lighter forms can be easily reversed to strike with the butt-end. This is applied in the familiar "staff fighting" manner and allows for fast, strong, and deceptive blows. However, again, the hands and arms are far more vulnerable to swords than most martial arts fights and displays would have you believe. Against armored swordsmen, these techniques are also much, much less useful. This is why so many Medieval pole-weapons had elaborate metal blades.

At a certain range, the opportunity to bind or deflect the pole-arm is offset by the often greater chance of being quickly stabbed by it in return. Judging exactly what that range is and acting in time is the real art.

Varieties of hanging parries are very useful for defending against pole-arms because they can parry both high, low, and middle attacks with short, quick motions.

Chopping off the end of a pole-arm is not at all easy. They were designed to be resistant to this, and, besides, they usually move too fast to offer enough resistance to be cut. Also, metal strips known as *langets* were often attached to the shafts of many types of pole-weapons to prevent their being worn down or cut through.

The attack may be beaten or parried down and out or scooped up, depending on its angle. Either way, rapidly closing in to attack or grab and strike is the goal. Should the adversary break free or maneuver out of the way, quick recovery of a strong, flexible middle guard position is vital. Above all, the distance should be forced to the sword's advantage and not fought to the pole-arm's range. Simply facing off a pole-arm with its point threatening a few feet in front of you, but the opponent 10 feet or so behind it, is certainly not an ideal position to be in. You can't hit an opponent if he is not in range.

The closest target of the pole-arm is one that is very often overlooked and unprotected: the hands. A pole-arm fighter's hands can be quite vulnerable to simple gliding slices or quick chops. Don't forget: a pole-arm is essentially a two-handed weapon, and once opponents lose the use of one hand, they are no threat. Getting close enough to hit them is the problem.

The low stance is also very useful; it can be used to parry to the sides or lift to make hanging parries. Pole-arm thrusts can come in at any level from thigh to face. The low stance can intercept many of these with the cross-guard and afterward allows the blade to cut from underneath.

The key to defeating pole-arms lies in getting past the point. This is not easy, but once achieved, a pass, step, or lunge can be used to deliver a cut against either the arm (often the closest target) or the body/head. The pole-arm's weakness is in being tied up and trapped once a swordsman has closed past the tip. The pole-arm user is typically forced to pull the shaft back in defense, thereby moving the point off line. With the point out of the way and the swordsman close, the fight takes on a different character. The pole-arm fighter must retreat to a safer range or try to use the reverse end of the shaft.

Getting in on a pole-arm is necessary, but once there you must actually strike and waste no time allowing the adversary to recover, withdraw, or hit with the butt of the shaft.

The close guard is useful once contact has been made with the pole-arm and pressure can be maintained. From here, thrusts can be made by sliding along the shaft, or hanging parries can be employed to scoop it up and off as you step in.

Additionally, once the distance is closed this does not mean that the adversary cannot slip away again or pull out by parrying and passing back. Shafted weapons can have surprising agility when used properly.

Once the pole-arm is closed with, an immediate grab may be employed to seize the shaft with one hand. The foot or shin may even be used to kick or step on the pole. Once the swordsman has grabbed the pole, it may be forced or maneuvered out of the way while a cut or stab is made. It can even be employed in defense by the swordsman should the adversary let go with one hand and draw a second weapon. Grabbing or trapping the shaft ties it up and prevents the adversary from using the reverse end to strike with. When you grab the shaft, it is vital to lower your hips and knees and stiffen the arm so as to gain leverage. In this way, your body weight can be put behind the seizure and strength can be added to the hold.

After parrying to the inside (left), the second hand can reach out to grab hold of the pole. Such precarious positions may exist for several seconds as the swordsman inches closer and readies his weapon to attack while the pole-arm fighter tries to free his weapon or consider other options.

Having a free hand, which is quicker and easier to grasp with, can be more effective against a pole weapon than keeping both hands on the sword at all times. The swordsman needs to be instantly ready to let go with either hand and grab or deflect the shaft of the pole-arm. The cross-guard can also be put to considerable use in opposing the shaft to close the distance or in holding it off or pushing it away.

245

Basic techniques against a pole-arm include using a middle stance and readying against an attack. As the pole-arm comes in, it must be carefully judged and greeted in order to parry and step in. Continuing on, the blade can glide along the shaft, thereby keeping pressure and closing to striking range. The initial parry and closure of the shaft is not easy as its attack often feints or disengages. All the while, the pole-arm will try to stay at its optimal range. Surprisingly, the low guard can be employed effectively to lift up suddenly and deflect the pole away with a hanging parry and bind and then countercut. A high stance may even be used cautiously to invite an attack in and then strike down forcefully on the shaft to knock it away before closing (although this is usually *very* risky).

With a pass forward, the distance can be closed and the point safely bypassed. From here, striking to the opponent's hands or lower legs is easy.

The hanging guard is versatile and against pole-arms can parry them safely up and away with a rising cut made underneath the shaft. The second hand can also quickly grab the shaft from this position and allow time for the sword to then cut around with force.

Opposition against the shaft can be maintained by using the body as well as the weapon. When necessary push against the shaft with your hips, waist, forearms, and back.

As the blade successfully opposes the weapon, letting go with one hand to grab the shaft immobilizes or at least holds the shaft while the swordsman prepares to deliver a blow. The pole-arms's point must still be bypassed or deflected, and opposition must be kept up so that the shaft cannot pull out or disengage.

Getting past the point of a pole-arm can be even harder when it has a blade head with hooks or prongs. Also, the heavier the blade head, the stronger cut or blow it can make.

Another effective pole-arm technique to be wary of is slipping, or the slip-thrust. To make an even quicker attack, the shaft can be thrown out in a one-hand thrust, slipping through the first hand's grip. Although having less force, this can significantly alter the range of the attack. It can also leave the pole-arm vulnerable on the recovery should it fail.

There are a multitude of techniques for fighting against pole-arms, and these examples represent only a few of them in order to describe the nature of the fight and the elements involved.

A halberd, bill, or any pole-arm with a cutting blade is a formidable tool. However, they are slower and not nearly as difficult to fight as long thrusting spears. By entering with the opponent as he lifts the pole-arm back or high before striking, the swordsman can close the distance.

Though slower, pole-arms are also better for fighting closer. Blows can be aimed directly at the sword to knock it away or trap and bind it. These weapons can strike at incoming sword attacks to deflect them and cut back before the sword can recover or parry. A pole-arm's leverage allows it to hook and unhook more easily than the sword. Shorter pole-arms can also strike with their back ends, and this greatly enhances their offense and defense. One end can intercept and deflect cuts, while the other instantly comes around to strike. This can be repeated again and again in a "staff fighting" manner. A fighter in heavy armor with a cutting-blade pole-arm can also be much less concerned about a swordsman's getting in close.

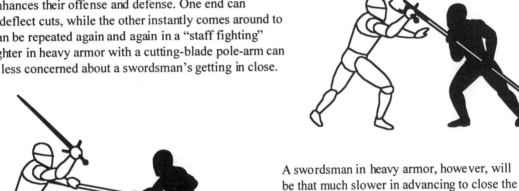

A swordsman in heavy armor, however, will be that much slower in advancing to close the distance and use entering techniques or grabbing. Regardless, seizing and pinning, immobilizing, or just delaying the shaft until you are close enough to strike is still a fundamental technique to use.

One-hand reaching cuts are also useful against pole-arms because they greatly increase the range and there is less fear of a slow recovery. The pole-arm's threat is limited to more specific attacks than other weapons, and this makes one-hand attacks easy to apply. Getting the chance to generate the necessary momentum to strike with is still not that easy.

Just as when fighting any weapon, there are no hard-and-fast rules for victory when fighting pole-arms. There are, however, discernible principles that can be applied effectively if they are learned well and practiced frequently. Pole-arms are ancient weapons that exist in endless forms in most cultures. No sword skill or training is complete without reference to them. This was the case especially for Medieval swordsmen.

THE TWO-HANDED SWORD

Because I have already described in some detail the handling of Medieval long-swords, it is important to state that there are many actions that are clearly better suited to one type than another. Most, but not all, of the fundamental techniques and general concepts described here are applicable to fighting with every form of Medieval long-sword. Techniques possible or more viable with a spadone, for instance, may not be as useful with a larger great-sword. Some techniques effective with great-swords may be slightly less so with war-swords. In the end, to know what any individual sword is best capable of is a matter of the skilled and knowledgeable swordsman handling it personally.

When it comes to the largest swords, the true two-handers of the late Middle Ages and early Renaissance, it is important to know something about them and how they differ from the long-swords. Although this study does not include them, there are several distinctions that should be noted. In Germany and Switzerland during the Renaissance they were used by the *Doppelsöldner*, the strongest fighters who received double pay. In battle they protected the banner and leaders as well as charging into pike and halberd formations to clear paths for others.

True two-handed swords can't actually be used in the same manner as Medieval long-swords and great-swords. They are simply too slow to hold for long in high, middle, low, or inside guards. They can be used more effectively in back, close, and hanging guards, or by placing them at the ready across the shoulder. With a two-handed sword, the sheer force of its blow can create its own opening. Its length and momentum can make it difficult to block since it can often knock lighter weapons aside. However, when closer in it lacks agility and speed, as well as perhaps versatility.

Working extensively with replicas that are too heavy, too light, or poorly balanced is a good way to misunderstand a great deal of using any historical sword. It is one thing to train alone doing drills with a replica two-hander or even spar with safe simulated versions, but it is quite another to practice with an accurate replica in a realistic manner. To realize how such a large sword functions differently than smaller ones, it is necessary to not only test its ability at chopping, cutting, and slicing, but also its maneuverability (and lack of it) at parrying and binding. For practitioners today to truly appreciate the handling and functioning of a two-handed sword (or Medieval sword, for that matter), it is imperative that they use a model that is historically accurate in its weight and balance. The limitations and advantages of such a weapon cannot be accurately simulated or understood in any other way. Cheap reproductions weighing half the weight of real swords or hollow, foam versions are simply not acceptable replicas. On the other hand, 10- or 12-pound stage combat props are hardly suitable either. Two-handed swords were heavy compared to other swords, but they were not the super slow, unmanageable ones often depicted in film and stage fights (where they are often confused with great-swords).

A two-handed sword does not "swordfight" in the same manner as a long-sword, nor was it intended to. It is a slower and more cumbersome weapon but with its own unique style. With such a large sword, the on-guard or ready stance is far more vertical. The sheer weight of the weapon prohibits it from being held in most long-sword guards for very long, if at all. Maneuvering one requires strength as well as more time and force to not only bring it up to speed but also apply sufficient force. Other than its tremendously powerful blows, its only redeeming factor really is its long reach. Two-handed swords have great momentum to their swings and a heavy follow-through. Blows that miss tend to travel in a wide arc and can leave the user quite vulnerable and open to a shorter or nimbler weapon. Parrying with a two-handed sword, although it has substantial length to defend with, is not easy, either. Moving the weapon down or over to block can be cumbersome and slow in contrast to "lighter" Medieval swords. Additionally, much of the striking power can be lost when riposting (counterattacking) from a parry. This is yet another reason why emphasis was placed on passing moves and stepping in timing with strikes.

The two-hander is adept at using the hanging and close guards for this reason. The elbow of the second hand must often be raised quite high and even over the head to strike low or on an upward (hip to collar) angle. From this position the pommel is also placed conveniently to deliver a blow. A wide grip is required to gain the leverage needed to strike, and this necessitates a very long handle and a large, counterbalancing pommel. An extralarge cross-guard is needed as well to make up for the lack of defensive agility. To protect the hands, many two-handers had side-rings, and such guards provided protection from quicker weapons, as well as clashing pole-arms.

Most two-handed swords had dull, thick edges at the shoulder. Gripping this "false-grip" (or ricasso) also allowed the two-hander to be able to make powerful thrusting attacks. This portion was also sometimes wrapped with leather and was virtually an extended handle. Using this false-grip/ricasso allowed the grip to be lengthened, thereby shortening the blade and allowing the weapon to be more maneuverable when the user was closer to an opponent. This is often used in more easily torqueing the weapon around to aid in recovery or continuing attack. Of course, an opponent can also take advantage of this and may try to gain control of the sword by grabbing it there, too.

Many forms of the two-handed sword had small pointed lugs or flanges called *Parrierhaken* (parrying hooks) jutting out of the blade just above the hilt. They are quite distinctive, and other than two-handers only a few great-swords have them. These parrying hooks can act as a secondary cross-guard when gripped below. The hooks even could be used to keep the opponent's weapon out that much farther when weapon to weapon and allow the two-hander more opportunity to better use its reach. By turning the blade slightly when an opponent's weapon (typically another sword or a pole-arm) has been blocked against the flanges, the sword can slip free to strike. These flanges can even be used to attack if the lower portion of the blade ends up hitting or the weapon is swung from the tip end.

The big advantages of a two-hander are its obvious reach and powerful cut. However, its length also makes it far less agile and requires it to travel in wider arcs. It also requires a greater range from which to strike successfully, and in close a faster weapon can be decisive. By closing in on an adversary, the larger weapon can be forced to defend, thereby binding or trapping it so the edge is unable to move out or its tip to lower.

In many respects a two-handed sword could be used almost like a big club or even a staff weapon. It can function very much like a good pole-arm. This further distinguishes it from swordsmanship with other Medieval swords. And there are many long-sword techniques that are simply inappropriate, impractical, or impossible for the two-handers. A definitive study of this unique weapon has yet to be done, and it would surely be welcome by students and scholars of the sword.

SUMMARY

It is the changing of range by altering cuts from the shoulder with cuts from the elbows and using false attacks from the wrists that, when combined with proper stepping, makes the long-sword such an effective weapon. In skilled hands its suddenly changing distance and strong cuts, with the threat of thrusting or closing to use the hilt, make it quite dangerous. When all this is added to the weapon's parrying potential and guarding and the ability to pass forward and back in evading attacks while counterstriking, it is clear why this form of fighting developed into a martial art of its own. This then, is the nature of the Medieval long-sword.

A profound element in the art of swordsmanship found expressed within the Medieval manuals is one that seldom seems to be grasped by modern students: When engaging an adversary, do not think in terms of "swordfighting" or "fighting with a sword" or even of "fencing." Your attitude should only be that of "fighting" the adversary. Whatever actions you make, however you manage to do it, everything is for the goal of getting the opponent in a position where you can then use your weapon to injure him. That is what it is all about.

This survey of Medieval swordsmanship is far from complete. The three most important weapons of the Medieval warrior of any century were the spear, sword, and dagger. This book has only examined one of them in depth. Much more could be said of the long-sword versus pole-arms or versus the sword & shield. There is much material that could have been added regarding the single dagger alone or against the long sword as well, but because of space limitations it must be omitted. The same applies to the long-sword against the long-axe, the hand-axe and shield, and hammer, mace, or flail and shield. The fight of Renaissance sword & dagger against the long-sword is also an intriguing practice. All of these will have to be left for future volumes.

The Medieval sword is not merely a cultural object of ceremony and leadership, an archaeological artifact or artistic curiosity, or a piece of military history or costume accessory; it is also a deadly and effective weapon of a time long past. All that has been attempted in this presentation is to bring some clarity and focus to the modern study and replication of Medieval swordsmanship and to illustrate a historical foundation for its study. Medieval swords and swordsmanship cannot all be lumped together as one generic system. There are essential differences between early Medieval swords, later arming swords, and the many forms of long-swords. There is much to appreciating the elements of using the sword & shield or understanding exactly the significance of a long-sword. In combination with shields and in association with armor and other weaponry there are many important considerations. At its core, Medieval swordsmanship is a diverse and vibrant subject.

It cannot be overstated just how different safe reenactment and the practice of re-creational swordfighting today is from the life-threatening violence of the historical reality. Battle was an exhaustive task. If a fight was prolonged, whether individually or for whole armies, fatigue easily took over. We can only speculate about how much theory and how many rehearsed techniques might have been forgotten or ignored once actual battle was joined. If the similar weapon arts of Asia and elsewhere, as well as the sports of fencing, wrestling, and boxing, are any example, training must have centered not only on the physical execution of movements, but upon conditioning the individual mentally, emotionally, and psychologically. Honor and courage had to be called upon to overcome fear and stress. There are numerous examples of this understanding throughout Medieval literature and in Renaissance fighting manuals. The true art is not some spectator sport version, nor merely done in a manner to entertain crowds and audiences. Yet, for modern students and scholars to earnestly follow the "Way of the Sword" and be a warrior, it is not necessary to go to war or to kill or even be violent, but only to practice diligently and humanely with a martial spirit.

As with any sword, true skill is partly a matter of physical conditioning, technical proficiency, and mental development (i.e., understanding of distance, timing, and intention). Beyond mere technique exist an infinite number of tactical combinations, which require a proper understanding of preparation and movement. This experience comes about only through practice and fighting. Skill with the sword cannot be obtained by merely reading about it or theorizing and fantasizing about it. Skill is gained only by training hard and sparring. It has been said that true swordsmanship cannot really be taught, but that it must be self-learned. It has also been said that it cannot even be learned, rather it must be self-taught. Train hard and you'll perform techniques naturally. It is only through intense, long-term effort and practice that the marvels of swordsmanship will reveal themselves. To all would-be swordsmen I say, never stop practicing, never give it up, and never think you alone know.

CHAPTER ELEVEN

Practice and Sparring

"There is a difference between interest and commitment. When you're interested in something, you do it only when circumstances permit. When you're committed, you do it no matter what, no excuses."

—Art Turak

In many ways, swordsmanship is the neglected martial art. It is difficult to teach it without sparring or practice cutting. On the one hand, safe, simulated weapons are needed for contact, and on the other, an actual sharpened blade is required for cutting-practice. Other martial art weapons may have flashy twirling motions or colorful spinning actions and such, but swords just basically cut, parry, and thrust. Much of swordsmanship consists of subtle feinting, beating, and waiting, against an opponent who might hesitate to charge a 3-foot piece of sharpened steel. Real swords do not allow beginners to feel a sense of immediate gratification from learning some flashy and dexterous move. They are not simple sticks, staffs, or clubs. Users must sharpen their minds and senses as much as they must do repetitive and endless drills. More than any other martial art weapon, swords have an immediacy and a lethality to them that cannot be ignored. Some swordsmen even maintain that swordsmanship is the pinnacle of all martial arts. There is evidence that the earliest systematic methods of unarmed fighting originally evolved from those first developed from using swords. It has even been said that at its highest level, swordsmanship is synonymous with strategy.

Swordsmanship is learned like most any other martial art. Individual techniques are practiced until the student is proficient. All the while, students must pay attention to the correct performance of these techniques until combinations of them can be applied easily. But unlike other physical activities—such as dancing, in which the movements are either prearranged or random—the choice of technique in battle depends also on the opponent's actions in the situation and necessitates the development of heightened perceptions and spontaneous, unconscious reactions in order to use techniques and control the combat distance and the timing of moves. This is achieved by repeating techniques until they become "internalized" and reflexive. No time is wasted in having to give thought to actions (and nothing is given away to the opponent). It "just happens." This is why at the higher levels swordsmanship is an art.

To develop this intuitive aspect of sword use (or of any hand weapon) requires more than technical skill, repetition, and physical conditioning. It requires the subtler and more complex psychological factors that are gained only through serious, long-term free-sparring. Only sparring reveals to us our inadequacies and deficiencies and teaches us application of tactics. It is by comparing and contrasting our skills with those of others that we come to know ourselves;

otherwise, no matter how well intentioned practice drills may be, they are really just supervised dancing and playing. Classroom drills and noncontact practice is good, but real ability can only be gained through fighting.

The method today's practitioners use to train and spar with is crucial in determining what level of understanding they develop and what kind of skills they learn. Particular techniques are quite often available only to certain systems of sparring under particular sets of safety rules. Sparring comes from the Middle English word *sparren* (to strike rapidly) and is defined as fighting for practice. This definition pretty much sums up what it's all about. Skill cannot be acquired from a mere book; it has to be gained through hands-on learning and sparring. Books can supplement, they can augment, but they cannot themselves instruct. The individual must achieve skill alone.

Sparring in its most basic form can be defined as engaging in mock or practice-fighting for the purposes of freely applying techniques, principles, and concepts to practice them against another combatant. It consists of using strikes or hits in a manner that would be lethal with actual weapons. It is true that sparring in a sense is a form of pretending. It must be bound by certain safety constraints, whereas real combat has few, if any, rules. But sparring is still much more than mere play-fighting or acting out an imaginary fight. Sparring can be considered any manner of intentionally noninjurious fighting practice, but free-sparring is best defined as each party openly trying to "defeat" or best the other for the time being. Free-sparring is therefore much more than an arranged drill or structured exercise.

Sword or weapon sparring has three main categories: *semi-contact, contact,* and *full-contact.*

1. Semi-contact
   - Pros
     - Uses blunt steel or wooden weapons
     - Teaches control and finesse as well as respect
     - Is useful for training
   - Cons
     - Has limited and inadequate contact or force
     - Confines target areas
     - Disallows many techniques and actions for safety reasons

2. Contact
   - Pros
     - Uses padded weapons or wooden weapons with armor
     - Allows for speed, full motion, good impact, and a wide array of techniques and actions
   - Cons
     - Is still not full-force
     - Limits some target areas

3. Full-contact
   - Pros
     - Allows maximum force and power
   - Cons
     - Involves a loss of apprehension/hesitation
     - Still limits some techniques as well as certain target areas
     - Has higher equipment costs
     - Is inherently dangerous

It is important to stop for a moment and define exactly what constitutes "full-contact" sparring. The phrase is used often, but rarely is the real thing encountered. The key word here is *contact.* Full-contact weapon-sparring involves not just using speed, but the intention to strike, *along with the awareness that hitting can and does occur.* You can't just strike forcefully while allowing the other party to parry and evade. Nor does true full contact mean just whacking weapons together. Pulling your blow short before connecting doesn't count either. Full-contact sparring means to truly hit your sparring partner's body at full strength and full speed. You cannot say you are sparring with full contact and then add that no one ever actually gets hit. You have to actually be trying to contact your opponent, not just "banging blades" with enthusiasm. To practice-fight this way using wooden sticks or blunt steel or even padded weapons is inherently injurious. If it isn't, it's not full contact. Full-contact sparring, therefore, by definition demands protective armor and helmets.

Contact-sparring, as opposed to the full-contact kind, can be defined as that form of free-sparring that does not necessarily allow for, or require, full-powered strikes. Hence, full protective equipment (helmets and armor) is not mandatory. Contact-sparring does allow for considerable speed, force, and impact on an opponent, but not in a manner that causes intentional injury. It is a method of practice-fighting that consists of making contact by using techniques realistically yet safely. It is well beyond semi-contact sparring (in which little or no connection can be made against targets), yet not to the degree where blows are delivered at full power, regardless of danger, as with true full-contact sparring.

In effect, no one sparring method is perfect or allows for everything. Each has advantages and disadvantages over one or both of the others. It is the combination of all three that provides practitioners with a fuller understanding of the art. Each offers particular benefits to learning techniques and fundamental concepts.

MEDIEVAL SWORDSMANSHIP AS AN ACTIVITY

A leading expert on swords once stated that swords are designed with specific uses in mind, and that each sword requires a specific technique and specific techniques require specific swords. Yet, occasionally, it seems that some people have a psychological need to find the "ultimate" type of sword or the one that lets you do the "superior" technique that no other can. This is a useless myth. Confidence and advantage do not belong exclusively to one particular sword, one comparable weapon type, or even one historical class of warrior. It is only that some types of weapons will reveal things that others do not or allow more techniques and expose us to insights that others cannot. The same is true for the method or system one uses to conduct practice-fighting or safe sparring in the course of training and learning.

Although learning a martial art is itself mostly a conscious, cognitive process, developing true skill involves a lack of thought and a "blank mind." Thus, you must think to learn and train, but later "consciousness" of your actions will be forgotten and replaced with an "empty" attitude. Learning is often a paradox in this sense. It takes a conscious, thoughtful effort (and will) to train and practice until what is learned is "forgotten" in the mind but not the body. As well, the more you learn, the more you realize your previous ignorance. It is well known that a beginner's movements and actions are at first very natural and raw. They are untainted by learning

(whether correct or incorrect). They can be awkward and unrefined but still unpredictable and fluid. As you later learn the actual techniques, you can become stiff and hesitant. As your mind stops to ponder what it is your body is trying to do, you will become vulnerable to those who perceive it. It is no secret that as this process continues and you develop the coordination and competence to execute proper movements, your actions will become reflexive and natural. This continues until your use of swordsmanship is unconscious and fluid once again. You return to the mind-set of a beginner, and the "circle of learning" closes. There is nothing mystical about all this (or a need to make it so), only wonderment when we realize it.

As with any physical art, fighting can be described as 10 percent physical and 90 percent mental. But to tap and apply that 90 percent we have to spend virtually all our time developing the physical. The mind in this case can really only be reached through muscle and nerve. Strength and reflex must be developed first before deeper principles can be mastered. There is no other way. Although one may have certain physical limitations that prevent a broad approach to training, this should not be an excuse. If you are not physically inclined or conditioned to perform well, then perhaps you will just have to train all the harder. The idea is not to accept your failings as they are, but to teach yourself how to minimize and perhaps even overcome them. It starts with an awareness of our limits and the knowledge that we can extend them. There are ways of emphasizing or amplifying our strengths while preventing an adversary from exploiting our weaknesses. As with everything else, this demands great perseverance and commitment to develop. As you make the effort, you will develop the very discipline required to achieve it.

In any event, Medieval swordsmanship requires stamina, agility, reflexes, forearm strength, hand-to-eye coordination, balance, quickness of foot, and myriad other qualities. However, the continual practice of swordsmanship will itself provide those very qualities (and improve them if already present). Originally, swordsmanship was about the violent and efficient destruction of our fellow human beings in combat. Much has been written on the psychology and philosophy of studying martial arts. It has been suggested that our modern fascination with the warrior arts is a way of touching that primitive emotional core within us that understands the inherent violence that underlies the daily struggle for survival. It has been said that the practice of a martial art is a way of realizing our own mortality by facing and confronting in small, palatable increments our natural fear of death and dying. It is a form of expression for our primitive, violent impulses and a means of channeling and redirecting them into something positive. There is an emotional level to violent encounters for which no amount of pretend practice and preparation can truly capture. For those now following their passion for the sword, these are thoughts worth pondering. Only those who have faced injury or death at the hands of others can understand this.

Today, for its students and reenactors, the practice of Medieval fighting skills is about mental and physical exercise, historical research, creative expression, stress relief, and even self-defense. Many practice for the sheer love of the craft itself and appreciation for the history behind it. Through this, some do achieve higher skill, some never advance very far, and others progress not at all. There are some people for whom the illusion and escapism of play-fighting is the only thing that matters in this subject. There are those who do not even believe that anyone else could possibly know more about swords and swordsmanship than what they do. Strangely, they just don't believe that any others could have learned something more than what little they've stumbled upon. These people will often not even believe that there is anything more to learn. Nor, apparently, can they fathom that there is "research" that could be done other than by watching movies, looking at a few library books, and just playing around. They simply don't grasp that playing tag with sticks or foam toys is hardly equivalent to serious full-contact sparring with proper equipment or extensive test-cutting practice with sharp, real blades. Their knowledge of the basic actions and fundamental techniques of swordsmanship is typically based on fantasy theories or narrow theatrical experience. Their understanding of just what real, steel swords are and how they actually handle is decidedly limited. They are also just as unknowing about the value of the historical Masters.

In their hearts, these people know that they are just pretending and somehow must assume everyone else must be too.

This singular element is these people's primary obstacle to real learning. Indeed, such people may not really wish to learn or be taught by anyone else. Sharing knowledge with them, rather than being an act of giving and educating, can instead become one of robbing them of their comforting ignorance. For such unfortunate individuals this book may not be of much value at all. Enthusiasts in most re-creational groups and fantasy societies do not seem to develop much actual ability. They don't learn because typically their sparring rules either just don't teach good form, or, more profoundly, the rules don't handicap them for *not* learning. In other words, the rules either don't demand higher performance or there's no penalty for using inferior technique.

True achievement comes from expectation and effort. If we demand a standard expectation for performance and insist upon a certain effort, then there will be achievement—out of which develops self-esteem. To try and obtain such self-esteem otherwise is a form of false pride: feeling good about accepting mediocrity does not serve anyone very well. All that is required is to properly motivate and support the effort. To motivate performance we can give support, promote confidence, and set an example. We can teach good skills, but we cannot create results without effort by the individual. Effort comes from within each of us only when we have motivation. Setting the expectation of achieving a standard is itself a motivation. If you set a standard, expect results, and nurture the efforts, higher performance will be achieved. None of this is easy. It takes discipline, but forging this discipline is what the process is all about. There is no shortcut.

Of course, long-term training and practice require particular motivation, especially when we do so alone or without the benefit of a traditional, established school, master, or group. It is motivation that pushes us to discover and extend our own physical and mental limits. Most people are influenced by "external" motivations (those things that are immediate and tangible), such as avoiding pain, looking good, or gaining prestige. Some people require structure, competition, or instant reward to be motivated. Others only need direction and aim. To attain higher skill in swordsmanship, as with other martial arts, it eventually requires internal motivation, which is deeper and more personal. Internal motivations are things that compel one to compete against the self rather than others and to excel. You train and practice to improve yourself, not to impress others or defeat and ruin them. This kind of internal motivation is uncommon and not found on the more or less superficial levels at which most practitioners train. Going beyond the superficiality is what the higher level of swordsmanship teaches and why it is a creative art that can affect, and improve, one's consciousness.

In swordsmanship, it has been said that the true opponent is and always has been one's own self . . . our ego, fears, and inadequacies. These are what must be overcome and defeated. After this, any other adversary will fall easily. But it is an endless struggle, for perfection is a path not a destination.

THE CRAFT OF MEDIEVAL FIGHTING TODAY

Today, serious students of European weapon arts practice to understand historical arms and armor and improve ourselves. We certainly won't ever be using them for real any time soon. At the most, the discipline, physical conditioning, and mental preparedness that can develop may provide us with advantages in times of personal self-defense. Individual techniques and concepts might even find employment with everyday objects (e.g., sticks, brooms, baseball bats, tire irons, umbrellas). Unlike for systems of unarmed martial arts and self-defense, there's no direct opportunity for real-life testing and use of the methods of Medieval swordsmanship and weaponry in our modern world. We are not likely to run into sword attacks outside a local bar or be challenged to a sword & shield duel in a mall parking lot. People don't go around anymore facing mail-clad assailants armed with shields and spears and axes. Thus these techniques and methods of combat are now restricted only to demonstrations, re-creations, and mock encounters—but they should not be construed exclusively as escapism and fantasy fulfillment.

It is important to realize that these methods were never intended as a sport. Nor were they meant for playing games or as a product to be marketed to kids and adolescents. They were about killing and survival. Fighting was a very violent and bloody affair; it was not about dressing up and play-acting. (This does not at all mean that martial exercises cannot be practiced with revelry and fun.) The techniques and methods were instruments of war, and their dire historical foundation should never be forgotten nor disregarded.

Just as with the practice of popular forms of Asian martial arts—where one can choose between a "hard" or "soft" style of karate or an "external" or "internal" style of kung fu, and note fundamentally different attitudes between a taekwon do and a jujutsu class, or between aikido and tai chi as opposed to Thai boxing and jeet kune do—so it is to some degree with Medieval and Renaissance weapon practice. In both arts, a student finds an approach that fits his needs and interests.

Around the United States and the world, Medieval and Renaissance swordsmanship and weaponry are being studied, practiced, and explored by a wide range of groups, organizations, and individuals. The groups reflect a diverse range of approaches, personalities, goals, and motivations. The Internet is full of different sites devoted to these pursuits. In these groups are members who attempt to realistically simulate actual weapons and how they handle, while others only act as a means of playing safe "touch-hits" with mock weapons. There are those who emphasize chivalry and knightly tournaments and those who focus on Dark Age skirmishes. There are individuals who attempt to simulate large battles, people who try to re-create cavalier dueling, and others who practice the theatrical theories of choreographed performance. Still others follow the directions of some sport-fencing experts or pursue some imagined role-playing agenda. Some groups try to influence one another, while others prefer to train in isolation and obscurity. Some seek prestige and renown, and some wish to sincerely promote swordsmanship and weaponry. There are those interested only in fantasy fulfillment and those concerned with their own personal development. On one end there are enthusiasts trying to reproduce real martial arts, and on the other those merely playing at swords and combat. In between lie a myriad of others. Each person must find where he fits and where he wants to go from there. Only time will reveal whether the knowledge gained was worth the effort.

The level of commitment and martial-spirit varies according to the goals, attitudes, and methods of the participants involved. But there is, so far, no recognized way of classifying these different approaches other than by subjectively experiencing them firsthand. Yet, remove the element of role-playing, remove the element of staged performance, and you completely alter the focus and character of this activity, whose objective then becomes martial and historical, not fantasy and pretend. This key distinction is certainly something not all enthusiasts comprehend—nor do some even want to know.

Let us be blunt. Some popular historical societies and Medieval combat organizations today claim that their manner of re-creating Medieval combat is "historically accurate." Some will even assert it is the "most authentic" manner in which one can safely engage. In reality, however, many of these societies and organizations are continually promoting fallacies about what Medieval combat and fighting skill is all about (many are little more than pseudo-Medieval fantasy groups that deal ahistorically with their activities). Although the practice of historical fighting should be a matter of open, objective investigation and research, this is not always the case. With some Medieval combat practitioners and re-creators, what often becomes more important is supporting the status quo of their organization's rule structure and the large investment its members have made in it (financially, emotionally, and socially). For some groups, following their own interpretation of Medieval fighting is more than a matter of simply having different views on what historical aspects to re-create or emphasize. It is often a matter of consciously holding a narrow, self-serving view and conducting biased research to defend it. The main motivation for this seems to be the mind-set produced from a focus on fantasy fighting and costumed role-playing as opposed to a purely martial investigation of the subject. Many Medieval combat societies and organizations may actually be quite sincere and vigorous in their efforts, but they can be quite wrong nonetheless.

When trying to re-create aspects of historical fighting from the diverse range that occurred in the Middle Ages, you must make certain assumptions, as well as admit certain restrictions. However, what you can't do is start with a particular premise of how to reproduce an "ideal" version of Medieval combat and then apply that version to all circumstances that occurred during the age. One cannot go out and pick and choose data to support a preferred interpretation while ignoring anything that undermines it.

Neither can one practice-fighting under a set of limited, artificial conditions only to later selectively gather research to back up results that have already been accepted in the first place. Such an approach is not an honest exploration of Medieval fighting. For anyone supposedly seeking to re-create authentic fighting skills, this should be an intolerable situation. When the facts of historical reality contradict our preconceptions, it's time to update and change our theories—and our practices. We can't go around disregarding whatever doesn't agree with our preferred interpretation and accepting only those things that do.

In devising any method of engaging in a safe re-creation of Medieval combat, we can't just fabricate an imaginary "generic" version. We must first decide whether we are setting up an idealized form for play-acting or are attempting to reproduce a close facsimile of historical fighting using simulated conditions. To avoid oversimplifying Medieval combat, the historical model we choose as our basis must be specific. Then we must decide whether we will be reconstructing the open conditions of battlefield warfare or, instead, the specialized circumstances particular to certain tournaments. We cannot have it both ways with much accuracy when using the same sparring rules. We must also decide whether we will simulate fighting in the age of plate or that occurring with earlier forms of lighter armor. Again, we can't realistically have it both ways with identical safety guidelines.

Some individuals, when presented with information, experience, or skill that conflicts with their association's long-held assumptions on weapon-sparring—regardless of its obvious historical significance or accuracy—treat it as virtual sacrilege. When the emotional investment is so high in an activity, the need for one's personal pet organization to "be right no matter what" tends to override honest inquiry.

The fighting structure of some organizations apparently develops too much momentum to be questioned. Its diehard adherents typically reject the suggestion to examine their method critically and admit and then improve historical deficiencies. Instead, anything that undermines, discredits, or weakens the "official" prescribed version of fighting will tend to be disregarded, bypassed, and feebly explained away. When this phenomenon occurs in groups that purport to practice historically based Medieval combat re-creation, it is the saddest hypocrisy. It seems that they would rather cling to their own preferred, comforting nonsense than face the hassle of having to change the insipid rules of their sparring system.

It is evidently not easy to avoid an idiosyncratic, stylized version of Medieval weapon-sparring that consists mostly of "getting good at using rules." Instead, a large number of role-playing, costumed theorists in certain historical societies seem to consciously overlook evidence contrary to the fundamental premise of their sparring systems. What we often see by the apologists of some combat groups are attempts to rationalize artificial, stylized versions of Medieval weapon-sparring. They grasp at obscure accounts and twist facts to justify contrived rules that are unsupported by historical conditions. Some will even stretch historical incidents, distorting their significance, and misuse the relevance of historical references in an effort to justify fighting rules for an interpretation that, at its core, is fallacious.

The attempt to safely re-create a close facsimile of Medieval fighting reflects both a set of expectations based on history and a set of results based on modern experience. Factors that come into play in this attempt are the types of mock weapons used, the types of armor worn, the materials armor and weapons are constructed from, the range of suitable techniques available, the target areas allowable, what will be considered the result of a strike or hit, and the degree of force behind blows.

Sparring rules that put unreasonable restrictions on target areas or place artificial results on hits and strikes must not be blindly accepted by participants. Any time such rules and restrictions inhibit the actions of free, spontaneous sparring, an organization should have to strongly justify the effects of any such rules. Nor should the mantra of "safety first" be allowed to override reasonable objections to any such restrictions. Far too often the cry of safety in sparring is used to mask what, in reality, are only flawed and poorly conceived rules. Serious practitioners today, regardless of their group affiliation or exact period of historical interest, must have the honesty and courage to critically examine their preconceptions about how mock Medieval fighting can be conducted.

If theories on what forms of Medieval combat were actually like and how best to re-create or practice them safely are to be claimed as "realistic" and "accurate," they must be tested by open inquiry. This cannot be legitimately achieved under a set of questionable, exclusive assumptions and insular conditions. Doing so invariably results not only in your experiences becoming self-referential, but in your becoming closed to insights others might have discovered through alternative interpretations and practices. You can't train under preconceived and restricted conditions and then study to support conclusions that have already been accepted as indisputable. Such "research" is not an honest exploration of historical fighting, nor is it worthy of claiming to represent our Western martial heritage.

Advice to the Reader

"It has been said, some training is better than no training, but no training is better than bad training."

—Anonymous

There are perhaps three main reasons why it is so rare to find skilled martialist swordsmen and so difficult to find quality instruction today: (1) it is not cheap or common to own an accurate, quality, replica sword; (2) you have to actually cut things with your sword to fully understand it, but you can't normally go around finding suitable materials to practice cutting; and (3) you have to engage in some realistic form of simulated "combat" to test your techniques and skill against others, but without a safe method of serious free-sparring most people will refrain. If the earlier two elements are excluded as well, an aspiring student of the sword will be left in the fantasy land of pretend play with ineffectual techniques and flawed fundamentals.

This brings us to the issue of how to proceed with the learning and training of Medieval swordsmanship today. How do those wishing to learn the martial art of Medieval swordsmanship today go about it? How do we practice? Besides the obvious necessities of free-sparring, test-cutting, and drilling techniques, exactly what exercises and routines should we do? Although this book does not offer lessons, it does present practical guidelines and suggestions. There are many pieces of good advice that can be offered to

people conducting Medieval swordsmanship today, regardless of their method of practice or period of historical interest.

1. *Question everything.* No one has all the answers, and you should suspect any individual, group, or organization that proclaims, or just implies, that it does. Even when a particular theory or technique seems fully established and valid, there can always be exceptions to it or flaws in it. The best way to proceed in studying historical fencing is to assume that most everything is tentative and always be ready and willing to reexamine ideas.

2. *Cross-train.* Whatever form of historical fencing you are pursuing, realize that training is a continual, never-ending process. Seek out as many varieties and methods of swordsmanship and weapon-sparring as you can find. This can have tremendous advantages. It can allow for a freedom in exploration devoid of stylistic conformity to one set of sparring rules or one manner of fighting. Almost any method has some virtues to offer, and practicing exclusively with only one method is limiting. Always endeavor to engage as many sparring partners as you can, particularly the better ones. The better the opponent, the more you will

be challenged and the more you will learn about yourself. Training with only inferior opponents will not bring you to your highest level and can even lead to lazy habits. Do not neglect either sparring or live-blade practice.

3. *Research.* Read and study everything you can find on the subject and pay special attention to the works of the historical Masters. The most important thing to keep in mind is that although the historical manuals divulge many techniques, there are still many others that they do not. In addition, over time many techniques become obvious to students as they learn how the weapon itself operates. It has even been suggested that many of the historical manuals were less guides for students of the day than promotional advertising and that no real master would have revealed his carefully guarded methods so carelessly, despite how uncommon books and reading were at the time. Besides, the methods would have been impossible to put in one volume. Thus to those who question the validity of techniques and movements described in this work, my advice is to practice them without restraint— and then to practice them again. But I must reiterate that this book is certainly not "everything" there is on the subject.

Don't exclude the wealth of information that can be attained in sport fencing or Asian martial arts, but also don't forget that to inquire by doubt and question is also part of our Western heritage. It is strongly recommended that you consult the original historical sources and not just secondary ones or general books on Medieval warfare and arms and armor. It is from reading primary, sometimes obscure, references, rather than relying solely on other's views, that more profound insights and details may be gained.

4. *Practice.* Although it's a cliché, the three most important things in gaining true skill with the sword are practice, practice, and practice! Also, there is really no substitute for proper fencing instruction. Don't treat it as a short-term activity. Whether instruction or cross-training is available or not, there are still numerous exercises, drills, and routines that should be followed. But remember that what one does in mock fighting and re-creation combat is not the historical reality.

5. *Take whatever techniques, strikes, or moves you use in a fight and attempt them with a real, historically accurate sword* (not against another person, of course). After practicing this way, if your style, your method, or your moves do not completely translate, then you should stop immediately and closely examine why. You must seriously consider just what it is about what you do in your sparring that a real blade can and cannot do. What cuts, what parries, what stances still carry over? What is there that you do only as a result of the particular rules you follow? Stop and ask yourself how your current training method would change if you knew that in six months you had to fight a duel to the death with real weapons? This is the attitude you should try to maintain all along. It is in this way that the nature of historical weapon use will become far more apparent and relevant, as will the limitations or merits of whatever sparring system you use.

SUGGESTIONS FOR MEDIEVAL SWORD TRAINING

- Practice cuts and strikes at full speed and power (for proper delivery, angle, and recovery).
- Practice footwork and stepping in coordination with strikes and parries.
- Practice full-contact strikes at a fixed soft target or pell (for power and focus).
- Practice controlled strikes and cuts at fixed and mobile targets.
- Practice defensive and offensive shield motions.
- Practice use and coordination of a second-hand weapon (i.e., axe, mace, dagger, buckler).
- Conduct contact-sparring with safe, padded weapons (or either wooden or blunt weapons and proper armor protection).
- Spar at full speed with intent.
- Spar at half-speed with exaggerated, casual intent.
- Spar without verbal comment or instruction.
- Spar by alternating offense only/defense only.
- Spar against multiple opponents and groups (2 on 1, 3 on 1, 4 on 1, etc., and 2 on 2, 5 on 5, 10 on 10, etc.).
- Practice with a single sword alone without any shield (by both single- and double-hand gripping).
- Practice with the sword held in the opposite hand.

- Practice with single dagger alone against sword, and dagger against dagger.
- Practice both against and with pole-weapons.
- Practice routines with a historically accurate replica blade.
- Conduct test-cutting with a sharp replica blade.
- Do some aerobic exercise for stamina.
- Do some form of weight training for strength.

A good method advocated for studying the sword uses four training implements:

- Wooden weapons for practice
- Blunts for training
- Sharps for test-cutting
- Padded contact weapons for sparring

In ages when warriors trained for real battle, they were obviously far more accepting of danger and realism in their practice than we are today. Although we know that wooden weapons were used historically, we don't know much about their details (were they just sticks, or were they shaped to resemble the weight and balance of real weapons?). We know that from time to time blunted steel versions were also used, but we do not know how common or widespread a practice this was. We can certainly assume that a degree of practice and test-cutting with sharps (live steel) was also done as well (how else to tell whether a blade is battle worthy?). Although warriors of past ages could rely on experience in warfare and actual life-and-death encounters, we cannot. Thus, to supplement training and practice with wooden and steel blades, contact sparring serves as a substitute. Not only does this serve to test the mechanical and tactical effectiveness of our technique, it helps us to develop the all-important fundamental principles of distance, timing, and perception. Besides, it's great fun.

The combination of these four instruments as a method of practice will definitely provide a well-rounded understanding. Wooden weapons ("wasters") have a certain aesthetic quality, can be easily carried about with little care, and are very practical both for beginners and experienced swordsmen. They are also ideal for solo practice, two-person strike-and-parry drills, and even light, semi-contact touch-sparring. Blunts are less common and wear out sooner, but like wooden weapons, they are extremely useful for teaching control and finesse. These are also good for teaching the basic stances, actions, and movement. Above all, they enable a practitioner to get a feel for the play of steel on steel and the feel of handling a real sword. However, since few blunts function identically to true swords or are even accurate reproductions, they are not an end in themselves. Thus, only using an accurate and sharpened replica of an authentic blade will teach a swordsman the subtle and crucial elements of handling the weapon. As has been emphasized, sharps should be used to practice their purpose: cutting. Test-cutting (and thrusting) should be available as soon as a student is able, for it will give a clearer understanding of what a sword is all about. Additionally, padded contact-weapons safe enough for unarmored sparring should be used. It is vital that they be designed with a rigid core and be as accurate as possible in their weight and balance. The early introduction of contact-sparring will produce a quick understanding of these vital concepts. Although forms of sparring can also be undertaken using wood or blunts, the virtue of padded ones is that they can be used for firm and solid blows, thrusts, and slices whether the swordsmen wear armor or not.

There is no real order that is necessary for the use of any of these tools, except that sharps should, of course, never be handled by complete novices. But the use of the other implements, including those for contact-sparring and two-person drills, should begin almost immediately. Relying too much on the use of any one of these alone (but particularly blunts and contact-weapons) will distort understanding and skill. If one wishes, Medieval fighting arts can be seen as a combative system. A combative system, as once defined by the International Hoplology Society, is "a body of organized, codified, repeatable movement patterns, techniques, behavior, and attitudes, the primary intended function and design of which is to be used in combative situations." Fighting is not an overly complicated matter, nor should it be made so. For instance, stand with your weapon in a reasonable and comfortable position, have your sparring partner repeatedly attack, and simply defend yourself. Have your partner increase the aggressiveness of the attacks, and over time the most efficient and effective ways in which to respond will become clear. Further, it will become obvious that the best defense is a good offense, for the adversary can make himself vulnerable when he attacks. Of course, this works both ways (for defense as well), and therein lies the fight. Provided we do not delude ourselves with contrived, false projections of what is and is not possible or restrict target areas unrealistically, the natural secrets of swordsmanship can reveal themselves in time. It is only a matter of long-term, committed practice.

There is another matter regarding training and learning that should be commented on. Given that fighting is too dynamic and unpredictable to be reduced to preset patterns or arranged motions, no choreographed rehearsing is necessary for practice. But, for instructing beginners, a useful training aid— for fundamental movements only—can be solo drills. Early on they can assist individual practice. Such routines, however, which consist of only the very fundamental cuts, parries, and stepping, are no substitute for the understanding of principles acquired through sparring and training. Repeated cutting-and-blocking routines with emphasis on strength, speed, and precision should not be viewed as an end in themselves. Solo drills are not the art itself, but merely a temporary tool; they are not, for example, the equivalent of the kata, or forms, of Asian martial arts, nor should they be made so.

There is something to consider when acquiring sparring partners. Finding opponents who can match particular levels of ability may be difficult. Quite often potential partners are either noticeably superior or inferior. Though you may practice with individuals you outclass and can readily defeat, it is important to not allow yourself to become lax. We must resist the urge to fight softer or to quit trying in an effort to somehow make things "more interesting and challenging." This attitude does a disservice not only to your true skills, but also to your sparring partner by not offering him an honest test. Practice like this surely leads to bad habits and weakens one's edge. This is not to say that when

facing clearly inferior opponents you should always crush and overwhelm them. Not at all. In those cases you obviously need to teach and instruct without diminishing an individual or breaking his spirit. On the other hand, if you face partners who soundly beat you, you must avoid the urge to view it entirely in terms of something you failed to do or something the opponent did. This is not useful. Victory or defeat is always a matter of that which we do or fail to do *in combination* with what an adversary does or fails to do. Sometimes the two are indistinguishable.

Keep in mind that although there are certain universal concepts of fighting (e.g., perception, distance, timing, technique), every method of swordsmanship or weapon use has its own historical context. No style or form should be viewed as a be-all and end-all ultimate method. It is as much mental (psychological) as physical. Above all should be the realization that this activity takes discipline and physical conditioning; it does not work well with a light-hearted, weekend pastime approach. It is a martial art and really should be treated as such. If you begin to feel inadequate or lacking in skill, this is a good sign; it means you are honestly recognizing that you could be better and that there is more to higher skill than you yet know. The desire to improve is a further step along the path. What has been imperfectly presented here is not any cultural tradition or aesthetics, nor even one particular historical simulation, but rather fundamental skills and knowledge of Medieval sword use. As with any art, it has introspective and contemplative qualities that can be experienced with dedicated training.

It has been said many times in many ways that the true purpose of swordsmanship is the destruction of the ego, of the self. It is intended to improve the character of the person wielding the sword. In the words of an anonymous swordsman, "If you would seek skill in the sword, first seek sincerity of the heart, for the former is but a reflection of the latter."

Afterword

"Knowledge of arms and weapons, which defends life, country, and honor, is a most fitting subject for the author's pen and for glory of his lord. Here it's shown not as a matter of violence and aggression, but of a higher, nobler purpose for the greater social good."

—From a 1594 English book on swordsmanship

The reality of hand-to-hand combat in any warfare is a brutal and unromantic subject, but its drama and honor is richly deserving of study. The hand-to-hand fighting of Medieval warriors has been the subject of much investigation and reenactment, despite the fact that there is limited historical evidence available to understand it precisely. All that has been presented in this guide is a simple overview of the techniques and methods of Medieval swordsmanship as historical fighting skills uncontaminated by ideas of modern sport-fencing, stage-combat, or techniques derived from Asian martial arts.

To think that we can go from first doing mock-fighting based on some limited preconceptions to then understanding what the real thing was all about is misguided. This is an ass-backwards approach. What we should, and must, do is first reconstruct Medieval fighting as a true martial art. We must redevelop it as legitimate fighting skills first before we attempt to simulate it with a limited set of pretend rules. Obviously, we cannot (nor should we want to) engage in lethal combat with real weapons. But there are alternatives to just playing. Imagine what the state of traditional Asian martial art forms would be today if there were no surviving schools or instructors, only people dressing up and playing with sparring gear. What would be the nature of their skills? Could these people with their narrow understanding be expected to reformulate actual, lethal combat techniques realistically? Could they go on from this to re-create a historical killing art? Hardly. However, such is the state of much of the stylized sparring today that currently passes for Medieval (and Renaissance) swordsmanship and weapon fighting.

The sword has always stood not for destruction but for freedom, strength, and justice. The history of the sword has often been called the history of humanity. Despite its obsolescence, no other weapon in the world has the heritage of or the reverence for the hilted blade. Indeed, when we consider how ubiquitous swords are on flags, emblems, signs, and statues, among other items, it is surprising in some way that its tradition has not been kept more alive in the West. Although it is often forgotten, the influence of the sword through the ages can still be felt in everyday life. For example, in some countries it is still customary to drive on the left because people once walked on the left. They did this because, most being right-handed, they would draw their swords to the right and would need the space. Men's coats are buttoned left over right so that a gentleman could unbutton it with his free left hand while engaged in a duel. For similar reasons, a gentleman escorts a lady on his right arm, keeping both his sword-arm free and his weapon out of her way. These customs come down to us in the same manner as those for shaking right hands (thought to originally have been a Germanic custom for showing that the weapon hand was empty) or the military salute (a remainder from armored knights' lifting their visors to identify themselves).

In pursuing historical swordsmanship today, whether as a personal martial art or organized *martial-sport* activity, there are certain abstract fundamentals to realize. The practice of swordsmanship has often been described as being a path and not a destination. One never truly masters it. You just go farther along the path. The point at which you enter the study will differ for some, who may join farther along and move more quickly. Others may get sidetracked or wander off. To begin, you bring only what you have within yourself, mentally and physically. In this way it is analogous to a mirror that reflects only what is brought before it—in all its glory or its flaws. In the long run, what swordsmanship offers, other than the physical benefits of exercise and stress relief, is a change in the character of the person wielding the sword. The requirements of self-discipline, commitment, perseverance, and patience are transferable outside the art. So, too, is the need for self-control and focus, both mental and physical. At the highest level (for there are higher levels), the development of perception, insight, and intuition can eventually begin to alter our perspective on life. As with any martial art that is practiced with sincerity and commitment, it has been said that true swordsmanship cannot be taught, it must be self-learned. It has the goal of defeating the ego, the self, and few ever realize that this is the constant and ultimate opponent to overcome.

Most practitioners today have had to learn through self-discovery and research, but no one can really say, "I am a self-taught swordsman" unless he has lived alone on another planet. We all learn something whether we realize it or not from every book on the subject we have perused and every swordfight film, good and bad, we have seen. We also learn something about ourselves every time we spar

or practice with someone else. In addition, we may have been taught something of traditional sport fencing, Asian sword styles, or the standard techniques of some historical fantasy organization. With a great many enthusiasts, a good portion of what they have discovered has been what they have picked up practicing with friends in a backyard or the local park. But, for the most part, seriously learning swordsmanship today is a very personal undertaking. Neither martial skill nor martial spirit comes naturally. It must be learned in battle or through skillful practice. Today, a student must first procure a source of this martial knowledge and then work hard to acquire the skills. Hours of attentive exercise and drilling should be followed with contemplative, relaxed time spent reflecting on the craft at hand. Unfocused, clearheaded repose can be an invaluable asset to learning and improving skill.

Lacking an established tradition of instruction to follow in the course of studying and reconstructing Medieval swordsmanship, we may come to ask, "How is it we are to know what to do; how can we know exactly how to learn?" Those are reasonable questions. How *do* we know when we are practicing real moves or actual techniques and not just basing things on wishful thinking, stylized rule conventions, or even our own naive illusions? Often we receive answers such as, "*Well, it seems to have worked so far . . . against those I've encountered . . . at least I haven't seen anything too different or that really worked any better.*" Whether we possess a coherent, systematized theory of swordsmanship or not, these doubts can still sometimes be present. We should turn them into a positive force: we can learn to use them as inspiration to further our study and continually train.

There is more to studying this subject than the age-old problem of scholarly research versus hands-on training. Theoretical practice versus practical application is the issue now just as it was in the brutal times of the Medieval period. In historical fighting there were no rules, and if something did not work it was discarded. It has been said that a successful warrior must be able to adapt to his opponents, to perceive their ability and threat, and simply do the unexpected. Anyone who is today ostensibly a "master" of historical European weaponry should be well scrutinized. After all, should not "masters" have to prove themselves against other "masters" and not just their own students? But the vast majority of enthusiasts today have no real way of telling whether the instruction they encounter is good, bad, or bogus if they themselves don't know much either. I hope this work has helped to arm students of the sword to understand this issue better.

Occasionally, when I am asked exactly where I learned my skills, I respond, "From the wind, from the trees, from the sky." Nonsense! Yet, there is a small metaphorical ring of truth to such a silly answer: that is, much of swordsmanship must be self-taught. Regardless of our sparring partners, sources, and instructors, it must be acquired alone through personal, disciplined, committed practice. I acquired my proficiency through long, dedicated training and a wide range of study. There is no other way. As they say, you can't buy it off the shelf or just take a pill—otherwise everyone would have it. Through historical sources, I was guided to inquire further and to ask more questions. In one sense, I really did learn from reading books and watching TV: I learned what not to do, as well as what was silly and false.

Like many others, I searched for the "real thing" and asked why one would do this or do that in a fight and how best to respond. The discovery of the works of real historical masters opened a whole new dimension. I personally had always found sport-fencing too restrictive and not historical enough, and the traditional Asian martial arts were far too ritualistic and structured for my tastes. I also found that the more common forms of Medieval re-enactment and stick-fighting were limiting, stylistic, and historically inaccurate. As with numerous other practitioners and students, this led me in a different direction of investigation. Once the role-playing and pretend performance were removed, what was left utterly changed the character of my approach: it then became purely martial and historical.

As a practicing swordsman and martialist, I eventually realized that for a great deal of my early experiences I had not been particularly more skillful or knowledgeable than others I encountered. Rather, my opponents had themselves been decidedly inferior, and that perhaps accounted for a good deal of my early success. I had also been lucky in possessing natural ability that benefited from not being stifled by one limited, stylized training method

or limited rule system of sparring. These factors combined resulted in the opportunity to commit myself to a serious, lifetime pursuit of sword skills and the accumulation of related knowledge. I became dedicated to the reconstruction and replication of historical European fighting skills from both the Medieval and Renaissance periods.

In Medieval swordsmanship, we discern the fundamental principles and concepts, we practice the basics, we try them out, we refine them, and (we hope) we continue to further reevaluate them. Scrutinizing and critically examining all forms of armed fighting that we are exposed to becomes a central factor in our learning. It is also a dominant characteristic of all modes of Western empirical thought. Although one may not necessarily possess the physical ability or conditioning necessary to be a highly effective fighter, merely possessing knowledge is not enough. Knowledge must be applied. When it comes to fighting, one cannot simply assert theories. Too often someone who has been thoroughly outfought and surpassed in free-sparring will utter something like, "Oh, that may have worked just now on me, but you shouldn't do that"—as he gets hit yet again. To justify high regard or earn respect, skill must be *demonstrated* through successful fighting . . . with no excuses. The way of the sword (any sword) is not something one just does the way one "does" tennis or bowling. It is not something one adapts to his life; it is rather something one adapts his life *to*. It has been said that there is a point at which training and discipline become a philosophy and vice versa.

In swordsmanship, often what you *do not* do is almost as important as what you do: avoiding incorrect form or erroneous technique is also a part of developing proper skill. Learning what to do and what not to comes about only through discovering one's errors, flaws, and misperceptions. It is a continual process of self-examination. It seems clear that the majority of students of the sword never come close to this attitude in their efforts. Too many apparently believe that they "know it all" or that there isn't any higher level of learning to be achieved. How very wrong they are. Sadly, many Medieval combat enthusiasts today are more interested in playing at swords than in recovering historical skills or legitimate martial ability. Personal development can only be achieved through education rather than entertainment, history instead of fantasy, and reenactment over role-playing. It is only through disciplined, serious sparring that understanding can be gained about striking, parrying, and moving in any form of swordfight. However, swordsmanship is not just applying technique. It is also a creative, intuitive interaction (physical and mental). It is necessary to comprehend both the value and the limitations of techniques. Once this is achieved, true skill in swordsmanship begins.

The task now challenging committed practitioners is to recover and learn Medieval swordsmanship and fighting skills and to disseminate them. Once more, these lost arts are becoming modern skills to perform.

That we can begin now to fully appreciate and realistically study Medieval swords and Medieval fighting manuals is for many a new and exciting prospect. That we can respectfully practice their skills as a true martial art is the challenge.

Be not wise in thine own conceit, in thinking that thou hast learned all the skill which is to be learned already, farre deceived are thou if thou thinks so, for if thou live (til) thou art olde, yet thou mayest learne still.

—Joseph Swetnam
The Schoole of the Noble and Worthy Science of Defence, 1617

On Obtaining a Real Sword

Finding a good antique blade in fine condition is out of the reach of perhaps 99 percent of those now pursuing historical fencing. Few can spend $5,000 or $10,000 for a specimen, and those who could would hesitate before risking damaging such a piece of history. So we must instead be content with as accurate a replica of a real sword as possible. Purchasing a realistic, historically accurate reproduction of a Medieval sword is often not an easy task.

If you want a piece just to hang on the wall or wear with some costume, it hardly matters whether it's real or fake. But if you want to know that your $300 was not spent on just a metal toy or stage prop, but rather on a real weapon (sharpened or not), you need to be much more discriminating. No one would purchase a gun that couldn't fire, but many will readily plop down good money for a useless facsimile blade from any retailer with a sales pitch about Rockwell scales and handcrafted spring-steel. One may not intend to ever do any test-cutting with a blade, or perhaps even bother practicing with it, but it's at least better to understand whether it is real or complete junk. So, the question arises of how to tell how "real" or historically accurate a replica sword is.

There are currently available far more varieties of replica swords that are make-believe or historically fake than there are those that are made in the likeness of real-life models. It seems that copying historical examples from a museum or private collection is of much less interest to swordmakers and swordsmiths now than are their own "original" interpretations or product marketing. This is understandable because, as artists and vendors, they do not want to just redo other people's work over and over. They need to create and express, or at least push sales of their product to ignorant consumers. This would seem to be no big deal—people are certainly free to make and sell whatever they want. There shouldn't be any difficulty in coming up with alternative yet legitimate designs or fulfilling customer's requests. Except doing so comes with a price—a price that serious students of the sword must be wary of.

During the Middle Ages, tens of thousands of young men used real swords for real life-and-death fighting. Their swordmakers came up with practical and beautiful styles and stuck with them. These warriors knew what sword forms worked and why, and they knew how to handle them. In a process of deadly natural selection they tried and discarded those that were inferior. As a result, thousands of examples have survived for us that represent designs for defeating a variety of different opponents and armors.

Yet, today, we now have modern, self-taught Medieval swordmakers who presume to create their own imaginary designs according to whatever aesthetics suit their fancy, regardless of functionality. This would be no problem if these makers could either admit that an original fantasy design is impractical or that it violates an established principle of use. Typically it would appear they cannot. If they could respect the knowledge of skilled practitioners and adhere to the fundamentals of what makes a comfortable, balanced, and functionally sound hilt or blade, there would be no need to write this.

After all, who is there with the authority to tell them? Who among them would listen anyway? They focus on the science and art of their craft (metallurgy, forging, and tempering) instead of whether it is functionally sound. They are artists and craftsmen, not slaves to the opinions of self-proclaimed swordsmen. They can label their work as "historical" or "historically accurate" based on their own subjective criteria (although some presumably do their own sword training as well).[1] However, because of their own creative whims, technical limitations, and marketing notions, they pass their fantasy swords off to an unassuming and unquestioning public. Some will even argue, "Who's to say they didn't have a sword like this back then?" or "Maybe they just didn't get around to doing a design like this." In their asserting that a particular design is "real," they ignore their responsibility to provide reference and historical evidence for the design and expect others to prove that it isn't.

In a perverse reversal of the ancient relationship in which skilled warrior-swordsmen provided to swordmakers the crucial feedback on sword-handling characteristics and performance, we have the opposite today. Often it is the fantasy swordmakers themselves who tell their customers what a sword should be able to do and how it should respond when doing it! When these blades (those few that are capable) end up being used by performers of stage-combat and jousting shows, the claim is then made that they are "real" and "battle-tested." This is hardly the case. The limitations and artificial premises of staged fighting and theatrical combat routines with their special requirements are a far cry from really wielding a sword to cut or kill, or just to train realistically today.

Rather than a relatively light and agile real blade accurately copied from an actual historical model, some people, out of ignorance, are more impressed by ornate hilts on what they expect should be ponderously heavy blades. These are not swords. These do not represent the ancient heritage of true weapons. They are "wall-hangers" suitable only for display. Many swords commercially available today are completely fake. The only thing that makes them "swords" is the fact that they are shaped liked them and happen to be metal. The cheapest of these "swords" are incapable of even holding much of an edge and will quickly be dulled or even dented if used for test-cutting. But then, most people don't sharpen them very much, not to mention actually practice-cutting with them.

Bending the blade a few inches by hand can easily check for a good temper. The blade should flex and spring back into shape easily. If it's too thick to bend or stays bent, it's not good (and that's putting it politely). Even when a blade is made of quality steel, expertly tempered for flexibility, and is able to hold a keen edge, there is no guarantee that the maker understands the proper weight and balance it should have.

Many Medieval and Renaissance swords commercially available on the Internet, in catalogs, or at festivals, flea markets, and cutlery shops are cheap pseudo-swords. Their quality typically ranges from just bad to awful. Many of these swords contain chromium or other trace metals for that high gloss, silvery sheen, and mirror finish. Others are simply polished stainless steel, which makes the steel too soft to hold a keen edge for very long. These blades invariably have false tangs that are far too short for proper, full-powered swings. A short tang, crudely welded on the blade, will break once enough torque is applied in swinging it for a cut. Because of the softer, poorly tempered metal used on most, these blades are often much thicker (and heavier) than historical swords. If made too thin they would bend or droop under their own weight (as some "cosmetic" blades notoriously do when held horizontally). On many, by looking closely one can also detect the telltale signs

---

[1] This stands in strong contrast to the situation in Japan today; Japanese swordsmiths are considered national living treasures and their products are officially regulated to control quality. Producing or importing cheap fake swords is not even allowed.

of machine-grinding in their minute, scratchlike surface. To counterbalance these heavier blades the guards and pommels are often extralarge or at least made of soft, heavy brass or bronze. This is particularly so for stage-combat blades that are used for endless (and unrealistic) banging edge on edge.

It should be obvious, but perhaps it must be explained: stage or theatrical swords invariably are not real swords. Although they are admittedly dangerous objects, and some versions could be honed to a serviceable edge and indeed kill, they are still not actual sword weapons. They are intended for practice and show, not cutting (see Appendix B). Stage blades are squared-off with flat edges, whereas a true sword has a tapering cross-section with very thin edges. Real sword edges need to retain their sharpness, not simply take lots of gouges and dents. The ability of a blade to withstand repeated beatings is irrelevant if the adversary's sword is twice as fast and sharp. Swordsmanship does not consist of banging swords together. It is about moving and cutting. Although unedged practice swords ("blunts") can be valuable training tools when well made, they are not good substitutes for accurate replicas in serious practice.

When choosing a real sword, there are two types to consider. First, if you can afford it, you can have a weapon personally made by a smith who, likely through trial and error, manages to produce a good facsimile of a Medieval sword. In which case, you hope it is forged and tempered properly and has some guarantee. Second, you can choose a sword that was patterned directly after an existing historical weapon, crafted only after an expert on Medieval weaponry has certified to its accuracy and quality. In the second case, ideally, you want an opinion not from a knifemaker or blacksmith, but from someone who has traveled to leading arms museums and sword collections, handled and inspected their weapons, measured them for weight and balance, and then supervised the reproduction of a replica. Ideally, you want a sword copied from a prototype, which was tested for quality as well as cutting power before being declared satisfactory to offer at an affordable price. Fortunately, such swords are indeed readily available from a few manufacturers.

You should avoid mystical claims of "magic" swords, or swords "tuned" to a user or metaphysical notions that blades "choose their owner." Even if it's a deadly weapon, a technical marvel, or a work of artistry, it's still just a piece of steel. To superstitious warriors of ages past, the mystery of what went into the making of a good blade was a matter bordering on the paranormal if not outright supernatural. Why it held up well and kept a good edge was often considered beyond mere physical attributes. But in the end, skill and ability depended upon the individual warriors themselves, and neither gods, demons, nor magic charms made a difference.

A real Medieval (cutting) sword essentially needs to be able to do three things well:

- To cut, but cut strongly and still retain its edge
- To withstand impact and flex or "return true"
- To fight, or rather to be agile enough to strike and recover

Remove any one of these three as a result of inferior steel or tempering or because of poor design and you do not have a true weapon. It will be at best a blunt training tool and at worst a prop. If a sword cannot maintain a keen edge it will not cut effectively even if it strikes accurately and strongly. If it cannot take a beating, it will break or warp and stay bent. If it is heavy or ill balanced, it will be sluggish and slow and leave you vulnerable while parrying or after striking. Understanding these three elements is to understand the nature of a Medieval sword and the nature of a swordfight.

The problem of inferior, poor-quality hilts on replica swords is another important issue. One of the most irritating things that can happen is to take your expensive, finely made replica out for a few minutes of practice cuts, only to have the leather or wire wrap unfold and the pommel begin to twist in your palm each time. What's even worse is to have a brand-new sword fall apart on you, leaving the thing virtually useless. The typical hilt defects associated with the better replica swords are the tang's snapping, the blade's breaking at the handle, and the side or finger-rings' cracking. Another problem includes loose, ill-fitting handles that cause the tang inside to shift when the blade is swung forcefully. This flaw is often caused by softer wood that has expanded or by the drilling of too large a hole for the tang. If you ever have the splendor of examining actual antique blades you can see their guards are typically of one solid piece, perhaps hot-forged together. By contrast, today's imitation hilts are usually spot-welded while cold. Thus, they are weaker and unable to take the abuse that real ones could. Understand that no sword is indestructible, to be sure. But they should be able to take some abuse without their hilt's falling apart in your hands. Nowadays, the better swordsmiths have been able to produce some excellent blades, but most cutlers who make the hilts have a long way to go. Even the best replicas pale in comparison to historical (real) swords. That's not to say that today's replicas can't be as great, just that the real ones are very impressive. Keep in mind that no matter how well-forged and carefully tempered a blade itself is, as a weapon (or as a training tool), it's really only as good as its hilt.

It will take some time, perhaps another generation, before sufficient Western re-creational swordsmen become knowledgeable and skillful enough to compel the many fantasy makers to respond to the swordsmen's expertise, thereby creating more historically accurate weapons. Until then, the preponderance of inaccurate replicas and fantasy versions will continue to mislead enthusiasts and retard modern reconstruction of the art. The masses of misinformed and uninformed sword fans will continue to be taken advantage of and sold inferior merchandise. Practitioners are advised to avoid the many "costume" swords on the market. The majority of these reproductions are inaccurate, poorly tempered blades of inferior steel. Most also lack proper weight and balance. The peddlers of many of these often ridiculously priced props (for that is what most are) are not about to inform their potential customers of these facts—even if they are fully aware of it themselves. Buyer beware.

The Problem of Stage-Combat

The subject of historical Western fighting arts or swordsmanship cannot be addressed without encountering the practice of stage-combat or theatrical fighting. There are many clichés of choreographed swordplay so pervasive that in certain circles they have become accepted as legitimate actions of fighting. Although mostly fantasy and illusion, the clichés have so permeated the public's consciousness that there are some enthusiasts who don't even understand that they are imaginary. As obvious as it may seem to experienced fighters, this problem is worth taking the time to discuss.

Let's be honest. By its very definition, stage-combat is about faking it. Stage-combat practitioners do not really fight, nor do they even try to learn to really fight. By "really fight" I do not necessarily mean to kill, but rather actually trying to hit an opponent with force. However, in their enthusiasm and increasing self-reference, few stage-combat adherents seem to concede this fact easily (I leave it to the reader to ponder why).

It is a sad thing that sword students practicing and sparring today can be seen trying fictional stances they saw on *Highlander* or some ninja movie, and twirling their blades around because they saw "Hercules" do it once on TV. The make-believe fighting of movies, plays, and live-action amusement park and dinner shows is about illusion. It is about creating the appearance of fighting, not about accurately exploring or simulating it. Remember that the shows only want to entertain, and they have no obligation to present the fighting realistically or to educate the viewer.[1] Doing so is often considered boring. Additionally, the weapons most often used for film and stage are usually inaccurate: to withstand constant pounding, they must often use extra-thick, double-weight versions that distort true fighting performance. At other times, flimsy, half-weight versions or aluminum blades are used to increase the weapons' agility and the actors' speed.

Unlike what passes for Medieval (and Renaissance) swordfights in the movies, where the fighters seem to do everything but try to cut or stab one another, the art of swordsmanship is usually far less animated and much more cautious. For dramatic effect, choreographed fights must exaggerate both the importance and the frequency of blade-to-blade

---

[1] Perhaps in the same way that actors in commercials will say, "I'm not a doctor, but I play one on TV," it wouldn't hurt for some theatrical fighters and performers to give their own disclaimers, such as, "I'm not a swordsman, but I play one on TV."

contact—and this is by far their most significant defect. In the usual staged swordfight, blades are banged on each other (invariably edge on edge) for minutes at a time. Combatants are shown basically whacking at each other's sword (they "fight the weapon not the actor"). Sometimes we witness the combatants making every attempt to place their own swords in the direct path of their opponents so that the blades will be banged around dramatically. Usually the performers can be seen making extrawide strokes and broad, exaggerated parries. Anything more realistic (i.e., effective) is improper. In the worst swordfight scenes, one even notices that were the performer to just lift his sword out of the way, the opponent would cut through empty air and miss by two feet or more.

Typically, the fighters are shown unnaturally making swing after swing and delivering blow after blow without ever moving to feint or fake out their opponent. Seldom do the fighters pause to out-time or deceive their adversaries (such actions are contrary to the craft). Virtually every swing is blocked by the opponent or even strikes some other unintended object. Few blows seem to ever miss or to be evaded. Often the swords are used as if they weighed 10 pounds or more. They are swung as if their momentum is so great that the user cannot help but follow behind. The openings and vulnerability thus created are ignored; the opponent can never seem to move his own "heavy" weapon in time to counter properly. It is ludicrous how often we see fighters unintentionally hit everything in sight except for their supposed target. Sometimes if a blow does miss, it serves to cause the attacker to "fall off balance" while the defender is able to make an agile dodge or step in to punch and kick. Such occurrences are improbable at best in the real art.

Although fighters historically relied on anything to win, most instances of knees in the groin, elbows in the face, dramatic pauses for dialogue, and kicks to the backside commonly seen in choreographed swordfights are fiction. Most such moves are either worthless when compared with the effect of hitting with a weapon or would probably get the fighter killed very quickly in the attempt.

Among the more notorious and common clichés of choreographed swordfighting are the following:

- Long, dramatic pauses as the actor-fighters clutch each other closely so that they can deliver face-to-face dialogue
- Punching and kicking when there is an opening instead of just cutting
- Closing in to hit with the hilt or pommel instead of the sharpened blade
- Finishing off the enemy with a simple stab after minutes of nothing but trying to hack at him throughout the fight
- Uselessly spinning and twirling the sword in one hand in the middle of combat
- Circular parries that disarm and throw off the opponent's sword (try that one!)
- Beats that easily knock a heavy sword out of the opponent's hand
- Swinging at a disarmed opponent yet still missing him over and over and over
- Missing a strike so that the inertia of the blow spins the attacker around
- Telegraphing a blow so much that the opponent has every opportunity to get out of the way
- Having the hero lose his weapon and then recover it

There are, of course, many, many more that could be added to this list, but the point is made.

Choreographed swordfights are also notorious for displaying any opportunity for one opponent to grab, push, pull, and knock the other—and in the process missing just about every chance to do what he is supposed to be doing with his weapon: kill the opponent. Take a good close look at most one-on-one fight scenes and it becomes clear that the actors are less interested in connecting with attacks than in following their programmed moves. The fights frequently appear overly rehearsed and dancelike. Even in the better choreographed (or "telegraphed") fights, you can even catch the pauses as the combatants freeze their actions just until their opponent is ready.

Remember that Medieval swordsmanship is fundamentally about cutting. Making an effective cut depends on three major components: grip, edge placement, and blade motion. Although these elements may be present in good contact-sparring, they are all but nonexistent in stage-combat performances—where parries and pretend blows must be exaggerated for safety and dramatic effect.

To be efficient, and therefore more effective, both parries and strikes need to be made with minimal motion and not with wide, revealing action; they must be subtle and imperceptible to the adversary. A fighter should move as if trying to out-time and counterstrike an adversary, not greet and welcome an expected partner. But all this is the converse of stage-combat.

Even when done quite well, choreographed swordplay is still rarely more than a fantasized version. It is about following a prescribed pattern, not freely and spontaneously moving. There are fundamental differences between contact-sparring and choreographed fighting, and professional fight arrangers understand this. Unlike swordsmen in a fight, choreographed performers are not looking for openings on adversaries, trying to deceive and counter them. In many ways, choreographed fighting is the exact opposite of free-sparring swordsmanship. In choreographed swordplay, instead of trying to conceal true intentions and read the adversary (as one would in combat), one projects one's actions and intentionally avoids any and all deception. Instead of trying to outmaneuver and actually connect, one must be wary not to hit and or accidentally touch the opponent's sword. The elements of choreographed swordplay are contrary to the very nature of all real fighting.

The simple truth behind it is that fighters seek to hit, actors seek to miss. Staged, simulated fighting can allow for almost any action or technique, no matter how silly or suicidal, to be made to look effective and useful. Visually appealing movements frequently are the entire purpose. This should never be forgotten.[2] Stage-combat is not about practicing how to effectively engage and defeat an opponent (real or simulated), but is instead only about convincing a viewer that what he sees is real. What true martial ability can come out of stage-combat, and what true historical skills can be replicated through it? Any elements of weapon handling, physical action, and the mechanics of movement taught in theatrical combat can be learned far better through study of the martial art form. Choreographed fighting is essentially acting with weapons.

Many of the standardized conventions of faking combat follow the traditional formula of theatrical stage-fighting. To increase the action and quicken the pace, choreographers and fight directors must often resort to a variety of familiar routines and slapstick. Some stage-combatants even feel that rather than presenting realistic, historical violence, putting on "a good show" is what is really important. Early stage-combat was notorious for inappropriately adapting the moves of épée sport-fencing to Medieval prop swords. Today, we can often see the recognizable and equally inappropriate moves of Chinese kung fu or Japanese kenjutsu being similarly used.

It must first be realized that, above all, the fundamental concern of all choreographed fighting is (naturally) safety. Everything is subordinate to this, and everything is controlled. Therefore, the majority of techniques that would realistically be used must be excluded because of either the danger of injury or the inexperience of the performers. The second concern is dramatic license. The fight must be made to "look good" and fit the story and characterization. No matter what, it must be "entertaining." The director may also call for actions that, although highly artificial for a real fight, must be included because of the script. The general public, ignorant of the subtle complexities of swordsmanship, doesn't know any better and merely wishes to be entertained by the swordfights. Capable, experienced, real fighters can be patient and cautious, even when intensely engaged. Although it's only for a brief instant, fighting might appear to be in limbo because of a lack of quick movement, but this is not really the case. Much of the action of real fighting is too subtle, too quick, or just too chaotic to be of interest to most fight-scene directors. Faced with this, fight directors and performers wish to avoid the two most likely possibilities: the fight would be very quick and brutal because one fighter was totally outclassed and killed, or it would be drawn out and slow because neither party took any action for some time.

Quite often actors involved in stage-fighting will have little real experience in handling a sword and may even be in poor physical condition. At other times they may have only a very short time in which to prepare. They may be instructed by a fight director or stunt coordinator whose sword experience

---

[2]The element of humor that occurs in some theatrical fighting, although entertaining, is a distortion of its brutal reality. Swordsmanship is not supposed to be a "Three Stooges" routine.

might be limited to basic sport-fencing (épée/foil/saber) and maybe some Asian martial arts thrown in (usually kendo or kenjutsu, or some Chinese swordplay).³ Certainly, the actors can apply the fundamental physical mechanics of sword use in a "historical" manner, but the rest is pretty much just made up. Thus, what is typically created is a hybrid "nonstyle" of swordsmanship. Indeed, a great deal of what theatrical fighters typically do is utter nonsense, and the participants display little ability other than timing movements together. It seems rare to find a cinematic or theatrical swordfight in which the choreographer has gone out of his way to include historically appropriate movements or actions fit for the weapons being used for a given era (though this is slowly changing).

Rather than having skilled, martial artist swordsmen today influencing stage fighting, it is the stage-fighters who seem to frequently present themselves as the martial authority (as if somehow they alone are the preservers of our surviving Western martial culture!). Yet, a stage-combat fight director is not necessarily a "master swordsman" or even a real martial artist. Instead, the director must be, first of all, someone who can prepare, arrange, and safely act out motions that appear to be a fight. There is the tacit assumption at work that such individuals are also capable fighters, rather than the greater likelihood that they are only performers. Yet, they often get recognized as "experts" or even "masters" in Western swordsmanship by mere virtue of their performances. Arbitrarily calling such performers "expert swordsmen" is like calling someone who shoots blanks a marksman.

Consider that when it comes to films featuring Asian style martial arts, the fight scenes are, for the most part, created and performed by skilled martial artists. They are typically choreographed by highly experienced, real martial arts masters who are able to create fairly realistic and entertaining fight scenes. These martial artists know real techniques and can actually fight. They are able to effectively control their actions and avoid injury or mishap while demonstrating their ability. They also have a complete, preexisting, and fully established martial system of real techniques and fighting experiences to draw upon to begin with! Fight arranging and stunt work is a secondary function to most, if not all, of them.⁴ This is not the case with Western fighting skills of historical swordsmanship.

In contrast, rather than witnessing actual martialist swordsmen during Medieval or Renaissance swordfights in film and on television, we have instead a cadre of professional stunt fighters and stage-fighting directors. They are taught the fundamentals of theater, safety, and choreography. Real martial arts or fencing experience is secondary (as if this alone can somehow fill the gap). Films and shows featuring forms of European swordsmanship appear to consist primarily of performers who are either relatively unskilled as fighters or invariably mere sport-fencers.

Despite the fact that they often create entertaining and well-played scenes under sometimes difficult conditions, it is outrageous to consider that stage-combat is itself somehow a form of true martial art. The craft of stage-combat is a performance art, not a fighting art (no matter how much some instructors and proponents pretend otherwise). Although it is becoming increasingly more sophisticated and historically accurate, by its very nature stage-combat must always be more ballet than fence, more pretend skill than martial skill.

It's not surprising, then, that with all the hundreds of books available on Asian martial arts styles, there are no such titles on "Asian martial arts stage-

---

³ Theatrical fight directors do not automatically have any particular grasp of Medieval fighting skills by virtue of their also being sport-fencers. Sport-fencers (collegiate or Olympic) are not necessarily martial artists either. The earliest cinematic and theatrical swordfights were little more than modern fencing mixed with sheer fantasy. Yet this influence was pervasive in a whole generation of today's leading fencing coaches. Much of their own ideas on what Medieval fighting skills were came from comparing movie fights with their own refined modern sport. The fencers then helped established stage-combat theories in a circular and self-referential process of mutual delusion. Exacerbating the problem are certain historical role-playing societies that practice forms of mock fighting that almost anyone can see are nowhere close to what Medieval combat must have surely been like.

⁴ Such experts also readily admit the great differences in attitude and style, not to mention technique, between what they do in a movie and how they fight in a tournament or on the street. However, a good deal of the weapon practice witnessed in some Chinese kung fu is not based on ancient battlefield effectiveness or skills of some isolated monks, but on the old operatic gymnastics of troupes of traveling actors. Rather than being for pure self-defense, their skills were presented as exaggerated, stylized, theatrical movements to entertain the crowds. This is not generally admitted to naive Western students eager for "Asian fighting powers."

combat." Nor are there any such "schools" dedicated exclusively to "Asian martial arts choreography." This fact is revealing. It points directly to the nature of the two activities. Why, then, should stage-combat be looked upon as anything other than entertainment? It is very sad that for historical Western swordsmanship there are far more published works available on the false fighting of staged "swordplay" than there are on the true art.

Consider it this way: What if instead of there being martial arts movies starring experts ranked in some martial style (e.g., Bruce Lee, Chuck Norris, Steven Seagal), there were instead only professional stunt fighters? What if rather than being skilled, trained martial artists who were actual masters at various systems of fighting, they were merely people who knew how to safely fake it? Could the general public tell the difference? Would people have the same respect and admiration for the fighting arts they were portraying? Yet such is the state today of virtually all film, television, and stage depictions of historical European swordsmanship and fighting from both Medieval and Renaissance periods. It is no wonder that many find it so difficult to accept that effective forms of true Medieval European fighting arts can still exist.[5]

Although stage-combat adherents may feel tht they are greatly concerned with "proper technique," they are seriously handicapped in what and how they can study. Martial artists and historical combat re-creationists, on the other hand, might sometimes not have much structured training, but they will apply whatever works in free-sparring to (safely) defeat an opponent. Ordinarily, the most serious drawback they face is only the rule structure they spar under or the limitations of the method they train with.

Stage performers or theatrical fight choreographers, in contrast, have to have something to base their actions on, since they are not "fighting" in the first place. They have no real tactical freedom, and their moves are based on whatever interpretation the fight arranger and performers can imagine. The possibility of applying any one particular technique may often be an arbitrary decision based on what looks good or seems fitting. When one has only a tiny fraction of actions to employ within a preset scene or narrowly defined circumstance, there is really nothing else to concern them (excluding the issue of safety) except reference to a handful of "historical techniques" and dramatic embellishments. Face it, by not having to earnestly use the principles and concepts of swordsmanship to counter an adversary actively trying to oppose you, it leaves you pretty much free in stage-combat to talk theory all day long. This is a far cry from what occurs in the adversarial contact-sparring of a true martial art.

The better stage-combat performers will admit that in their craft they must make considerable alterations to realism for the sake of safety and drama. They will admit that real combat unfolds very differently. It is at this point that we must then ask, if they can't do most realistic things but do include many false things, just what exactly is it they are doing? The answer obviously is that they are faking it. It is this very pretense of presenting martial skills that is so misleading. Just going through the motions and footwork of striking and parrying is hardly the same as using techniques and fighting principles in a tactical context. Learning false parries against false attacks certainly will not serve a swordsman well at all in free-sparring. This is something like trying to learn to hit a home run by just swinging a baseball bat at air. You have to have a ball actually thrown at you or you can't do it.

No one would think to learn to box, say, by watching the *Rocky* films of Sylvester Stallone (although they might perhaps be inspired to do so). In these films, through the efforts of a fight director, choreographer, and a coach, Stallone managed to pass for a professional boxer—to the untrained eye. Of course, no one would seriously think to learn boxing by watching those films and then going to classes just on fight arrangement. There are no schools that specialize in "how to box like Rocky Balboa." Instead, to learn real boxing, you have to go to a real gym and find a coach and sparring partners who could care less about how it's done in the movies. Yet, today, aspiring swordsmen flock to stage-combat classes in hopes of learning something about the real thing.

---

[5] When someone today says that he practices Western swordsmanship, people will often ask, "Oh, do you perform at the Renaissance Fair?" These people would never think of asking this sort of question of someone who announced that he was a student of kenjutsu or iaido. This illustrates both the sorry state of Western sword arts and the very different attitude fostered by the pretend nature of stage-combat.

For some students of the sword, their first introduction to the subject comes through taking a college course in theatrical combat or visiting performers at a Renaissance festival. Many of these students first get involved with stage-combat instruction out of a real love for swords rather than a great interest in theater or acting. For others it's just the reverse. Presented for the first time with a systematic method that breaks down movements and actions, they cannot help but be impressed. But few seem to realize that performance art is not a martial art. They have no way of understanding just how limited and narrowly specialized an approach stage-combat is.

A true martial art form can be described as a set of organized, systematized, reproducible techniques, actions, and concepts, whose main function is for use in violent encounters. Although certainly a physical art form, stage-combat, in contrast, consists of prepared, mutually agreeable, sequential movements adapted for the purpose of acting out an arranged display. Other than using the same tools and fundamental motions, the only thing that stage-combat displays and the practice of historical fighting arts today have in common is that neither intends to do real harm to the parties involved. The problem of why so many stage-combatants are deluded into thinking theatrical fighting is "martial" is that both the displays and the fighting arts employ "pretend" blows. In all other areas of offense and defense the two are contradictory. Although they both use the basic fundamental principles of fighting, they employ them quite differently:

- Where stage-combat shares perception, a martial art provokes misperception.
- Where stage-combat uses safe distance, a martial art uses proper distance.
- Where stage-combat involves timing, a martial art involves countertiming.
- Where stage-combat involves rhythm, a martial art involves broken rhythm.
- Where stage-combat embraces acted intent, a martial art demands earnest intent.
- Where stage-combat applies recognized technique artificially, a martial art applies individualized technique tactically.
- Where stage-combat avoids contact, a martial art seeks contact.

- Where stage-combat requires a theatrical sense, a martial art demands a fighting spirit.

The two activities, though superficially similar in their tools and actions, are really fundamentally and profoundly different in their nature, methods, and goals. They foster two very different and incompatible attitudes among their practitioners. To believe otherwise is foolishness. To confuse and blur the two is naive. Of course, to fake it well one must certainly have some ability. But the less you know, the less real it looks, and the less able you are to know better. Consequently, the more you know, the more you understand just how hard it is to make something fake look real. It is absurd that those who only study the restrained and highly altered methods of fighting required of modern stage-combat will then presume to describe or teach how real swords "could" or "might" be used.

The rhythm of swordfighting is not the cliché 1, 2, 3—1, 2, 3 of stage-combat routines, but rather an unpredictable broken pattern of something more like 1—2, 1,3 . . . 2—3, 3, 1 . . . 1, for example. Yet, staged choreographed fighting lacks the feints, deceptions, false attacks, and constantly altering distance that is the signature of free-sparing bouts. It is this which allows a superior fighter with greater technical skill and perception to successfully countertime his opponent.

Make no mistake: stage-combat swordplay is a necessary and respected part of entertainment and theatrical history, but it is not historical swordsmanship. It is practiced as entertainment, not conflict resolution or personal growth through martial skill. Training exclusively in stage-combat or choreographed fighting builds a distorted and artificial sense of distance, timing, and rhythm, and, frankly, does not lead to any legitimate fighting skill. There are those who will suggest that learning the theatrical form is somehow beneficial. This is nonsense. No instructor of karate or jujutsu would dare ever say to his class, "Okay, tonight we will disregard learning to kick and punch properly in favor of pretending to get beat up." Why should it be otherwise with this subject? It would be just as senseless for fencing coaches to teach their students to win competition bouts by acting out pretend fights. No one would imagine that you could become a skilled unarmed fighter or martial artist merely by the practice of faking it, yet with regard to swordsmanship, this is indeed what occurs among many stage-combat performers.

There are those who will argue that time spent choreographing and arranging fights is beneficial, that it even helps to improve their understanding and skill. They will assert that when done realistically, stage-combat is a useful tool for studying the real martial arts. This is a very poor excuse and one that does not stand up to either historical texts or common sense experience. To this we can respond: Why not then just spend that valuable time studying the real thing? If you enjoy fight direction and showmanship for its own legitimate ends, then have fun. But do not think that time spent doing it is in any way better than time spent free-sparring and drilling in realistic techniques. There are no actual fighting arts, whether Asian or Western, that waste effort in stage-combat pursuits in place of genuine martial practice. There is no theatrical playing in the curriculum of boxing, fencing, kenjutsu, jujutsu, or jeet kune do.

Please keep in mind that nothing in the preceding was in any way intended to discredit or devalue the time-honored craft of theatrical swordplay, but only to place it in context with the emerging practice of the historical methods. The theories of modern theatrical combat, though fine for the structured scenes of film and stage, just do not appropriately prepare fighters for free-sparring or serious martial practice. They are not tools for replicating historical fighting skills. Those seeking to learn the true craft must study elsewhere. If the historical Western fighting arts were fully reconstructed and reestablished, if skilled, expert swordsman and instruction were commonplace, there would be no need for such a lengthy dissertation such as this on why stage-combat is not a martial art. Stage-combat, which has done so much to entertain and thrill audiences, which has done so much to popularize swords, has also done a great disservice. In almost all its forms, it perpetually asserts the mantra that "the public doesn't know any better." By following a formula of fantasy and falsehood, it helps to ensure that the public never will. In the end, all this does is validate theatrical nonsense at the expense of our true martial heritage.

Methods of Weapon-Sparring

nthusiasts today have a range of options for conducting safe sword & shield or Medieval weapon free-sparring. These methods vary in their degree of historical accuracy and physical intensity. Many organizations and clubs of note exist to pursue forms of Medieval combat. Some have been active for decades. It is worthwhile for practitioners to explore what they have in common, the points where they differ, and how far they diverge. Too often, people's personal preferences for one group's rule system or established style prevent an open dialogue and free exchange of experience.

The approaches to re-creating and exploring Medieval combat range from the silly and juvenile to the outright dangerous. In between these extremes are many valuable options. There are those methods that attempt to realistically simulate actual weapons and how they handle, while others only act as a means of playing safe "touch-hits" with mock weapons. There are those that emphasize chivalry and knightly tournaments, and there are those that focus on Dark Ages conflicts, battle reenactments, and small skirmishes.

One of the most common forms of weapon sparring uses foam swords, popularly known as *boffers* (typically, hollow PVC or bamboo covered with ethyl foam or pipe insulation). These have been around in various homemade forms for about two decades, and commercial versions are increasingly being used in Asian martial arts (where they are assumed to be recent inventions). Some boffers use thin fiberglass, carbon rods, or even nylon rods wrapped in camping-pad foam. Boffers are notoriously light and flexible, often "whipping around" when swung. They are essentially "Nerf" swords. They offer the advantage of making it difficult to injure an opponent accidentally. However, they perform nothing like real weapons and tend not only to inhibit authentic techniques, but also to promote fictitious ones. Boffer sparring is really only suitable for adolescents and children. (This issue is significant enough to be addressed elsewhere in its own appendix; see p. 289.)

Bamboo swords (kendo *shinai*) are also popular weapon substitutes. Some people use them covered in cloth or foam. Shinais were invented in 18th-century Japan and were originally wrapped in leather. But like boffers, shinai are also ridiculously light and behave far too unrealistically to simulate Medieval swords accurately. On the other hand, solid-wood weapons can be excellent training tools, and historically they were used as such. There are a number of variations to this approach, and it is among the oldest being practiced.

Many approaches use rattan, a relative of bamboo and similar to sugarcane. It is favored because, like sugarcane, it breaks cleanly without splinters. But it, too, is also fairly light. Stick-fighting in heavy armor padding with rattan is a popular method that offers the advantage of relatively safe, true full-contact practice. It particularly allows for the experience of fighting in and against various types of plate armor. Unfortunately, it has drawbacks in its limited target areas and somewhat rigid padding and armor requirements. It invariably restricts sparring to fighting against other armored opponents only and tends to lead to a rule structure (the method of discriminating target areas and accounting for blows) that is somewhat idiosyncratic and stylistic.

Other wooden substitutes consist of carved oak, ash, or hickory swords (often called *wasters, bavins,* or *cudgels*). Some of these can be very realistic and well made, with excellent balance and weight. They are a form of real weapon in themselves. In addition to training exercises and practice drills, these wooden swords can be used for light, semi-contact sparring (a practice common in kenjutsu). This method teaches control and finesse as well as caution. It can vary in intensity, depending on the safety equipment worn and the experience of the participants. Using wooden weapons saves wear and tear on expensive steel blades, and they are certainly less conspicuous than metal ones to practice with and carry around. But wooden weapons also have drawbacks: the amount of force and the types of techniques that can be employed. Unlike metal blades, they do not have thin sides and slender edges that cut through the air. Wooden weapons, though very useful, are still distortions, not duplicates of metal ones.

At the other end of the spectrum is *live-steel*, a term often applied when metal blades are used. Although actual training with a sharpened sword is highly recommended for test-cutting, real blades are useless for sparring purposes. However, using blunts (dulled swords) offers valuable insights. Although practice with handling steel on steel can certainly teach finesse and control (like wooden swords they involve many restrictions), it is inherently limited for free-sparring because of the danger involved. Many types of blunt swords can also be quite unrealistic. Typically, they can be too thick and heavy, too slow, or too soft and flimsy. Some sparring methods use different versions of blunts and require the wearing of full plate armor and padding. This offers interesting opportunities, but for safety, the manner of contact is limited, as is the range of target areas and the techniques that can be applied. Other versions of live-steel involve only "semi-contact" or even weapon-only contact. These are not real means of free-sparring as much as forms of unrehearsed, live theater for battle performances or reenactment displays. By its nature, live-steel certainly has the virtue of being realistic in some aspects, but not in others. This practice is significant enough to be addressed in its own appendix (see p. 285).

It is worth noting that the vast majority of traditional Asian martial arts that feature weapon training are known to have little or no contact-sparring and virtually no true full-contact fighting (with the notable exceptions of kendo and certain forms of Filipino stick fighting). Instead, for various reasons, modern weapon practice among traditional Asian martial arts invariably focuses on proper form, style, ritual, and structured rehearsing—although the exceptions to this are increasing. However, it is one thing to do only repetitive, dancelike routines or endless classroom drills, and an altogether different one to constantly fight in mass battles and duels as most Medieval combat students do. This lack of true weapon sparring may come as a surprise to many. Unfortunately, in the Asian martial arts establishment today, despite diligent practice, far too many people seem to just "dance" with their swords and weapons. Becoming so concerned with the minutiae of form and style over substance or utility, they can often miss the battlefield application of ancient armed fighting methods. Additionally, it is one thing to use farming implements and peasant tools to supplement the learning of unarmed fighting and quite a different one to study battlefield weapons used for armored warfare. This situation is significant enough to also merit being addressed in its own appendix (see p. 309).

Although safety must always be the paramount concern in any system of weapon sparring, there is another important element for the serious student to be aware of. What often goes ignored is how the rule structure affects the type of skill and understanding students can obtain. Whatever the rule structure under which sparring takes place, it will come to dictate what techniques can be used. As fighters practice to get good at sparring "under the rules," this structure reinforces those very techniques that the rules allow for (and discourages those it doesn't). This, in turn, reinforces the rules themselves: fighters begin to prefer rules that allow them to do what they have now "become good at." There is a circular dynamic at work in this. Unless sparring rules are very inclusive to begin with when it comes to the variety of applicable techniques and allowable target areas, their use will lead to serious errors about what Medieval fighting was all about. This is something that serious students of Medieval swordsmanship should consider in depth, whatever method of practice fighting they follow.

Today's approaches to weapon-sparring and sword training obviously can be very subjective. The perceived element of risk or possible injury can vary considerably from group to group and individual to individual. For example, traditional Japanese kenjutsu practitioners have used wooden swords (*bokken*) in forceful semi-contact training for centuries. Yet, other practitioners would view any stick sparring with great hesitancy. Still others fight with full power and full contact today with sticks and armor. Practitioners of certain styles of arnis and escrima do likewise, using rattan but with minimal padding or protection. Traditional kendo artists use bamboo shinais but demand stiff armor padding and place severe restrictions on cuts and thrusts. Still others can comfortably employ the same shinais with minimal force and no armor whatsoever. There are many who use toylike foam swords for "touch-hits" and will cringe at any greater degree of contact. Yet, many martial artists can use the very same foam weapons to enthusiastically and safely go at it with full power. Still more practitioners can use foam-padded "swords" that are heavy, rigid, and realistic enough to require the wearing of armor. There are also those using blunted steel merely for semi-contact "bouts" when only light armors are worn. Others use virtually the same steel blades and system, but manage to fight with full contact in plate armor without injury. There are even those who engage in forms of limited "non-contact" theatrical practice (you can't really call it "sparring") with blunted weapons, using no armor or padding whatsoever. From this perspective, it can be understood how every way of sparring can be seen as

crazy or unhistorical by someone.

It seems, then, that the idea of "safety," like that of historical accuracy, is very subjective. Sometimes it develops out of the experience of only a few participants who then pass it on. With others, it is a sort of general consensus formed by committee and made official by habit and selective research. Safety in any athletic event really depends on four factors: proper physical conditioning beforehand, adequate ability and skill, use of protective clothing and equipment, and adherence to recognized safety rules.

The bottom line is that we often cannot fully appreciate the subtle insights that all these approaches bring to simulated weapon combat or the teaching of fighting skills. Because different systems of simulating Medieval combat can reflect different aspects or emphasize certain characteristics, the wider the range of rules under which a practitioner gains experience, the greater will be his overall understanding. It is the nature of how one goes about sparring that becomes the issue. Naturally, some systems of safe sparring rules will promote aspects that others do not. Some methods will allow more technique than others or expose us to insights that others won't. Until practitioners spar under different rules or dissimilar systems that allow for other elements of fighting, how are they to realize they may be limiting themselves?

Almost every method now practiced of re-creating fighting with Medieval weaponry seems to have some parallel developments, but can also have its own innovations and original touches (for better or worse). Why do so many enthusiasts have preferences for following only one particular approach? Some do it because they don't know any better and it is all they have ever been shown. Others do it merely out of habit and pride. Still others will say that they understand their approach is limited, flawed, or inaccurate, but that they can't change the system. Of course, as the old saying goes, if you are not part of the solution you are part of the problem. All it takes is for enough people to stand up and say what is wrong and that they will no longer accept it when something better is available.

CONTACT WEAPONS

Ideally, a weapon-sparring system that includes

the widest range of techniques and target areas is best—if your goal is to develop real martial skill and not just play fight. Any method of realistic weapon-sparring should balance realism with safety and simulation with practicality. It should allow for full-body targets, full contact, and a range of historical armor types (from none to light to heavy). Of sparring weapons, swords in particular should be as historically accurate as possible in weight, balance, and shape (i.e., as flat as possible). They should not whip, bounce, or stick. The "edges" on blades must be clear and discernible (not round). They should allow for chopping, stabbing, draw-cutting, and slicing. This approach is neither impossible nor unknown, and there are many groups that continually work to refine such a method. The foundation of such a historical approach must be a martial spirit, and not one of fantasy, theatrics, or role playing.

Thus, we can discern two important factors that must be met for the conduct of safe, realistic Medieval weapon-sparring:

1. The simulated weapons used must be able to deliver substantially solid blows, yet not be capable of causing real injury.
2. The "weapon" must simulate a real one's action as much as possible.

How to meet these factors safely is the problem. One solution is to make the weapon soft enough to make strikes safe and yet rigid enough to solidly block, beat, and bind. Such a sparring tool can be achieved by connecting edges of high-impact foam padding to a solid, rigid core. This can be shaped into a thin, flat, simulated blade. The core can be properly weighted and balanced by the inclusion of various suitable materials.

With such a padded "contact weapon" fighters can spar unarmored and even unhelmeted, provided that they use a small degree of control to avoid unprotected target areas and limit the force of blows. But using the same such contact-weapon, fighting can also be conducted with full contact without restrictions when proper armor and helmets are worn for protection from the force. In this way, instead of requiring the force of blows to be felt through padding and armor, it acts strictly for safety and historical simulation. When wearing metal armor and safety equipment and hit by a stick or blunt sword (assuming, of course, that you aren't injured), you can say either, "I did not feel that at all," or "I think if that was for real it would have wounded/killed me through my armor." Of course, without having actually cut at real armor and at meat and bones with real weapons to see how it transpires, the accuracy of this is debatable. In contrast, with properly weighted and balanced padded contact weapons, a hit can be made that is easily discernable as simply good (killing or wounding) or too light. There's really nothing in between to cause confusion. Contact-sparring, therefore, does not require wearing heavy armor or safety equipment; thus, safe fights can be conducted by unarmored or variously armored opponents, making for more realism and historical exploration. When armor or padding is included, however, contact-sparring can then be freely conducted with full force (full contact).

There are some reasons why padded contact weapons are sometimes overlooked or disregarded by serious combatants. The first is because they are confused with boffers. It is believed that padded (foam-based) weapons have already been tried and found wanting. What most people do is pad a stick with pipe insulation and then whack at each other. They usually learn rather quickly the unsuitability of sparring with a heavy, solid core surrounded by thin, unsuitable foam. Pipe insulation, it must be realized, is not intended for impact; it is insulation. A solid core also has too much mass to strike with safely. Sparring with such items can be painful (and is not all that different from a wooden sword). What frequently happens next is that people will go to the other extreme. They will try to use a material with a lighter core (invariably, hollow PVC pipe, bamboo, carbon-fiber, or fiberglass of various diameters). This results in a foam sword that is little more than a toy and has the worst possible characteristics for learning and practicing swordsmanship. Such a sword is too light, unrealistically fast, and often requires soft "touch" strikes to avoid painful stings. Of course, all this is avoided when proper high-impact, closed-cell foam is used in the right thickness over a rigid, yet suitably weighted and balanced core. In this way a superb contact weapon is produced for use in hard sparring.

Experience has shown that at first this method of weapon-sparring makes some enthusiasts uncomfortable. Either they feel awkward striking at someone else who is unarmored/unpadded, or they feel apprehensive if not using such protection themselves. Still others will object to having to defend their full body as a result of the targets that now become available (i.e., the lower legs and hands). Also some practitioners resist having to use (or learn) any degree of control against lightly armored adversaries. In fact, to some the very idea of "control" in weapon-sparring is anathema. Either they are inhibited by not being able to "go all out" or they are already too accustomed to the freedom of full contact to change.

In response to the above concerns all that really can be said is that enthusiasts must first spend some time really trying such a contact-sparring system. Control is not that difficult to employ when fighting unarmored adversaries, and it does not seriously diminish the experience of fighting. However, it does take time for one to develop it to an effective level. In fact, in many Asian martial arts great control is considered a sign of mastery. When contact weapons are employed with full armor or padding, control is no longer even an issue.

To be sure, some practitioners just don't do well with this method. They may have habits and a style developed under a different rule structure. They may have techniques perfected only for a narrow set of sparring guidelines. But by being receptive instead of inflexible toward new weapon-sparring methods, such a contact-sparring system as this can quickly reveal its many virtues and insights. Padded contact weapons (when properly weighted and balanced) offer an excellent alternative if constructed with a discernible edge. They can be ideal sparring tools for delivering safe, yet substantially solid and satisfying blows ("contact fighting")—without any flexing "whip action." They are inexpensive, easy to construct, nearly unbreakable, and perform realistically. However, they do not simulate the feel and blade play of metal blades or the firmness of wood well enough to offer a complete picture. In the end, one should endeavor to supplement whatever sparring method preferred with cross-training with other methods. Training exclusively with only one means of sparring is limiting and eventually leads to a narrower interpretation of both technique and skill.

Blunt Steel and Plate Armor Sparring

One manner of re-creating Medieval combat is that of fighting in reproduction plate armor with dull, unedged, metal blunts (live steel). A number of organized groups and performance troupes currently promote this practice. Many rely heavily or even exclusively on its use. Replica plate armor, some with a high degree of authenticity, is not all that difficult to construct (although fake versions of tin and aluminum are not uncommon).[1] For some, its popularity has do to with the sense of romance, excitement, and invulnerability one feels when wearing it. Certainly, it has a high safety value: sparring in plate can be conducted with full-contact force using blunted steel (or solid wooden) weapons. Reproduction plate armor also has great theatrical qualities in its appearance, and this, too, is reason for its popularity among Medievalists.

While it demands the most stringent equipment requirements, sparring with metal blades and weapons while wearing plate armor is something that all serious students of Medieval combat should explore at some time. The sparring presents a particular aspect of late Medieval combat, that of fighting in full plate armor, with a degree of realism and intensity found with probably no other method. Such sparring is certainly admirable and among the most physically challenging methods. But it also presents some obvious problems that are well worth pointing out in detail. Despite the benefits of using steel weapons and full-contact strikes, this method is by no means a complete representation of Medieval swordsmanship.

This method of sparring fundamentally involves wearing historically accurate, steel plate armor (or as close to it as possible) with the addition of extra padding and cushioning for comfort and safety. Steel swords and other weapons with all sharp ends ground off are used in making essentially full-power blows. Usually, fighting continues until the opponent concedes, tires out, or is pinned and immobilized (although various other rules may be applied). Overall, although this method requires stamina, strength, and fortitude, and is a good facsimile of Medieval plate-armor fighting, it is certainly not the "most realistic re-creation of Medieval swordfighting," as many of its proponents sometimes claim.

[1] There is also the problem of practitioners who, for various reasons, insist on using plastic to simulate iron armor despite the obvious fact that it weighs only a fraction of the real thing! How they can even imagine that they are in some way experiencing or simulating plate armor fighting is strange, to say the least. Protective plastic padding worn under garments for sparring safety is one thing, but to pretend it's metal plate is farcical.

The blades required for this form of sparring are typically extrathick, extraheavy, inflexible swords of softer steel. These are necessary to withstand the heavy banging and excessive blade-on-blade contact (far more so than real swords ever had) inherent in the method. Admittedly, there is nothing like the feel of steel on steel, but these kinds of swords just don't handle or perform with anywhere near the agility or speed of the real things. Bashing with them is not exactly the equivalent of trying to place a good cut.

Fighters using this method today must also particularly avoid any and all serious thrusting, lest someone get stabbed through a visor, face plate, or space in the armor—which would in fact be those very sword techniques most particular to and most useful against plate armor. This means that the fighters have far fewer techniques at their disposal than they do with many other methods of sword sparring (though some sword attacks would be inappropriate or ineffective against plate armor anyway). This fact, combined with the known restrictions on movement that do indeed come about while wearing heavy armor, is enough to make nonsense of any assertion that this form of sparring is the closest to "real sword fighting." The merit this method does have is that it is the truest form of full-contact plate-armored tournament sparring. It closely simulates this form of late Medieval knightly combat—certainly no small accomplishment.

Still, sparring this way is further restricting and limited because, for safety reasons, combatants typically will not and cannot strike to the lower legs (i.e., knees, shins, and feet). These were all legitimate targets in actual combat (with the exception of certain tournaments). The significance of excluding such obvious and crucial targets as these cannot be understated. It seriously alters the distance of the fighting, the timing, and the range of offensive and defensive movement the combatants must employ. You can't just overlook a third of an opponent's potential target areas and expect to still be closely simulating historical sword fighting. The legs were vulnerable to certain blows even when wearing plate armor. There can be little doubt that ignoring the lower legs when sparring instills a multitude of habits and misconceptions about what Medieval sword skill was (see Appendix F).

Furthermore, sparring under the conditions imposed by the very nature of live steel and plate armor must completely dismiss fighting against any and all *unarmored* or lightly armored opponents. Fighters in plate armor who use blunt steel cannot freely spar with those who don't wear armor. After all, you can only have full contact with steel weapons when all parties are fully and safely protected in heavy armor. If you fight under such "equal terms" (heavy armor against heavy armor), where's the contrast? How can you understand the advantages and the disadvantages of heavy armor without comparing it with the alternatives? Opponents in lighter armors surely do provide different challenges in both their movements and techniques that balance their obvious vulnerabilities. More significantly, how do you realize the *advantage* of plate armor if there aren't any opponents with less defense to have advantage *over*?

It's ironic that the quality of swordsmanship in the Middle Ages is thought to have suffered during the "age of plate." It is important to realize one thing: swords don't cut through plate armor. A good number of tests and experiments have demonstrated this. Sword techniques against those in heavy armor were basically limited to trying to knock the other guy's weapon clear enough so as to get a stab in to his weaker gaps and joints. A few techniques have involved trying to puncture a space or even a larger plate. Otherwise, all one could do was to bash him, and swords are far less equipped for this than specialty weapons (e.g., maces, flails, halberds, pole-axes). Certainly not all foot soldiers were equipped with full plate armor either.

When we consider just how far removed from other forms of historical Medieval *swordsmanship* this method of fighting in plate armor with a steel weapon really is, it's almost ludicrous to consider claims that it is the "closest thing to real sword combat." It has been pointed out that one might as well replace the swords with baseball bats and it would make little difference in this method of sparring. Swordsmanship is about cutting and thrusting and about parrying and riposting, not simply beating on armor until someone tires.

The only unique value of full-contact free-sparring in plate armor is really the experience of striking full force on an opponent with a steel weapon. For safely re-creating *exclusively plate-*

286

armor combat as practiced with maces, hammers, and clubs, this method does so admirably. The equipment requirements may make it impractical for most enthusiasts, but this sparring is an area of practice worthy of deeper investigation. However, claims of greater skill in swordsmanship gained through this method must be considered absurd. It has many restrictions and teaches techniques clearly particular to its own fight.

There is also another form of *semi-contact* live-steel sparring that must be mentioned. This form involves the use of steel blunts and lighter armors, such as mail or even padded leather. In this method blows are not thrown at full speed or power. They are restricted more or less to "touch-hits" on the limbs and torso or thrown with greater force at shields and other weapons. Sometimes blows are even "telegraphed" (as opposed to "choreographed"). This is common in many styles of demonstration fighting and combat shows. With this approach to mock fighting, blows are often exaggerated for effect. Strikes to the joints, face, neck, hands, and groin are almost always disallowed, as are any thrusts. The vital elements of feinting and countertiming are also severely restricted.

This method of "sparring" is popular among many living-history and battle-reenactment groups (especially in the United Kingdom and Australia) and among performance troupes. Although it is a very limited form of sparring, it actually involves considerable martial skills and requires serious practice. You can't safely swing a piece of steel at another person without great care and precision, nor can you receive such blows without being able to protect yourself from mishap. As a training tool, such semi-contact, live-steel methods have definite use, and experience in it is highly recommended. In many ways it is equivalent to drills and exercises using blunts or wooden weapons. Of course, since such pseudo-fighting is not intended for much more than simulated exhibitions, it has obvious limitations. It teaches a restrained understanding of weapon use and reproduces only certain elements of Medieval combat, at a loss of many other important ones. In this it is not unlike the practice of stage-combat complete with many of its same failings. It is no substitute for the value of full-speed, full-contact fighting with far fewer target restrictions.

When free-sparring, you cannot limit the target areas, the force of strikes, and the techniques allowed, and then claim that you have not limited your skill as well. This is a matter of common sense and applies whether one uses live steel in semi-contact sparring or full-contact fighting in heavy armor. Again, the virtues of these methods diminish when practiced to the exclusion of all else.

Medieval Fantasy and "Boffer" Sparring Methods

Given the popularity of the previously mentioned boffer sparring method, especially with Medieval fantasy and live fantasy role-playing groups, some attention must be given to this practice. Surprisingly, there is actually very little in real/historical swordsmanship that is transferable or applicable to this kind of light sparring and play fighting. These boffer toy swords used (and the associated rules that go with them) function so differently from actual swords, or from any serious simulated versions, as to be *almost incompatible* with real swordsmanship techniques. This should come as no surprise since these toy swords are meant to be harmless. However, there are those who in their enthusiasm will argue differently, and this must be addressed.

Such fundamental factors as the weight, balance, and feel of these swords are obviously so different from those of a metal sword that they do not handle at all like a real weapon. Their speed is so great and their mass so insubstantial that they have a distinctly different blade play, significantly altering the action of a strike, including follow-through and recovery. The same applies to the manner of applying a parry, deflection, or beat. These toy weapons allow users to do things that one would never attempt with a real blade, or for that matter with any accurately designed sparring contact weapon. Naturally, since they do not simulate real weapons, they do not teach real fighting. They are not meant to. As a result, the user is introduced to a distorted and artificial understanding of various factors (e.g., range, movement, speed).

The boffer form of lighthearted, fantasy swordplay does definitely have its place among younger or less serious enthusiasts and their games. Indeed, it also has some small martial value. However, it must be realized (and admitted) that it is not, and never was, intended as a serious historical simulation or approximation of Medieval combat. It is a game only. From a martial perspective it can even be strongly argued that use of such sparring tools promotes and encourages an observable level of silliness and sloppiness in both style and technique. With boffer-type weapons, fighters essentially just slap out at each other to see who can touch first—even when used at full force. It honestly creates a form of sparring that is really little more than playing sword "tag."

It has even been suggested that the *inability* to apply true techniques and principles of swordsmanship when using this kind of toy weapon is part of its very popularity. The swords have the effect of creating a certain "standardization" among users. It is inherently impossible to apply much strength, ferocity, or higher techniques with such toy swords. Reach and speed are the sole dominant elements in their method of sparring. The boffer's light, extremely fast "whipping" nature has a neutralizing quality that roughly equalizes ability among users. So few concepts and principles of actual fighting are applicable with it that a certain balanced uniformity of skill among users results. It can almost be compared to fighting with balloons: no matter how good you manage to be with one, you can't really get that much better than anyone else.

This kind of fighting has been described as really nothing more than a glorified pillow fight. As when fighting with a pillow, there is nothing much one can do with these toy weapons except swing as fast as you can and hope you hit something. You can feint some and maybe dodge a bit, but little more. Because of the very nature of using such extremely light and flimsy mock swords, and the method of "touch" hits, this is all that serious practitioners can really expect from the experience. There is little to offer those seeking a more historical or "martial" experience. There is no genuine countering or parrying and little of anything else, no matter how seriously you approach this type of fighting. A fighter can have zero apprehension or caution about getting hit even if he is intent on its not happening. It is simply a game, and to skilled, experienced swordsmen it only resembles swordsmanship in the most primitive and superficial manner. Apparently, however, these conditions are enough for a multitude of enthusiasts (not all of them young) to have taken it up as a safe form of mock Medieval/fantasy fighting. The boffer method has also found renewed life among some Asian martial arts schools that are starting to use versions to allow for safe, extralight sparring.

There is no discounting the strong fantasy element involved. For a great many sword enthusiasts the role of make-believe plays a large part in establishing rules for a sparring system. Some systems are consciously designed to allow anyone to pretend he or she is someone else (e.g., Conan, Xena, or a ninja). Some may even argue that they don't "need" realistic rules since historically accurate,

serious, or realistic weapon sparring is not the goal.[1] If so, why then have any rules with any resemblance to historical reality at all? At what point do you say this is unreal and good but something else is unreal and bad? There have to be some criteria by which to judge what realism-based rules and what fantasy-based rules will be used. The criteria are invariably determined by the quality of the participants involved and the level of skill that they have or aspire to. To many boffer fighters, swordsmanship and battling activities are just ways of playacting and passing time. It is a casual, light-hearted escapism, not for serious effort. Many are frivolous about it (and some just insincere). They can feel good about doing it, relish in the amusement and occasional ego boost it provides, but not put in the time or effort to achieve higher skill. Nor do they wish to be reminded that there is anything more.

This has not been stated to disparage these individuals; they have a right to pursue their fun. However, real swordsmanship is not about role-playing or even "feeling good"; it's about making a dedicated effort at acquiring skill. Ability and real skill provide self-esteem, not vice versa. There is no doubt that some practitioners enjoy (and even need) this softer, carefree "swordplay." In any kind of martial activity, one can't ignore the psychological elements sometimes at work. For some people, there is an emotional need to believe they are doing something for real, regardless of any contrary evidence. Perhaps it is part of the illusion and fantasy escape provided by role-playing (which often is the primary motivation). For the true martial practitioner and student of the sword, fantasy is not enough. There is nothing wrong with fantasy play-fighting in itself, far from it. It is only when adults who never developed any real martial skills themselves go on to instruct their juniors in a play-fighting rule system they know to be inaccurate and imaginary that there is then a problem. Individuals who have no expertise end up spreading their erroneous knowledge to those least able to question or inquire on their own. There is a saying that toy swords make toy swordsmen.

In contrast to forms of historically accurate Medieval weapon-sparring, we have the near

---

[1] The term *historically accurate* is often heard, but just what it means can be ambiguous. What it should refer to are factual conditions and documented circumstances that can be identified or approximated to a high degree of confidence and verification. After all, the value of historical realism is that it really is our sole example of what is believed to have actually been.

irrelevance of "Medieval fantasy." Though often historically inspired, Medieval fantasy art, literature, films, and games are a fundamental source of misinformation about Medieval weapons and fighting. In modern fantasy literature, especially, there are numerous examples of supposedly realistic fight scenes that are, to put it mildly, highly unlikely. Usually arms and armor are depicted in an impractical, misleading, or even juvenile manner. Weapons and armor are often shown as not only historically inaccurate, but also as impractical, outlandish, and in some cases outright useless. It should go without saying that one shouldn't believe everything you see in a Boris or Frazetta painting or that can happen in *Dungeons & Dragons*. Fantasy artists and authors have creative license, to be sure, but many people assume that things are authentic or they just don't ever learn to care about the differences. Suspending one's sense of disbelief does not mean suspending one's sense. Just because something is fantasy or imaginary does not mean that it also has to be absurd. At the center of this is a powerful historical illiteracy. Fantasy escape is all very fine (when it's juxtaposed with a framework of historical reference). Far too many do not have this and instead possess only the vaguest notion of the Medieval period or what its social and military conditions were.

But when people do something long enough, they begin to believe that it has value despite anything to the contrary they may encounter. Newcomers don't know any better; as long as it's fun it eventually takes on a momentum of its own. After a while no one is about to question or doubt and thereby risk learning that he's been wasting his effort all along. There is too much invested already and too much at stake to upset the status quo. Thus, little ever changes or advances. From the perspective of legitimate skill, light boffer methods are more a parody of fighting than any simplified version. They invariably revolve around a whole repertoire of imaginary rules designed not to challenge us to a higher level but to limit and make the lowest common measure of skill the standardized norm. When a weapon's true cutting power, weight, length, and agility are all nonfactors, then any bizarre claim about its capabilities or handling can be asserted. Claims can be made regardless of historical or practical reality and without having to demonstrate anything except under the contrived (and silly) conditions of fantasy play-fighting. From this fantasized system, claims of fantasized skill cannot be far behind. It is time to point out that such efforts, as amusing as they sometimes are, really do little to promote our Western martial heritage.

The Importance of the Full-Leg Target in Weapon-Sparring

The idea of excluding the lower leg as a target in weapon-sparring is a fundamental error. It is limiting, unrealistic, and historically inaccurate. Doing so promotes a misunderstanding of Medieval swordsmanship and weapon use. Hits to the lower leg should not be excluded in any weapon-sparring.

The most noticeable effect of not targeting the full leg is that fighting distance is distorted, which can have numerous repercussions. Without including lower-leg target areas, there is no need to stand back and use a weapon's natural reach. Instead, fighters can only strike by getting in close to hit around and behind shields. Once at this forced short range, the longer, more historically correct weapon can become a hindrance.

With the full leg as a target, fighters are forced to be much more wary and fight farther away to prevent their legs from being easily cut out from under them (even when they are using shields), or they have to reduce the distance for closer blows. But in doing so, one opponent or another has to first move across ground, thereby making his legs momentarily vulnerable. If an opponent does get in close, the other one can still block high and strike down low or simply step back. These are common fighting techniques—*when lower-leg targets are included.* Otherwise, we end up exclusively with the step-right-up, in-your face, slug-it-out method so common in forms of popular full-contact Medieval stick fighting.

Excluding lower legs as targets also has the effect of virtually doing away with passing steps or long cutting slashes. The result of excluding lower-leg targets is often a typical toe-to-toe bashing away at one another, in which there is no need to use decent footwork in maneuvering, passing, or evading. Instead, it's all reduced to point-blank, over-the-top/around-the-back whacking that only uses small steps and snapping, clublike hits. This style is hardly swordsmanship.

This also explains the popularity among some of such shorter swords in fighting that excludes lower-leg targets. Why bother with a historically accurate blade length if the rules inherently favor shorter ones? There's no need to have a blade long enough to threaten an opponent's legs *from a distance* or capable of blocking attacks against one's own. It is laughable how anyone can claim to be doing "historical" fighting and then flat out ignore the length of the vast majority of real Medieval swords.

Without having to defend the lower legs the entire nature of fighting is changed. This is the single, most significant result of excluding lower-leg targets. *Targeting the whole body* is what opens up real tactical and technical possibilities. Having to defend the lower legs requires the use of lower parries and wards (i.e., moving the weapon down). This, in turn, obviously necessitates learning to cut and block from positions other than with the weapon held up, behind, or resting on the shoulder. Yet this understanding of weapon use is disregarded as a result of eliminating hits to the knees and lower. By being oblivious to the lower legs during sparring, a good number of fighters are cheating themselves of a fuller combat experience. Just hitting to the thigh is not enough and doesn't make up for this crucial loss.

In addition to obviously reducing the number of potential targets, excluding the lower legs has the affect of decreasing the number of possible cuts and attack angles. More profoundly, this limits the stances, positions, and parries a fighter needs to learn and practice. This exclusion *further* reduces the number of practical techniques available and all feints that go with them. If no attacks are made to the lower legs, then no parries are needed there and no feints are made there. Therefore, no stances or positions are ever taken that realistically guard or threaten the whole body. One does not train to fake hits on or make blocks for areas that are off target. Thus, there is a *substantial decrease in overall fighting moves (and corresponding ability) simply because the lower legs are not available for attacks.*

When fighters are jammed together in mass combat, the problems created by excluding lower legs are even more evident. In historically accurate fighting the full leg would be vulnerable; in fighting that excludes the lower leg there is instead a jumbled, static collection of fighters huddled shoulder to shoulder with no need for wider stances or room to step and maneuver. Often a bent knee is the closest target available, and it is most easily struck when foes are packed tightly and cannot maneuver. But this never occurs when lower legs are forbidden as targets, and so the style of group fighting is also affected.

Anyone who has switched from sparring under rules that exclude lower legs to sparring under those that don't will see the difference. If he is accustomed to sparring under confined conditions that limit leg blows, a fighter may at first find his legs open to attack and easily hit. However, with

effort he will quickly learn to deal with the new conditions. Eventually, his skill in attacking and defending the legs will become second nature, and he will wonder why he didn't fight this way sooner. The sheer increase in tactical options and sparring fun makes it essential.

The reasoning behind excluding lower-leg hits originates almost exclusively from ideas of "safety." Prohibiting lower-leg targets is standard practice in a number of Medieval combat systems. If fighting with full contact with wooden sticks or live steel, even a blow of only few pounds of force can shatter a kneecap and possibly cripple an individual for life (even through plate armor). This is certainly something to avoid. However, when it is examined closely, there are strong reasons not to buy the "excluding the lower leg because of safety" argument.

First, are we really expected to believe that after more than 30 years of massive experience and expertise in armor and padding, modern Medieval combat practitioners have never been able to come up with a way to safely pad and protect the knee? Has no one ever thought to combine thick padding with extra steel? Historical warriors found their armor sufficient enough for real weapons. After all, is the kneecap really all that different from the throat, the bridge of the nose, or the hand? Yet, these are all legitimate (and safe) target areas.

If we buy the safety claim about targeting the knee, why then allow hits to the thigh but not the shin? Can hits to the lower thigh not potentially strike the knee just as hits to the upper shin might? To this, we often hear the claim that blows skipping down to the shin "might" hit the knee by mistake. If so, then why exclude the foot at all? There is certainly no chance of being hit in the knee when someone is hacking off your foot! Excluding the foot makes no sense whatsoever (forget about leg wounds, how can you fight with half a foot?). Yet the safety argument proponents ignore this fact of physiology.

Some will even argue that the foot is a "useless" target. They say that going after the foot (and even the shin) exposes one too easily to an attack from above. Well, obviously—when the opponent *knows* you *can't* hit anywhere else in between! How can one force an opponent to guard his knees or shins if, when you lower your weapon, he can count on knowing exactly where you intend to strike—the foot.

To make lower-leg targets viable and force an opponent to be wary, the *whole* leg must be included. You can't attempt a strike or feint on the foot without also threatening the knee and the shin in the process. The same can even be said for blows aimed at the thigh. In fact, the threat value of striking the thigh (and hip) is actually increased when an attack can easily drop lower and hit farther down. After all, historically, warriors *did* often have to armor their shins and feet.

It is here that the concept of using padded contact weapons reveals one of its many virtues. With contact weapons the safety argument disintegrates. Padded weapons virtually eliminate the claim that fragile knees will be smashed. When the combatants wear armor or padding, even full-contact blows on any part of the lower legs (or the body) can be delivered satisfyingly and safely. All that is left is the unwillingness of certain participants to face battle where their deficiency in defending their lower legs will show. Can you blame someone for not wanting to enter into a practice fight where he'd quickly get his shins swiped right out from under him?

Another reason the lower legs are often ignored is because some enthusiasts argue that there are indeed accounts of historical tournaments where participants were not allowed to strike there. This is true to a certain degree. But there are also accounts of combatants fighting with wooden barriers between them and even with whalebone swords, yet no one tries to simulate that. To single out one reference to one form of tournament and then narrowly and exclusively focus on it is to misconstrue and misrepresent Medieval fighting. This is particularly so when the motivation is not to re-create that exact tournament form, but instead to use it as a convenient excuse for inferior rules. Such an approach is limiting and, yet again, forces practitioners to become stylized in their sparring for reasons having little to do with historical accuracy or fighting prowess.

There were late-Medieval tournaments that excluded *all hits below the waist* (not just the lower legs), but they were uncommon. In fact, for every reference to tourneys excluding legs, there can be found two or three that didn't. The vast majority of Medieval tournaments had no such prohibition against striking anywhere. Besides, in real battle there were no exclusions on any target areas. Restricting

hits on the lower legs is not about some distorted conception of "chivalry" in fighting; it's about poor attitudes in weapon-sparring.

What is really astounding is that many individuals have come to believe that lower-leg targets are somehow irrelevant. By the fact that they themselves don't bother to have experience with the targets, they seem to feel that making strikes against lower-leg targets has little value. This excuse is like people playing in shallow water arguing that swimming isn't important anywhere because they never had to learn to swim. Here we have fighters, without any real experience in lower-leg targets, telling us all how it doesn't matter in combat anyway.

Sometimes the sport of kendo is even cited as another justification for limiting leg targets. As a ritualized form of sword duel, kendo does not hit anywhere below the waist, let alone to the legs. This is due entirely to matters of etiquette and other issues having nothing to do with either safety or effectiveness of blows to the lower legs. The same thing can even be said of modern foil fencing, which targets only the torso, and saber fencing, which targets only from the waist up. Yet, the modern sport of saber fencing did not even outlaw the legs until sometime in the *first two decades of this century,* and épée fencing has always included the full body. Even in the 1890 book *Broadsword and Singlestick* (a rare work on 19th-century European stick-fighting sports and sword arts), C. Phillips Wooley complained that without flats on their singlestick, many men didn't learn how to *hit with the edge.* Worse yet, he states that because not everyone used the full leg as a target, they learned a *flawed defense.*

Examination of historical arms and armor alone reveals that the lower legs were protected more often than not and that weapons were usually designed with the length to strike the legs. It's worth recalling the wound interpretations of the remains of combatants of the Battle of Visby, as described earlier. As well, listings of early Frankish military equipment specifically included lower-leg armor (mail *chausses*) along with helms and mail coats. A good deal of Medieval artwork shows figures wearing leg protection as their only apparent armor defense. To be sure, there are also plenty of illustrations of armored warriors without leg protection. This would indicate that, like most choices of personal weapon and armor to use, it is a matter of what advantage to balance against what handicap.

In one sense, it's arguable that the lower legs can sometimes be more vulnerable when a shield is used than when fighting with a sword alone. A shield user can often be made to lift his shield and momentarily blind himself, thereby becoming vulnerable to an incoming blow's changing its line of attack downward. People who really believe that the lower legs are irrelevant should try fighting with someone good at hitting them there. A practitioner may not bother striking his opponent's lower legs, but he will fast learn the mistake of exposing his own.

Why then among certain organized Medieval combat associations do so many enthusiasts continue to ignore the lower legs in sparring? It seems fairly clear that among certain Medieval groups, there is an apparent effort to avoid alternatives to protect the knees and, instead, assert all manner of excuses for not doing so. This is due to something deeper. There are reasons at work that go far beyond lame assertions that hitting the knees and below is impractical, unsafe, or not worth simulating.

The reality is that there is a strong clique in certain Medieval combat groups that *does not wish lower-leg targets to become commonly accepted or allowed.* The reason is obvious. It opens up a whole new world of fighting techniques and tactics for which the majority of these combatants are ill prepared. Anger and resentment can occasionally surface from leg-exclusion adherents when this issue is even brought up.

Some Medieval combat enthusiasts may simply be heavier, slower, or older. They may have pet moves and skillful techniques perfected specifically for their method of toe-to-toe, close-in fighting used under sparring systems that ignore lower targets. Keep in mind that nothing about allowing full-leg targets would prevent anyone from using any "close-in techniques"; *it would only make them significantly less valuable than they were before.* It is this very problem that is the real cause of so much opposition to full-leg targets from some quarters.

Let's face it: allowing lower-leg targets gives an advantage to more agile and more mobile fighters who can move in and out and sidestep as necessary to protect their legs while hitting away on the enemy's (just as in real-life battles). This advantage

is especially apparent when the opponent trains only to fight with a style that excludes lower-leg hits: face-to-face with a sword pulled in tight against his cheek and shoulder. This is almost useless from a farther distance.

Less agile fighters are invariably unable to use the necessary quick footwork and stepping required in fighting at the realistic distances created by including the entire leg (i.e., the whole body). Many of these enthusiasts are well aware of their inability to move their feet as necessary to avoid lower-leg blows (to properly control fighting distance). They prefer instead to stand shield-to-shield and head-to-head, slugging it out, bashing away, and not having to move about in the manner that swords and weapons demand. Thus, their weapon-sparring rules *consciously* take this into account.

Some fighters are averse to having to move much in the first place. From the very beginning they have never had to learn to properly step, turn, or maneuver during their Medieval combat experience. For them to start doing so now might even be unsafe. Consider, for instance, the large number of injuries that occur in friendly amateur games of basketball, volleyball, or softball. Players are always twisting ankles and popping knees merely by turning or stepping wrong (and this is without anyone trying to hit them!). This is usually the result of inadequate conditioning and preparation. Yet, on the other hand, in such activities as fencing, kendo, and soccer, we often see even elderly participants doing fine with no problems at all. Is it because that in such sports they learned from the very beginning to move properly and to bend their knees and that they kept at it? It would seem so.

The truth of the matter is that after considerable time spent in training and fighting without regard to parrying below the thigh, many fighters have too many habits they'd have to break. If you spend all your time getting really good at close-range striking, virtually standing still, and ignoring shins and feet, why would you ever want rules that would allow people to hit you there from farther away? For some fighters, the mind-set against full-leg targets is apparently too embedded to change. These individuals feel that they would not directly benefit from realistic leg rules. Everything is built around the false premise of not having to protect your shins, ankles, and feet—*everything*. Take this way, force

296

them to defend down low, and their fighting theories will deteriorate quickly.

To retrain and relearn to properly defend one's legs and fight from a truer distance is demanding. It means having to break old habits and admit previous inadequacies or ignorance. It means having to attempt footwork that a fighter may not be physically built for. A lot of Medieval combat enthusiasts can't handle it and refuse to try. They will not stand any other rules that will alter their skill or adversely affect their prestige and status as fighters.

The lower legs may only be a quarter or so of total body area, but fighting without regard to them has a disproportional effect in sparring. The feet and the legs are the foundation from which we fight. There is nowhere an opponent goes without first changing his stance or taking a step. Instead of presenting combat as a complete "circle," excluding them creates only a "180-degree" understanding and restricts and focuses fighting on the upper torso without regard to the human body's natural inclination to move when striking. Training and practice that ignore the full leg only give half the proper understanding.

It is incredible how people can think that they are sparring realistically when they don't know how to defend their lower legs or deliver effective attacks there. Practitioners who ignore the lower legs are deluding themselves. No matter how much they tell themselves that their legs aren't vulnerable, no matter how hard they try to believe they couldn't be hit there, the reality is otherwise. All they have to do is fight with full-leg targets against someone practiced at it and they will quickly see the cold truth.

Medieval combat fighters like to assert that their skills are legitimate and authentic, but this simply does not hold true under rules that insulate participants from ever having to properly learn and gain realistic ability. Teaching Medieval fighting without making sure to protect one's own legs or take advantage of the enemy's vulnerability there is foolish. It's ridiculous to train and practice without regard for some of the most vulnerable and obvious targets on an opponent's body. It is also naive to believe that true fighting capacity is being developed without sufficient effort to protect and defend one's own vulnerable areas.

Kneeling Down in Weapon-Sparring Rules

The rules governing many popular Medieval combat weapon-sparring systems include a requirement that fighters go down on their knees when hit in the legs (whether it be full-leg target or just the thigh). This is sometimes referred to as the *kneeling-down rule*. The general idea is that if your leg is wounded, you're immobilized; you cannot stand and must fight from your knees. Seems reasonable enough. If you're hit in the arm, you can't use your arm, right? But this does not hold up after serious consideration. Those wishing to conduct more realistic and more martial practice must stand up (figuratively and literally) for what makes sense. Kneeling-down rules must be disregarded because they are silly and unrealistic and encourage poor skill. But because such rules are so pervasive among practitioners and organized groups, it is important for this topic to be fully addressed and its significance established.

First, consider this: if an arm is *slightly* wounded, perhaps you won't be able to use it. It could be disabled, and you'd drop anything you were holding and hold the arm in close. But if an arm takes a serious blow, face it, it would be hacked off—severed clean. The average blow from a sword or axe would easily do it. No doubt about that. If a fighter loses an arm in the middle of combat, he will surely die. In his moment of

shock and pain, an opponent would finish him. At the very least, he couldn't continue. Few would argue this. Now, apply this to the leg—a much larger mass of muscle and bone. If your leg is cut off, you die. The question is what about a blow that doesn't cut off the leg but still disables it?

The solution for many sparring systems, whether playful fantasy ones or serious methods, has been to drop down and fight from the knees. Although this is a very poor solution, it has been the rule for so many organizations for so long that no one seems to ever question its validity, notice its flawed reasoning, or contemplate anything else. It is obvious that something is wrong and it's time for a change when one can hear such things at a practice as, "Watch out for so-and-so; he's really good on his knees!" or "Don't hit what's-his-name in the legs; you'll be sorry." This is nonsense. It's like saying, "Don't cut off his right arm, because his left one is even better." Historical artwork depicting battle scenes is completely absent of any instance of a warrior fighting from his knees. You never hear of ancient armies crawling into battle on their knees or read about Lancelot fighting toe-to-toe with some poor sap sitting down in front of him. It is only the delusions of a few members of a certain Medieval society that originated this rule notion, which ever since almost

299

every organized sparring system has blindly copied.

Answer this simple question: Can you kneel down for longer than you can stand up? No, of course not. Give it a try. Kneeling down is *more* stressful on the legs since it actually requires the use of *additional* muscles. If you are in a position where your legs are damaged, kneeling or even sitting down is *harder*. It is certainly harder to do than standing on one leg and dragging the other. Besides, if you are hit in the knee itself, *how could you then possibly kneel?* This is even more so the case when we consider blows that damage the hipbone.

Unfortunately, this obvious piece of physiology is completely missed by many Medieval weapon-sparring systems *precisely* because the rule structure permits, and even encourages, "ground fighting" from a kneeling or sitting position. This blinds one to the *natural disadvantages* of fighting from the knees. Many individuals (and some groups) have elevated kneeling down from a clear position of disadvantage into one of comparative advantage—*thus defeating the entire reason for rules making a leg-wounded opponent sit in the first place!*

The kneeling rule has had an unintended side effect. By creating *contrived* rules to protect (and, in some cases, even give advantage to) those fighters who have "lost" their legs, it practically creates a *beneficial* position from being wounded. This is outrageous. By a twisted logic, rules have been constructed in some sparring systems that virtually favor combatants positioned on their knees. The whole problem of this "advantage" is magnified under rules that exclude the lower legs (knee, shin, foot) as legitimate targets or that disallow pushing against a sitting opponent's shield to begin with. Those on their knees have even more advantage in this way. They know exactly where and how the standing opponent will try to hit them, and they can expose almost any part of their own legs in leaning forward to hit. The problem is increased even further under rule systems using superlight, Nerf-like, boffer swords. With little effort required to swing them for "touch kills," those on the ground can easily make the required (soft) contact.

The target areas on a kneeling/sitting fighter are typically made so limited that the standing attacker is forced to expose himself to an effective counterattack. When he leans forward to strike, he is instead hit by the kneeling or sitting fighter who has far fewer targets exposed. Instead of being a handicap, kneeling down this way actually seems, contradictorily, to improve the grounded fighter's defense. By this kind of reasoning, we could claim that standing on our heads is a "good fighting position." Even more insane are accounts of uninjured fighters getting down on their own knees in order to fight under "equal" conditions!

Under some sets of sparring rules, the standing fighter cannot even make use of the one greatest benefit there is to remaining *standing* while fighting: shifting around. Circling around is usually outlawed, and opponents must be faced frontally. Taking "advantage" of a wounded opponent by sidestepping and striking from the flank or rear before a grounded foe can turn is forbidden. Fighting from the ground then becomes a pseudo-tactic. Under these rules, taking a wound in the leg is barely an inconvenience. It should also be pointed out that the kneeling party is in fact *not* hurt, but can freely twist and turn even when on the ground. Yet, the uninjured, standing fighter is restricted in *his* movement actions. This is ludicrous. Granted, many of these nonsensical rules are based on a fictitious sense of "chivalry," but their true reason for existence, as with similar rules, is to protect those fighters who cannot move well or defend their legs (this is what is often called "playability for everyone").

When one considers all the many hours of fighting that are lost, all the opportunities for stand-up experience that are missed, it is astounding. Particularly in large group battles, it is immensely silly to see isolated fighters sitting waiting for someone to come and hover over them. Rather than be busily engaged in shifting, sidestepping, and lunging, warriors are marooned around the battlefield sitting on their knees. They have to stand up, walk over to someone who agrees to stay there and fight, and then sit right back down. Sometimes fellow combatants are required to "lift" a wounded fighter, carry him to a new location, and then place him back on his knees in order to continue fighting. This is just plain silly. If the person can stand to walk around to re-engage, why not just let him walk *and fight?*

Rules requiring kneeling when wounded also affect the very tactical choices a leader has for maneuvering forces in simulated group battles. If some members of the force must stop to sit down, how can they possibly be maneuvered around the field? A commander can't rally warriors to outflank, break through, or regroup if they are sitting all over the place. How can there possibly be any true tactical mobility? The whole battle turns into a slow, unrealistic, isolated sit-in with a few wanderers straggling around (hardly the exciting, classical clash of arms and men a battle should invoke). The entire pace of fighting is reduced. Of course, if real tactical ability is not something one cares about, and not something one would even recognize, then this would not be a big deal, would it?

Some people claim that the kneeling rule helps fighters remember they've been hurt. Are serious practitioners really going to forget they've been "wounded" in the leg because they are standing up? Are other people that fearful that there are dishonest participants who will do this? If so, then why have hits based on honor at all? Surely, fighters can act as if their legs are injured just as is done with injured arms?

There are usually rules, completely lacking in common sense, that are related to kneeling down, such as not allowing a limb to be "re-hit" once it has already been struck and disabled. There seems to be a bizarre reasoning that a leg is somehow "specially protected" or has a greater defense by virtue of its status as a wounded limb! This makes no sense. If a limb is hurt once, it can be hurt again and again until it is severed or the person dies. The leg is not considered amputated, so there is just no cause to exclude it as a continued target (if it was, how could anyone continue on?). The true basis—as everyone knows but few will admit—is really to excuse inferior fighters and "give them a chance" instead of compelling them to improve.

All these problems detailed here occur among a range of various weapon-sparring systems because fighters are simply not allowed to stand and hobble, nor to drag a wounded leg while fighting. The real reasons behind all these apparently unrealistic kneeling rules is simple: it is about "playability." That is, these rules reflect a lack of martial spirit, which is very much the case with the more lighthearted and playful fantasy groups. This has the cumulative effect, of course, of reducing overall skill to the lowest common denominator instead of promoting real fighting ability (a sort of "anyone and his grandmother can participate" form of mock combat). It is a shame because, with only simple changes, more rigorous rules could be tremendously beneficial.

Aside from the negative effects on fighting, there are a multitude of anatomical and physiological reasons why the kneeling rule is ridiculous, some of which have already been mentioned. Could we really imagine a Medieval warrior, wounded in battle, on his knees, shifting and twisting to face enemies charging at him from various directions? Could he survive even a few seconds from such a position? This is pure stupidity. The fact is one can't stand, kneel, or even sit still, let alone continue fighting, without a leg, a shin, or even a foot. Take a serious blow at the hip, knee, or shin and a person would be in agony. A blow to the legs serious enough to keep one from standing would surely be so painful as to keep one from fighting. Even accounting for courage and adrenaline, a person would just not be able to function. So where are we to draw the line between playability and realism?

If fighters can't be considered killed by just having a wounded leg, and they can't be expected to lie down and moan, what then? The alternative is the *limping-leg rule*: a combatant may not run or walk after a disabling leg blow, but he may *still stand* and fight. Movement is limited to limping by dragging the wounded leg (no hopping). One could also kneel on the good leg, but *not* the injured one. If a leg is hit again, it must certainly count again (no excluding it). This rule is the intelligent and effective alternative.

Of course, none of this in any way prevents fighters from *voluntarily* kneeling down any time they feel like it, injured or not. It is only to prevent the position from being insulated from the realities of combat, to prevent standing fighters from being unnaturally restricted, and to realistically increase the amount of available targets.

The standard leg hit rules have become a virtual institution among most Medieval combat groups. Many individuals are reluctant to "give them up" and lose the "consolation prize" that the kneeling position gives them. Changing the rules would mean that they have to fight *almost* the same way with an injured leg as they do unhurt—without special provisions. The truth is, in sparring it is *harder* to keep fighting when you have to remember that a leg is wounded and keep it stiff or drag it.

Some would say, "Yeah, that's true, it *is* harder; so why do it?" Ah, but here we see that being harder really is the matter of it, isn't it? By having to *remember* the injured limb and having to drag it or just keep it stiff you really *are* distracted and fighting at a disadvantage, not just mimicking something. Because someone is still standing and fighting with a wounded leg, if he makes a lunge or step out and exposes a leg to another hit, he knows he *will* "die." This is a big difference from the supposedly awkward position that kneeling down was originally intended to cause.

If you accept an assumption (such as "you must sit and you cannot stand") without ever analyzing it, how will you ever know if it is faulty, illogical, or just inferior to something else? Assumptions create ramifications far down the road that are usually quite subtle. This is the case with kneeling-down requirements during any sparring that simulates any manner of Medieval combat.

Many participants refuse to reconsider issues of rules. They do this out of apathy and indifference (the "it works fine, why change it?" attitude), out of tradition or nostalgia for the "original rules," out of bias and favoritism for "their personal rules," and out of familiarity with the current rules. If some individuals find themselves growing angry while reading this critique of kneeling-down rules, perhaps they should ask themselves why and scrutinize their own preconceptions. Kneeling down while sparring is a bad idea.

Although this may surprise some and shock others, knowledgeable weapon fighters would agree, because the arguments, though debatable, are solid and irrefutable. Only those who are not serious would consider this matter unimportant in sparring.

The suggestion offered here about fighting on the knees is simply this: experiment. Just try out this alternative for a decent length of time. The results will certainly show if practitioners are honest with themselves. If you have to ask what's with all this bitching about fighting from the knees, then you may be missing a lot more in sparring and fighting than just what has been presented here.

Weapon-Sparring in Martial Arts

"Dulce bellum inexpertis."
(Sweet is war to those who have never experienced it.)

—Latin proverb

Medieval weapons have both an immediacy and a lethality not found in the unarmed martial arts. They are tools of warfare. Their use is about killing. It is not about disarming, dissuading, discouraging, or even performing simple self-defense. Swords in particular are not about barroom encounters, street fights, or basic protection. They are about war and killing. Their use is not a matter of immobilization of potential attackers or evasion; it is about lethally wounding, maiming, and decisively killing. Although they have been used in the past as tools to settle "duels of honor" with deadly and not-so-deadly results, they are primarily weapons of the battlefield. They are about men brutally slaying one another. Despite all efforts at philosophizing about character development, etiquette, and artistry, the ominous purpose behind a weapon such as the Medieval sword is self-evident. It is perhaps for this very reason, above all others, that expert instruction and knowledgeable teaching in the art is so rare.

Occasionally, those unfamiliar with the versatility and depth of historical European fighting arts as practiced today declare that they are martial "sports" rather than martial arts. The same people say that this is because no actual schools or authentic styles of Medieval fighting have survived and that modern practitioners have had, for the most part, to reconstruct it from scratch. Some even suggest that emphasizing technical efficiency rather than "aesthetics" devalues the effort of re-creating historical European fighting arts. The same people suggest that focusing on historical reenactments or regulated competitions robs such re-creations of true martial character and reduces them to just a game of rules rather than exhibitions of personal skill and art. Most of this kind of thinking, but not all, is unwarranted and incorrect. Such opinions confuse the informality of and conformity to practical guidelines for equipment or safety with a lack of earnestness. Taking this attitude might even be construed as a cultural bias on the part of some. Our European martial legacy is regularly seen as either unrealistically romanticized or else aberrant, whereas the esoteric martial traditions of Asia are frequently viewed as aesthetic and even humanistic.

Such thinking is perhaps understandable, given the poor representation that much of Medieval, as well as Renaissance, swordsmanship has gotten in films and commercial festivals. Modern sport-fencing shares some of this blame, too, because it does not often present a very martial character.

303

Invariably, when historical European arms and armor are written about it is by art historians and academics alone, while equivalent Asian tools are routinely discussed as cultural treasures and living skills by proficient followers. Why this disparity? Primarily, there is the lack of a preserved, continuing tradition of European martial skill that causes its importance to be so readily overlooked and unappreciated, which is unfortunate. A more open dialogue between traditional Asian stylists and skilled Western martialists (of Medieval and Renaissance methods) would benefit everyone (not to mention allowing excellent opportunities for intense sparring).

Unlike historical Medieval swordsmanship and weapon skills, the concern in traditional Asian fighting arts is more for the accurate transmission and preservation of style rather than the individual's development or self-expression. In contrast, most Medieval combat students today have had ample opportunity to test themselves freely in mass battles involving dozens or even hundreds of fighters per side. They have been able to fight against groups of opponents armed with a wide array of weapons and wearing various armors. This is a practice completely unheard of, and in many cases almost impossible, among practitioners of traditional Asian martial arts. It is a training opportunity of tremendous advantage and learning potential and one that is commonplace for most practitioners of Medieval European weaponry. It is still surprising how many martial artists today studying historical Asian weaponry have never sparred against multiple opponents, have never been in a massed group battle, never faced armored adversaries, and never even free-sparred against pole-weapons or shields (not to mention never having practiced cutting at test targets with a live blade). Two-person drills, whether arranged or unarranged, are not the equivalent of free-sparring, and there is far more to combat technique than classroom theory and tournament exhibitions.[1]

It is generally accepted that a martial artist expert in unarmed techniques can employ a knowledge of weapons use. Inherent is the idea that weapons are merely an extension of the body or the hand and that they merely supplement the "higher" method of unarmed fighting, but originally a warrior was supposed to supplement his skill in weapons and armor with unarmed technique, not the other way around. Historically, the two methods—armed and unarmed combat—were rarely viewed as being separate. Even though many self-defense techniques are not suitable for the battlefield (and are not meant to be), a proper study of historical weaponry incorporates ideas of disarms and weapon recovery, pugilism, grappling, wrestling, and kicking. The classical European manuals on fighting are full of such techniques. Historically, a warrior fought with his weapons and then, if somehow caught out or left unarmed, resorted to continuing with whatever he had.

However, it is obvious today that classical weapons are, for the most part, irrelevant in most modern self-defense situations. For the most part, in the modern martial arts, weapons have, naturally, been relegated to training aids. Nowadays, they are primarily used to supplement unarmed methods or taught almost incidentally—out of curiosity. Historically, warriors have always been *armed*—and usually *armored* too.[2] Over the centuries, many more forms of personal weaponry and armor have come into existence than have unarmed techniques for dealing with them. There is a certain myth promoted today in the martial arts that the "body" is the "ultimate weapon." From this follows the notion that the body can be trained and conditioned to make weapons unnecessary in personal combat. This is sheer nonsense, and it has also been misunderstood. Bodies cannot withstand blows from swords and axes, nor can they inflict more damage. There is no foolproof method that ensures that a highly trained unarmed fighter can prevail over any weapon-carrying warrior. Instead, what the notion of the body as being "ultimate"

---

[1] It is entirely possible to find an instructor of Asian martial arts who, though quite competent in unarmed fighting, is nonetheless completely inadequate when it comes to weapon use. For example, one such instructor cashing in on the increasing popularity of swordsmanship offered "weapon instruction" out of his large, highly visible school. He maintained that he "only taught the basic movements" and that these were enough. According to him, "no sparring or cutting was necessary once you got the correct movements down." Rubbish. This is martial malpractice. What if that attitude was applied to his own unarmed fighting? *"You don't need to spar or do drills, just go through the movements of kicking and punching, and you'll do fine."* This is far too common, and such "instructors," it seems, are merely indulging their students' curiosity to prevent them from straying to other sources of information or training (and taking their money with them).

[2] Two notable exceptions, perhaps, were the ancient Chinese monks and Okinawans, both of whom still included a great deal of weapons in their unarmed fighting methods.

means is that it is the *mind* within the body that is the real key to controlling how we train, how we fight, and how we win. Flesh and bone are no match for cold steel. Weapons have a huge advantage in reach and damage over empty-hand techniques.

Even in the most advanced Asian martial arts instruction, students are advised that if they face an attacker with a knife or a stick they should be prepared to get cut and be hit. The general idea is this: When an unskilled attacker with a weapon (assuming that it's not a firearm, of course) faces a skilled fighter without one, the trained fighter is expected to survive. His training is supposed to allow him to overcome the weapon. For the most part this is sound. However, if the attacker is himself a skilled weapon user the outcome can be expected to be very different. There is simply an innate power to weapons that few knowledgeable martial artists would dispute. When it comes to "battlefield conditions" and personal duels, armaments are decisive.

As tools, weapons have always been the great equalizers, whether in offense or defense. Understanding this has been displaced by many modern martial artists' not knowing the purpose of classical weapons. Let's face it, learning how to defend yourself against an axe, spear, or even a shield is not going to prepare you for what can happen on the street or in some bar. Historically, it was only when people were faced with the *necessity* of having to fight *without* weapons (because someone *armed* had taken them) that unarmed techniques finally became more highly developed. Unarmed techniques did not simply come about because someone figured that the techniques were somehow "superior" or on some other level.

Fundamentally, humans are tool users. We work better with implements than with our empty hands. We progressed and succeeded precisely because of our tool use. It is far easier to dig a ditch with a shovel or cut a tree with an axe than with an empty hand. Because we had no natural weapons or defenses, weapons for war were among the first our Neolithic ancestors created. Fighting arts first began when our ancestors realized that they could hunt and kill from a distance, whether with a rock, club, or pointed stick. Throughout history, armies have gone into battle armed and armored—not empty-handed, prepared to wrestle, punch, or kick.

Sadly, humans likely first learned to kill their own kind by use of weapons. Compared with the natural weapons of other animals, which evolved parallel with their instincts and social structure (if any), those of humans evolved much faster (perhaps too fast). It has been speculated that with our early hominid ancestors the natural barriers that protected intraspecies violence were essentially broken down by our newly acquired weapons. Weapons kill very easily compared to having to actually make physical, hands-on contact and to struggle clawing and biting. The effort required by hands or teeth to hurt another human is far more personal than that required in bashing him with a stick or throwing a stone. After all, throwing a spear or a rock at a fellow hominid was not all that different from throwing one at a caribou or bison. Perhaps competition with rival species of closely related hominids was also a factor that contributed to breaking down the barriers of using weapons against each other.

In some traditional Asian martial arts today the very idea of weapon fighting seems to disturb the unarmed purists (though others consider weapons indispensable). Despite the extent of some practitioners' hand-to-hand training, some people must feel that a trained warrior with a weapon could make all the difference. For instance, an individual with only a few months' training can learn to handle a spear or shield and axe sufficiently to endanger the most advanced karate or kung fu student. Consequently, despite what is typically shown in the movies, an expert with such weapons can upset even the most skillful unarmed master.

It seems that there are few schools of Asian fighting arts in which individuals seriously train and contact-spar full time with weapons or swords. Many schools and styles today will have an obligatory weapon kata, such as a staff, and teach a few disarming or countering techniques, but true full-contact weapon-sparring is almost unheard of. Additionally, much of the instruction seen is generally by and for students who themselves seem ignorant of how to really fight with the weapons. It is one thing to show how to disarm an assailant armed with a knife or a baseball bat-wielding attacker and quite another to fight against a trained swordsman or spearman. The real value of practicing an unarmed countertechnique to a sword cut is questionable, to say the least, if the student is making a move that no skilled swordsman ever would. Those who practice swordsmanship more earnestly and in a way that is more honest to its heritage know better. Indeed, assuming a kicking or grappling stance, for instance, can have very little effect against a mail-clad Medieval swordsman carrying a shield and even less against one in plate armor.[3]

In the traditional Asian martial arts community today there are few avenues by which to display weapon skills that involve actual fighting. Teaching methods that consist of set drills and programmed routines are often little more than ballet recitals. Indeed, the complaint is occasionally heard that there is little in much traditional weapon instruction today that qualifies as *martial*. One would be hard pressed to find in the martial arts establishment any place where true, serious, free-style, high-impact, full-target weapon free-sparring is practiced (including kendo and escrima/arnis), especially where a variety of weapons and armor are included. The great majority of weapon training in schools of Asian martial arts today has been criticized (from within its own community) as mere ritualized dancing with semi-contact drills thrown in. It is rare even to find competent instruction where swords are actually used for practice cutting. When there is sparring, invariably it is of the semi-contact form and strictly controlled. Also, the weapons themselves are rarely anything other than of the boffer variety (despite many recent efforts to develop alternatives). One common criticism is that the ritualized formality of practice and the limitations placed on target areas and strikes are very often far too restrictive. Other considerations can reduce realism even further.

Surprisingly, there are many traditional Asian stylists who dismiss the value of weapon-sparring altogether. They prefer their customary preset routines, arranged drills, and highly structured exercises for weapon practice. There are even those who consider weapon-sparring a hindrance to truer skill! Where is the evidence for such a view? Where are the individuals who have actually attempted long-term, serious contact-sparring and then rejected the result? Has there already been somewhere an organized body of traditional martial artists with extensive practice and experience in contact-weapon sparring who have discovered that weapon-sparring had a detrimental effect on their skills? The answer is no to every question. Excluding the approaches found in both the sport of kendo and the practice of escrima/arnis, a frequent complaint is that there is very little actual contact weapon-sparring going on in the traditional Asian martial arts.

In fact, from many traditionalists in a number of styles there is almost exclusively an a priori rejection of the idea of weapon contact-sparring. There are many who simply will not accept the sparring's training potential and benefits and refuse to take advantage of modern materials for the design of sparring tools. They simply will not attempt to do so. Yet nowhere have any traditional Asian stylists experimented extensively with serious contact weapons and found them to be without value or a hindrance to acquiring real skill. To the contrary, there are active movements in the Asian martial arts community to incorporate more contact weapon-sparring. These efforts are long overdue, and, despite the occasional setback, they have been gaining in popularity for years. Such efforts have, of course, met resistance from traditionalists and those objecting (reasonably so) to "boffer" styles of training, which they believe will only lead to "play-fighting."

Still, this is no excuse for automatically rejecting serious contact-sparring or refusing to properly explore it. We can only speculate about the motivations of some of these traditionalists (not the least of which is the fear of revealing their own inadequacies and loss of reputation that can bring). This question comes to mind: Why do the vast majority of Asian martial arts instructors who teach weaponry avoid conducting any serious contact-sparring? Well, the excuse is often that "it is not real, so we don't do it." To which I must respond, "Oh, so you only do it for real, then?" Of course, they never do do it "for real," and certainly any training for "the real thing" is inadequate without some sort of practice at fighting. Obviously, no one can practice "real" fighting to really kill, but this does not mean

[3] Although man-to-man fighting, whether armed or unarmed, does have its universal principles (such as those described throughout this work), there are also significant differences. Unlike hand-to-hand combat, the use of weapons in battle is not based on such concepts as leverage, balance, or redirecting force. It is based primarily on power, speed, and resistance.

that we cannot approximate such fighting to a high degree; doing so is what serious contact weapon-sparring is all about. There can be no doubt of its value in this regard. Providing that we avoid the pitfalls of a playful, frivolous approach, such sparring can indeed teach us legitimate fighting skills and allow us to practice them realistically.

It is unfortunate that weapon-sparring is rejected; after all, it can be quantified with objective criteria about what is and is not a lethal blow, far more so than with unarmed sparring. In other words, you can easily tell what would have killed or disabled your partner. Instructors and students of Asian fighting arts would be well served to follow the example of Medievalists and re-creationists and adapt methods of safe, realistic weapon-sparring for their training.

When learning something new, people are often willing to cede control and suspend their doubt; this is particularly so in martial arts instruction where structured guidance is necessary. But acceding to someone with superior knowledge or experience does not excuse any of us from the personal responsibility to inquire, even if it means that we must doubt, question, or ask for demonstrations of proof. This is how we exchange and develop knowledge, as well as refining our craft—as long as we avoid being sarcastic or cynical in the process. Skepticism and engaged curiosity are healthy in the long run only if those offering instruction are competent and confident. Otherwise these instructors are exposed to unexpected and unwanted scrutiny.

The impressive fighting arts of Asia found in so many schools across this country and the world are a rich, wonderful resource of our collective human culture. These arts have some of the most codified, systematized, and profound understandings of unarmed fighting and conflict, as well as an established, effective teaching tradition that has preserved their practice. However, when it comes to historical weaponry they hold no monopoly on technique, fighting skill, or warrior knowledge. They represent only one possible perspective of armed personal combat. Indeed, it can now be persuasively argued that European arms and armor of the Middle Ages and Renaissance are in a great many ways unsurpassed for use in the art of war. It is up to today's skilled proponents to demonstrate this for everyone's greater enrichment.

THE CHALLENGE OF CROSS-TRAINING

Many Medievalists and proponents of European weapon skills today are frustrated in their inability to contrast their techniques and abilities to those of their Asian colleagues and counterparts. For most, chances to engage in cordial, friendly, full-contact, cross-system free-sparring are lamentably scarce. The differences in the methodology of training, the nature of the instruction, and even the personalities involved can make such opportunities uncommon. For some of the more traditional Asian martial arts stylists, it seems that avoiding offers of friendly sparring encounters and cross-training has become an art in itself. The same can be encountered among leading sport-fencing coaches and classical fencing instructors. Some of us may come across the occasional Asian martial arts novice or young foil fencer who is eager to spar, but encountering skilled senior instructors of the same attitude is apparently rare. There are many reasons offered that seem to have become a cliché:

- "You can't appreciate the subtleties of my art and are not worthy of facing my skill." *The appeal to ignorance.*
- "You cannot compare with my power and would be injured." *The appeal to insult.*
- "I don't need to prove anything to myself or to you." *The appeal to ego.*
- "I cannot reveal my secrets to a nonstudent." *The appeal to mystery.*
- "I am forbidden to use my knowledge for anything except real combat—which I never do." *The appeal to circumstance.*
- "I know I could defeat you for real, so why bother doing it for pretend (i.e., this is just for show and makes me feel special)?" *The appeal to theory.*
- "Why should I risk my prestige and reputation on a nobody like you (i.e., I have nothing to gain by beating you, but should I lose and look bad . . .)?" *The appeal to reputation.*
- "I'm worried that I'm actually not very good and don't want to prove it to myself, so I won't take the chance." *The appeal to isolation.*

These reasons may be familiar to some readers

and are just what they appear to be: lame excuses to protect pride and ego and prevent loss of face. The excuses become less and less tenable as modern technology allows us numerous methods of safe, serious, and realistic weapon-sparring. Sadly, some students have never been exposed to any other view and can only regurgitate what they have been told. Martial artists and fencers are ordinary people who just don't want to risk having to prove themselves, not so much to others as to themselves. They can sometimes be more comfortable with believing than acting (it's a lot easier). This is a form of false humility that martial arts are supposed to teach one to transcend. For those practitioners of European fighting arts who have also encountered responses such as these, be comforted. You're not alone.

Understanding Swords and Martial Arts in America

After World War II, servicemen returning from occupied Japan brought back to the United States literally tens of thousands of antique samurai swords and other weaponry. The occupying authorities had collected these confiscated swords, and many soldiers took a few home as curios and souvenirs. Many of these blades had been in families for hundreds of years and were priceless works of art, as well as being some of the finest edged weapons ever made by man. Others were just factory-made weapons. In either case, they were also legitimate war booty for the winning side.

In the succeeding years, U.S. servicemen stationed in Japan won over the Japanese people through their character, generosity, and new-found friendship. In return, these same servicemen attained an appreciation for Japanese culture and were exposed to their impressive martial traditions. These war arts were presented at first in the form of "rituals" and "sports" so as not to cause alarm and be banned as too warlike. By the 1950s, returning servicemen, along with Japanese-Americans and newer Japanese immigrants, brought the more or less "traditional" Japanese *budo* (war ways) to the United States. Particularly in California and Hawaii, these "new" martial arts took on a more humanistic,

socially positive (and commercially viable) character. Later, arts from other Asian nations, such as China, Korea, and the Philippines, were introduced into the United States, and the rest, of course, is history.

However, there is something that is overlooked in all this. For the most part, the Westerners first exposed to these refined fighting arts were relatively ignorant of anything other than rudimentary boxing, some basic Greco-Roman wrestling, and maybe a little streetfighting. The same thing applied to previous Western visitors and tourists in the Orient at the turn of the century and earlier. Even when such naive European and American visitors had some fencing experience, their understanding of Western sword history was limited to what could be done with foils or épées and just maybe a military dress saber. This much is clear from reading their narratives. It is understandable that when presented with such systematic and well-developed systems of fighting with long traditions of instruction as in Japan, these Westerners could not help but be wide-eyed, drop-jawed impressed. It's no wonder most of them "went native." In the past 40 years, this process has been continued by consecutive generations of Americans and Europeans trained in friendly neighborhood dojos and community center classes and exposed to a multitude of mass-media martial arts films.[1] Westerners conditioned by technology and rationalism are very often hungry for something esoteric and metaphysical. In an age of fast-paced change and daily rushing they long for connection to something "traditional" that they find in these formidable martial arts.

However, unlike with the unarmed Asian fighting arts, when it comes to swords and swordsmanship, the situation is somewhat different. Those swords and other memorabilia that were brought back from Japan by servicemen eventually fell into the hands of militaria and gun collectors.[2] Eventually, realizing their historical significance as well as their artistic and monetary value, collectors began to preserve and study these beautiful works of art and technical achievement. Organizations (often called *token-kai*) dedicated to the appreciation, preservation, and inspection of samurai swords and associated Japanese arms and armor now exist in virtually every major U.S. and European city. Their members are well networked, dedicated, and highly informed. Over the years they have "rescued" thousands of these priceless objects from flea markets, pawnshops, basements, and attics. Similar collectors groups exist for U.S. and European militaria.

Besides education, a major concern of these groups is the acquisition, trade, and resale of items for investment purposes. These swords can easily range in value from $500 to $20,000 or more. It is not an inexpensive pursuit, and pieces are becoming rarer to find every year. Although classical Japanese sword arts such as kenjutsu, iaido, and kendo would be natural areas of interest for these collectors and enthusiasts, they appear to be peripheral activities for them with somewhat limited followings. The majority of these individuals can be compared to classic car buffs who rarely take their vintage 1960 Ferrari out on the street and never, ever race it. They are more interested in aesthetics, rather than "driving."

It is here that the all too common ignorance of most Americans about their own Western martial heritage comes into play. The general misconceptions most people have about Medieval and Renaissance swords (derived mostly from TV and movies), combined with the convincing teachings (and commercialization) of traditional Asian martial arts, lead to an often unwarranted and dismissive view of European swords and fighting arts as unimpressive, unsophisticated, and brutish. This view is then perpetuated by these "authorities."

Unlike with European weapons, for Japanese swords there have always been dedicated special interest groups studying, training, preserving, and (most importantly) cutting with them. They have spent far more time in the last few centuries refining and continuing these practices while their European counterparts have not. Furthermore, in Japan today swordmakers are considered national treasures, and their craft is both subsidized and regulated by the government. Hard as it is to believe, imitation samurai swords and "replicas" are not even legal in Japan. Actual antique blades are even given papers of authentication. Unlike the vast majority of European blades, Japanese swords have been continually cared for and cherished for hundreds of years. Quite often these swords, many 400 or 500 years old and covered in beautiful, incredibly detailed metal work, are considered works of art first, historical and family heirlooms second, and weapons third.

In contrast, modern swordmakers and importers in the West typically turn out a variety of cheap, poorly tempered, low-quality fantasy blades and stage weapons. The vast majority of these swords (even when hand forged) are not historically accurate reproductions or even close replicas. They are props for role-players and other costumed theorists. Who is there to tell the manufacturers that their products are inferior or inaccurate? Who is there to authoritatively demonstrate the differences in how real European swords handle and function? Who is there to tell the purchasers and enthusiasts that their expensive, heavy, shiny wall-hanger is little more than a decorated metal prop? In Western cultures there is no recognized body or authoritative group to fill this role. Instead, it is more a matter of general consensus

---

[1] The popularity and success of Asian martial arts today also owes a great deal of its cultural exposure and commercial success to the attitudes and innovative career of the late Bruce Lee. Ironically, as a martial artist, Lee was a vocal nontraditionalist and passionate nonconformist.

[2] In fact, there are actually more samurai swords now in the United States than in Japan itself, and in the last decade many blades have been purchased by professional "sword-hunters" for return to Japan.

of the few informed and experienced.

Again, unlike with Asian swords, few ordinary people possess or can hope to obtain actual antique European swords in prime condition. Add to this the built-in self-promotion and marketing that Asian swords and weaponry in martial arts schools and films enjoy, and it's no wonder that misunderstanding of their Western counterpart swords is so common and interest in them so restricted. The problem is that, like many people, these Japanese sword aficionados and dealers have learned everything they think they know about Medieval or Renaissance European swords and swordsmanship from watching such movies as *Dragonheart* or *Princess Bride*. Only a few of them have even taken little more than a semester's worth of collegiate fencing—hardly long enough to acquire respect for it, let alone any understanding of how it is different from its formidable predecessors. Worse still, they witness the choreographed slapstick performances at Renaissance fairs, or the "chivalry"-obsessed fighters from groups that stand toe-to-toe (or kneel down) in heavy armor and bash away with baseball-bat swings. Once more, they see little worth taking notice of.

Add to this impression the *Dungeons & Dragons* fantasy crowd playing sword tag offers and you can further understand their viewpoint of their own heritage. It is an attitude shared by many serious practitioners of traditional Asian weaponry.[3] Not surprisingly, many Asian-born martial arts instructors have even less understanding of (or respect for) Western sword skills than do most Americans (why their Western students don't realize this is a mystery). Chinese, Japanese, Okinawan, Filipino, and even Indonesian weapon systems are seen as supreme and incontestable by virtue of their long-standing, surviving traditions rather than for the unique sociological conditions that kept them in their own preindustrialized "Middle Ages" for so long. Further, the more sycophantic students are not about to challenge their assumptions or prejudices. Whereas one can go down to any local bookstore and purchase dozens of books on "secret" Asian fighting arts and techniques, their Western counterparts are virtually unheard of. Ironically, the true secret arts today seem to be the works of such Medieval and Renaissance masters as Liechtenauer, Egenolff, Talhoffer, Agrippa, Marozzo, Carranza, George Silver, Joseph Swetnam, Capo Ferro, and Joachim Meyer.

Still, it never ceases to amaze how often instructors of Asian martial arts will make broad statements and proclamations about the similarity of Eastern and Western methods. Sometimes they will go as far as to say they are "essentially the same." How they can say this without having deeply studied or long practiced the Western methods in question, without having researched the old manuals, without having trained with the arms and armor, or without having free-sparred against skilled students is a question yet to receive an adequate answer. It is especially bothersome considering how much of Asian fighting arts is uniformly founded on metaphysical and even paranormal notions such as chi and ki and hara and other elements. These notions are completely foreign and irrelevant to European systems of the Medieval or Renaissance period.

In light of the magnitude of false assumptions and general ignorance that most Americans and Europeans have about their own martial culture, it is not hard to understand how certain Asian-born-and-raised martial arts instructors can know even less of it. To use an analogy, this is a little like a gourmet Asian chef who has never tasted French or Italian cuisine, but announces that all types of cooking are fundamentally the same since in the end they each satisfy the appetite. In a sense, it may be true, but it's misleading and simplistic.

One cannot make pronouncements on European swordsmanship or fighting techniques based on seeing a few movies or taking a short class in foil or épée any more than one could become a skilled martial artist after watching *Enter the Dragon* and reading Miyamoto Musashi. It is distressing how frequently some experts in Asian sword arts will presume to teach something about "Medieval" swords with no framework other than their own partial assumptions. There are indeed many fundamental, universal ideas and principles common to all forms of

---

[3] Considering the approach followed by many of those involved in studying historical armed combat today, this is not hard to understand. One can wonder what the state of the traditional Asian martial arts would be were they to exist under similar conditions. What if instead of skilled instructors and students, they were made up almost solely of people just dressing up and playing pretend? What if their demonstrations of fighting skills consisted mostly of choreographed events and fantasy games? Sadly, such is the state of much of what passes for historical European fighting arts today.

fighting, but there are significant technical and conceptual differences between Eastern and Western systems. If there were not, the military histories, the swords, and the arms and armor of each would not have been so distinct. It's a shame to say that far too often a general ignorance of military history and misunderstanding of European arms and armor seem to be two of the major characteristics of students of most martial arts (the same can be said for the public at large).

Western civilization from the time of the ancient Greeks has always been a source of uniquely resourceful ideas and specialized innovation. For better or worse, the same technical ingenuity that was applied to classical arts and sciences was directed equally toward the weapons of battle and the skills of war. There is no reason whatsoever to believe that Medieval (and Renaissance) fighting methods were not vigorous and dynamic arts. Indeed, in the face of the demonstrable evidence from the times it would be foolish to hold an opinion to the contrary.

Yet in one sense, European martial culture is itself something that is still very much with us. But it now bears little resemblance to its Medieval and Renaissance heritage, which we have examined. The technological revolution in Western military science that swept the 18th century left behind the old ideas of an individual armored warrior trained in personal hand-to-hand combat. This itself is the Western martial "tradition." The Western way of war using ballistics and associated organizational concepts is now the model for all modern armed forces the world over.

As more and more students of the sword move away from mere role-playing and theatrics, a more realistic appreciation of historical Western martial arts will emerge. In an age of increased ethnic pride and sensitivity to cultural diversity, it is hoped that these prejudices will not stand forever. There are many out there dedicated to steadily reconstructing Medieval and Renaissance martial culture and reclaiming its methods from fantasy and myth. It is a formidable task, but fortunately it is one well under way.

Bibliography

MEDIEVAL MANUSCRIPT SOURCES

There are no sources like the material of the historical Masters. Anyone who asserts that there are no Medieval fighting manuals or that there are no real sources for historical Western martial arts is ignorant. Only a dozen or so of these are currently available in hard copy or microfiche, and most are untranslated from their native language and arcane phrasing. A few of these can be obtained from sources on the Internet (along with widely varying editorial comments) or in abridged formats within some of the published titles listed here. More works are being distributed as scholars and students of the sword share resources. A few other rare manuscripts and newly discovered works have yet to be made available to the public. The list below purposely excludes those many works after 1670 on small-swords, other blade forms (e.g., sabers) and classical fencing. It also does not list works for which only a title or author is cited in references and for which no actual copy is currently available. An asterisk indicates the more significant works.

* Anonymous 13th-century *Sword and Buckler* manuscript, "I.33" British Museum No. 14, E. iii, and No. 20, D. vi. (A short Medieval German work on the use of the sword and buckler. It is quite likely the earliest known European work.)

* Liechtenauer, Hans. *Hanko Doebringer's Hausbuch.* (German *Fechtbuch* of 1389 on sword use. It exists in portions only, most reportedly now lost.)

* Dei Liberi, Fiore. *Flos duellatorum in armis.* Italy, 1410. (This covers the long-sword/great-sword).

* Ringeck, Sigmund. *Fechtbuch* from 1440s. (His *Fechtbuch* offered interpretations of Liechtenauer's verses.)

* Talhoffer, Hans. German *Fechtbuch* of 1443 or 1467. (It covers swords and other weapons, as well as some Liechtenauer and Austrian wrestling of Otto the Jew. It actually consists of various editions from the 16th and 17th centuries.)

Harleian Manuscript 3542 (*The Man That Wol*). (A rare, short mid-15th century English work on two-handed swords.)

Feres, Boris. Milan, 1400.

313

Studer, Charles. *Das Solothurner Fechtbuch*. 1423.

* Von Danzig, Peter. *Fechtbuch* from 1452.

* Lew, Jud. *Fechtbuch* from c. 1455.

Kal, Paulus. *Fechtbuch*, circa 1465.

Tarcirotti. Milan, 1400s.

Vadi, Filippo (or Fillipe). *De Arte Gladiatoria Dimicandi*. Italy, 1480 or 1495. (This covers the long-sword/great-sword.)

* Lebkommer, Hans (or Lechkuchner)/Johannes Leckuechner. *Der Alten Fecter an fengliche Kunst. Fechtbuch*, circa 1482, (This covers the sword, falchion, and other weapons. It is said to actually be the work of a Christian Egenolff and to include materials from Andre Pauerfeindt's *Fechtbuch* of 1516 and Sigmund Ringneck's *Fechtbuch* of circa 1440. It now consists of various editions from the 16th and 17th centuries.)

Von Speyer, H. *Fechtbuch* from 1491.

Falkner, Peter. *Fechtbuch*, circa 1495.

Monte, Pietro. Italy, 1509. (This is about swordsmanship and other weapons.)

Pauernfeindt, Andre. *Ergrundung Ritterlicherkunst der Fecterey. Fechtbuch*, 1516

Le Jeu de la hache (*Axe Play*). (An anonymous 15th-century work on the use of the Medieval pole-axe, portions of which appear in Alfred Hutton's 19th-century *Old Swordplay*. It was recently retranslated by Prof. Sydney Anglo.)

NOTE: There are many more works, as well as a number of recently recovered works on German and English great-swords and two-handed swords, but it will be some time before they become generally available to students of the sword.

PRIMARY SOURCES & SUGGESTED READING

Amberger, J.C. *The Secret History of the Sword*. Vol. 1, 2. Baltimore: Hammerterz Verlag Special Publication 0101, 1996.

Beeler. J. *Warfare in Feudal Europe 730–1200*. Ithaca, NY: Cornell University Press, 1971.

Bull, Stephen. "An Historical Guide to Arms & Armor." *Facts on File*. New York: 1991.

Cole, Michael D. et al. *Swords & Hilt Weapons*. London: Weidenfeld and Nicholson, Multimedia Books, 1989.

Contamine, Phillippe. *War in the Middle Ages*. Paris: Presses Universitaires de France, 1980.

Devries, Kelly. *Medieval Military Technology*. Broadview Press, 1992.

Edge, David and John Miles. *Arms and Armor of the Medieval Knight*. Crescent Books, 1988.

Galas, S. Matthew. "Kindred Spirits—The Art of Sword in Germany & Japan." *Journal of Asian Martial Arts,* Vol. 6, No. 3 (1997).

_____. "The Flower of Battle—An Introduction to Fiore dei Liberi's Sword Techniques." *Hammerterz Forum*, Vol. 2, No. 3 (Winter 1995/96): 118 ff.

Gruett, Christopher and Christopher Hook. *The Norman Knight 950–1204*. London: Osprey Military Series, 1993.

Hawkes, Sonia Chadwick, ed., *Weapons and Warfare in Anglo-Saxon England*. Oxbow Books, 1989.

Humble, Richard. *Warfare in the Middle Ages*. Mallard Press, 1984.

Keegan, John. *The Face of Battle*. London: Jonathan Cape Ltd., 1976.

Koch, H.W. *Medieval Warfare*. Brompton Books, 1978.

Margeson, Sandra. *Vikings*. New York: Eyewitness Books, Alfred A. Knopf, Inc., 1988.

McGlynn, Sean. "Myths of Medieval Warfare." *History Today*, Vol. 44 (1) (January 1994).

"Myths of Medieval Knighthood and Warhorses." *Military History Quarterly* (summer 1995).

Newark, Timothy. *Medieval Warfare*. Bloomsbury Books, 1979.

Nicolle, David. *Medieval Warfare Source Book, Vol. 1, Warfare in Western Christendom*. London: Arms and Armour Press, 1995.

Oakeshott, R. Ewart. *The Archaeology of Weapons*. Boydell Press, 1960 (reprint 1994).

_____. *Dark Age Warrior*. Lutterworth Press, 1974.

_____. *A Knight and His Armor*. Philadelphia: Dufour Edition, 1961.

_____. *A Knight and His Weapons*. Philadelphia: Dufour Edition, 1964.

_____. *Records of the Medieval Sword*. Boydell Press, 1991

_____. *The Sword in the Age of Chivalry*. Boydell Press, 1964 (reprint 1994).

Oakeshott, R. Ewart, and Henry Treece. *Fighting Men*. New York: G. Putnam Sons, 1963.

Prestwich, Michael. "Armies and Warfare in The Middle Ages: The English Experience." New Haven and London: Yale University Press, 1996.

Shadrake, Dan and Susanna. *Barbarian Warriors: Saxons, Vikings, and Normans*. London: Brassey's, 1997.

Wise, Terence and G.A. Embleton. *Saxon, Viking, and Norman*. London: Osprey Military Series, 1979.

SECONDARY SOURCES

Ashdown , C.H. *European Weapons and Armor*. 1925.

Auerswald, Fabian von. *Die Ringer-Kunst des Fabian von Auerswald erneuert von G. A. Schmidt . . . ; mit einer Einleitung von K. Wassmannsdorf*. Leipzig: Acta Humaniora, 1988.

Aylward, J.D. *The English Master at Arms from the Twelfth to the Twentieth Century*. London: Routledge and Kegan Paul, 1956.

Baldick, Robert. *The Duel, a History of Dueling*. Spring Books, 1965.

Balent, Matthew. *Weapons & Armour*. Detroit: Palladium Books, 1981.

Bertrand, Leon. *Cut & Thrust*. 1927.

Blair, C.B. *European Armor circa 1066 to circa 1700*. London: T. Batsford, Ltd., 1979.

Brown, Terry. *English Martial Arts*. United Kingdom: Anglo-Saxon Books, 1997.

Burton, Sir Richard. *The Book of the Sword*. London: 1884.

Byam, Michelo. *Arms & Armor*. New York: Dorling Kindersley Limited, 1988.

Castle, Egerton. *Schools and Masters of Fence: From the Middle Ages to the Eighteenth Century*. London: 1885.

Clare, John D., ed., *Knights in Armor*. San Diego: Gulliver Books, Harcourt Brace Jovanovich, 1993.

Clements, John. *Renaissance Swordsmanship: The Illustrated Use of Rapiers and Cut-and-Thrust Swords*. Boulder, CO: Paladin Press, 1997.

Cooper, J., ed., *The Battle of Maldon: Fact and Fiction*. 1993.

Cowper, H.S. *The Art of Attack*. E.P. Publishing, 1977.

Davidson. Hilda R. Ellis. *The Sword in Anglo-Saxon England*. Suffolk, 1962.

The Diagram Group. *Weapons*. New York: Diagram Visual, 1980.

Duffy, Arthur Richard. *European Armor in the Tower of London*. London: Her Majesty's Stationary Office, 1968.

_____. *European Swords and Daggers in the Tower of London*. London: Her Majesty's Stationary Office, 1967.

Duval, Cynthia and Walter J. Karcheski, Jr. *Medieval and Renaissance Splendor: Arms and Armour from the Higgins Armory Museum & Works of Art Ringling Museum*. New York: Ringling Museum, 1984.

Featherstone, Donald. *Warriors and Warfare in Ancient and Medieval Times*.

Fiore de Liberi da Premariacco, Fior di battaglia. MS 383. New York: Pierpoint Morgan Library.

Froissart, Jean. *Chronicles*. Selected and translated by Geoffrey Brereton. London: Penguin, 1968.

Grafton, Carol, ed., *Arms & Armor—A Pictorial Archive of Woodcuts and Engravings*. Dover Books, 1995.

Gravett, Christopher. *Knight*. New York: Eyewitness Books, Alfred A. Knopf, Inc., 1988.

Hart, Harold, ed., *Weapons and Armor—A Pictorial Archive of Woodcuts and Engravings*. Dover, 1978.

Hooper, Nicholas and Matthew Bennett. *The Cambridge Illustrated Atlas: The Middle Ages 768–1487*. London: Cambridge University Press, 1996.

Hope, William. *The Scots Fencing-Master*. Edinburgh: John Reid, 1687 (2nd edition, London: Dorman Newman).

_____. *The Complete Fencing-Master*. Edinburgh: John Reid, 1692 (2nd edition, London: Dorman Newman).

Hutton, Alfred. *Old Swordplay*. 1892.

_____. *The Sword and the Centuries*. London, 1901.

Karacheski, J. *Arms and Armor in the Art Institute of Chicago*. Chicago: Bulfinch Press, 1995.

Limburg, Peter. *What's in the Name of Antique Weapons*. New York: Coward, McCann, and Geoghegan, 1973.

Lowy, F.A. *The History of Chivalry and Armor*. Kottenkamp, translator. New York: Portland House, 1988 (reprint of 19th century edition).

Mann, J.G. *An Outline of Arms and Armour in England*. London: 1960.

Meyer, Joachim. *Kunst der Fechtens*. Circa 1570.

Morrison, Sean. *Armor*. New York: Thomas Y. Cromwell Co., 1963.

Nicolle, D.C. *Arms and Armor of the Crusading Era 1050–1350*. White Plains, NY: Kraus International Publications, 1988.

_____. *Warfare in Feudal Europe*. 1981.

_____. *The Medieval Soldier*. London: Barnes & Noble (reprint 1993).

Norman, A.V.B. and Don Pottinger. *English Weapons and Warfare*. London: Barnes & Noble, 1966.

Norman, Vessey. *Arms and Armor*.

North, Anthony. *European Swords*. London: Victoria and Albert Museum, 1982.

Oakeshott, R.E. *European Weapons and Armour*. Guildford and London: Lutterworth Press.

Oman, C.W. *The Art of Warfare in the Middle Ages*. Ithaca, NY: Cornell University Press, 1953.

Pfaffenbichler, Matthias. *Armourers—Medieval Craftsmen*. London: British Museum Press, 1992.

Pierce, I. "The Knight, His Arms and Armour. c. 1150–1250." *Anglo Saxon Studies*, XV (1993): 251–274.

Pleiner, Radomir. *The Celtic Sword*. Oxford: Clarendon Press, 1993.

Reid, William. *A History of Arms*. Sweden: AB Nordbok, 1976.

Reinhardt, Hank. "Hype . . . As Ancient an Art as Sword Making." *Knives '87*. DBI Books, Inc., 1987.

_____. "There Is No Best Sword." *Knives '88*. DBI Books, Inc., 1988.

Robards, Brooks. *The Medieval Knight at War*. Brompton Books edition, 1997.

Rossi, Francesco. *Medieval Arms & Armor*. Magna Books, 1990.

Small, R.C. *Crusading Warfare 1097–1193*. Cambridge University Press, 1956.

Smith, A.G. *Knights & Armor*. Dover Children's Books, 1985.

Spalding & Nickerson. *Ancient & Medieval Warfare*. London: Barnes & Noble (reprint 1993).

Stone, C.G. *A Glossary of the Construction, Decoration, and Use of Arms and Armour in All Countries and in All Times*. Portland, ME: 1934.

Strickland, Matthew, ed., *Anglo-Norman Warfare*. Boydell, 1992.

Sutor, Jacob. *New Kunstliches Fechtbuch*. 1612.

Tarrasuk, Leonid. *The Complete Encyclopedia of Arms & Armor*. New York: Simon and Schuster, 1982.

Thimm, Carl Albert. *A Complete Bibliography of Fencing and Dueling*. London and NY: John Lane, 1896.

Thordemann, B.J. *Armor from the Battle of Wisby, 1361*. Stockholm: 1939.

Turnbull, Stephen. *The Lone Samurai and the Martial Arts*.

Verbruggens, J.F. *The Art of Warfare in Western Europe During the Middle Ages*. North-Holland, 1977 (first published 1956).

Wagner, Eduard. *Medieval Costume, Armour, and Weapons (1350–1450)*. London: Paul Hamlyn Ltd., 1958 (1962).

_____. *Cut and Thrust Weapons*. London: Spring Books, 1967.

Walsh, J.H. *Archery, Fencing and Broadsword*. London: Routledge, 1863.

Weland, Gerald. *A Collector's Guide to Swords, Daggers, & Cutlasses*. London: Chartwell Books, 1991.

Wilkenson-Latham R. *Guide to Antique Weapons and Armor*. Oxford: Phaidon Press, 1981.

Wilkinson , Frederick. *Battledress*. 1970.

_____. *Arms & Armor*. London: Paul Hamlyn, 1978.

_____. *Sword & Daggers*. New York: Hawthorne Books, 1967.

_____. *Edged Weapons*. London: 1970.

Wilkinson, Frederick and Robert Latham. *Swords in Colour*. 1978.

William, Reid. *The Lore of Arms: A Concise History of Weaponry*. Göteborg, Sweden: AB Nordbok, 1976.

Wise, Arthur. *The Art and History of Personal Combat*. London: Hugh Evelyn Ltd., 1971.

Wise, Terence. *European Edged Weapons*. London: 1974.

_____. *War in the Middle Ages*. Hastings House Press, 1976.

Wylde, Zachary. *The English Master of Defence*. 1711.

About the Author

John Clements has had a lifelong pursuit of (some say obsession with) nearly all forms of swordsmanship. He started studying historical weaponry in 1980 and has practiced cut-and-thrust swordsmanship for almost 18 years. He has practiced under five different weapon-sparring systems and trained in numerous sword arts. He started fencing at the age of 14, followed by an interest in martial arts, and in 1982 founded the Medieval Battling Club. He has spent time in Europe examining weapon collections, and his writings on swordsmanship and weapon-sparring have appeared in more than six magazines.

John is a member of the British Arms & Armor Association and taught two semesters on swordsmanship and Medieval battling at Western Nevada Community College in 1992. In 1994 he took first place in the Advanced Weapon-Sparring Competition of the U.S. National's Kung Fu Tournament in Orlando, Florida. He lectures on historical weaponry and is an ardent promoter of contact-weapon sparring and study with historical replica swords. He trains regularly in long-sword, sword & shield, sword & buckler, sword & dagger, Medieval spear, and rapier & dagger methods. He now teaches classes and seminars on Renaissance and Medieval swordsmanship in Houston, Texas, with the Historical Armed Combat Association (HACA).

John's first book was *Renaissance Swordsmanship: The Illustrated Use of Rapiers and Cut-and-Thrust Swords* (Paladin Press, 1997).

From the Author

In a work of this size, not every aspect of Medieval swordsmanship can be addressed with the necessary detail. Such additional elements of fighting as engaging, feinting, gaze, tense exhalation, aggressiveness, and types of attacks could all be addressed at length. Much could also have been said of the important and common fight of sword and shield versus pole-arm. Indeed, pole-arms were the dominant weapon of the Medieval battlefield, and going into combat armed with one was standard for many warriors throughout the period. However, in single combat a pole-arm or spear could meet its match against the skillful use of sword & shield. There is also much more that could be examined regarding use of extralarge shields. A larger shield, though supplying greater area protection, is far slower and less maneuverable. Too large a shield prevents many of the deflecting and striking motions that make a more traditional size so effective. An extralarge shield cannot cover two opposite lines of attack in short time. If the shield is raised high to cover the head, an attack can drop down to the legs. If a shield is lowered to protect the legs, a blow can shift up to the head and so on. The nature of Medieval sword & shield fighting does not lend itself to the static use of large, immobile planks that do not allow effective footwork and agile combinations. Too large a shield ends up keeping the user's own weapon from his opponent and becomes a wall behind which the adversary can also hide.

When it comes to weapon-sparring, it is also of great importance to stress that including the head as a target should not be neglected. Helmeted training and sparring is a necessity in gaining a proper understanding of both techniques and concepts. The head and face are major and important targets for both cuts and thrusts and are not as easy to defend as is commonly thought. The ability to directly strike to a combatant's head or face can be quite enlightening to those who are unused to it. Thrusts to the face can be particularly dangerous when one has not developed proper responses and counters. The experience of learning to effectively attack to as well as defend the head cannot be ignored without creating significant deficiencies in a fighter's skill. Although unhelmeted practice and sparring is certainly an effective and reasonable means of learning, it nonetheless has obvious limitations (especially in sword & shield fighting). For realistic sparring the head is an obvious and vital element that really must be included. In studying Medieval swordsmanship, sparring that regularly or continually excludes the head should rectified as soon as possible.

Finally, keep in mind that Medieval martial culture is varied and diverse. Only portions survive of how warriors taught and trained in the use of arms. But we know that they did put considerable effort into the craft. Among the earlier Vikings and Anglo-Saxons the sword was often the weapon only of the leading warriors. Their great love of single combat and duel also made the sword a favored weapon. A man who could no longer rely on his sword was a second-class citizen. His property and home had to be protected by others. He had to hand over his sword and the defense of family to his heirs. One exercise of control practiced at Anglo-Saxon courts consisted of throwing sword blows at a participant's eyebrows! If he flinched he was deemed unworthy of further training. The Vikings were said to have had a similar method of sword and shield training called the *Worod*. Part of this consisted of swinging swords at the foreheads of young students. Those who flinched were dismissed. To the Vikings, certain fighting skills were sometimes known as *Riddaraskap*. Saxo the Dane tells us of such a warrior: "taught by fencers, he trained himself by sedulous practice in parrying and dealing blows." He also tells of a king's decreeing that his soldiers learn "from champions the way of parrying and dealing blows." Yet, no training, no matter how good, can prepare a man for the reality of battle. The most that can be done is to instill basic responses and physical conditioning. But training together also gave men the sense of camaraderie that was especially essential for a tight-knit group of fighters in an age when fighting man to man occurred more often than not by being close enough to look your enemy in the face.

The chronicler Roger of Howden wrote in the 11th century that "without practice the art of war did not come naturally when it was needed." For the knightly classes there was the always idea of "Preudome," or being a "man of prowess" skilled in military arts. Prowess in arms was itself one of the fundamental tenets of chivalry. Early knightly tournaments were intended very much to train men in the use of their arms between wars and were much more martial and brutal and with far less pageantry than later ones. The earliest were conducted as "grand melees" in a large field. Later on there were

also informal challenges issued such as the *pas d'armes*, or "passage of arms," wherein a group of knights might invite all others to meet them in honorable combat at a specific place and time. Although not generally to the death, some of these fights became quite bloody. We also know that there was at one time a distinction made by knights between forms of combat conducted *a'plaisance*, or with blunts, and that which was *a'outrance*, with sharps.

Late Medieval texts even describe young knights training with weapons of double weight in order to develop strength. But Medieval warrior skills were for the most part the indigenous fighting arts of an entire people and not specifically limited to the knightly warrior classes (who by far had the better arms and armor). Unlike his peers in Germany, Italy, and elsewhere, the traditional Medieval English weapons expert essentially was a "blue-collar" commoner whose profession was looked down on. Often this Master-at-Arms taught only in private, or at least without official permission. From as early as 1286 an edict in England had forbade private schools of fence within the city of London–ostensibly to "control villainy" and "prevent criminal mischief" said to be "associated" with such activities. Yet, despite being ill armed, the common folk always had need to protect themselves and if called upon even to defend the kingdom from invasion. By the late Middle Ages there were sword-masters fighting experts both teaching and fighting for pay, yet they themselves were typically commoners.

Today, students of historical fencing will often take too much of a technical approach to swordsmanship. This is natural in the early stages of learning, but later they may obsess with "technique, technique, technique" and overgeneralize them. They scour the historical manuals searching for clues and techniques while overlooking principles. They will theorize and theorize rather than examine the practical applications of physical actions with weapons. Techniques are merely the execution of the mechanics of a move. They are never done in a vacuum, but in reference to what the adversary himself is doing or not doing. Even at the highest level, when a technique is selflessly and reflexively executed, there is still the unconscious recognition of the target's immediate action. Techniques must involve reference to understanding underlying principles.

The effectiveness of a properly handled Medieval shield & sword combination is formidable. However, this is not that easy to realize because its proper use is all but absent in most movie and theatrical combat presentations, as well as in Medieval fantasy societies. The conditions under which they must operate are not conducive to either the aggressive hitting techniques that are common or the subtle and tight movements it sometimes uses. Instead, performers and choreographers prefer hitting directly at the shield, having the fighter pull it out of the way as they are attacked, and even acting as if it is somehow an encumbrance. None of this is consistent with the physical realities of the tool or the actions and motions of employing it effectively. Fighting with a weapon is not about technique alone, nor is it about simply technique and physical actions. There are considerable mental elements that must be understood in order to be more effective. General principles of fighting lie at the very heart of any understanding of weapon use and any tactics applied. The four major principles of personal combat are *timing, distance, technique*, and *perception*. They could all be addressed at length on their own. All fighting involves understanding timing, controlling distance, applying technique, and utilizing perception. These familiar elements, defined in various ways, have been identified and stressed by masters in countless martial arts.

They are fairly self-evident ideas and serve only to coherently direct how we think about actions. They are concepts that should not be ignored. None is really more vital than any other, and no one alone ensures victory. It is by comprehension of their mutual relation and interaction that they can then benefit a fighter. It is when these principles and concepts are openly violated that a fighter falls into bad habits and becomes vulnerable to an opponent who better understands and applies them. These principles cannot really be taught but must be learned by each individual and developed through practice and experience. When we understand timing (measure) we know when to strike and when not to strike. When we can control distance we know where we can strike and where we cannot strike, and where the adversary can and cannot strike. When we can

apply learned technique with proficiency, we can fluidly attack and defend with both speed and intensity. When we can use our perception on a higher level, we can foresee, anticipate, and respond with immediacy and efficiency. The German Medieval masters expressed the idea as *Fuehlen* (feeling), or the gauging of an opponent's "pressure."

If we don't know timing, our actions will be off and we will leave ourselves vulnerable. If we can't control the distance, our techniques will be too short or too long and we will leave ourselves exposed. If we don't learn proper technique we will not be able to attack or defend well, and we will be hopeless. If we don't develop our perception we will function only on the simplest level and miss all the greatness of the art. It is these general principles together that essentially represent and embody personal fighting skill. Skill can make up for lack of strength, but strength alone is hard pressed to replace skill. Weapons alone do not win fights. Physical ability alone does not win fights. Mental ability alone does not win fights. But all three together can.

There are really very few general "truths" to what one should or should not do in a sword fight and they can be summed up as: (1) Hit the opponent. (2) Don't get hit. Just how to go about this is where things become a little more complex—which is exactly why it's called fighting! There are of course other ideas that are present in fighting and swordsmanship, but which are themselves more obvious and inherent principles, such as aggressiveness, caution, and speed. The Northern Italian master Fiore dei Liberi himself makes regard to the ideas of audacity, prudence, celerity, and strength. By this he is acknowledging the concepts of initiative, caution, quickness, and force. These ideas go without saying because, without aggressiveness we cannot take or keep the initiative in a fight. However, we should never become overly aggressive to the point where we are reckless or foolhardy. This is where caution and prudence are needed. The balance between the two is a matter of experience. While defense is passive, it is also safer and allows for strong countering. But offense is active and allows openings and vulnerabilities in an adversary to be exploited. Each swordsman will find his own preference between fighting offensively and defensively.

The fundamental concepts of swordplay must be

learned accurately to avoid bad habits and long-term errors that will inhibit greater skill. Later on, as you develop ability, your own personality will emerge in a "style." But the basics will always need to be practiced and relearned. To grasp the correct martial attitude for realistic training, we must practice with passion. In both drills and sparring attacks, parries, and other techniques must all be committed with enthusiasm, speed, and energy. They cannot consistently be made "lightly," "theatrically," or just semi-fast. Of course, to do this with earnest appreciation for the underlying principles requires safety equipment.

Unfortunately, exclusive reliance on any form of mock weaponry alone leads enthusiasts to experience significant misunderstanding of the nature of Medieval swords (as well as other arms and armor). Certain types of blunt props and fake sword substitutes can seriously distort the nature of swordsmanship, and the significance of this must be underscored. It is practice with accurate replicas of real swords that will reveal just how different they function from any mock versions. In the end, one should endeavor to supplement whatever method preferred by cross-training with others. Training exclusively with only one means of drilling, exercising, or sparring is very limiting and eventually leads to a narrow interpretation of both technique and fighting. Serious practice requires much more than drills and exercises. It requires forceful, full-speed free-sparring to the full body target–i.e., contact-sparring. In contact-sparring the presumed value of fixed drills and arranged practice routines often crumbles in the face of a skilled adversary who uses unorthodox and unrehearsed actions to earnestly hit. The longer you train and study Medieval weaponry and fighting arts, the more readily apparent this becomes.

John Clements
November 1998